Housing the Urban Poor

Policy and Practice
in Developing Countries

Edited by

Brian C. Aldrich
Ranvinder S. Sandhu

Zed Books
London and New Jersey

Housing the Urban Poor: Policy and Practice in Developing Countries
is first published in South Asia by Sage Publications, Post Box 4215,
New Delhi 110048, India, and in the rest of the world by Zed Books Ltd,
7 Cynthia Street, London N1 9JF and 165 First Avenue, Atlantic
Highlands, New Jersey 07716, USA in 1995.

Cover designed by Andrew Corbett
Printed in India by Chaman Enterprises, Delhi
Bound in the United Kingdom by Biddles Ltd, Guildford and King's Lynn.

A catalogue record for this book is available from the British Library.

US CIP is available from the Library of Congress.

UK ISBN   1 85649 359 8 (HB)
          1 85649 360 1 (PB)

For
Lynn, Robert and Michael
and for
Jasmeet and Sandeep

For John Stafford,
Master of the New International Language

Contents

List of Tables and Figures

Figures

Foreword

This volume is a benchmark in the interplay among data, research, theory, and policy in Third World housing. Until the 1960s, Third World nations were still viewed in the context of awaiting the 'takeoff' of their economies on a trajectory of development; lagging behind, but imitating the housing of cities in the First World. In the decades since then, globalization and the complex interdependence it represents have become established as the context for the understanding of housing, as also of urban and economic development.

For housing theory and planning this has meant that much more attention needs to be focused on what local efforts by governments, community groups, and self-help initiatives can teach us about successful upgrading of housing, and much less on efforts to implement 'top-down' housing plans from the already developed world. To implement the new local perspectives, relevant housing data and research are needed. In this volume, Brian Aldrich and Ranvinder S. Sandhu, themselves representing a collaboration between the First and Third World, have provided a *systematic* series of case studies of Third World housing in 16 countries ranging from China and Brazil to Cuba and Zambia. With this standardized data base and the trends it presents, this volume lays the basis for further transformation of perspectives on housing poverty in the Third World.

Sylvia F. Fava
City University of New York

January 1995

Acknowledgements

Throughout our work on this book we have been assisted directly and indirectly by a large number of people. First of all we would like to thank the Department of Sociology and Social Work for inviting Ranvinder S. Sandhu to be a Visiting Professor in 1991-92. The secretarial staff of the Department, headed by Connie Koza, handled extensive international correspondence with efficiency and care. Linda Duffy, an undergraduate assistant, learned how to take the manuscripts which came in, scan them at the computer center and download them onto a disk. She followed through with this task by correcting or filling in all of the words and tables which did not scan. John Stafford, the system manager for the computer center, volunteered the scanning services of the center and patiently taught Linda how to use the facilities. In a world of computers and international scholarship he facilitated communication across the globe and between cultures. Tiffany Carstensen, an undergraduate student assistant under Dr. Brian Aldrich·assisted with a portion of the editing process, by tying up all the loose ends in each chapter that would allow for the best possible finished product.

Preface

Our book is an effort to bring together the research and experience of the best scholars on the issue of housing poverty in the Third World, i.e., societies not highly industrialized. The idea for this book developed while Ranvinder S. Sandhu was a Visiting Professor at Winona State University, in Winona, Minnesota in 1992. Together, we compiled a list of people who had already contributed to the understanding of habitat issues in the Third World. We were greatly helped by the fact that Ranvinder S. Sandhu is a board member of the Committee on Housing and the Built Environment. The Committee is an adjunct group organized within the International Sociological Association. Its members interact with and participate in a number of other professional organizations concerned with habitat issues around the world. Despite the Committee's connection with the discipline of sociology, it is a very. interdisciplinary group—the issue of housing not being confined to one profession. Membership of the group is reflected in the disciplines of the authors of the various chapters, who are architects, planners, engineers, anthropologists and others, *along* with sociologists.

Members of this group and others were selected for their record of scholarship and experience on the housing issue. A letter was sent to each one of them asking them whether or not they would like to contribute a chapter to a volume on 'slums and squatter settlements' in the country of their expertise. The questions were:

1. What is the history and development of slums and squatter settlements in the country?
2. What are the main characteristics, and current extent and patterns?
3. Review the available research on slums and squatter settlements.
4. What strategies have been utilized to ameliorate the conditions in these settlements and their critiques?
5. What is the status and future of these settlements?

One hundred or more scholars and experts were contacted. Sixteen country case studies were selected for inclusion in the book along with two chapters which help frame the global context of housing poverty.

One of the early responses to our request was a rejection of the term 'slums and squatter settlements' by several of the contributors. We learned in the process of putting the case studies together that the term 'slum' was used at one point in the development of policy and practical responses to housing poverty as justification for clearance and relocation. We also learned in the process of editing this book that the term 'squatter settlements' is both too broad and too limited a term; that there are large numbers of settlements now designated 'illegal subdivisions' or some equivalent term. It means that a systematic but informal market process is at work in several countries to subdivide land and construct houses without going through the formal process of housing construction. These are not 'spontaneous settlements' or ad hoc developments on marginal or vacant land. These are much closer to the formal market provision of housing and that process creates special kinds of problems for the occupants. Since many authors are still comfortable with the original terms, we continue to use them as indicators of a crisis in housing. We use the term 'housing poverty' to include all of these different aspects of habitat.

The two editors would seem to have very different concerns about housing, as one is active in India, the soon-to-be largest country in the world, and the other is from one of the lowest density cities in the United States. Our concerns are the same, however. Brian Aldrich has done neighborhood organization work within the city of Chicago, studied the role of neighborhood organizations in the United States and in Southeast Asia, and was in Manila the morning the city government first used troops to clear the old city center of squatters. These squatters were relocated many kilometers from the heart of the city with no infrastructure whatsoever and with no jobs. Since then he has continued to work with, study and visit squatter areas in Southeast Asia. Ranvinder S. Sandhu has a dual concern of how to bring housing development and support to areas outside the direct control of the controlling political parties and political center of his country. Both his research and work have been directed towards understanding the habitat problems of smaller, less central cities in the Indian subcontinent.

The country case studies are organized in terms of their level on the Human Development Index (HDI) developed by the United Nations Development Program. The use of the Index helps place each country in the distribution of well-being on the planet as measured by life expectantcy, literacy, and low income. It should come as no surprise to the reader that there are fewer cases in the high human development category than in the medium or low categories. The extent of housing poverty is negatively associated with high human development in the nations of the world.

Reading the chapters of this book will allow students of housing at whatever level of interest and experience to gain a detailed understanding of housing poverty in a representative group of countries around the world as well as the larger global context in which this problem is defined, policies supported, and funds provided.

Brian C. Aldrich
Winona, Minnesota
Ranvinder S. Sandhu
Amritsar

PART I

HOUSING POVERTY IN THE THIRD WORLD

Each chapter in the book takes the long view: looking at housing poverty in particular countries over a long time frame, or looking at it from a global perspective. In Chapter 1, the editors begin by examining the length and breadth of the problem of Third World housing poverty, and then define and describe the terms 'slums' and 'squatter settlements' and see how they are used as indicators of crisis in housing. The general problem of habitat is described as housing poverty, a term used in Chapter 2 as well. The sources of variations in housing problems are reviewed, including imposition of norms from industrial societies, the role of the World Bank, local versus global interests, the Cold War, level of economic development, the role of national and local elites, and the problems of land use and bureaucracy. They go on to describe the global process of urbanization as it impacts Third World cities, and different theories which have been suggested to explain what is happening with housing poverty. They also review the variations in housing policies and practices. The United Nations Development Program (UNDP) measure of the level of human development is introduced and the countries are compared. Finally, the UNDP model of human development is presented with its emphasis on the conditions leading to increased choice by citizens of a society.

Chapter 2, 'The Role of the World Bank in Housing' by Cedric Pugh, looks at recent changes in World Bank policy, i.e., since 1990, in light of the negative consequences that traditional World Bank attempts at long-term macro-economic stabilization and adjustment policies have had on near-term income and housing. The chapter evaluates these traditional policies and practices with specific case studies to document the negative results. The emphasis then shifts to the newly evolved, but untested, current policy which maintains a policy commitment to near-term consequences of their long-term stabilization policies. In this chapter, Pugh recognizes a New Political Economy model which provides the legislative, institutional, and financial framework whereby entrepreneurship in the private sector, in communities, and among individuals can effectively develop the urban housing sector. It describes the importance of government protection of housing and income from World Bank austerity programs associated with loans to national governments. Since this is a very new policy shift on the part of the World Bank (since 1990), *much of this chapter should be seen as a prescription for the housing problems described in the chapters which follow.* The chapter provides an important review of a major global institution, how its policies have affected housing poverty and how it is altering its policies in order to have a more positive impact on near-term income and housing.

1

The Global Context of Housing Poverty

Brian C. Aldrich and **Ranvinder S. Sandhu**

There is a crisis in housing in the Third World. Large increases in the urban population of Third World countries have dramatically increased the demand for housing. Sao Paulo, Brazil, for instance, has grown from under 3 million in 1950 to almost 24 million today (Dogan and Kasarda 1988). A production-oriented, Marxist–Leninist regime, traditional values, and large increases in urban population have resulted in the deterioration of housing conditions in China's largest cities (Kirkby 1985, p. 168). Shanghai has over 7 million people. Beijing and Tianjin have over 5 million each (Chen 1988). In India, the estimates of inadequate housing of the urban population run as high as 20 to 25 percent (Nagpaul 1988, p. 265). Housing in the large cities has continued to deteriorate over the last 30 years (Nagpaul 1988, p. 268).

Cairo, Egypt has over 8 million people (Khalifa and Mohieddin 1987). Yet so few housing units have been provided that an estimated 1 million people live in an ancient cemetery called 'The City of the Dead', another half million people occupy roof-tops, and millions of others live in illegal squatter settlements or unauthorized housing divisions (Khalifa and Mohieddin 1988). Tropical African cities have had fewer housing problems until recently. New city residents in West Africa were absorbed through traditional forms of land use, while those in eastern African cities were kept from migrating to cities or developing illegal settlements by colonial powers (O' Connor 1983, p. 185). But the old constraints have been loosened. The poor are especially hard hit. They are not able to afford a house with amenities and therefore try to find shelter for themselves in areas which lack the services essential for a healthy and adequate life.

What have governments done to handle this crisis? What social and political processes have been at work to solve these housing problems, or to exacerbate them? Is this a national problem or a global problem? Each country has a seemingly unique set of factors which have played a role in the history and development of urban housing and related policies (Hardoy and Satterthwaite 1989). Scholars, experts, and practitioners do not agree on how the inadequate levels of housing came about, why housing is in the state it is in, and what needs to be done to effectively deal with the crisis. The chapters which follow provide answers to these and other questions on a country case basis. The remainder of the chapters provide an understanding of the context in which these housing problems occur.

The global context of housing, i.e., the recognition that the provision of housing in the Third World, or the lack of it, is not just a national problem but that it is also a consequence of transnational structures and processes linking all the societies of the world by one degree or another, will be developed in a number of ways. First, this introduction will put Third World housing in a global economic context which relates housing scarcity to industrialization and the growth of Third World cities. In Chapter 2, Cedric Pugh analyzes the role of international agencies, especially the World Bank, in the development of housing. Several country case examples are included and the policies and practices of the World Bank on housing are reviewed. In the introductory chapter, the country cases will be examined within levels of the Human Development Index (HDI) (UNDP 1990). Each of the country case studies can thus be viewed comparatively. Each country case study describes and analyzes the emergence of the housing crisis in a country. In the concluding chapter, Choguill examines the various strategies and tactics which have been used in the provision of international technical aid, and suggests new directions in planned housing projects.

SLUMS AND SQUATTER SETTLEMENTS: HOUSING POVERTY

It is very difficult to get reliable estimates of the number of people in the Third World who are housed inadequately (UNCHS 1992). However, some attempts have been made. According to the United Nations, by the year 2000, half of the population of most Asian cities will live in slums or squatter settlements (Murphy 1990). In most Asian cities, inadequate housing is characteristic of 25 to 80 percent of the population. Inadequate housing in African cities ranges from a minimum of 33 percent to a maximum of 90 percent (Parmar 1991). Various sources indicate that the proportion of inadequate housing varies from country to country and between regions because each nation has its own unique, complex mix of economic, social, political, ecological, and demographic characteristics which influence the form that urbanization takes, as well as the types of housing problem that emerge (Van Vliet 1987; WHO 1988). There are also significant differences between cities in the same country (Van Vliet 1987; Sandhu 1989). These variations result from factors such as differences in size, rate of growth, location, and functions of the city in which these settlements are located (Sandhu 1989). Detailed analysis reveals that even within a housing settlement there are important differences among the residents (Seely 1979; Stokes 1970; Van Vliet 1987; Sandhu 1989).

The presence of slums and squatter settlements in a society is a clear indication of the failure of a society and government to provide adequate habitat for human development. The term 'slum' is used to indicate housing which falls below a certain level which is necessary to contribute to human development. The term 'squatter settlements' is used to indicate housing that is either the result of illegal occupation or has been developed in an unauthorized fashion (World Bank 1992). The amount of squatter housing is one indication of the extent of housing poverty in a society. It indicates a crisis because squatter housing generally lacks the primary, fundamental requirement of certainty of tenure. Used together, the presence of slums and squatter settlements indicate a habitat which fails to contribute to human development, and/or lacks the most fundamental guarantees necessary for the building of human communities. The presence of either of these two conditions is indicative of housing poverty.

Slums and squatter settlements are often difficult to separate. However, slums generally refer to housing, regardless of tenure, which has fallen into such disrepair that it constitutes a general condition for a neighborhood or community. A squatter area could also be a slum. Generally such areas are in the older central parts of cities (Nagpaul 1988).

Squatter settlements vary in their conditions, and the characteristics of their occupants. In India, they may consist of low-income and low-status persons who have been forced to live outside the bounds of tenured land-holding (Nagpaul 1988, p. 266) in order to survive in an urban setting. In some societies the squatter population may consist of large, integrated urban areas with housing, factories, shops, and services with a million or more people, i.e., Karachi (Yap 1990). Squatters may occupy parks, river banks, railroad right-of-ways, and other small pieces of urban land, and include professionals because of the scarcity of land, e.g., Manila (Aldrich 1985).

The main characteristic of squatter housing is the lack of formal ownership of the land on which the squatters live. The uncertainty of their tenure situation creates problems for capital improvement in the physical structures and social commitment to the larger neighborhood and community (Angel, et al. 1983). But even where government is willing to assign land or formally register it, additional problems of site improvement charges, bureaucratic breakdown, and political corruption may keep people from getting adequate housing.

Much of the conflicting analysis of squatter settlements centers around whether the people in these settlements are part of the problem or part of the solution. Early views by experts on urbanization in the Third World were based on industrial societies (Weber 1899; Wirth 1938). The term 'overurbanization' was coined to describe societies where there were more urban workers than urban industrial jobs—a supposed deviation from earlier patterns of industrialization. One consequence of overurbanization of Third World societies was said to be economic stagnation and slowed development (Timberlake 1985). Such views supported regimes in their efforts to limit migration to cities. Failing in that, these views often provided a rationale for bulldozing unwanted settlements as well as the forced removal of squatters.

Analysis by other experts suggests, however, that there is more to the growth of Third World cities than meets the eye. For instance, the labor pool formed by the large number of new residents may actively contribute to the economic growth of a society, and might even be the basis for such growth (Kelley and Williamson 1984; Portes 1985). The people living in slums and squatter settlements, the reasoning goes, subsidize the formal economy (and perhaps the world economy) by not requiring large amounts of capital for housing and related services. Slums with their physical deterioration, and squatter settlements built by their own residents with marginal or cast-off materials, minimize the need for capital from the formal sector. The financial resources which have been saved in this process could be used elsewhere. Two examples in contrast to this situation are Singapore and Hong Kong. Both these societies have directly subsidized their labor forces by extensive housing projects. Singapore housing has been subsidized with a 23.5 percent social security tax on workers and business. Housing in Hong Kong has been subsidized by massive relocation and resale of former squatter lands for commercial purposes (Aldrich 1985). These two instances are indicative of the massive amount of capital necessary to rehouse a large urban population and the level of economic activity required to allow for major subsidies to their labor force. Societies with lower levels of economic resources, the argument goes, use the cheap labor but do not bother to provide housing and related services. Thus the labor market is subsidized in an indirect fashion.

The country case studies show a great variety of social, political, and economic conditions associated with slums and squatter settlements. The cases in this book take a qualitative approach to these questions (AAAS 1976; Castells 1978). The authors(s) of each case has/have been asked to describe the extent and pattern of slum and squatter housing in the country. The available literature is then reviewed along with the description and analysis of strategies which have attempted to ameliorate the conditions of squatter housing and slums. This is followed by concluding remarks on the present and future status of slum and squatter housing.

SOURCES OF VARIATION IN HOUSING OUTCOMES

One major variable in the case studies is the impact of international housing norms and expectations brought in by international organizations or by exposure to the levels of housing development in First World countries. In Chapter 2, Cedric Pugh clearly describes the role of the World Bank in the provision of housing in the Third World. The policies, resources, and activities of the World Bank have had very mixed results in the provision of adequate housing. More subtle, perhaps, is the cultural hegemony associated with the transfer of Western norms of what constitutes acceptable forms of housing. These norms are transmitted by national elites who have been exposed, through education, training, travel, and social interaction, to housing expectations in such places as Boston, London, Tokyo, Amsterdam, or Paris (Drakakis-Smith and Rimmer 1982). One major source of variation described in the country case studies is the conflict between local culture, history, and expectations, and those of the expectations of the political elites. Often funded by governmental and nongovernmental international organizations, these 'top-down' solutions to housing often contributed as much to the problem as to the solution. The case studies raise questions about the efficacy of solutions imposed from the outside. Not only have many resources been wasted, but their imposition has often been associated with a good deal of suffering, dislocation, and conflict.

The post-World War II division of the world into two camps around the twin poles of the Cold War has played a major part in the imposition of external norms and values upon local housing problems. The collapse of the USSR has suddenly altered the conditions which led to competing models of industrialization and the provision of amenities such as housing. The ideology, under certain forms of Marxism, that housing was a nonproductive capital expenditure and thus not a priority, created major housing shortages in some socialist and Marxist countries (Kirkby 1985). The country cases of China and Cuba show different interpretations of this ideological tradition. Marxist–Leninist land and labor controls also had the effect of dampening the movement to cities. Variations on this ideology affected housing decisions in some African societies as well. On the other hand, societal elites supporting policies which left the housing market to the invisible hand of capitalism or to separate nongovernmental agencies, with free movement of labor, evidence another extreme in experience. Major population movements ensued, resulting in high levels of urbanization and low levels of provision of housing services.

Cutting through all the imported solutions is the issue of the level of economic development. In the best of circumstances nothing can be done if the economy is not working, or the nature of the tie to the global economy means that stability is impossible. The Sub-Saharan countries in the study are good examples. Without a stable and/or growing economy, resources for housing and related services remain scarce. All of the countries under review here suffered from this problem to one extent or another. However, the relationship between the level of economic development and the level of human development is not direct and unambiguous (UNDP 1991). There are many factors which can intervene.

Another factor cutting through all of this is the role of national and local political elites (Field and Higley 1980, pp. 95–116). Single party systems may be helpful under some conditions and not so helpful under others. Competition among political elites in an open society, however, has often increased the power of squatters. They are able to use political pressure to obtain greater tenure guarantees or more services for their areas. On the other hand, slum and squatter dwellers have also been subject to the whims of political elites in their determination to 'build or bulldoze'. Cynical exploitation of the housing and service needs of these populations for political gain has also been widespread.

Perhaps no issue cuts more clearly across all of the case studies than the bureaucratic problem of imposing formal controls over land—its use and its distribution. The bureaucratic knife cuts both ways: landowners in Thailand, for instance, find it an exhausting and time consuming process to remove unwanted squatters from their land. Land reforms in Colombia become so enmeshed in the bureaucratic process that they are effectively nullified. Land, its ownership, land use controls, removals, prevention of occupation, and all the other related issues turn out to be more related to culture than to efficiency. The case studies strongly suggest that where formal controls are not part of the traditional culture, or where bureaucracy has become a realm unto itself, even the best housing schemes may end up in the dustbin.

Charles Choguill, in the concluding chapter, suggests that new skills are required for those who intend to work on housing problems in the Third World. These include the 'skill to promote and co-ordinate community development, particularly development from below...the skills of a diplomat...the skills of economic analysis...[and] knowledge of infrastructure...'. International experts are beginning to recognize that providing good, secure housing in Third World countries is not just a matter of bringing in new methods and techniques, but a recognition of the fact that housing programs must take into consideration local political, economic, and social variations in order to be effective.

ALTERNATIVE MODELS
OF URBANIZATION AND HOUSING

At the present time, the interpretation of which global processes are at work in Third World countries, and the related question of how housing fits into the process, is an open question. There are several competing models of the process of urbanization which might be related to the development of slums and squatter housing. The basic demographic or population model emphasizes the conditions which contribute to movement from rural areas to urban cities. The second model posits a global hegemony of capitalist countries which drain the resources from the Third World countries in a one-sided exchange process. The third model emphasizes the interaction between the national economy and the dynamics of an international market. A fourth model has been developed by the United Nations Development Program which emphasizes the necessary role of economic development, and also looks at the significant role of active political elites with a commitment to human development. Any of these models, or some combination of them, may be explanations for why housing is so inadequate in Third World countries.

Since the end of World War II and the collapse of European colonialism, people in Third World countries have been actively relocating themselves from rural to urban areas with a vengeance. As populations increased due to medical and other advances, the carrying capacity of rural land was exceeded (Krausse 1977). Large numbers of rural residents relocated to the largest cities which had been the seat of colonial administrative and economic activities. Many of these cities were primate or first in size, with no near size contenders. Consequently, large numbers of people were 'pushed' out of rural areas because there were too many people to be supported on the land, and/or 'pulled' to the cities by the attraction of jobs, higher standard of living, and more variety (Firebaugh 1979).

This form of urbanization, however, was not typical of the process in the industrializing West (Berry 1981). In the West, the population movement was more incremental, moving in stages from smaller to larger cities since industry was concentrated in rural areas for a long time. It also consisted of massive interstate and intercontinental emigrations. Urbanization in Third World countries is not an analogous process. Unlike the sparsely populated rural hinterlands of most of the countries where this early urbanization and development took place, many Third World hinterlands have, for long centuries before Western colonial expansion, been characterized by dense populations, e.g., wet rice cultures such as China or Indonesia. In other parts of the world where this 'push' took place, the rural areas were characterized by subsistence, nonmonetary forms of agricultural activity. This was not the commercialized agriculture characteristic of most early industrializing European or European-dominated societies.

Furthermore, the sociocultural forms were radically different in the industrializing countries than they are in the Third World countries of the present (Berry 1981; Lenski, Lenski and Nolan 1991). The 'pull' to cities has much to do with the lack of alternatives in the local village. In societies dominated by large, colonial administrative centers with few cities of an in-between size, the forces of the market place have not created a hierarchy of cities which support the growth of local economy and a commitment to the local area (Lenski 1966; Eisenstadt and Shachar 1987). If residents want to go where the action is they have to move to the large city. There are no other alternatives.

It should come as no surprise that rural residents get up and leave these densely populated rural areas, or wish to leave the rural areas for the opportunities of large, administrative market centers. None of the factors which appear to be at work here look like the kind of rural life in industrializing countries like England, Germany, France, the United States or Australia.

The Dependency model asserts that the financial and raw material needs of the industrialized countries (including the Second World of Socialism) are supplied by countries in the Third World (Frank 1972; Harvey 1973). Sugar from Cuba and grapes from Chile feed the populations of the industrialized societies. Local elites and multinational corporations, the argument goes, create common cause to exploit the resources of people and the land in the interests of making a profit (Timberlake 1985; Smith 1987). Populations in the Third World are then entirely dependent upon the global economy for their jobs. Nothing is left for development because the local elites export all their share of the profits to more lucrative (and stable) investments in industrial societies. Under this scenario, the people of the Third World get poorer and poorer and there are no resources available for housing.

Changes in the economies of industrial countries over the last decade or two show that this model holds some truth. All the evidence is not yet in (Horowitz 1977; Light 1983; Portes 1985). A recent study by Bollen and Appold (1993) concludes that trade interactions between Third World countries and the fully industrialized countries are the key factors in predicting industrialization and the absorption of labor into the labor market. The amount of foreign investment was not a significant factor. Presence of a Marxist–Leninist regime did make a difference in the level of industrialization during some periods. These global economic processes appear less and less to be the conspiracy of corporate executives and local rentier elites (Logan and Molotch 1987) and more and more a result of the process of deconcentration of the global economy (Teune 1988, p. 365), and concentration of populations in cities resulting from factors of geography, market resources, elite decisions, and the culture of civilization (Eisenstadt and Shachar 1987; Teune 1988).

Econometric and Ecological–Evolutionary models are interaction models. They assume that there are both internal and external factors which affect outcomes. In the Ecological–Evolutionary model, some of the important internal factors are the level of development achieved under former types of civilization (Lenski and Nolan 1984). That is, did the society attain a typical level under the advanced agrarian civilization with the development of a full complement of economic specialization, bureaucratic organizations, and cultural universalism? An examination of the different regions of the world shows that much of Asia developed along these dimensions as did Russia, Europe, the Middle East, and central America. Each of these areas have their own social, organizational, political, and economic history (Eisenstadt and Shachar 1987). Consequently, their contribution to the interaction with another new and rising civilization, Western industrial democracy, varies and affects the level and process of industrialization, the build up of infrastructure and the provision of housing to the population.

Econometric models also look at internal and external factors and build in interactions and feedback, negative and positive, into their models. The most important of these studies shows that the price of oil and gas is a major factor in economic activity which in turn affects the size of cities in the Third World (Kelley and Williamson 1984). Instead of the self-contained population models used by demographers to predict trends in city growth, these models focus on the movements between institutions and across space, emphasizing the role of wages, prices, geography, demographics, and other market factors to guide transformation (Kelley and Williamson 1984; Eisenstadt and Shachar 1987; Bolland and Appold 1993). Advocates of this model make the assumption that the informal sector—the squatter settlements—are not just 'holding pens' for people waiting to get into the economy, but are an integral part of the economy with labor that actively participates in the wage and price process, transfer of skills, etc., across sectors. The movement of immigrants to cities in the Third World, according to this model, must also take into consideration the rents they have to pay and such things as the cost of food (Kelley and Williamson 1984).

The Kelley and Williamson Econometric model predicts that the population in Third World cities is a function of cost of inputs (oil and gas), the level of demand in the industrialized countries, and the level of acceptable housing services available in the cities. This model predicts that the urban transition in Third World countries will be completed roughly by the year 2000. Their analysis clearly shows that industrialization creates slums and squatter settlements in Third World cities. But it also predicts that urban land values will cease to surge at rates far exceeding output and employment growth in cities, and that rising densities, congestion, and rents will increase relative to the cost of movement to the cities. When this transition is complete there will be a decline in housing problems due to the rapid population growth, and an increased emphasis upon investment in housing, along with city building and service activities for the poor in the informal sector (Kelley and Williamson 1984).

The Evolutionary–Ecological model emphasizes an interaction between the global forces which are impinging upon Third World countries, and the internal characteristics of each society. Housing quality is treated as an outcome in the process of human development, exercising a pull upon rural peoples considering migration for jobs. It is consequence of the process of policy making and resource allocation at work in a society which in the present context means the operations of the global market. The reasoning in this model includes the rural to urban migration factor. It includes the fact that these Third World societies are producing for a global economy. But it also recognizes that these internal shifts in population have housing consequences with feedback upon the decisions of rural and urban migrants. For example, during the Great Depression in industrial societies there were large return migrations to the rural areas. In the Philippines of a decade ago, as the economy began to fail and outside investments were falling, large numbers of Manila area residents returned to rural areas or emigrated overseas to other sources of work. Models which are based upon these broader assumptions seem to be doing a better job of predicting the course of housing shortages than those which fail to take this interaction into account. The country case studies will be more qualitatively detailed along these dimensions.

HOUSING POLICIES AND PRACTICES

The case studies show the policies and practices undertaken by different countries to cope with the problems of slums and squatter housing. These policies are put into a historical process describing how they are connected to one another, as reactions to or developments from, as well as how they grew out of political, economic and social developments in that society. In the case studies, discussed later, these policies can be seen converging from opposite directions over the last several decades. On the one hand are the countries dominated by a single ideology of state Socialism. Cuba and China along with some African countries are examples of such cases. In these societies the movement of individuals from the countryside to cities was strictly controlled. This movement prevented, for some time, the large build-up of population and related housing problems in cities. But as most of these countries shifted to freer markets and more open systems, and the central government loosened control over the development process, the numbers moving to the cities increased rapidly. This has caused housing problems more recently in societies where housing was not defined as a service or a consumption item. Cuban response in the Socialist camp has followed a different policy. It has used social brigades to help rebuild poor housing. This practice was brought to a halt by the collapse of the Soviet Union and the economic problems which were part of that trade and political alliance. At the other extreme, there are more than a few cases where no attempt was made to control population movements, or the movement could not be controlled given the political and institutional resources. Cities in these countries became extremely crowded. What followed then were a variety of policies and practices which attempted to resolve the problems of population growth and housing. All these policies and practices are examined in the country case studies.

Since the squatters were not supposed to be where they were, one of the universal policies was squatter clearance. This policy generally involved destroying large amounts of housing near places of employment for this unskilled and semiskilled population and the relocation of its residents to a distant fringe of the city. This often meant a relocation to another urban squatter settlement. This approach has had limited success and resulted in the relocation of large numbers of urban residents to urban fringe areas or to other regions of the country. Almost without exception, the relocation sites were inadequate in terms of the infrastructure and services. Most of the time they were very distant from the jobs held by the residents. The families were often split up with some members living in other slums or squatter settlements near their work and commuting on weekends. In other instances, it only succeeded in moving residents to other slum and squatter settlements. These policies generally created a great deal of social unrest leading to injury, death, and often the development of major political unrest.

Another policy was of the 'If you can't fight them, then join them' philosophy. Under various regimes the squatters and the political elites reached an understanding in which some semblance of services were provided to squatter areas. The process, in a great many of these countries, involved various ways of coming to terms with political party representatives, government bureaucrats or elected officials in order to get some basic services such as electricity or water into the settlement. Changes in regimes complicated this process. In some instances this included political deals for various forms of temporary occupation permits or outright land tenure.

At a more formal level, and often with the support of international agencies, sites-and-services projects were introduced to try and upgrade these areas and provide higher levels of services. Slum and squatter areas were formally upgraded, densities lowered, and schools and other services added. In the most advanced cases, entire areas were rebuilt into high rise housing or more standardized units with the overflow going to adjacent sites.

Perhaps the most famous policy, 'autonomous housing', was to let the squatter groups construct their own housing with their own resources (Turner 1976). For a while this was considered to be the most effective policy. It generally involved providing some basic resources to the residents of an area to improve their own housing. In almost all of the instances of this policy, governments altered their positions from clearance to sites-and-services to looking the other way. None of these policies in the countries being examined here, were substantial enough, i.e., were supported with enough resources and time, to rehouse entire populations. Only countries bordering upon developed status, such as South Korea were able to generate the resources necessary to carry forward the more massive schemes.

These policies, both implicit and explicit, are described in each of the case studies which follow. These policies were not conceived and carried out in isolation, but in the context of the larger forces that are outlined above. The confluence of these various forces and the various policies make generalizations difficult. Nevertheless, the comparative perspective provided by the country case studies form the basis for a broader understanding of the problems associated with providing adequate housing. One important effect is to recognize the clinical nature of the problem, i.e., the need to take the empirical situation into account rather than proposing one policy or approach as a solution for all problems. The second important effect is to set housing policy within the context of the social, political, and economic processes of each country.

SLUMS, SQUATTER SETTLEMENTS AND HUMAN DEVELOPMENT

If generalizations are not easy to come by, and if housing problems need to be approached clinically and in terms of the in-country processes at work, then what parameters can be used to frame the problems of slums and squatter settlements? Our approach emphasizes that cities 'have generally been associated with human development' (Teune 1988, p. 351). Therefore, we propose to use the Human Development Index (HDI), developed in 1990 by the United Nations Development Program (UNDP 1990), as a comparative framework for the country case studies.

The HDI is a measure which ranks all countries on their level of human development. It is constructed, as revised in the 1991 report, by ranking each country from lowest to highest on the basis of 'longevity, knowledge and decent living standards' (UNDP 1991, p. 15). Longevity is measured by life expectancy. Knowledge is measured by adult literacy and mean years of schooling. A decent living standard is measured by multiples of the poverty level in which 'the higher the income relative to the poverty level, the more sharply the diminishing returns affect the contribution of income to human development' (UNDP 1991, Technical Note 2). Using a formula to calculate the position of the country on each measure relative to the highest and lowest scores results in an Average Deprivation Index. This index when subtracted from 1 becomes the HDI. The Index for 1991 varied from a high of 0.993 for Japan to a low of 0.048 for Sierra Leone (UNDP 1991, Table 1.1, pp. 119–21) for 160 countries. Additional versions of the Index take gender inequality and income inequality into account, as well as changes in the Index score from 1970–85 (UNDP 1991).

The purpose of using the HDI in this study is to provide a standardized measure against which all the countries can be compared. HDI comes closest to providing such a basis for comparison. The Index is also intuitively associated with the problems of poor housing represented by slums and squatter settlements. Using the Index allows the cases to be grouped into low-, medium-, and high-levels of human development so that the characteristics of critical habitat can be compared with others at the same or different levels. Other relevant measures from the UNDP report will also be used.

The figures in Table 1.1 rank the countries studied by level of human development. They also indicate whether the level of human development is higher or lower than would be expected on the basic level of economic development (GNP). The rankings of the countries in the book by the HDI give some idea of the range being examined. Bangladesh is next to the bottom on the Index, while the Republic of Korea and Costa Rica are up near the top. The figures in Table 1.1 also show that while gross national product (GNP) and the HDI are closely correlated, as a rule the countries in this volume are ranked higher on the Index than their level of GNP would suggest. The higher than expected HDI suggests that these countries are better than average in translating their economic gains into positive conditions for their citizens. The same pattern holds for countries in the medium ranks, with the exception of Cuba and Brazil. In the ranks of the low-levels of human development, all but Egypt are higher than would be expected based upon the level of GNP.

Table 1.1: Level of Human Development and Relation to Gross National Product for Countries in the Study, 1991

A. High Human Development

Country	HDI Rank	GNP Rank Minus HDI Rank*
Hong Kong	.934	0
Republic of Korea	.884	9
Costa Rica	.876	27
Mexico	.838	20

B. Medium Human Development

Country	HDI Rank	GNP Rank Minus HDI Rank*
Caribbean	.760 (approx.)	—
Brazil	.759	−2
Colombia	.757	22
Cuba	.754	−2
Thailand	.713	22
China	.614	51

C. Low Human Development

Country	HDI Rank	GNP Rank Minus HDI Rank*
Egypt	.394	−10
Zambia	.351	19
Tanzania		
Ghana	.311	4
Pakistan	.311	11
India	.308	9

* A positive figure shows that the HDI rank is higher than the GNP rank, a negative the opposite.

Source: UNDP (1991), *Human Development Report 1991*, Table 1. Human Development Index, All Countries, pp. 119–23.

THE UNITED NATIONS DEVELOPMENT PROGRAM MODEL OF HUMAN DEVELOPMENT

The housing crisis in the Third World must be put into the larger context of improving the level of human development in all countries of the world. The position of the UNDP is that political commitment is often more important than the level of economic development in determining the level of human development in a society (UNDP 1991, p. 1). Human development:

...is a process of enlarging people's choices. The most critical of these wide-ranging choices are to live a long and healthy life, to be educated and to have access to resources needed for a decent standard of living (UNDP 1990, p. 1).

Housing which meets adequate standards as well as cultural definitions of security of tenure is an essential part of a decent standard of living. There are a number of assumptions which go along with this approach. First of all, GNP growth 'is treated here as being necessary but not sufficient for human development' (UNDP 1991, p. 11). Second, human development for human beings is the outcome of the process—'the ultimate ends and beneficiaries of this process' (UNDP 1990, p. 11). In addition, human development emphasizes not just production structures but distributive policies as well (UNDP 1990, p. 11). Unlike the basic needs approach, which '...concentrates on the bundle of goods and services that deprived population groups need...the human development approach...brings together the production and distribution of commodities and the expansion and use of human capabilities' (UNDP 1990, p. 11). The objective is to concentrate on the complexities of the process of developing human capabilities and choice.

CONCLUSION

One of the most exciting aspects of reading through these country case studies on housing poverty is the impression gained that there is, in fact, a global community of organizations, institutions and individuals concerned with the issue of housing poverty—a true global context to the entire endeavor. And there are global processes which influence the level of housing poverty in each of these countries—economic, social and political. What is pervasive in these chapters—and in this effort—are the concerns of so many people. There is also, however, a remarkable diversity in the developments on housing around the world. The decisions of governmental leaders, the reactions of citizens, different cultural complexes, a variety of responses to development, and the local history of the development of cities all contribute to this diversity. The diversity of the cases suggests a clinical analysis of each of the cases but with an eye on the underlying themes or patterns, both at the global and the national level.

REFERENCES

Aldrich, Brian C. 1985. 'Habitat Defense in Southeast Asian Cities', *Southeast Asian Journal of Social Science 13*, pp. 1–14.
————. 1990. 'Relocation under Unified and Disunified Elites in Southeast Asian Cities', in Brian C. Aldrich and Ranvinder S. Sandhu (eds.), *Housing in Asia*. Jaipur: Rawat Publications, pp. 63–89.
American Association for the Advancement of Science. 1976. *American Values and Habitat*. Washington, D.C.: AAAS.
Angel, Shlomo, Raymon W. Archer, Sidhijai Tanphiphat and Emiel A. Wegelin. 1983. 'Reflecting on the Land Issue', in *Land for Housing the Poor*. Bangkok: Select Books, pp. 2–3.
Berry, Brian J.L. 1981. *Comparative Urbanization*. New York: St. Martin's Press.
Bollen, Kenneth A. and Stephen J. Appold. 1993. 'National Industrial Structure and the Global System', *American Sociological Review 58*, pp. 283–301.
Castells, M. 1978. *Cities, Class and Power*. New York: St. Martin's Press.
Chen, Ziangming. 1988. 'Giant Cities and the Urban Hierarchy in China', in M. Dogan and J. Kasarda (eds.), *A World of Giant Cities*. Newbury Park, CA: Sage, pp. 225–51.
Dogan, Mattei and John D. Kasarda. 1988. *Mega-Cities*. Newbury Park, CA: Sage.
Drakakis-Smith, D.W. and P.J. Rimmer. 1982. 'Taming "The Wild City": Managing Southeast Asia's Primate Cities Since the 1960's ', *Asian Geographer 1*, pp. 17–34.
Eisenstadt, S.N. and A. Shachar. 1987. *Society, Culture and Urbanization*. New Delhi: Sage.
Field, G. Lowell and John Higley. 1980. *Elitism*. London: Routledge & Kegan Paul.
Firebaugh, G. 1979. 'Structural Determinants of Urbanization in Asia and Latin America', *American Sociology Review 44*, pp. 199–215.
Frank, Andre Gunder. 1972. *Lumpen Bourgeoise: Lumpen Development*. New York: Monthly Review.
Hardoy, Jorge E. and David Satterthwaite. 1989. *Squatter Citizen*. London: Earthscan Publications Ltd.
Harvey, David. 1973. *Social Justice and the City*. Baltimore: Johns Hopkins University.
Horowitz, Irving L. 1977. 'Review Essay: Coming of Age of Urban Research in Latin America', *American Journal of Sociology 83*, pp. 761–65.
Kelley, Allen C. and Jeffrey G. Williamson. 1984. *What Drives Third World City Growth?* Princeton, NJ: Princeton University Press.
Khalifa, Ahmed M. and Mohamed M. Moheiddin. 1987. 'Cairo', in M. Dogan and J. Kasarada (eds.), *A World of Giant Cities*. Newbury Park, CA: Sage, pp. 235–67.
Kirkby, R.J.R. 1985. *Urbanization in China*. New York: Columbia University Press.
Krausse, G.H. 1977. 'Problems and Prospects of Low-Income Settlements in Southeast Asian Cities', paper presented at the Third World Conference, University of Nebraska at Omaha, Omaha, Nebraska.
Lenski, Gerhard. 1966. *Power and Privilege*. New York: McGraw-Hill.
Lenski, Gerhard and Patrick D. Nolan. 1984. 'Trajectories of Development: A Test of Ecological-Evolutionary Theory', *Social Forces 63*, pp. 1–23.
Lenski, Gerhard, Jean Lenski and Patrick Nolan. 1991. *Human Society*. New York: McGraw-Hill.
Light, Ivan. 1983. *Cities in World Perspective*. New York: Macmillan Publishing.
Logan, John R. and Harvey L. Molotch. 1987. *Urban Fortunes*. Berkeley: University of California Press.

Murphy, D. 1990. *A Decent Place to Live—Urban Poor in Asia.* Bangkok: Asian Coalition for Housing Rights.

Nagpaul, Hans. 1988. 'India's Giant Cities', in M. Dogan and J. Kasarda (eds.), *A World of Giant Cities.* Newbury Park, CA: Sage, pp. 252–90.

O' Connor, Anthony. 1983. *The African City.* New York: Africana Publishing Company.

Parmar, V. A. 1991. 'Urbanization in the Third World Countries', *Social Change 21*, pp. 10–21.

Portes, Alejandro. 1985. 'The Informal Sector and The World Economy: Notes on the Structure of Subsidized Labour', in Michael Timberlake (ed.), *Urbanization in the World-Economy.* Tokyo: Academic Press, pp. 53–62.

Sandhu, Ranvinder S. 1989. *The City and its Slums—A Sociological Study.* Amritsar: Guru Nanak Dev University Press.

Seely, John R. 1969. 'The Slum: Its Nature, Use and Users', *Journal of the American Institute of Town Planners 25*, pp. 7–14.

Smith, David A. 1987. 'Overurbanization Reconceptualized: A Political Economy of the World-System Approach', *Urban Affairs Quarterly 23*, pp. 270–94.

Stokes, Charles J. 1970. 'A Theory of Slums', in A.R Desai and S.D Pillai (eds.), *Slums and Urbanization.* Bombay: Popular Prakashan, pp. 55–72.

Teune, H. 1988. 'Growth and Pathologies of Giant Cities', in M. Dogan and J. Kasarda (eds.), *A World of Giant Cities.* Newbury Park, CA: Sage, pp. 351–76.

Timberlake, Michael. 1985. 'The World-System Perspective and Urbanization', in M. Timberlake (ed.), *Urbanization in the World-Economy.* Tokyo: Academic Press, pp. 3–24.

Turner, J.F.C. 1968. 'Housing Priorities, Settlement Pattern and Urban Development in Modernizing Countries', *Journal of the American Institute of Planners 34,* pp. 354–63.

United Nations Commission on Human Settlements. 1992. *A New Agenda for Human Settlements.* Nairobi, Kenya: UNCHS.

United Nations Development Program. 1990. *Human Development Report 1990.* New York: UNDP.

———. 1991. *Human Development Report 1991.* New York: UNDP.

Van Vliet, W. 1987. 'Housing in the Third World', *Environment and Behavior 19,* pp. 267–85.

Weber, A.F. 1899. *The Growth of Cities in the Nineteenth Century.* New York: McGraw-Hill.

Wirth, Louis. 1938. 'Urbanism as a Way of Life', *American Journal of Sociology 44*, pp. 1–24.

World Bank. 1992. *The Housing Indicators Program.* Washington, D.C.: The World Bank.

World Health Organization. 1988. *Urbanization and its Implications for Child Health—Potential for Action.* Geneva: WHO.

Yap, Kioe-Sheng. 1990. 'Capital Interests and Housing Policy in Baldia Township in Karachi', in B. C. Aldrich and Ranvinder S. Sandhu (eds.), *Housing in Asia.* Jaipur: Rawat Publications, pp. 191–201.

2

The Role of the World Bank in Housing

Cedric Pugh

The visual imagery of housing poverty in urban areas in developing countries is clear and well-known. Fetid slums are widespread in the form of overcrowded tenements and ramshackle buildings erected by the poor on patches of invaded land. Living conditions are frequently unhealthy and households compete and struggle for work, meager incomes, basic food, and access to shelter and inadequate urban services. This visual imagery expresses part of the reality, and it is so plain and obvious that the nature of the relationship between housing and poverty is seldom explored in-depth either by policy makers or by housing intellectuals. Although the literature on housing in developing countries has numerous examples of sociological surveys of slums, upgraded slums with improved urban services, and of sites-and-services projects, few authors go beyond the factual reporting of household living conditions. Consequently, the housing literature has insufficient analysis of the causal connections between housing poverty and income (or food) poverty. Lacking a good analytical basis and broad socioeconomic conditions of causes and connections between housing and poverty, policy tends to address the issues in fragmentary or misconceived ways, not in ways which create a broad sustainable reduction in housing poverty.

By the late 1980s, it was becoming increasingly obvious to international aid donors, policy makers, and housing intellectuals that notwithstanding extensive efforts to improve the living conditions of the poor, the level of effective achievement in relation to need and expectations was disappointing.[1] In their international review of popular (poor) urban settlements, Hardoy and Satterthwaite (1989) reported the realities on such issues as low-income access to housing, policy performance, the health-housing relationship, squatting, eviction, social segregation, and pollution. They found large gaps between what actually happened in these matters and what policy makers said should happen. The legal and institutional structure of government and its housing agencies were not coping; local government was deficient in responsibilities and resources; and in some instances the authorities bulldozed squatter settlements and repressed the poor. Amidst living conditions where crowding, disrepair, and insanitary environments prevailed, land rights were, nevertheless, traded in active commercial markets, even though many settlements had their legitimacy in question among the urban governing authorities.

In the early 1990s, the World Bank brought the issue of poverty to the center of its agenda in its development goals. The Bank's development and anti-poverty goals had been evident during the 1980s, but were somewhat relegated to the background owing to widespread macroeconomic destabilization and external debt problems among countries in Latin America and Sub-Saharan Africa. Macroeconomic destabilization and external debt problems have significant links with poverty and these will be discussed in due course. The Bank's 13th annual development report (World Bank 1990a) was devoted to a review and an analysis of poverty in developing countries. Using a meager poverty line (i.e., an income-food subsistence indicator) of some US$ 370 per capita per annum, the Bank estimated that developing countries continued to experience a massive burden of poverty, affecting over 1 billion children, women, and men. The large number, affected in itself, gives significance to poverty: this significance is not diminished by the progress which had been achieved in the previous three decades, 1960 to 1990. In that time the proportions of populations in poverty had decreased, and notwithstanding economic austerity programs in some Latin American and Sub-Saharan countries, better national performances had occurred in social indicators such as education, health, and nutrition. These social indicators express aggregate tendencies, of course, and it should be appreciated that economic austerity during the 1980s intensified poverty among some groups which were vulnerable and already experiencing subsistence poverty.

It also has to be appreciated that although assessments and analyses of poverty and inequality are related to each other, they are not the same thing. Inequalities may increase even though poverty decreases. This has been the case during the 1980s with the Bank (World Bank 1990a) reporting decreases in poverty, and the United Nations Development Program (UNDP 1992) revealing increased inequality. Since 1960, countries where the richest 20 percent live have increased their share of global economic income from 70.2 percent to 82.7 percent, being 60 times better off than countries where the poorest 20 percent reside. Comparative international inequality raises relevant questions about social justice and the causes of inequality, and whether the inequalities influence housing affordability in nations, especially with regard to proportionate income distribution in households below median-level incomes. For individual countries, development policies and performances which increase the income share of households below the fortieth percentile enable potential housing affordability among low-income groups to improve. Taiwan was an example of this kind from the 1960 to the 1990 period, with the rise in manufacturing which tightened labor markets and reduced unemployment. Apart from noting this general perspective the questions about inequality will not be pursued further in this piece of writing. The purpose here is to focus and give prominence to income poverty, housing poverty, and anti-poverty policies.

It is necessary to discern at the outset in exactly what ways the World Bank is addressing the renewed significance it is giving to income poverty, housing poverty, and their relationship to economic policies. The Bank's 13th development report (World Bank 1990a) does not have much to say *directly* on housing, but by inference it assumes importance in various indirect ways. These indirect ways include the Bank's favored policies for economic stabilization, for using markets and reformed state roles to increase the incomes of the poor, and for taking more urgent measures to ensure that social policies are formulated and designed so that they become more effective among the poor. Since 1990, the Bank has issued a specific report on urbanization in developing countries (World Bank 1991), and that report is a forerunner to one which is currently in preparation on housing. The housing policy review is being coordinated with the report on urbanization, and both of these are related to the 1990 13th development report. As will be seen presently, the Bank's evolving theory and practice of low-income housing has antipoverty aims, and its learning experience is derived from its post-1972 learning by doing with its varied program successes and failures. Since 1990, the Bank has issued a specific report on urbanization in developing countries (World Bank 1991), and that report was a forerunner to the Bank's strategic review of housing policy (World Bank 1992).

The foregoing clearly establishes the growing policy significance of poverty and housing, but, as was mentioned, the subject presently lacks adequate analytical and evaluative insights. In this piece of writing, the focus will be on the analytical, interpretive, and evaluative aspects of the relationships between income poverty and housing poverty. My approach to the subject will also provide discussions on the continually evolving theory and practice of low-income housing within World Bank loan finance since 1972. The Bank has been a major agent of change in developing countries, both in relation to its coordinated macroeconomic reforms with the International Monetary Fund (IMF) and its housing loan and policy activities. In housing, the Bank has participated in the finance of some 116 sites-and-services projects and complementary slum upgrading schemes with its average loan of some US$ 211 million in the period 1972 to 1990 in some 55 countries. Perspectives and explanations of housing and poverty are linked to the IMF and World Bank macroeconomic reforms in some developing countries. For example, policy requirements in macroeconomic stabilization to curb increases in public expenditure frequently lead to cuts in spending on infrastructure, consequently reducing short-term provisions of basic urban and housing services. Further elaborations of the macroeconomic links with housing and poverty will be made in subsequent discussions. Another feature of this article will be a review of the emergent 'best practice' in low-income housing, with reference to case examples in Madras, India and Sri Lanka. India and Sri Lanka are particularly important in the discussion of poverty and housing because some 50 percent of the poor in developing countries are in South Asian countries (World Bank 1990a).

The connections between housing poverty and income poverty are not straightforward, but rather they are somewhat complicated and vary according to the circumstances of time and place. For example, in times and places where housing is grossly undersupplied in relation to demand and need— such as was the case in Bombay in the 1970s and 1980s—households with middle and higher incomes will live in slum housing conditions (Pugh 1989). It is possible to be nonpoor in income, but to experience housing poverty. The criteria which determine that existence of housing poverty include high rent/repayment-to-income ratios, substandard and unfit housing conditions, and substantially blocked access to adequate housing. Income or food poverty is, in itself, a matter of households falling below some level of subsistence or deprivation. Although low income is frequently a major cause of housing poverty, such housing-related conditions as low supplies, ineffective land policies, inappropriate building codes, and imbalances in tenure and finance can be significant in assessments of housing poverty and affordability. These matters are central in discussions of housing poverty, all of which are to some extent affecting quality of life conditions in pavement dwelling, squatter settlement, slum living, and public policy responses to low-income housing problems. Housing poverty is also significantly influenced by general economic conditions including inflation, unemployment, rapid changes to the structure of an economy, and changes in rates of interest. Housing and poverty can be approached and analyzed in a number of ways. The approach taken here is to commence with a discussion of the causes of income poverty in developing countries. This will provide a conceptual basis and a context for further discussions on macroeconomic conditions, antipoverty policies, and case studies.

INCOME POVERTY

In developing countries income poverty is, as was indicated earlier, massive in scale, and it is predominantly associated with low-levels of economic development. Low-levels of economic development are explained by the structural conditions of such economies. As populations increase, rural land is insufficient to provide income generation for the labor force in agriculture, and consequently, the landless are pushed into urban areas for survival and opportunity. But in urban areas investment in the formal sectors of the economy is not high enough to absorb the increasing labor force. In fact, in urban areas levels of investment are too low to absorb the growing labor force from natural (i.e., nonmigratory) increases in urban population. This means that migrants from rural areas and many born in growing urban areas are dependent upon the informal sectors for their livelihood. The economic and legal conditions in the informal sectors result in large numbers in these sectors living in a state of poverty. However, some workers in the formal sectors are paid low wages with some consequent poverty in these sectors. But most urban income poverty is accounted for in the informal sectors. The relationship between income poverty and income generation in the formal and informal sectors of the economy is illustrated in Figure 2.1.

Figure 2.1 Income Poverty and Formal and Informal Sector Incomes

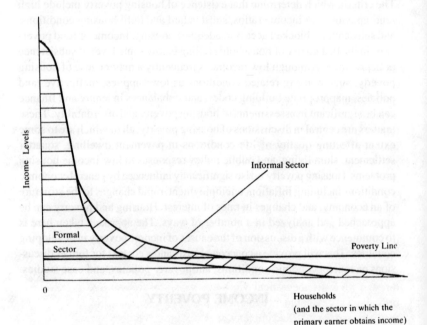

The formal sectors have legal recognition and are within national tax systems, whereas the informal sectors have no legal recognition and are largely outside tax systems. As shown in Figure 2.1, the formal sectors generate higher levels of income for some households, but most households have moderate or low incomes. The formal sectors are advantaged by having access to the finance provided in formal capital markets and financial institutions, along with the use of superior technology. The inaccessibility of the informal sectors to superior financial systems and technologies largely accounts for their lower income generation and their widespread poverty. Nevertheless, many individuals in the informal sectors are self-employed, and some have significant entrepreneurial talent. Often economists omit the contribution of the informal sector to GDP (i.e., to national income), and such contribution can amount to over 30 percent of GDP. As economic development proceeds, the formal sectors grow and the informal sectors decrease in their overall economic contribution.

The jobs available in the informal sectors are mainly occasional and intermittent; labor competition is intensive for the jobs; and sometimes the work is exploitive providing low cost labor and goods to both the formal and informal sectors. Housing conditions are closely related to informal sector economic activity. The dominance of low incomes in the informal sector means that the affordability to spend on shelter needs is very limited. For example, in India the very poor are constrained to spend some 80 percent to 85 percent of their household budgets on food, while the not so poor spend some 60 percent of their budget on food (Pugh 1990a). Clearly the pressed low incomes leave little in the way of surplus for shelter and other economic needs. Accordingly the poor economize by dwelling on pavements, crowding into tenements by often renting meager space on a roster system, and building makeshift housing on low cost land. Self-help housing in squatter settlements is, of course, often constructed by people whose labor time, access to materials, and holdings of capital are within the informal sector. The building work is sometimes contracted out or accomplished within family and friendship networks. It is the economic saving, investment, and labor activity which, like most informal sector work, is omitted from official statistics of the economy.

The World Bank has a theoretical and a policy action view of how structural poverty in developing countries can be reduced progressively through time. Its theoretical view has become something of a dominant orthodoxy in development economics for the post-1989 period. In the 1980s, the Bank and the IMF had implemented economic stabilization and structural adjustment programs in Latin American, Sub-Saharan African, and other countries. Loan finance was provided to enable governments to introduce economic reforms and reduce balance of payments deficits, to curb excessive deficits in public sector budgets, and to place economies into a medium-term reform to secure better performances in exports and economic growth. The new orthodoxy in development economics was based upon integrating national economies into international trade and finance, and upon establishing reformed relationships in state and market roles. The advocates for the new orthodoxy argued the virtues of free markets for their economic efficiency and dynamism in securing growth. State roles were regarded as appropriately constructed when they expressed enablement. Enablement took the form of ensuring secure private property rights, deregulating markets where regulation was inhibitory, achieving macroeconomic stability, enhancing the development of finance capital markets, and providing sector policy frameworks and institutional conditions which allowed the private sector and nongovernmental institutions (NGOs) to have an effective performance in sector development. As will presently be seen, all of this has relevance for housing and poverty.

In its broadest macroeconomic perspective, the aim of the new enablement orthodoxy is to increase economic growth in developing countries in order to reduce poverty. For an illustrative perspective, with reference to Figure 2.1, this means that general national income levels would grow and less households would be placed below the poverty line. One housing consequence could be that crowding in tenements, squatter settlement, and pavement dwelling would all decrease; but, as reasoned in later discussions, this would depend upon complementary changes in urban housing markets. The World Bank offers both evidence and argument in support of its favored policies for development. Evidence comes from experience in some countries: for example, in Indonesia from 1970 to 1990, poverty was reduced from 60 percent to 20 percent of the population within medium-term, continuous, economic growth (World Bank 1990). Taking this sort of evidence, and the precepts of enablement as the way to increase economic growth, the Bank gives shape to its antipoverty economic argument as follows (World Bank 1990a, 1991a):

- Central governments should provide a stable macroeconomic foundation to the economy.
- State roles should include the investment in people (i.e., human capital formation) in education, training, health, nutrition, family planning, and the alleviation of poverty: one aspect of these roles is to improve the targeting of benefits and any necessary subsidies to ensure that they reach the poor, sometimes using the NGOs in outreach programs.
- Other state roles would include responsibilities for ensuring that free market competition flourishes: this is regarded as beneficial for the

poor as well as the rich, because it would increase the productivities and income levels in the informal sectors.

The foregoing expresses prescription rather than reality for many developing countries, and its significance for housing is both general and indirect, rather than particular and programatic for the housing sector. However, it has relevance and realism in some countries because it summarizes their recent experiences and for other countries it forms part of loan supported World Bank and IMF economic reforms. Countries for which the above prescription broadly fits their economic experience in development include Hong Kong, Singapore, Taiwan, South Korea, and other Asian countries. Singapore, especially, has operated successful long-term reform in coordinating its economic development policies, urbanization, housing programs, and its performance in keeping poverty within moderate levels (Pugh 1984, 1985). Squatter settlement in Singapore was reduced in a coordinated set of planning provisions which included upgrading, rehousing a growing public housing program, and the reallocation of land for more intensive and modernized urban purposes. For countries undergoing economic reform within IMF and World Bank adjustment loan programs, the intention of policy reform is to achieve some useful elements in the prescription given earlier. Often this includes conditionality clauses in the loan agreements to alter policies, reform the public sector, and create institutional arrangements which are less harmful to markets. The elements of conditionality-induced reform which have special significance for housing include the development of finance capital markets, the deregulation of rates of interest, the curbs on the growth of public expenditure which often cuts spending on infrastructure, and taking direct production roles away from the state (including housing) in favor of enhanced private sector and NGO roles. Much of the antipoverty and housing impact of conditionality-induced reform is not yet realized, with evidence and evaluation unavailable: the reforms are set for medium-term periods, and evidence and evaluation will be available by the mid-1990s. But it is possible to discuss some poverty and housing-related consequences of economic stabilization and structural adjustment programs in Latin American countries and to show the large significance of macroeconomic factors in housing, including low-income housing programs.

With the onset of greater economic fluctuations and increasingly volatile markets in the global economy, among many developing countries during the 1980s, more attention has been given to the relationships among the wider macroeconomy, housing systems, and housing poverty. Buckley and Mayo (1989) have reviewed housing and the macroeconomy, arguing that it is important to distinguish on-budget from off-budget factors. On-budget factors include government loans, grants, expenditure subsidies, and taxation expenditures (i.e., tax remissions on housing assets), and other items which occur in public sector budgets. The off-budget factors comprise overt and hidden subsidies or costs lying outside public sector budgets, including loans at below-market rates of interest, land use regulations, and allocations to housing at distorted (nonmarket determined) prices. Buckley and Mayo found that the off-budget subsidies and costs were frequently larger in volume and more significant in their social and economic consequences than the on-budget matters which are nevertheless more conspicuous. In effect, the off-budget factors are significant in housing poverty because they impede flows of finance capital into low-income housing, and they reduce housing supplies by the excessive regulation of markets. The intellectual implications are that housing researchers will have to give these issues more attention in their housing poverty research, and the policy implications are that central and local governments need to reform institutional and regulatory relationships so that housing sector development becomes more effective. This is discussed further in the subsequent sections.

Examples of the housing-related consequences of IMF–World Bank stabilization and adjustment programs in some Latin American countries can be given. Stabilization programs and (structural) adjustment programs have differing but related aims. Adjustment programs are set to improve medium- and long-term economic growth: they address sectoral change enhancing growth prospects in those sectors which are internationally efficient, and in exports, integrating national economies with the global economy. By contrast, stabilization programs address the immediate causal conditions of excessive inflation and balance of payments deficits which get out of control: they are aimed at short-term impacts. Adjustment and stabilization programs are related. Stabilization sets the framework under which well-designed adjustment programs can have better prospects for effective implementation, especially in redeploying resources and finance capital to efficient growth sectors. In actual form, both types of programs include the elements of enablement discussed earlier, and they are attached to loan conditionality clauses. In their actual operation in the 1980s, and in their theoretical predictions in the short term, the programs can reduce economic growth and intensify poverty among some groups. Accordingly in the developing countries which have experienced either their own stabilization and adjustment programs or those under the World Bank–IMF loan programs, it makes appropriate sense to recognize stabilization poverty and adjustment poverty in income poverty.

Stabilization and adjustment programs in some Latin American and Sub-Saharan countries were introduced under conditions of urgency, without significant regard for the social costs and poverty intensification. This means that in the course of their implementation, the programs had adverse consequences for income and housing poverty. Accordingly the World Bank's learning experience has brought into significance the necessity to include policy elements which cushion the poverty-related social costs of macroeconomic programs, and to become more appreciative of the vulnerability of housing-related infrastructural investment when public sector budgets are tightly controlled, curbing public expenditure (World Bank 1990b). Presently the case for including consideration and well-designed policy elements to provide a cushion against the social costs of adjustment programs and to ensure that infrastructural investment is satisfactory, is propositional rather than actual in practice. The macroeconomic lessons from experience in Sub-Saharan African countries is that although stabilization is a precondition for improved economic development, it is not in itself sufficient: other necessary preconditions include skill formation in industry, increased private sector investment, and a deepening learning experience in the entrepreneurship of running internationally competitive firms. It is appropriate to consider a few examples from the 1980s with a purpose to discern in what ways adjustment and housing policies can be harmonized more effectively.

STRUCTURAL ADJUSTMENT, LIVING CONDITIONS, AND HOUSING POVERTY

Housing poverty is intensified when any combination of the following occurs—incomes are reduced, particularly among low-income groups; housing costs and interest rates increase, especially when the increases outpace any growth in incomes and the general index of prices; and utility services and infrastructure are undermaintained and capital installation programs are cut back in low-income areas where populations are, perhaps, increasing. Countries which experienced significant macroeconomic mismanagement— for example, in the late 1970s, Brazil, Mexico, other Latin American countries, and some Sub-Saharan African countries—often had severe problems with inflation, destabilized housing finance systems, economic recession, and pressures to cut back utility services and infrastructure in public sector budgets. The urban poor are vulnerable to these problems both directly in the impact upon their living and housing conditions, and indirectly in the housing-related consequences when moderate- and middle-income groups are adversely affected. When moderate- and middle-income groups experience higher housing costs and decreased incomes, housing supplies are curbed and competitive pressures increase in the housing system as a whole, with low-income groups then facing inadequate housing supplies and higher costs in growing urban areas. The indirect consequences often mean that slum living conditions, squatter settlement, and affordability difficulties in housing will increase, adding to the chronic long-term trends of growing numbers of the urban poor. The examples selected for discussion give insights into the ways housing systems respond to austerity-directed stabilization and structural adjustment programs.

Costa Rica

Costa Rica experienced problems associated with economic mismanagement and deterioration in export revenue in the late 1970s and early 1980s. In consequence, its government accepted IMF and World Bank loan program in the years 1981 to 1989, amounting to some US$ 200 million. The loan programs had conditionality clauses, requiring costa Rica to reform its macroeconomic policies in favor of anti-inflationary purposes and export sector development. The attitude of the IMF and the World Bank is that austerity packages for policy reform are necessary because deterioration in balance of payments deficits and in inflationary conditions is unsustainable, and that their 'orderly' approaches to adjustment are superior to 'less orderly' approaches outside the influence of their loan agreements. The World Bank's policy approaches and their effectiveness have been evaluated by Mosley, Harrigan, and Toye (1991). Their evaluation reveals that until the late 1980s, Bank adjustment programs emphasized macroeconomic urgencies for anti-inflation rather than social and poverty impacts, and that the Bank had to go through a learning by doing experience with necessities to achieve better coordination with national governments and with the IMF. As was mentioned earlier, the Bank has acknowledged the need to give poverty and social impacts more significance in the future (World Bank 1990b).

Chant's studies of household living conditions and migration patterns in the 1980s in Costa Rica, reveal the housing-related consequences of adjustment policies and macroeconomic austerity. She found that women-headed households sought an economic refuge in small- and medium-sized towns where they could economize housing outlays and live within their low-income constraints (Chant 1990b). The larger cities had unaffordable housing costs and greater inflationary pressures than the smaller towns. How is this change to be interpreted? First, housing systems reacted spontaneously to adjustment packages rather than being within protective policy formulation. Second, families often split up, with men taking work and rental rooms in larger cities where some work was available, and women migrating with their children. Beneria's study of similar conditions in Brazil in her surveys of household living conditions reinforces this interpretation (Beneria 1990). She found that some households remained intact with cooperation among men and women, but others dissolved with separation and divorce. This changed attitudes to gender and marriage, conventionally having been within the strong Catholic family unit advocacy and tradition for hundreds of years. In the long-term, split families will add to the housing demand, and sometimes to welfare support needs. Third, structural adjustment has impacts on the economic growth rates of sectors, with some declining and others increasing at various rates. This leaves some towns and regions with loose (affordable) housing markets and others with tight (less affordable) housing in the short- and medium-term. Housing policy, especially for low-income groups, will have to increasingly bring the sectoral–spatial effects of economic adjustment into account. Rapid sectoral change disturbs the balance of housing demand and housing supply, and it can lead to higher household formation by way of separation and divorce.

Kenya

The next example is Kenya, a country in Sub-Saharan Africa, which, although not with the severest intensity of poverty among Sub-Saharan countries, has, nevertheless, some of the economic problems associated with that region of the world. Economic and political crises in Sub-Saharan Africa have been receiving international intellectual and policy attention since 1985. The general features of these problems can be summarized as follows:

- high rates of population growth and birth rates, in a context of sluggish economic performance,
- rapid urbanization in a policy and economic context where inadequacies are significant in infrastructure, public sector budgeting, urban management skills, and where corruption is present,
- growing external debt problems in economies which are dependent upon primary commodities for export income and where economies have been in a state of stagnation,
- famine in some countries, often aggravated by political conflicts and bad government (Glickman 1988; Stren and White 1989; Parfitt and Riley 1989; Pickett and Singer 1990).

The World Bank has also reviewed countries in Sub-Saharan Africa, concerned that prospective futures will increase the proportion of world poverty in the region (World Bank 1989). In fact, the Bank's report on Sub-Saharan economies and their poverty marked a change in attitude and policy direction. The Bank became concerned about the quality and performance of governments, particularly because loan adjustment programs required government commitments and actions to improve the economies. By 1991, the Bank and other international aid donors were placing pressure on political leaders to introduce democratic political reform and to improve their record in human rights, associating this pressure with power to withhold loan assistance. The Kenyan President, Daniel arap Moi, has been under such pressure; and pressures have increased since the demise of international communism in eastern Europe and in some developing countries. Kenya's external debt repayments as a proportion of export income have increased from 8 percent in 1975 to 19 percent by 1982. In the years 1979 to 1991, it has been constrained to receive some US$ 500 million for economic stabilization and structural adjustment from the IMF and the World Bank. Economic growth performance had been satisfactory at an annual average rate of 7 percent in the period 1964 to 1973, but with deteriorating exports in 1974, the economy went into a recession from 1974 to 1984. This led to a loan agreement in 1983 with the World Bank in favour of adjustment, and subsequently public sector expenditure was constrained and its growth curbed.

The consequences for public sector investment in land, infrastructure, and housing were immediate and adverse. Capital allocations came down by 23 percent from 1984–85 to 1985–86: sanitation services in low-income areas were reduced to marginal allocations (Pugh 1992a). From one perspective, this raises questions about the intensification of housing poverty, and from another, it points to the need to find long-term solutions to the provision of utility and infrastructural services. An emergent new literature (Rondinelli and Shabbir 1988; Mengers 1990) is addressing long-term solutions in terms of innovation and new approaches. In some countries, even apart from austerity-directed adjustment programs, the population growth in low-income urban areas outpaces the capacity of government to provide infrastructure, and high-levels of poverty are likely to continue in many urban areas. Innovative approaches to the problems can take the form of joint ventures among governments, markets, NGOs, and community groups. Joint ventures require new institutional arrangements, being favored in the World Bank, UNCHS (Habitat), and UNDP advocacy of enablement. Initiatives by governments and local governments would be required in community development, skills training, provision of information, deregulation of some building codes, and in linking the poor to NGOs and to informal sector capacities in infrastructural services. Infrastructure and utilities would consequently be supplied by varied sources, not being entirely within government provisions. Self-help and group voluntarism would be necessary: an example of such initiatives will be outlined in subsequent discussions of housing reform in Mexico.

Brazil

Brazil presents a good example of interdependence between macroeconomic policies, external debt crises, structural adjustment, declining living standards among the poor (and higher income groups), and housing. The growing literature in these topics reveals the essential characteristic insights (Barbosa 1984; Helmers 1988; Klugman 1988; Simonsen 1988; de Azevedo 1990; Pugh 1991; Pugh 1992b; Valenca 1992). In the years 1983 to 1990, Brazil borrowed over US$ 1200 million from the IMF and the World Bank for the stabilization of its currency and structural adjustment. This followed macroeconomic mismanagement, large external indebtedness to international commercial banks, and global economic recession in the early 1980s, undermining consequently, Brazil's export earnings. The austerity stabilization and adjustment programs had severe effects upon incomes and poverty, and repercussion effects on Brazil's housing system and housing affordability. The social impacts were all the more intense because Brazil has one of the most inegalitarian distributions of income in the world. Some 5 percent of its population have 35 percent of GDP, and 70 percent have less than 30 percent of GDP. Living standards, housing affordability, and the poor were hit by high rates of inflation, high-levels of interest rates, economic recession, an economic collapse of housing markets, and disruptions in housing finance. The effects were experienced among middle-, moderate-, and low-income groups, and, following government action in 1986 to eliminate the National Housing Bank, Brazil was left with institutional gaps in housing.

The major economic issues and events took the following course. A military government was in power from 1964 to 1985. Its economic policy was to diversify and expand manufacturing industry and to continue high economic growth at some 10 percent per annum. Some priority was given to developing housing finance and housing sector development. In the 1970s, economic problems began to appear, although unlike Mexico (see subsequent discussions), Brazil kept its government budgets out of deficit. The major economic problem which had assumed great significance in the time of the crisis in the early 1980s was the adoption of indexation in wages, finance contracts, and other things. Indexation was widely used in attempts to compensate for high continuous rates of inflation. Along with indexation, the other contributory causes to triple digit inflation were looseness in controlling money supply, increased costs of imported goods, and delays in making appropriate public policy responses. Balance of payments deficits also became significant, and by 1982 the balance of payments deficit amounted to some US$ 16.3 billion and Brazil's foreign reserves were depleted. Investors feared a worsening macroeconomic performance and sent their finance overseas in capital flight. Meanwhile foreign debt grew and following the Mexican action in 1982 in declaring its inability to repay its debts, foreign banks withdrew their loans to Latin American countries. In the deteriorating circumstances the government devalued its Cruzeiro by 30 percent in 1983 and in the same year sought IMF loan finance for stabilization and structural adjustment. The IMF used its conditionality clauses to press Brazil into reductions in public spending, and switching expenditure in favor of growth sectors for effectiveness in structural adjustment. By 1986, Brazil had eliminated deficits in its balance of payments as imports were savagely compressed in austere economic policies; but inflation remained grossly high at 22 percent. It was not until 1991–92 that inflation was reduced; but it had not been adequately controlled in the early 1990s. The purchasing power of wages and incomes decreased in the years 1983 to 1990.

Housing was affected in a number of ways, including low-income households adjusting to austerity by favoring rental tenure, crowding into housing space, and by increases in squatter settlement. But for present purposes the main focus will be placed upon changes in the Brazilian housing finance system because the enlargement and development of housing finance systems is perceived by the World Bank as an important means of improving housing conditions for moderate- and low-income households. In fact, in 1963 the World Bank and the US Agency for International Development (USAID) held a conference in Lima, Peru with the purpose of encouraging governments in Latin American countries to restructure capital markets and to develop housing mortgage institutions. The military government in Brazil responded in 1964 by creating the Brazilian National Housing Bank. This signalled the commitment of the government to the policy priority of developing the housing sector. The National Housing Bank operated as the key coordinating and policy agency within the *Sistema Financeiro da Habitasao* (SFH). Financial sources to support the SFH and the National Housing Bank came from savings and loans institutions, mortgage repayments, and from the compulsory social insurance funds which collected 3 percent of formal sector wages. The housing finance and housing construction sectors grew substantially, and by 1982 some 40 percent of the housing stock was financed from the SFH and the National Housing Bank employed over 10,000 people.

Problems began to appear to the National Housing Bank finances in the 1970s. Loan allocations were diverted to the middle-income groups in reaction to constrained affordability and loan repayment difficulties among moderate- and low-income groups. The Bank's attempts to cross-subsidize financial costs from higher to lower income groups had failed. When the austerity stabilization and adjustment programs were introduced in 1983, worse was to follow. Middle-income groups also began to experience decreases in incomes. The Bank found that as a consequence, the defaults on loan repayments increased, but its depositors were bound to receive index-linked guarantees to compensate for inflation in their accounts. The Bank's sources of funds were also affected adversely: social security funds diminished as wages decreased, and unemployment led to prior claims for a call on these funds by the unemployed. Simultaneously, the savings and loan institutions faced decreased deposits because in economic austerity households reduced their rates of saving. Housing markets experienced rapid falls in prices and an excess supply of dwellings in austerity conditions.

Clearly the SFH and the National Housing Bank were in a state of financial crisis, and housing sector development had been disrupted. In 1984, defaults on mortgage repayments were running at some 50.9 percent. The government abolished the Bank in 1986, and did not create new institutional and policy arrangements for housing recovery. Although the demise of the Bank mainly directly affected middle-income households, the nature of the crisis had substantial repercussion effects upon lower-income groups. Housing supplies were cut back, leaving Brazil in a housing needs deficit of some ten million dwellings, consequently heightening price access problems among middle-, moderate-, and low-income groups. More significantly, the abolition of the National Housing Bank has forestalled any real possibility of developing housing finance systems specifically for the poor. Kaul (1990) has given attention to these possibilities in his studies of the poor in India. He found that the formal sector housing finance institutions seldom provide mortgage finance to low-income households, but that such households have a willingness to save for homeownership. He recommends the development of a small loans system, linked to the formal financial sector and relying upon NGOs to make savings and loan repayments effective. Innovative institutional arrangements would be needed because the poor have intermittent incomes and no collateral assets in land and property to secure their loan finance in the formal sector. The innovations would include a link institution between NGOs and formal financial institutions to raise finance from those institutions, and using their influence and controls through NGOs to ensure that the poor repay their loans. The NGOs would develop informational and community networks among the poor to create motivational contexts for saving and repayment, relying upon their direct contact with the poor. Affordable loan instruments could be designed, with some lower interest cross-subsidization for the poorest. Practical examples exist in Bangladesh in the Grameen banks and in self-help movements among organized women's groups in some Indian cities. More significantly in 1991, UNCHS (Habitat) and the UNDP jointly launched an Asian-based project to develop market based housing financial systems which would be responsive to low-income groups. In response, the Coalition of Housing Finance Institutions was created to link policy, research, and program development among leading housing financiers in Thailand, Korea, the Philippines, and India. By 1992, the Coalition was having an innovative impact on other Asian countries, including Vietnam and Mongolia.

Mexico

Mexico's experience during the 1980s presents some interesting features of housing-related responses to stabilization and structural adjustment programs. Like Brazil, the Mexican economy had a steady and good economic growth at an annual average rate of some 6 percent in the two decades before economic crisis occurred in the early 1980s. In 1982, Mexico declared that it could not repay its debts to international banks, placing dilemmas of serious possible instabilities in the international financial system. Mexico became dependent upon the IMF and the World Bank to rescue it from economic collapse: in the years 1983 to 1991, Mexico has borrowed some US$ 4200 million for stabilization and structural adjustment. This has been associated with austerity programs in the first instance in the mid-1980s, followed by controlled growth and restructuring in post-1987 economic policy packages. The 1980s have been characterized with external debt which grew from US$ 57 billion in 1980 to US$ 101 billion in 1989, with interest payments absorbing over 27 percent of export income. In attempting to deal with the external debt problems and some economic mismanagement from the 1970s, Mexico has experienced high rates of inflation, austerity policy-induced recession, balance of payments crises, devaluation, and decreases in living standards. By September 1993, inflation had been reduced to some 9 percent per annum, privatization and deregulation were well-advanced, foreign capital was flowing into Mexico, negotiations were proceeding on the North American Free Trade Area (NAFTA), and allocations to health and education in public sector budgets were increasing.

Owing to the very great significance of the Mexican debt crisis in 1982, the international evaluation and commentary on Mexico's economy has been substantial and detailed (Collins 1988; Cardoso 1988; Dornbusch 1988; Helmers 1988; Pugh 1991; Pugh 1992b). Since 1970, the significant events and economic characteristics have been as follows—By 1970, some 60 percent of Mexico's population was urbanized and it was on a growth path among the higher income group of developing countries. Mexico became a major exporter of oil, and although it was not a member of OPEC, its economy was influenced by international oil prices and the activities of

OPEC. For example, in the second OPEC oil crisis in 1979, OPEC doubled the price of oil: Mexican policy makers took this as a signal for long-term economic boom conditions and they accelerated public expenditure and their ambitions for economic growth. However, two factors made this a risky and vulnerable reaction. First, in 1979, Paul Volcker, Chairman of the US Federal Reserve Bank, decided to follow a strong anti-inflationary policy by severely restricting the growth in US money supply. Other countries were threatened in terms of speculative international currency movements, with investors being attracted by the high US rates of interest. In response to this they tightened their money supplies, raised rates of interest, and placed anti-inflationary aims as their priorities in macroeconomic policy. This lowered the demand for internationally traded goods and services, consequently undermining the exports of developing countries, including Mexico. Second, oil prices fell in 1985 as a reaction to lower international demand and increasing cost efficiency in the energy and manufacturing sectors of the developed countries. Instead of long-term economic boom, Mexico faced decreased export revenue and an overhang of debt repayment problems.

During President Echeverria's regime, 1970–76, deficits on government budgets had grown from 1 percent to 5 percent of GDP, and excessive expenditure policies were also pursued by his successor, President Portillo in the early 1980s. When President de la Madrid took over in 1982, inflation was running at 160 percent and foreign debt stood at over US$ 100 billion. Austerity macroeconomic policy was secured by the IMF in its conditionality clauses in the 1983 stabilization loan program, and attempts were made in 1985, 1986, and 1987 to restructure the economy. However, such were the magnitudes of Mexico's economic problems, and their context in a global recession with post-1985 lower oil prices, that the attempts to secure stabilization and adjustment had limited success until after 1988. But the austerity features in the 1983 IMF loan program—reduction of government deficits by 50 percent, wage curbs, anti-inflation policies, and better control of the exchange rate—had a clear impact. Living standards declined and imports were savagely compressed. All of this, together with inflation continuing to run at high levels of some 80 percent, had various adverse housing-related effects.

Some of the housing-related consequences of macroeconomic austerity are well-documented and reviewed by Gilbert (1989, 1990a), Gilbert and Varley (1990), Beneria (1990), and Connolly (1990). The profitability in formal sector tenements for rental purposes had been marginalized for decades and this was aggravated by the decreased affordability in the mid-1980s. But landlords in squatter settlements who sought to supplement their depressed incomes, and households with decreasing incomes were constrained to economize on their housing outlays. Accordingly the demand for letting rooms increased and squatter settlement populations increased. Homeownership among the poor decreased owing to the lowered incomes, inflated building costs, and high rates of interest on housing credit. In these circumstances the political discontent in squatter settlement was significant, and the Mexican government was inclined to regularize tenure (i.e., recognize it and give it legal legitimacy) during the 1970s and 1980s. Housing and urban living conditions became heightened in political significance, and this eventually led to creative reforms after 1987.

Significant economic and political changes occurred in 1986–87. The IMF and the World Bank recognized that austerity stabilization programs would not in themselves secure the reduction of external debt in Mexico. They were more disposed to emphasize new directions for structural adjustment which could secure medium-term economic growth. Within Mexican politics, Salinas de Gortari emerged as the key figure in economic and social reform and in Mexico's dominant political party, the *Partido Revolucionario Institucional* (PRI). He had a strong economic influence as the Planning and Budget Minister in de la Madrid's presidency, 1982–88, and in 1988 he became President. His policy had three important elements. He wanted medium-term stabilization to secure conditions for structural change and economic growth. Growth would be encouraged from open economy policies, by attracting foreign capital and repatriation of Mexican capital, from privatization, and from the negotiation of a free trade area with the United States and Canada. The basis for these economic conditions was established in the 1987 Pact for Economic Stabilization and Growth (PESG) which began as a determined intent to restrain inflation by cutting subsidies, curbing wage increases, and renewing attempts at achieving effective structural adjustment. By June 1992, inflation had been reduced to some 15 percent per annum, privatization and deregulation were well-advanced, foreign capital was flowing into Mexico, and negotiations were proceeding on a North American Free Trade Area (NAFTA). Salinas de Gortari added socioeconomic reforms at grass-roots levels to the international and national economic reforms. The day after Salinas de Gortari became President in December 1988, he launched his National Solidarity Program (Solidarity).

Solidarity was designed to achieve popular participation among the poor, using new NGO community development committees for improving access and standards in food, health, education, infrastructure, and housing. Government has been committed to expanding budget allocations to Solidarity programmes and coordinating these with additional resources for health and education. It also provided managerial, publicity and, administration support at decentralized levels of operation, including the use of power and influence to coordinate packages of necessary services from relevant government agencies. In housing-related aspects, Solidarity has expanded self-help housing in sites-and-services in some regions, linking such programs to low-income housing finance; in FONHAPO, a government housing trust fund. Additionally, Solidarity committees in the community have opted to improve sewerage systems, piped water, and access roads in squatter settlements.

Although Solidarity has some political motivation to secure support for the PRI it also is developing genuine participation in community development and in improving living conditions. Solidarity rests upon principles and learning experiences which Salinas de Gortari acquired in his doctorate studies at Harvard University in the 1970s. In those studies he found that political support was related more to participation of the masses in social programs rather than to the volume of public spending in social programs. However, since Mexico's economic recovery in 1989, Salinas de Gortari has expanded social policy budgets to make progress towards a 20 year programe to mitigate poverty and to redress the large inequalities in Mexican society. This constitutes a new way of thinking and operating in a welfare state. Welfare is understood to reside simultaneously in market efficiencies, household self-help, improved effectiveness in welfare state provisions, and in participation through organized community based representation in social development. Alongside Solidarity, the Mexican government of Salinas de Gortari has been reforming housing policy. The reforms include tilting public sector programs towards low- and moderate-income households, regularizing tenure and property rights in squatter settlements, and taking initial steps to expand and improve housing finance for middle- and moderate-income homeownership. As noted perceptively by Connolly (1990), housing reform has been possible because one of its sources of finance has been from mandated social security funds rather than in regular (and curbed) public sector expenditures.

The post-1989 results of PESG and Solidarity shared good early results. By 1990, some 442 Solidarity projects had been undertaken annually and 325,000 land plots had been regularized in squatter settlements. Inflation decreased by some 9 percent by 1993; Mexicans repatriated funds sent into capital flight in the early 1980s and foreigners (including banks which had retreated in the early 1980s) provided a sharp increase in investments; and growth rates were sufficient to restore and improve living standards after 1989. Mexico obtained greater flexibility and more time for meeting its foreign debt repayment obligations: in 1990 it secured an agreement with international banks to restructure some US$ 48.23 billion of its US$ 101.5 billion debt burden.

What is the general and wider international significance of Mexican experience with macroeconomic and housing reforms, especially in their impacts upon living standards and poverty? Clearly bad economic management accumulates problems which eventually require attention, and bad economic management is adverse to housing sector development. Then in the stabilization and adjustment policies, the immediate and short-term effects can further destabilize housing finance and housing production systems. This is particularly the case, if, as occurred until 1988 in IMF and World Bank macroeconomic programs, antipoverty purposes were not included in program design. But stabilization and structural adjustment leave some resource slack in the economy for the medium-term process of change. Salinas de Gortari was quick to recognize this and used the opportunity to develop the housing sector as a means of enhancing economic recovery on the one hand, and of furthering social and political purposes on the other. In fact, the housing-related potential in structural economic adjustment has been receiving significant attention in the modern housing literature (Woodfield 1989). Research in housing economics by Strassman (1976, 1978, 1982) indicates that housing investment has wider benefits in economic growth and that specific types of housing programs have importance in mitigating housing poverty. Investment in housing has useful multiplier economic benefits in employment generation in other sectors, and housing is less likely to drain away scarce foreign exchange than many other sectors. Low-income housing programs can be particularly beneficial with regard to income and employment generation, especially when programs are aimed at the broad dispersion of small loan/assistance packages among the poor. Salinas de Gortari was following these kinds of approaches to housing sector development. Moreover, he created novel institutions in linking state, market, self-help, and NGO roles; and as Strassman (1978, 1982) notes, it is the absence of appropriate institutional frameworks rather than matters of housing design standards which have impeded the required rate of progress in low-income housing.

Overview

The foregoing discussion has elaborated the relationship between income poverty and housing, revealing a diversity of relevant factors. Income poverty, though decreasing, remains significant. It is significant in terms of the mass population in poverty and with regard to such things as macroeconomic destabilization and external debt crises in some developing countries. The macroeconomic factors are relevant to housing through issues like inflation, recession, increasing rates of interest, and curbs in public spending, particularly in infrastructure services. These macroeconomic factors can affect the distribution of income among households, and they may accentuate the burdens on the poor. The poor can be affected both from direct income and housing-related consequences and from indirect impacts such as reduced housing supplies.

Experience with bad economic management and structural adjustment programs in some Latin American countries has left highly specific consequences in housing. In Costa Rica, men and women split their households, with women and children often being constrained to migrate to poorer regions where housing outlays could be economized. Sometimes this added to separation and divorce with long term consequences for living standards and the demand for housing among split households. Kenya and Mexico provide indications of what may happen in structural adjustment: in Kenya, public spending on infrastructure in poor neighborhoods was severely marginalized, and by contrast in Mexico, opportunity was taken to innovate, with collaborated arrangements among government agencies, NGOs, and the community to improve utility and infrastructural services. In fact, since 1987 in Mexico, President Salinas de Gortari has used housing as a lead economic sector in structural adjustment for economic growth and reform. However, in Brazil, macroeconomic destabilization and austerity adjustment programs undermined the National Housing Bank's financial viability, leading to the abolition of the Bank and a large gap in housing development. Obviously the results in housing vary and depend upon economic circumstances and whether policy makers have positive or negative dispositions towards housing. This raises the question as to whether it is possible to design and formulate a prescriptively useful housing policy which would operate effectively in reducing housing poverty. Attention is now being given to this question.

POLICIES TO REDUCE HOUSING POVERTY

My approach to the design and formulation of effective policies for reducing housing poverty is derived from a variety of considerations. Some of these considerations can be presented as summaries of economic principles which have been elaborated in detail in my earlier writing (Pugh 1990a). Others are more practical and experiential in nature, drawing upon on-locational observational experience in India's metro cities, in Sri Lanka's million houses program (and its subsequent developments) in the 1980s, and in Kenya's attempts to develop a national housing policy in the years 1973 to 1989. Finally, yet other considerations are derived from the foregoing experiences in Costa Rica, Brazil, and Mexico under circumstances of macroeconomic destabilization and structural adjustment during the 1980s. For present purposes the policy prescription will be written in the form of operating guidelines rather than an abstract theory, though principles, concepts, and theories do underlie the guidelines.

First, in the most general way we can agree with the World Bank (1990a) that policies which raise the income generating capacity of the poor will contribute towards reducing housing poverty. Such policies will include programs to enhance informal and formal sector markets, state, and other provisions to add to the skills and human capital of the poor in the labor market, and steps to improve infrastructure in the urban areas where the poor live. Furthermore, both as an endorsement of experience with structural adjustment programs in the 1980s and as a desirable objective, we can agree that the reduction of poverty should be secured in macroeconomic policies (World Bank 1990b). Austerity programs were insensitive to their impacts upon the poor until the late 1980s, and some new learning by doing experience is necessary. The World Bank is also correct in drawing attention to the variable consequences of good and bad governance on the opportunities for the poor: its report on declining and slow economic growth in Sub-Saharan Africa reveals the adverse results of bad governance and cumbersome institutions (World Bank 1989). More is said about creating good institutional conditions in subsequent discussions.

Second, it is recognized that housing markets in developing countries will often express demands, even though the demands sometimes lead to housing poverty in squatter settlement. Demands, of course, do not always coincide with needs, including safe and sanitary housing. Such needs can be transformed into demands in such programs as well targeted subsidies, cross-subsidization in sites-and-services programs (Pugh 1990c), and in lowering relative prices in low-income housing markets by increasing housing supplies. In fact, in the developing countries reforms and enhancement are often required on the supply side of housing markets rather than on the demand side.

Supply side impediments can consist of many things including inappropriate technology, disorganization of the construction industry, inadequate finance and credit provisions, excessive and distorting government regulations, and land policies and land management practices which restrict supplies of serviced land. Examples can be given to show the significance and policy thrust of these points. Simple technologies in slum upgrading and sites-and-services schemes to ensure basic sanitation standards are more appropriate than high cost public housing provisions. Slum upgrading and regularization of tenure in squatter settlements can, under the appropriate conditions, be the most effective approach to reduce housing poverty. In housing finance, initiatives to develop credit are necessary where developers have to rely upon occupiers' arrangements to raise finance rather than upon banks and financial institutions. Developers need short-term credit and finance to achieve assured and continuous supplies of housing. As will be shown presently, initiatives to enhance the development of financial systems may have to come from government action. Excessive and inappropriate regulations can retard housing supplies, even in cases where official government and World Bank sites-and-services schemes have achieved some effectiveness for low-income households. For example, in the post-1977 programs in Madras, cross-subsidized housing in sites-and-services projects reached the ninth income percentile (poverty incomes reach to the 35th percentile), but programs did not expand. Potential expansion from the private sector was inhibited because town planning and building regulations prevented developers from creating similar sites-and-services housing to those built under government auspices.

Land price inflation in many urban areas in developing countries exceeds general price inflation and income growth rates among the poor. Also, land management practices often have gaps in registration of plots, surveying, titling and property rights, and land acquisition for urban development. Town planning practices sometimes require lengthy and cumbersome approvals' processes, and have aims which conserve undeveloped land rather than transform it for housing use. Examples of good policy and practice are available, but they cannot always be repeated in countries where policies and practices are less effective owing to political constraints. Vested interests among landowners run in favor of restrictions which raise land price inflation. Nevertheless, it is important to reveal good practice. Thailand has achieved simple and rapid approvals' processes, consequently achieving low land cost components in overall housing prices (Mayo 1991). Taiwan and South Korea have devised joint private–public sector land acquisition and planning policies which increase the supply of serviced land. This keeps land price inflation within reasonable bounds and enables some infrastructure to be financed from land sales (Pugh 1992a).

The third operating guideline for designing good low-income housing policies switches the emphasis from the microeconomics of markets to macroeconomic considerations. It was established in an earlier discussion that bad macroeconomic management can lead to destabilization and failure of an economy to adjust structurally. Among many countries experiencing these circumstances, Costa Rica, Kenya, Brazil, and Mexico provide examples of various adverse housing-related consequences. These range from decapitalization in housing finance, through intensification of housing poverty and income poverty, to severe cuts in public spending on infrastructure. Even when economic austerity packages are introduced with World Bank and IMF loan support, the social and economic impact upon the poor has often been ignored, except for some policy correction since the late 1980s. It is the policy correction which becomes the useful operating guideline in policy formulation. As a prescription this means incorporating antipoverty provisions within macroeconomic stabilization and adjustment programs. In Mexico, since 1987 under the influence and power of Salinas de Gortari, this means creating new institutional arrangements to bring together organization and resources from central and local governments, NGO outreach programs, and from household and community self-help. In housing, such initiatives can sometimes secure infrastructure service improvements, housing improvement, and supporting social development in education, health, and women-targeted services. In short, antipoverty and low-income housing policies can be coordinated, and when structural adjustment leaves a medium-term slack in overall resource use, housing sector development can be used both for lead growth sector purposes and for economic correction for some unemployment. Adjustment programs provide potential opportunities in low-income housing, but in practice policy makers seldom take up such opportunities.

Fourth, it is clear that infrastructure service provision requires some reformist attention. Reformist attention is perceived as necessary in the context that some countries (e.g., in Sub-Saharan Africa) have such weak administrative systems and such pressed economic adversities that public sector resources are inadequate. In addition, as revealed earlier, countries undergoing adjustment programs experience short-term pressures to economize on infrastructure in housing development. Apart from the solutions taken under Solidarity in Mexico under Salinas de Gortari, the subject has obtained new significance in academic literature (Rondinelli and Shabbir 1988; Mengers 1990). Prescriptively good policies in the aforementioned contexts would link government agencies, NGOs, popular mobilization of the people, and self-help initiatives. Arrangements for financial support, information, and training would have to be highly adaptive and flexible. The program agenda would include the installation and maintenance of infrastructure, the regularization of settlement and tenure, deregulation of inappropriate town planning codes, mobilization of the information sector, and carefully accounted financial support.

Fifth, housing policies would be improved under review processes which set low-income households as a policy priority. What sort of policy outcomes might ensue? Perhaps the in situ upgrading of slums would have greater priority because in many instances the squatter settlements have the highest concentrations of income and housing poverty. Deregulation may assume importance because inappropriate regulations in building and town planning codes may restrict housing supplies or exclude some productive at home income generating activities. Other aspects revolve around supply restrictions referred to in the earlier discussions of housing markets, including the need to ensure competitive building industries, land policies which curb land price inflation, and land administration with competence in titling, registration, and surveying. Gaps in housing finance also frequently impede low-income households in fulfilling their housing aspirations. Low-income households are perceived as risky among formal financial institutions owing to their lack of collateral to secure loans and their intermittent flows of income. Examples exist where NGOs and voluntary link institutions can reduce some risks and link low-income households with the wider financial system, supplying small loans at affordable repayments (Kaul 1990). Initiatives for reform in low-income housing finance are an important element in the prescription for low-income housing policy development.

Sixth, attention should be given to tenure and access to housing for low-income households. On the one hand, this involves recognition of occupancy rights in informal settlements, including the range of recognitions from de facto acceptance to the regularization of tenure. This is justified on both humanitarian grounds and for facilitating housing investment (including self-help investment) in low-income housing. Households and owners will feel secure in making housing investment only when they are safe from eviction, fire hazards, and various forms of (un)official harassment. But housing tenure policy for low-income households should extend beyond these important considerations. Policy can be designed to achieve a balance of tenure provisions and flexible access among tenures. Homeownership enables households to acquire and manage assets in a context where most low-income households would otherwise lack land, property, and other substantial assets. For feasibility, homeownership requires a setting where other aspects of low-income housing policy are fulfilled. As argued above, this includes policy provisions in finance, land policy, infrastructural services, deregulation, and in ensuring a competitive building industry. Homeownership in itself—including in such provisions as sites-and-services schemes—is seldom sufficient in low-income housing policy. Rental tenure is also significant. Consider Figure 2.2, depicting (individual) per capita income and life cycle.[2] Poverty risks are greatest among children in low-income families, and among the aged. For some households, poverty is chronic and evident throughout life, but for others it is less intense with concentration among young single adults and older (working) couples who have accumulated some modest savings and who have less childbearing expenses. At the poverty-risk periods in life, rental housing will be important. Rental housing enables households to begin their housing careers in a flexible way, before

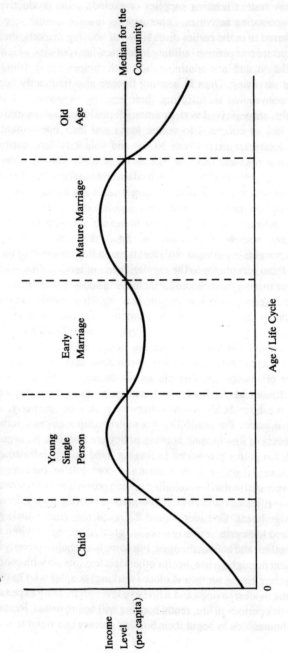

Figure 2.2 Per Capita Income and the Life Cycle

taking long-term decisions on their work careers and childbearing; and it forms a safety valve for times when homeownership is unaffordable or inappropriate. Rental housing can originate in informal sector entrepreneurship, in extensions of space by homeowners seeking supplementary income, and from formal sector landlording. The essential policy prescription is that in tax law, town planning regulations, and housing policy the rental sector be facilitated so that supplies meet demands.

The foregoing policies to reduce housing poverty are to be regarded as a set, with the various elements being reinforcing. They can be interpreted as resting upon two important foundations. The first foundation is conceptually based with some reasoned principles for the relationships among households, their housing, and the wider society. Households are viewed as resource systems which produce and consume goods and services. They produce both at home and out-of-home goods and services. The at-home goods and services include meals, laundering, housekeeping, and, in some households, childbearing. Childbearing adds human and social investment to society, providing human capital and socialized humans for future labor forces and civilian responsibilities in adult life. Childbearing incurs economic expenses in terms of rearing, feeding, clothing, and generally bringing up children. The costs fall upon parental labor, especially mothers, and these costs are not directly repaid by the (grown) children, employers, and governments. In a sense, the household sector as a producing and childbearing sector may subsidize other sectors of the economy (Pugh 1990b). For low-income households in developing countries, at-home production often also includes work and goods for hawking and contracting in the informal and formal sectors of the wider economy. Households will determine their personal, their gendered, and their age-wise division of labor in at-home production, childbearing, out-of-home production and work, and consumption. Some of the household's production, consumption, and saving-investment will be in its housing decisions. These include self-build labor in house construction, housing loans taken up, outlays on housing expenses and so on. Own labor in housing construction is economic saving and investment, even though the labor is not financed, that is to say it has economic value (Pugh 1990b). Viewing the household as a resource unit in the foregoing way enhances the economic significance of housing because it is seen as economically productive in itself and for future societal development. This reinforces the argument for giving significance to low-income housing within housing sector development. Also, it widens the meaning of self-help in housing and social policy.

In the world of housing practice, the conceptual foundation requires an action-oriented institutional foundation. At various points in the earlier discussions, institutional conditions have been mentioned and elaborated; for example, joint venturing and collaboration among central and local governments, NGOs, and households have been reviewed in low-income housing finance and in the provision of infrastructural services. Taking a wider and more general perspective, the point can be made that housing sector development in most developing countries involves some combination of state, market, NGO, and self-help elements. These elements have to be defined and operated in the division (and coordination) of labor among self-help, NGO, market, and state roles. The roles have to be differentiated and practiced in varied role emphases because 'housing' is a complex and many-sided thing. If housing is to be properly understood in modern policy making, it has to be regarded as bringing together land policies, developers' finance, investment, saving, occupiers' finance, infrastructure, competitiveness in the building industry, a relationship to urban policies, and a coordination with macroeconomic policies. From within the housing system as whole, low-income and antipoverty housing policies will require specially formulated institutional arrangements combining state, market, NGO, and self-help roles. It then becomes largely not a question of asserting opposing causes for either the state or the market, but rather one of improving both market and state roles where these roles are interactive, not independent. More will be said about this in subsequent discussions which review housing policy development in the World Bank.

THE EVOLUTION OF WORLD BANK HOUSING POLICIES

Since it entered into low-income housing projects in developing countries in 1972, the World Bank has exerted a powerful influence in the development of housing theory and policy. Some of its influence and power arises from its role as a major financier because it is able to express its favored policy reforms in the conditionality clauses attached to loan agreements with governments. Conditionality is negotiated with governments in a context where the Bank has the power to withhold loans and governments are ready to assess the political feasibility of reforms. Although the Bank's approach to housing is frequently associated with in situ slum upgrading schemes and sites-and-services projects, policy development has, in fact, been wider and evolutionary. The Bank has, itself, been in a learning by doing experience, with considerable significant change in a comparatively short period of two decades. Accordingly it is important to discuss the Bank's policies in their evolutionary context, as the changes will reflect varied perspectives on housing poverty. Policies have achieved contrasting success–failure characteristics, often depending upon the qualities of administration in different countries and the lessons from learning by doing. As will presently be seen in elaborated discussions, the Bank's basic theory of political economy has also been evolving, commencing in the 1970s with a market favored neoliberalism and then by the 1990s enjoining this with more attention and sophistication for government roles.

At the outset it is appropriate to obtain some insights into the volume and character of World Bank involvement in housing. In the 1972–90 period, the Bank participated in 116 sites-and-services projects and complementary slum upgrading schemes in some 55 countries, with an average size expenditure of US$ 26 million (Mayo 1991). The projects were successful in so far as they demonstrated the feasibility of implementing low cost provisions. Slum upgrading schemes were more successful than sites-and-services projects in reaching the poor, mainly because they were directed at areas where the poor lived whereas sites-and-services plots were allocated to selected households which could repay costs. The antipoverty thrust of sites-and-services projects also depended upon the extent to which households traded their housing rights to higher-income groups. Beyond this, as noted by Mayo and Gross (1987) the cost recovery objectives of projects were sometimes undermined by hidden subsidies in low rates of interest and write downs in land values. More aspects of the character and performance of sites-and-services projects and slum upgrading schemes are discussed later in the case study of Madras.

Figure 2.3, highlights the main features of the Bank's housing policy development. Commencing its housing involvements in 1972, the Bank was intent upon reform with an invasion and succession of new theories and practices. In order to understand the reforms, it is appropriate to consider the approaches adopted in the earlier period, i.e., the years from 1950 to 1972. In those years the dominant public policy in low-income housing was based upon the states' roles as providers of public housing, in the form of permanent construction units, these often being apartments. It was intended that public housing replace squatter settlement. Public housing was a way of doing things in some developed countries and it was transplanted without giving much thought to the differing contexts of developing countries.

The actual reality in developing countries was that most low-income households were out of sheer necessity finding their shelter solutions in squatter settlements and crowding in slum tenements. But the underlying assumptions of public housing were that it would be affordable, effective, and eventually eliminate the insanitary conditions and professionally perceived disorder of squatter settlements. These underlying assumptions were eventually criticized by intellectuals such as Turner (1967, 1968, 1971, 1972a, 1972b, 1976) and Mangin (1966, 1967) on the basis of their on-location research in developing countries. Turner and Mangin saw positive value in self-help and in the poor resolving some of their shelter problems within affordable limits and without direction from centralized bureaucracies. In short, Turner and Mangin favored sites-and-services projects and in situ slum upgrading schemes. The World Bank and international aid agencies were ready to add their own reasons to those of Turner and Mangin in support of sites-and-services and slum upgrading approaches. Whereas Turner and Mangin argued that self-help develops a personal sense of achievement in housing (i.e., 'housing is a verb'), the Bank was conscious of the fact that economics must become feasible. Low-cost and affordable housing were advocated as a means of fulfilling loan repayments in low-income housing.

Faced with rapid urbanization and increasing squatter settlements, governments in the developing countries pressed the World Bank in the 1960s to extend its range of development loans to urban infrastructure and housing. The Bank was inclined to enter these new spheres, but only upon the basis of a root and branch review of the prevailing public housing approach to low-income housing. In its publications (1972, 1974, 1975) the Bank formulated a radical departure from public housing, favoring sites-and-services projects and in situ slum upgrading. The first phase of the Bank's theory and practice of low-income housing can be expressed in the hyphenated term affordability-cost recovery-replicability. The intention was to make housing affordable to low-income households without the payment of subsidies, in contrast to the heavily subsidized public housing approach. Housing standards and methods of construction were to be set within affordable limits using budget limits to define feasible standards rather than to follow professionally derived building standards to determine excessive budget levels. Cost recovery would reinforce affordability. It could be implemented to make the 'user pays' principle overt and real; projects could be brought under financial control; and expenditure on land acquisition and infrastructure would be repaid. Essentially, cost recovery was regarded by the Bank as a way of avoiding a self-perpetuating and limitless expansion of subsidies which were unaffordable in the government budgets of developing countries. In principle, cost recovery would hold housing finance capital intact, consequently enabling replicability of investment projects and the eventual means of eliminating squatter settlement.

The affordability-cost recovery-replicability theory and practice of housing can be interpreted as a relatively simple political economy. Its essential political economy was 'neoliberalism'. State roles were confined to facilitate household self-help construction either from self-build or from households contracting building services from the informal and formal markets. The

Figure 2.3 The Evolution of World Bank Housing Policies

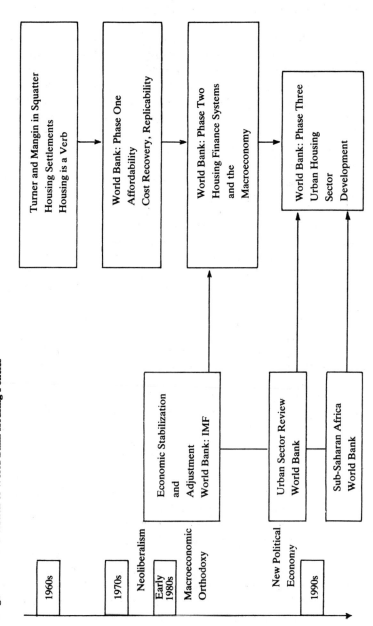

state's supportive and complementary roles came in the form of installing infrastructure, providing tenure rights to occupiers, and sometimes taking initiatives in the social planning elements in low-income settlements. In application, neoliberalist practice was envisaged as operating only in designated projects, not in the wider spheres of housing finance, whole urban sector development, and broader program and policy frameworks. The first phase theory and practice assumed largely separated actions by markets, states, and people in its division of labor. For example, it was not envisaged that states should take initiatives in such things as creating housing credit systems and reforming property rights to ensure that markets could work effectively and rapidly. In its learning by doing the Bank discovered that housing required more sophisticated and interdependent relationships among markets, the state, and self-help among households. Neoliberalist approaches had placed their emphasis upon individualism, free markets, and user pay principles.

The second phase theory and practice of low-income housing involved appreciation of the fact that housing was closely connected to macroeconomic conditions (see earlier discussions) and the need to create and use housing credit institutions. Innovations in the creation and use of housing credit institutions occurred in the US Agency for International Aid (USAID) in the early 1980s. The World Bank adopted the innovations in 1983. USAID used its housing guarantee provisions to expand housing supplies. In effect, USAID could raise debt finance in the US finance markets on favorable terms because liabilities to investors were guaranteed by the US government. Such guaranteed funds were then on-lent to developing countries such as India, Sri Lanka, and Pakistan, using the housing finance systems in these countries to intermediate the loans for housing sector development (Woodring 1984; Buckley, Khadduri, Struyk 1985). In both timing and connections, the second phase approach by the World Bank had implications in macroeconomic reform, including the Bank and IMF structural adjustment loan programs. The new macroeconomic orthodoxy for the 1980s emphasized tighter fiscal and monetary policies, deregulation in financial markets, and anti-inflationary policies. In housing finance markets in many developing countries, the Bank found economic problems and inadequacies. Problems included excessive regulation, existence of privileged circuits and sources of finance to government institutions, and attempts to set rates of interest below free market rates. Such problems impeded the development of saving, investment and flows of funds to housing. In short, in some countries reform was required, and in others initiatives were necessary to create new housing finance institutions.

The Bank's second phase theory and practice of housing had various implications for housing poverty. First, the Bank's strategic housing policy review (World Bank 1992) and Mayo's commentaries (1991) indicate the nature of the reforms for the third phase. Second, the new approach led to a more rapid disbursement of loan funds, but in the early years this was feasible only in those countries where housing finance systems had been developed to critical thresholds. This often means that the poorer countries lag in feasible applications of the new approach, with consequently less alleviation of housing poverty. In later years the poorer countries may develop suitable housing finance systems. Third, as discussed earlier, the formal housing finance institutions often bypass the poorest households, leaving the necessity to create new institutional linkages by using NGOs to connect the poor to flows of saving and investment in housing (Kaul 1990). Fourth, as compared with the sites-and-services or slum upgrading approaches, the second phase of reform focused on the housing system as a whole and on increasing housing supply. This set the context for a widening of housing objectives for the entire urban housing sector development in the third phase (see below). Finally, it has to be appreciated that the second phase did not replace the first phase provisions of sites-and-services and slum upgrading approaches, but rather encompassed them in a wider policy framework.

The third phase theory and practice of housing was developed in the years 1986 and 1992. It evolved from the second phase concerns of housing finance and macroeconomic conditions. The main thrust of the third phase is the growth and development of the entire housing sector in its urban and national context. The third phase joins together the Bank, the United Nations Center for Human Settlements (Habitat) (UNCHS), and the United Nations Development Program (UNDP). In 1986, these international institutions collaborated in founding the Urban Management Program with the aim of improving performance in developing countries in land management, municipal finance, infrastructure services, the environment, and building up the capacity of urban management institutions. An important aspect of the third phase theory and practice of housing is to link housing to the wider urban economy, and to develop both the housing sector and the urban economy as vehicles for promoting general economic growth and productivity. It is envisaged that these aims can be made more operational and coherent by giving appropriate meaning and applicability to the idea of enablement.

The idea of enablement has been refined and elaborated in a succession of UNCHS documents and publications, and it has been endorsed in the General Assembly of the United Nations (UNCHS 1987; UNCHS 1990). The essential characteristic of the global strategy for shelter is that human settlements be regarded as contributing positively to economic and social development, rather than simply as a social expense of industrialization. Enablement is defined as providing the legislative, institutional, and financial framework whereby entrepreneurship in the private sector, communities, and among individuals can effectively develop the urban housing sector. Government roles are seen as enabling sector development in a historical context where the first phase project by project approach had neither generally promoted whole housing sector development nor eliminated squatter settlement and housing poverty. Enablement is a key part of the new political economy (NPE)—a theory of political economy which was adapted and developed from the earlier neoliberalism.

The NPE gives greater attention to the roles of government than the simpler and earlier neoliberalism. Some of its historical roots are associated with the public choice theory which was elaborated in the United States in the period 1955 to 1971. The major authors of public choice theory were Downs (1957), Buchanan and Tullock (1962), and Niskanen (1971). Taking different perspectives in their theoretical foundations, each of these authors had a common attitude to government and its institutions. Politicians and bureaucratics were seen as pursuing narrow interests rather than broad beneficial public interests, and consequently, it was important to constrain both their power and the power of the government. In more recent times public choice theory and NPE have been modified to embrace a more positive attitude to government roles. For example, Meier (1991) and Klitgaard 1991) support good governance, institutional reform, and sophisticated roles in government in order that liberalism and enablement succeed. In this context state roles would include audits of the (in)effectiveness of its regulations, creation of new institutional arrangements to enhance market performance, provision of public goods, and programs to reduce poverty. By the 1990s, the World Bank had recognized the need to achieve good governance, after being influenced by more favorable attitudes to government roles with its experience in Sub-Saharan Africa (World Bank 1989).

The new enablement and NPE political economy can be contrasted with the first phase theory and practice of low-income housing. In the first phase, neoliberalism had assumed simple divisions of labor among individuals, markets, and the state in sites-and-services projects. The new enablement opens up requirements for partnerships and interdependence among state agencies, markets, NGOs, and individuals. For example, in land management state roles would include reforms in property rights, land registration systems, and in ensuring adequate supplies for expanding housing markets. Sometimes land acquisition and housing development may involve partnerships between government agencies, NGOs, and households in creating community land trusts among low-income housing groups (Matthei and Hahn 1991). In earlier discussions similar partnerships and interdependence have been elaborated in housing finance for the poor, in infrastructure, and in the Solidarity program in Mexico. The third phase theory and practice also adds an important dimension to housing poverty: it accepts the legitimacy of subsidies providing that these are effectively targeted and limited to poverty groups. The World Bank's post-1989 favored form of subsidy is the one-off capital grant for the poorest households, carefully assessed in terms of affordability and eligibility. It will be recalled that the phase one theory envisaged user pays and cost recovery principles without subsidy.

In 1991, the World Bank published its urban policy review for the 1990s, developing the ideas and context for the third phase theory and practice (World Bank 1991b). Although the urban policy report was wider in scope than housing, it nevertheless had direct significance for the 1991–92 review of housing by the Bank (Mayo 1991). The Bank's current 1991–92 housing review work is being made entirely consistent with the urban policy review report, and some authors of the housing review were also authors of the urban policy review report. The urban policy review report was written in the context that urban populations in the developing countries would increase by some 600 million in the 1990s; that the urban share of GDP in developing countries would rise; that the productivity of economies in developing countries would be clearly linked to their urban economies; and that some 25 percent of urban populations in the developing countries were living in a state of poverty. All of this indicated that the Bank's share of lending to urban and housing investment would rise in the 1990s, and that urban policies would have to be formulated to enhance the prospects for economic growth with regard to the realities of large-scale poverty. The Bank's loan programs for the 1990s give primary importance to mediation via housing finance systems (see previous discussions) and to the provision of municipal development funds.

The scope and interest of the new urban policy agenda was wide-ranging. It aimed to connect urban growth to macroeconomic policy, assuming the conditions of the new 1980s macroeconomic orthodoxy, i.e., anti-inflation policies, market determined rates of interest, and the development of finance capital systems. Urban policy was to be formulated at national levels to be connected with macroeconomic conditions, especially in reforming housing finance institutions and legislation on land development and town planning. At the municipal-city level urban policy was to be formulated to fill gaps in management, financial capability, and in creating linkage and partnership institutions among government agencies, markets, NGOs, and households. The prescriptive aims were to overcome the limitations in the first and second phases of policy development. Affordability-cost recovery-replicability had been too simplistic and narrow in its project by project approach. The second phase development of housing finance systems had gone beyond narrow project by project approaches, but it was self-limiting because it was confined to finance, omitting land policies, construction industry, infrastructure, and deregulation in town planning.

The direction of the third phase of World Bank theory and practice of low-income housing is reasonably clear. Mayo (1991), a Bank housing policy analyst at the Bank has indicated the nature of the reforms for the third phase. The thinking for reform takes the following direction:

- it connects housing to the macroeconomy and to urban sector development, being understood as the development of the housing sector as a whole,
- it addresses issues such as urban poverty, constraints which inhibit urban economic growth, environmental conditions, and research which improves understanding of urban housing sector development,
- the focus for operational attention in housing sector development will be in seven spheres: (i) housing finance systems and mortgage finance, (ii) the targeting of subsidies, (iii) the development of property rights, especially in regularizing tenure in squatter settlement, (iv) infrastructure improvement, (v) introductions of regulatory audits to ascertain the extent to which inappropriate town planning regulations inhibit housing sector development, (vi) the improved organization and competition in the building industry, and (vii) the reform and creation of institutional frameworks which will link government, market, NGO, and self-help roles.

The overall package of reforms is comprehensive. From one perspective it is very demanding, requiring well-developed public administration, effective coordination among participants, and complex systems of cooperation. Some countries and city-regions will not have the capacities and the political–institutional conditions to administer and manage urban housing sector development as comprehensively and effectively as envisaged in the third phase prescriptions. However, the World Bank can influence the building up of institutional capacity on the basis of loan financed training programs and the conditionality clauses in housing sector development loans. In fact, the third phase Bank reforms will expand the purposes and functions of loan programs beyond those of the second phase which focused upon housing finance. Loan programs will be designed to influence policy and performance in the diverse elements which are within housing sector development. The Bank is also aware that the progressive development of housing sectors can be positively influenced by findings from comparative research. Comparative research can indicate the reasons and contexts which explain success in some places and failure in others. Such evaluations will be important in the antipoverty intentions of third phase policy development. As yet, the Bank has not formulated in detail the scope and characteristics of housing poverty programs. Moreover, in the World Bank's 1990 report on economic development and poverty, housing was not given any full and significant attention (World Bank 1990a). The earlier discussions in this piece of writing gave indications of policies to alleviate housing poverty. These are compatible with the World Bank's third phase theory and practice of low-income housing. The third phase approach is characterized by a holistic view of the institutional and economic conditions which are relevant to whole housing sector development, compared with sites-and-services conceptualization in phase one which was limited by a project by project perspective. Further evaluation of the third phase will be given in the concluding section. Meanwhile, useful insights can be obtained from a brief review of case studies.

CASE STUDIES

The housing literature contains numerous examples of failure and disappointment in sites-and-services projects and slum upgrading schemes. Sometimes such failures are interpreted as evidence for argument against the self-help and the affordability-cost recovery-replicability approach to low-income housing. However, a more sophisticated evaluation would help discern situations where there has either been some significant success or where a valuable learning experience ensues from the implementation of policies. This defines the purpose of this section which takes Madras and Sri Lanka as its case examples. The post-1970 experiences in these places will enable us to draw some general conclusions about conditions in which low-income housing policies can achieve some success.

Madras, Tamil Nadu—India

Madras is significant in low-income housing policy development because it became the setting for a vast World Bank loan program in the 1970s from which substantial learning by doing experience emerged. What follows is a summarized review of that experience, with further detail elaborated in some of my earlier writing (Pugh 1990a, and 1990c). In 1976, the Bank opened up negotiations with the Tamil Nadu government with the aim of implementing a large volume program of sites-and-services projects and slum upgrading schemes within the first phase theory of housing, the affordability-cost recovery-replicability approach. Some political–institutional conditions in Tamil Nadu were particularly favorable for low-income housing reform. The ruling AIADMK party was well-disposed to giving housing policy political significance to increase its electoral popularity, and Tamil Nadu had recruited some young and active housing professionals who were well-versed in the (then) new theories of self-help in housing. In the negotiations for securing loan agreements, the Bank wanted to tilt budget allocations in favor of low-income households and to switch emphasis from redevelopment to in situ improvement in squatter settlements. The Tamil Nadu government readily conceded these conditionality terms in the loan programs.

The implementation of the affordability-cost recovery-replicability approach in Madras demonstrated features of an emergent best practice. Land was purchased in suitable locations where low-income households could generate incomes. The allocation and pricing of plots in sites-and-services projects enabled some useful cross-subsidization from commercial to housing uses and from higher to lower-income groups. Clauses in contracts limited the retrading of land and housing to higher-income groups. Social planning provisions and employment were linked to the self-help housing project. Cost recovery was effective to a level of 96 percent of liabilities in sites-and-services projects, but somewhat less effective in slum upgrading schemes. In the sites-and-services projects, the allocations did reach low-income households, with access to households as low as the ninth income percentile.

In implementation, the experience in Madras revealed that the affordability-cost recovery-replicability approach was incomplete as an overall housing policy. It focused upon specific projects rather than housing sector development as a whole. Also, the scope ignored significant spheres such as land policy reform, the development of housing finance, and the demands upon local government in managing and maintaining infrastructural services. Land price inflation threatened the future of sites-and-services projects because the operation of the 1894 Land Acquisition Act and the 1976 Urban Land (Ceiling and Regulation) Act restricted the supply of serviced land, thereby leading to speculation and the land cost element in housing prices rose to a point where affordability could have been undermined. Housing financial institutions were undeveloped and limited in scope in India in the 1970s. Informal sector lenders set very high rates of interest; the government institution, the Housing and Urban Development Corporation (HUDCO) had limited funds which were insufficient to meet the demands and needs of low-income households. In the formal private sector, the Housing Development Finance Corporation (HDFC) was purposeful and innovative, but only in its first years of operation in the late 1970s. In the overall perspective, it can be said that the housing finance system was undeveloped and had gaps in meeting low-income needs.

The World Bank loans were adequate for providing basic utility and infrastructural services. But these provisions covered only the initial capital installations, not the ongoing needs of management and maintenance. These ongoing needs and responsibilities fell upon local governments which lacked the managerial, financial, and technological capacity to fulfil them. When the Bank had commenced its involvement with low-income housing in developing countries it had favored metropolitan-wide town planning and housing agencies as the appropriate institutions, with doubts about smaller local government jurisdictions. However, in operation it became clear that local governments would need to be involved in the programs, and the effectiveness of their roles depended upon substantial reforms in finance, management, and training. Finally, although the projects in Madras were undertaken with the intention of demonstrating the efficacy and practicality of new methods in low-income housing, the private sector did not respond. The reasons included the gaps in land policy and housing finance already referred to, and, in addition, the town planning regulations which inhibited private developers from creating affordable plots for low-income households. It was necessary to reduce regulatory standards and to revise town planning regulations.

The learning by doing experience in Madras in the years 1977 to 1984 has been significant in low-income housing policy, especially in leading towards whole sector housing development. In whole sector housing development, the emphasis is upon policies, institutional reform, and achieving useful roles in combining markets, self-help, and government agencies. This occurred to some extent in Madras, widening the scope of policy and action.

In Figure 2.4, the production–consumption economy is shown in formal and informal market supplies of goods and services linking firms and households. The capital market and the housing capital market are linked to the housing system. The housing capital market is expanded by virtue of the second phase theory and practice of low-income housing in which the World Bank on-lends funds to housing finance institutions. Also, the Bank supplies loans to a municipal fund which is used to increase the institutional capacity of local governments to manage and maintain infrastructure. Government roles are significant in policy development, deregulation, ensuring that serviced land is adequately supplied, and in supporting infrastructural provisions. Generally government has a reformist and enablement role to play in order to improve prospects for market, self-help, NGO, and other participants in housing sector development. Although not specifically identified in Figure 2.4, from earlier discussions it will be recalled that government also has important housing-related roles in formulating macroeconomic policies. The housing system has resource and financial flows originating in goods markets, capital markets, and from government budgets. The ultimate

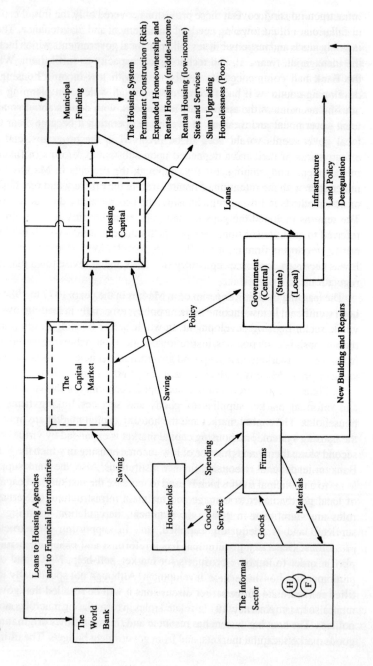

Figure 2.4 World Bank Policies in the 1990s

impact upon housing poverty depends upon the extent to which resources and finance are tilted towards low-income households. The ways in which this can be done are partially evident in the political–institutional conditions of Madras in the years 1977 to 1984, and more fully elaborated in the discussions on housing policy for antipoverty purposes in the earlier sections of this writing.

In Madras, some progress has been made in the institutional reform for whole sector housing development. Experiments have been introduced to achieve better supplies of serviced land, using joint venture schemes between developers, landowners, and government agencies (Pugh 1990c). A municipal fund has been created to encourage local governments to improve the maintenance of infrastructure. In the national (central) government policy in India, steps were taken in 1988 to formulate new policies for expanding housing capital markets. The process of reform is incomplete and its experience has not been long enough for intellectual evaluation. But it is clear that the stakes are very high. One consideration is the large number of households which experience housing poverty. Another is that housing sector development has significance for the growth of the economy. Housing contributes some 3–5 percent of GDP and some 25–50 percent of fixed capital formation. Housing sector development is a good means of contributing to economic growth in developing countries. The World Bank's third phase theory and practice of low-income housing—whole sector housing development—is designed to contribute to urban economic development and to the growth of national incomes.

Sri Lanka

Housing policy development in Sri Lanka presents an interesting example of the intent to deal with mass housing poverty and to adapt policy to changing economic and political circumstances. Sri Lanka won independence from the British colonial rulers in 1948 and its various governments and policy makers have consistently placed priority upon social policy development, including health, education, state welfare programs, and housing. Accordingly, although Sri Lanka is among the poorest of nations in the developing countries, it has achievements in nutrition, life expectancy, health status, and literacy which surpass those of richer developing countries. Antipoverty and egalitarian purposes have held an enduring and significant place in Sri Lankan politics, state budgets, and in competition among political parties for electoral support (Kearney 1973; Jayatnam 1974; Sharma 1988). Housing policy development has been influenced by a number of conditions within social and economic change, including the changing theory of development economics, electoral politics, macroeconomic policies, the dilemmas of pursuing low-income emphasis in housing, and the changing pattern of low-income housing policies by USAID and other international donors. It is appropriate to give some brief introductory attention to each of these conditions of change in order to provide a useful interpretation of housing policy development.

The dominant political economy in development economics in the years 1950 to 1975 relied upon state-guided indicative planning, usually in the form of five year development plans (Hunt 1989). Its application in many developing countries invited policy makers to extensively use state roles in regulating the private sector, restricting trade, and in creating state enterprises in production. This broadly defines the position in Sri Lanka in the period 1956 to 1976 when power was held by social democrats and left-wing elements led by S. Bandaranaike until his death in 1959 and then by his wife Mrs Bandaranaike. However, by the mid-1970s the economic problems consequent upon misplaced government intervention in the economy were becoming conspicuous and damaging. Economic crisis loomed with a fall in export revenue, an increase in external debt, rising unemployment, and low economic growth. Campaigning for the 1977 election was dominated by economic issues, with some increased significance also given to housing. The 1977 election was won by the United National Party (UNP), a center–right political party intent upon restoring economic growth and achieving political popularity in its housing programs.

The economic reforms of the UNP included cutting subsidies and targeting them for antipoverty purposes, liberalizing trade and investment, devaluing the currency, and reducing unemployment. The reforms were supported by the World Bank and the IMF, being in affinity with the stabilization and adjustment programs favored in the 1980s in response to external debt problems of developing countries. In fact, in 1986, the IMF supported the restructuring of the Sri Lankan economy with a structural adjustment facility loan. The conditionality clauses in the loan were designed to reduce inflation, decrease government expenditure, improve the balance of payments which was in deficit, and to achieve further growth so that external debt could be more readily repaid. As will be presently seen, all of this macroeconomic change influenced the course of housing policy reform. Housing policy reform was strongly advocated and executed by Premadasa who succeeded Jayawardene as Prime Minister in 1988. Premadasa favored self-help solutions in low-income housing, set within a massive small loans program development. In effect, these policies commenced national housing sector development, but in the process as difficulties became evident, they stressed the necessity of reforming policies.

Sri Lankan housing policy development falls into three periods, 1948 to 1969, 1970 to 1976, and post-1976. The first period, 1948 to 1969, was typical of conventional ways in developing countries. Public housing was provided in a limited way in the form of rental flats; a national housing fund with subsidized interest rates was created for some middle-income households; and large spheres of spontaneous low-income squatter housing were left largely outside the scope of policy. The public housing supplies fell well short of demands and needs, amounting only to some 3,000 units by 1969. Low-income households tended to trade their rights to public housing in favor of higher income groups, leading to ineffectiveness in policy performance. The second period, 1970 to 1976, was marked by some continuity of policies and some significant innovations. The ineffective public housing approach was continued, with some 2,800 units built, costing as high as Rs 30,000 per unit. Government took more active stances in squatter housing, with emphasis upon the (now) discredited eviction of residents and demolition of self-help shelter. More significantly, the left-wing government of Mrs Bandaranaike introduced a self-help program for low-income households in rural areas: this was the Aided Self-Help (ASH) program. The ASH program provided for community participation and low-cost self-help, with loan finance from government at some Rs 6,000 per unit. Although the ASH program fell short of its targets, it provided a basis for the subsequent development of high volume self-help housing programs.

It will be recalled that the campaign for the 1977 election was fought from 1975, with economic and housing reform being the central issues. The UNP proposed new directions for housing in its proposals for the 100,000 housing program. The new program occupied the years 1977 to 1983. It extended the concepts in the ASH program to urban areas and to a national all-island significance. Government roles included the acquisition of land, the provision of house designs, the planning of neighborhood layouts, assembling building materials, and the provision of technical advice for self-help construction. Finance came from government sources, with the disbursement of small loans on an average of some Rs 14,000 per participating household. The public housing program continued, but its importance dwindled as the small loans self-help approach became more acceptable to the people on grounds of affordability and suitability. Also, after 1977, the approach to squatter settlement switched from eviction and demolition to in situ upgrading. The 100,000 housing program fulfilled its quantitative targets, though in implementation some problems had arisen. These problems included shortfalls on loan recovery, gaps in the analysis of affordability for low-income households, and cost overruns. Furthermore, the program had been introduced without an overall review of housing needs and demands.

In 1981, both a housing census and review were undertaken to establish factual information on housing standards and to give future policy clearer directions and targets. An additional survey in 1984 estimated that Sri Lanka would need to build some 38,000 units per annum for a decade to fulfil housing needs.

The UNP government took positive and determined steps in launching a new million houses program (MHP) for the years 1984 to 1989. This was a much enlarged self-help, small loans program. It offered a 'housing options and loan package' (HOLP) with 19 choices on loan sizes and use of loan for new building or rehabilitation. The program had a strong low-income emphasis with 16 of the 19 options reserved for low-income households. Loans were available at concessional rates of interest from 3 percent to 6 percent with 15 year repayment periods. In operation the program fulfilled its targets, and in selecting the loan options households chose 50 percent for upgrading, 31 percent for new housing extensions and latrines, and 15 percent for completely new housing. Whereas the 100,000 housing program had mainly been aimed at new construction, the MHP included upgrading, extensions, and housing rehabilitation. This program developed the national housing sector, adding to the economic strength and activity in the building and building materials industry. Housing poverty decreased, with better quality housing and lower occupancy rates (i.e., more rooms per capita). Some problems did arise in the program operation. First, the National Housing Development Authority (NHDA) which was responsible for the program had to find local means of disbursing loans and collecting loan repayments. It used the Thrift and Credit Cooperative Societies (TCCSs), having to encourage the formation of new TCCSs where none previously existed in some localities. Gaps in financial administration led to problems in loan collection, worsening in 1988 when politicians waived repayment among some poor. Others then became reluctant to repay their loans and the financial administration of the program was partially undermined.

The economic issues surrounding the program and its successor for the years 1990 to 1995, and the 1.5 million housing program (1.5 MHP) have wide relevance in designing and operating mass low-income housing programs. Sri Lanka was able to finance the programs because its foreign reserves and government budgets were supported extensively by international donor agencies. By 1991, Sri Lanka was receiving some US$ 500 million aid for projects; and in housing, USAID was providing some US$ 60 million funds under its housing guarantee program. Without such international assistance the housing programs could not have been sustained. Nevertheless, even with such foreign economic support, steps had to be taken to tighten economic and financial control because the subsidies on the concessional rates of interest were hidden and running out of control. This led to program reforms whereby one-off capital grants were targeted to the poorest households and supplementary and other loans were priced at commercial rates of interest. All of this came in the context of further macroeconomic reform in the 1980s as the Sri Lankan economy experienced further crises. The IMF had to provide an adjustment loan for reform so that Sri Lanka could reduce its external indebtedness and improve its balance of payments. Structural adjustment required a variety of reforms, including curbs on public spending and the development of capital markets. For housing policy this meant that subsidies had to be controlled, and that housing finance would be reviewed in the general development of capital markets. The prospective aims in the review would be to enlarge housing credit, using housing as a motive to increase household saving and investment. It is anticipated that the course of reforms in housing credit will increase household economic contributions, thereby reducing burdens in public expenditure.

The MHP and 1.5 MHP represented substantial innovation in housing policy. Government roles changed from direct provision to the enablement of self-help. By placing the emphasis upon loans it became possible to undertake a mass assault on housing poverty. Households were enjoined in the housing process as participants. They acted as contractors to builders, sometimes as builders, and they took roles in decentralized community development associated with the new approaches to housing. The 1.5 MHP was connected to the Janasaviya antipoverty program which provided income support and savings schemes for welfare and for employment. All of this meant that the NHDA had to undertake internal reforms, changing from a building agency to a manager of loan finance and community development programs. In terms of social mission and idealism, Sri Lankan policy makers saw the new programs as the means of empowering the poor and giving them self-fulfillment in life. The programs have a strong flavor of participatory idealism. Although the programs are not under the auspices of the World Bank, they are partly influenced by the evolving theory and practice of the Bank. For example, capital grant subsidies are targeted and made explicit, and the programs have whole housing sector development purposes. The Sri Lankan innovation is to join community participation with a mass small loans approach. This innovation has some dilemmas which have to be reconciled in the future, including impacts upon public expenditure, integration with macroeconomic controls, and qualities of administration in community development.

The case studies of experience in Madras and Sri Lanka show that it is possible to innovate and to make progress in low-income housing policy. The circumstances have to be conducive in their particular settings. In Madras, the political and institutional conditions favored housing reform; the World Bank provided loan finance and encouraged speedy reform; and in operation both theory and practice were adapted to improve prospects for success. The learning by doing experience in Madras contained substantial change: the policy framework began as a project by project approach and ended with an emerging emphasis upon whole sector housing development. In Sri Lanka, the political conditions favored antipoverty, egalitarian, and housing reforms. The UNP was able to reform housing alongside macroeconomic reform. The self-help approach and international donor aid made it possible to formulate and operate mass low-income housing policies. Housing program operation and reform was influenced by ideas from USAID which has a theory and practice of housing closely in affinity with the World Bank. In fact, the Bank was influenced by USAID in the early 1980s, particularly in the on-lending of funds to financial institutions in developing countries. Sri Lanka's reforms have been centered on the disbursement of small loans through the NHDA and the TCCSs. In the general overview, although Sri Lanka has had to adjust and restructure its housing and welfare state programs in the context of macroeconomic constraints and political change, it has related social policy development to the pattern of its economic growth.

SUMMARY AND EVALUATION

In capitalist developing countries urban housing has a configurated mix of government, market, NGO, and household self-help roles. The particular configurations and balances of roles vary among countries in accordance with their particular political–institutional and stage-of-development conditions. The prescriptive theory of low-income housing emphasizes whole sector housing development, thus encompassing, but being broader than earlier sites-and-services projects and slum upgrading schemes. In the overall perspective, the whole sector housing development approach has the following conceptualization and operation of housing—housing is variously connected to infrastructural services, land policy and land management, to capital market and financial systems, and to macroeconomic conditions. It is interdependently linked in causal and consequential ways to national and city-regional economic development. In developing countries low-income housing reform has to often focus on supply side factors such as land policy, developer finance, appropriate technology, the organization and degree of competition in the building industry, and activating community and self-help potentiality. All of the foregoing is relevant to the alleviation of housing poverty within the context of housing system reform. The antipoverty focus emphasizes upon income generation, increasing housing supply, and ensuring that access is affordable within economic costs and, in some instances, with some carefully targeted subsidies. Ineffectiveness in housing policy is often caused by unwieldy institutions. The process of change of the 1990s and for the 21st century places urgency upon institutionally loaded reform. Urgency is relevant because the number of households experiencing poverty is massive and growing. The importance of institutionally loaded reform is that whole sector housing development depends upon creating good policies and establishing an effective division of labor and cooperation among government, market, NGO, and self-help roles. This will often involve joint venture and linked roles, for example, in infrastructural services, in some innovations for linking the poor with housing finance, and in developing self-help.

In the overall perspective, it is important to be clear about the welfare components in policies for housing and the reduction of poverty. The welfare components are located in various parts of economic and political systems. They include some redistributional aspects in government budgets and in housing-related public expenditure. But they go beyond this to the welfare components in macroeconomic performance, in policies for economic development, the generation and distribution of income in goods and labor markets, and in self-help in households. The welfare components can be identified and evaluated with respect to needs-based considerations in such social spheres as education, health, nutrition, income transfers, and price access conditions in the budgets of poor households. From the themes and arguments in this piece of writing, the prescriptive welfare components can be summarized as follows:

- The short- and medium-term stabilization and adjustment policies in macroeconomics would include antipoverty and housing objectives among their overall set of objectives. The post-1988 policies in Mexico can be seen as positive and creative.
- Development policies are favorable to antipoverty when income generation, income distribution, and employment favor labor markets in the lowest 40 percent of the income distribution. This is consistent with post-1990 concerns in the World Bank to reduce poverty, and the exemplar is Taiwan in the period 1960 to 1980 when high rates of economic growth were associated with labor-intensive income and skills growth.
- The state's public budget roles include policies and allocations in the social benefits aspects of infrastructure and other housing-related provisions. Social benefits arise from policies and resource allocations in which benefits are not confined to private firms and individuals in

direct market operation, but spread more widely in the community. An example in infrastructure would be the reduction of contagious diseases in low-income housing areas, thereby increasing health and income from work activities. Less sickness leads to more work, and more work leads to more income. Some antipoverty subsidy may be justified for securing social benefits and for basic needs in poor households. The policies and allocations have to be brought within general macroeconomic and development policies, and not left to run out of control. Sometimes the social benefits from public budgets can be linked to joint ventures with markets, NGOs, and self-help in households. The post-1988 exemplars are Sri Lanka and Mexico, but with a need to monitor progress and adapt policies in the light of evaluation.

- The state's roles go beyond public budgets and the provision of infrastructure. They include reform in property rights, in the institutional linking of government agencies, markets, NGOs, and self-help in households and community development. The scope includes development policies, macroeconomic policies, housing policy reform, institutionally loaded reform, and clear and sensitive policies to reduce corruption, ethnically associated poverty, and inefficiencies among economic producer units. These sorts of policies are in their introductory phases in World Bank activities and in national policy development in some developing countries.

- Households are units of economic production and consumption. Self-help is not confined to housing construction, housing improvement, and community development: it also includes household decisions on the basis of age and sex, division of labor, childbearing, housing saving and consumption, and decisions by household members to improve skills, education, and income generation. This self-help is often influenced by male dominance within households, cultural and religious factors, macroeconomic fluctuations, and the state's policies which impinge upon the household (e.g., family law, social policies, laws on discrimination, and economic policies). The efficiency of the household and its internal distribution of income and goods are relevant for price access to basic needs goods, including housing.

- Household policies are in need of formulation and development, especially in terms of the intent and the program activities by the World Bank, the IMF, and national governments in developing countries. Households have increased responsibilities and burdens in post-1990 directions for housing and economic policies. They are required to generate income, to save and spend it in prescriptively useful ways (though within a context of some freedom), and to pay for significant proportions of basic needs goods. Households also produce some of these at home goods and services, including housing maintenance, housing improvement, meals, housekeeping services, and self-help in education and entrepreneurship. In developing countries household self-help can be enhanced by state policies which improve economic conditions in the informal sectors, enable households to link their domestic production with at home commercial activities (e.g., revising restrictive town planning regulations), and through gender sensitive policies which improve the economic status of women and children.

Clearly the welfare components are many and varied. They depend upon a wide variety of related policies, upon efficiencies in markets, and institutionally loaded reform. The welfare components will not always follow in any simple way if and when economic growth occurs. Welfare components have to be related specifically as targeted needs to income generation, economic policies, and housing policies. This requires specific antipoverty policies and the monitoring of performance with reference to social needs indicators, including social indicators in housing. In short, welfare has some limited prescriptive elements as well as some dependence upon the freedoms and the entrepreneurship in capitalist societies. Effectiveness in antipoverty performance is likely to vary depending upon national policies in developing countries and the conditionalities written into loan agreements by the World Bank, IMF and other international aid agencies. Welfare has some elements which harmonize with economic freedom, and some which have potential for conflict. Housing reform for low-income groups has much that is friendly to economic freedom and which can be pursued by extending some economic freedom and market competition. This is particularly so in supply side policies directed at the informal sectors, land management, and in housing finance. The conflicting elements arise in the size and sector allocations in public budgets, in aspects of subsidy programs, and in divergence between social benefits and private benefits at the intersection of markets and state economic activity.

The discussions in this piece of writing have ranged widely, mainly because housing poverty can be understood only with a relevant selection of theory, practice, case studies, and reviews of policy change. It has been possible to present a prescriptive set of policies to reduce housing poverty. Some actual policies, including those of the World Bank, have been evolving in the direction of useful prescription. In all of this there are grounds for some optimism, though it must be cautious. Reform will vary in acceptance and effectiveness. Whole sector housing development, with its dependence upon institutionally loaded reform makes heavy demands on policy making and the quality of performance in government agencies, markets, and self-help among households. These demands include concurrent effectiveness in many institutions, in coordination, and in the motivations of the poor. Good reform will be won hard, with the likelihood that failures will occur alongside successes. Successes occur in an opportunistic way. In Mexico, Salinas de Gortari took the opportunity in post-1988 economic restructuring to use housing as a means of wider economic change, linking it to mass popular participation institutional change (i.e., the Solidarity program). For Sri Lanka, housing and antipoverty have been politically significant since 1948, but economic and political change have led policy makers to turn housing programs from a limited welfare state basis to a mass national program of small loans. Self-help and community mobilization have been brought together with the help of the small loans program. Nevertheless, the state's economic and social roles remain significant: the state provides antipoverty targeted one-off capital subsidies, it innovates in linking housing with infrastructure and community development, and although economic dilemmas occur in short-run situations, it relates the social policy aspects of government spending with long-term economic growth. In Madras, the World Bank and the Tamil Nadu government took a large set of sites-and-services and slum upgrading projects towards a more comprehensive housing sector development. Opportunism has no planned prescription, but the conditions under which success occurred can be analyzed and written into operating guidelines. This was done in the earlier discussions.

Finally, it is clear that recent and some prospective housing policy reform largely falls within the new political economy (NPE). At the economic level, the NPE has both macroeconomic orthodoxy and an acceptance of markets in microeconomics. The macroeconomic orthodoxy is closely associated with IMF and World Bank learning by doing experience in their loan programs for stabilization and adjustment in countries facing external debt problems and accumulations of bad economic management. The orthodoxy runs in favor of anti-inflation policies, monetary and fiscal restraint, curbs in the growth of public expenditure, liberalization of trade, and market determined interest and exchange rates. This orthodoxy has spread to many developing countries, the post-socialist transforming countries, and some developed countries. It is a globally dominant political economy. The microeconomic elements in the NPE have been in a state of evolution in the late 1980s. Before that, microeconomics was often a simple advocacy for neoliberalist (free markets). But in the World Bank and from appreciation by some intellectuals (Klitgaard 1991; Meier 1991) it is now understood that government roles in policy-making and in institutional development are critically important. For developing countries the general thrust of the macroeconomic elements in the NPE is that improvement has to be sought across all fronts, in markets, NGOs, self-help in households, and public administration. One short- and medium-term consequence of the NPE is that in some countries unemployment increases, greater inequality occurs in the distribution of incomes, and policy dilemmas arise in providing safety nets for the poor and simultaneously reducing the growth in public expenditure.

The NPE is a practiced social theory. It has political biases, its own persuasive language, inconsistencies, and relationships with power. Its dominance since the mid-1980s is readily explained. Structural economic change and the global integration of national economies undermined conventional theories and practices in macroeconomics and development economics. Stalinist socialist economics (and some adaptations of state socialism) were abandoned owing to their failure in economic management and their suppression of freedoms. State socialism had also failed to secure satisfactory standards of living for large sections of the population. The NPE was often adopted by governments for pragmatic necessity rather than as an ideological choice. Few options were available in its historical context. It filled a void, and conditions for its acceptance have been pressed by the technocrats in the IMF and the World Bank. However, as we have seen, the technocratic imperative has revealed a capacity for adaptation in the light of experience, and it contains some post-1989 elements favorable towards antipoverty purposes and policies. The NPE also contains come indirect economic and political power through which developed countries influence the course of reform in developing countries. The Group of Seven industrialized countries influence policies of the IMF and the World Bank, and they have greater power in developing and monitoring global economic performance and policy.

As a social theory and practice, the NPE has its varied critics. For Colclough and Manor (1991) it has an excessively cynical attitude to government and it contains biases from orthodox neoclassical economics. The criticism has relevance, but needs to be modified in the light of the evolution of the NPE towards positive acceptance of improving government (Klitgaard 1991; Meier 1991). Government has varied important roles in NPE, especially in creating property rights and effective institutions. The NPE and its earlier versions, with relevance to self-help housing policies, have been criticized by Marxist intellectuals (Burgess 1977, 1978, 1982). The Marxist line of reasoning is that self-help connects to capitalist markets and it thereby becomes exploitive and inegalitarian, with no ultimate solution to housing poverty. Elsewhere (Pugh and Lewin 1990, 1991) the Marxist approaches to housing theory have been critically reviewed. Essentially the problem with

Marxist theory is that although it provides a useful critique of capitalist societies, it has no operational blueprint for managing a socialist economy and its housing sector. In actual housing practice, socialist countries in the developed and the developing world have performed badly in housing. Socialist housing has been underresourced, undersupplied, inegalitarian, and full of economic and organizational problems (Mathey 1990; Pugh and Lewin 1990, 1991; Pugh 1992c). The socialist failures in housing do not imply that the NPE is the only means of guiding housing policy development. Other social theories may be worthwhile in principle and useful in practice, but presently the NPE has no real competition in the mainstream. What is clear is that in the NPE or the (partial) socialist political economies, it is necessary to restructure and review government roles in their public spending. Housing subsidies can be better targeted for antipoverty purposes, infrastructure can be developed within joint ventures among government agencies, NGOs, and organized self-help groups, and overall public expenditure has to be related to taxable capacities and medium-term economic growth.

Social criticism of the NPE does not have to be limited to socialist alternatives. The French social theorist, Michel Foucault has some ideas which can be applied to the NPE approach to housing (Ranibow 1984). Foucault argues that social and economic theories become linked to state power, obtaining practical acceptance at particular moments in history. As argued above, the NPE came to dominance at a period when state socialism demised and some developing countries experienced severe problems in repaying external debt and in macroeconomic management. In practice, social and economic policies are set in a pattern of administrative norms. This is a process of using power to prescribe and implement norms (i.e., 'normalization'), involving setting conditions, administering eligibilities and exclusions, and favoring particular approaches such as those consistent with the NPE ideology and practice. For example, in post-1972 World Bank housing loan programs eligibilities were attached to agreements with governments, with allocations to financial institutions, and with rights to access in sites-and-services projects. Housing standards are bureaucratically normalized in the economic–administrative systems which are operated within a low-income housing system. The NPE housing policies have their own characteristic jargon, for example, terms such as 'affordability' 'enablement', 'market friendly', and 'institutionally loaded reform' approaches. In all of this the practical, ideological, and the advocacy merge, sometimes in hidden ways. Sometimes NPE housing policies will fail in their aims for efficiency and effectiveness, including low-income purposes. The central thrust of

Foucault's ideas is to ensure critical evaluation of history, the conceptual foundation, and application of dominant theories and practices of housing.

What does the evidence of NPE housing approaches reveal by the early 1990s?—On the one hand, policies which have been appropriately fine-tuned and adapted have performed positively in low-income purposes, for example, policies in Madras and Sri Lanka have achieved some effectiveness. On the other hand, some inherent problems are contained within the NPE housing approach. The problems include possibilities that loans channelled through financial institutions can favor the middle classes, government administrative capacities could fall short of whole sector housing development, and that austerity packages in macroeconomic policy ignore adverse housing impacts. Above all, the new housing policy approaches depend upon formulating and operating sophisticated institutional linking between government agencies, markets, NGOs, and self-help in households. Self-help is regarded here as a choice made in households to earn, rear children, work at home, respond to incentives, and to build and maintain housing and infrastructure. Risks of failure are many, varied, and real. They would exist not only in NPE-type policies, but also in the application of social theories in general. The particular characteristic of the NPE is its association to capitalist market inequality, and to the willingness of political elites and the middle classes to support and deliver antipoverty housing policies. In housing, low-income purposes also depend upon the political–technocratic conditions within the IMF and the World Bank. These conditions and the ideas underlying the favored theories have been evolutionary, rather than static. Low-income housing policies remain in need of a learning by doing experience and an ongoing critical evaluation. This piece of writing has identified and discussed the significant issues from principles, practices, and economic dilemmas in housing sector development as well as antipoverty program development.

In the final evaluative comment on low-income housing development, two major points can be made. First, though often misunderstood and neglected, the reality of squatter settlement has had positive features, notwithstanding the fact that it represents poverty and health risks. Households have engaged in jobs which lead to economic development and necessary urbanization. The authorities have *in time* recognized and accepted the settlements, and in many instances property rights for individual and social property. Without secure property rights, economic functioning would be retarded, fraud would increase, and high risks would add to the economic and social costs of life. The assets in squatter settlements, though sometimes appearing meager and unhealthy, represent impressive saving, investment, and entrepreneurship. Second, the third phase World Bank housing policy can be widened with innovation in low-income housing development. The possibilities are many and varied, with useful examples from the history of international experience. In varied ways, market–state interactions in land policies in Taiwan, South Korea, and Sweden (since the early 1990s) have kept land cost components in housing comparatively low. Statutory urban and housing development corporations, e.g., South Australian Housing Trust and new towns corporations in Britain have promoted private sector development with social principles, some cross-subsidization from commercial to social spheres and from high-income to low-income housing. The possibilities for progress are wider than those expressed in the World Bank's third phase housing policy development.

NOTES

1. The subject development economics has experienced discontinuities and ideological controversies during its post-1950s history. During the 1950s, development economics was in its formative stages; by the 1960s it was dominated by intellectual advocates of state-led development in the form of five year plans; the 1970s gave greater emphasis to income redistribution in development; and the 1980s was influenced by the IMF and World Bank stabilization and structural adjustment experience and favor to enablement policies (Colclough and Manor 1991; Dornbusch and Helmers 1988; Hunt 1989; Krueger 1992; Pomfret 1992). The present post-1989 World Bank and IMF orthodoxy is based upon freedom for market capitalism and a view of the state which emphasizes the negative attitudes of public choice economics. Public choice economics had its roots in the 1960s and its advocates regard bureaucrats as self-serving in securing their careers, enlarging their power and bureaucratic imperialism, and consequently favoring big government and large state economic roles. The new World Bank–IMF orthodoxy is aimed at significantly restraining government–bureaucratic economic imperialism and interference in markets.

2. The commentary and the diagram, Figure 2.2, need some qualifying points. Although the diagram expresses continuous incomes among poor households, income flows will often be intermittent and highly variable. Cultural, religious, and social attitudes to marriage and male–female partnerships will vary among countries and ethnic groups. For example, common law marriages are frequent in some African countries and male partners often live and work in towns and females in rural area where they rear the children and work on the land.

REFERENCES

Barbosa, E.M. 1984. 'Household Economy and Financial Capital', in J. Smith et al., *Households and the World Economy*. Beverly Hills, CA: Sage.

Beneria, Lourdes. 1990. 'The Mexican Debt Crisis: Restructuring the Economy and the Household', XII World Congress of Sociology, International Sociological Association, Madrid, 9–13 July 1990.

Buchanan, J. and G. Tullock. 1962. *The Calculus of Consent*. Ann Arbor: University of Michigan Press.

Buckley, R., J. Khadduri and R. Struyk. 1985. *Housing Development Finance Corporation of India: Evaluation of the Housing Guarantee Loan*. Washington, D.C.: USAID.

Buckley, Robert and Stephen Mayo. 1989. 'Housing Policy in Developing Countries: Evaluating the Macro-economic Impacts', *Review of Urban and Regional Development Studies 1 (2)*, pp. 27–47.

Burgess, R. 1977. 'Self-Help Housing: A New Imperialist Strategy? A Critique of the Turner School', *Antipode 9 (2)*, pp. 50–59.

———. 1978. 'Petty Commodity Housing for Dweller Control: A Critique of John Turner's Views on Housing Policy', *World Development 6*, pp. 1105–33.

———. 1982. 'Self-Help Advocacy: A Curious Form of Radicalism: A Critique of the Work of John F.C. Turner', in P. Ward (ed.), *Self-Help Housing: A Critique*. London: Mansell, pp. 14–37.

Cardoso, Eliana and Santiago Levy. 1988. 'Mexico', in Rudiger Dornbusch and F. Leslie Helmers, *The Open Economy: Tools for Policy Makers in Developing Countries*. Oxford: Oxford University Press and World Bank, pp. 348–72.

Chant, Sylvia. 1990a. 'Gender, Migration and Urban Development in Costa Rica: The Case of Guanacaste'. Unpublished Paper, Department of Geography. London: London School of Economics.

———. 1990b. 'Gender, Households and Seasonal Migration in Guanacaste, Costa Rica'. Unpublished Paper, Department of Geography, London School of Economics.

Colclough, Christopher and James Manor (eds.). 1991. *States or Markets? Neo-Liberalism and the Development Policy Debate*. Oxford: Clarendon.

Collins, Susan. 1988. 'Multiple Exchange Rates, Capital Controls, and Commercial Policy', in Rudiger Dornbusch and F. Leslie Helmers, *The Open Economy: Tools for Policy Makers in Developing Countries*. Oxford: Oxford University Press and World Bank, pp. 128–64.

Connolly, Priscilla. 1990. 'Housing and the State in Mexico', in Gil Shildo (ed.), *Housing Policy in Developing Countries*. London: Routledge, pp. 46–59.

de Azevedo, Sergio. 1990. 'Politics and Housing Policy in Brazil', XII World Congress, International Sociological Association, Madrid, 9–13 July 1990.

Dornbusch, Rudiger. 1988. 'Overvaluation and Trade Balance', in Rudiger Dornbusch and F. Leslie Helmers, *The Open Economy: Tools for Policy Makers in Developing Countries*. Oxford: Oxford University Press and World Bank, pp. 80–107.

Dornbusch, Rudiger and Leslie Helmers (eds.). 1988. *The Open Economy: Tools for Policy Makers in Developing Countries*. Oxford: Oxford University Press and World Bank.

Downs, A. 1957. *An Economic Theory of Democracy*. New York: Harper and Row.

Financial Times. 1992. 'Avuncular Provider of Advice: Lewis Preston Talks to Michael Prowse and Peter Normal', 27 April 1992, p. 30.

Gilbert, Alan. 1989. 'Housing during Recession: Illustrations from Latin America', *Housing Studies 4 (3)*, pp. 155–66.

———. 1990a. 'Housing Under Salinas: The Art of the Possible'. Paper presented to the Society for Latin American Studies, Jesus College, Oxford University, 30 March–1 April 1990.

Gilbert, Alan and Ann Varley. 1990. *Housing the Poor in Urban Mexico*. London: Routledge.

Glickman, Harvey. 1988. *The Crisis and Challenge of African Development*. New York: Greenwood Press.

Hardoy, Jorge E. and D. Satterthwaite. 1989. *Squatter Citizen: Life in the Third World*. London: Eathscan.

Helmers, F. Leslie. 1988. 'The Real Exchange Rate', in Rudiger Dornbusch and F. Leslie

Helmers (eds.), *The Open Economy: Tools for Policy Makers in Developing Countries.* Oxford: Oxford University Press and World Bank, pp. 10–36.

Hunt, Diana. 1989. *Economic Theories of Development: An Analysis of Competing Paradigms.* Hemel Hampstead: Harvester Wheatsheaf.

Jayatnam, W. 1974. *Politics: Sri Lanka 1947–1973.* London: MacMillan.

Kaul, Sanat. 1990. *A Housing Finance System for Low-Income Households in India: A Proposed Model. Vinod Dixit Foundation.* New Delhi: National Institute of Public Finance and Policy.

Kearney, R. 1973. *The Politics of Sri Lanka.* Ithaca: Cornell University Press.

Klitgaard, R. 1991. *'Adjusting to Reality: Beyond State versus Market' in Economic Development.* San Franciso: ICS Press.

Krugman, Paul. 1988. 'External Shocks and Domestic Policy Responses', in Rudiger Dornbusch and F. Leslie Helmers (eds.), *The Open Economy: Tools for Policy Makers in Developing Countries.* Oxford: Oxford University Press and World Bank, pp. 54–79.

Krueger, Anne. 1992. *Economic Policy Reform in Developing Countries.* Oxford: Blackweil.

Mangin, William. 1967. 'Latin American Squatter Settlements: A Problem and a Solution', *Latin American Research Review 2 (3),* pp. 65–98.

Mangin, William and **John F.C. Turner.** 1966. 'The Barrida Movement', *Progressive Architecture 1 (3),* pp. 34–49.

Mathey, K. (ed.). 1990. *Housing Policy in the Socialist Third World.* London: Mansell.

Matthei, C. and **R. Hahn** 1991. *Community Land Trusts and the Delivery of Affordable Shelter to the Urban Poor in Kenya.* Nairobi: Ford Foundation.

Mayo, Stephen. 1991. 'Housing Policy and Housing Research: The View from the World Bank'. Paper for European Network for Housing Research, Conference, Housing the Urban Poor. Istanbul, Turkey, 17–20 September 1991.

Mayo, S. and **D. Gross.** 1987. 'Sites and Services—and Subsidies: The Economics of Low-Cost Housing in Developing Countries', *The World Bank Economic Review 1 (2),* pp. 301–35.

Meier, G. 1991. 'Policy Lessons and Policy Formation', in G. Meier (ed.), *Politics and Policy Making in Developing Countries: Perspectives on the New Political Economy.* San Francisco: ICS Press, pp. 96–113.

Mengers, H.A. 1990. *Aspects of Privatization of Basic Infrastructure in Developing Countries.* Rotterdam: IHS.

Mosley, Paul, Jane Harrigan and **John Toye.** 1991. *Aid and Power: The World Bank and Policy-Based Lending, Vol. 1, Analysis and Policy Proposals.* London: Routledge.

Niskanen, A. 1971. *Bureaucracy and Representative Government.* New York: Aldine, Hawthorne.

Parfitt, Trevor and **Stephen Riley.** 1989. *The African Debt Crisis.* London: Routledge.

Pickett James and **Hans Singer.** 1990. *Towards Economic Recovery in Sub-Saharan Africa: Essays in Honour of Robert Gardiner.* London: Routledge.

Pomfret, Richard. 1992. *Diverse Paths of Economic Development.* Hemel Hampstead: Harvester Wheatsheaf.

Pugh, Cedric. 1984. 'Public Policy, Welfare and the Singaporean Economy'. *Annals of Public and Cooperative Economy 54 (4),* pp. 433–55.

———. 1985. 'Housing and Development in Singapore', *Contemporary Southeast Asia 6 (4),* pp. 275–307.

———. 1989. 'The World Bank and Urban Shelter in Bombay', *Habitat International 13 (3),* pp. 23–49.

———. 1990a. *Housing and Urbanization: A Study of India.* New Delhi: Sage.

———. 1990b. 'A New Approach to Housing Theory: Sex, Gender, and the Domestic Economy', *Housing Studies 5 (2),* pp. 112–29.

Pugh, Cedric. 1990c. 'The World Bank and Housing Policy in Madras', *Journal of Urban Affairs 12 (2)*, pp. 173–96.
———. 1991. 'Housing Policies and the Role of the World Bank', *Habitat International 15 (1/2)*, pp. 275–98.
———. 1992a. 'Land Policies and Low-Income Housing in Developing Countries: A Review with Reference to Kenya and India', *Land Use Policy 9 (1)*, pp. 47–63.
———. 1992b. 'International Finance and Housing Policies in Developing Countries', *Cities 9 (2)*, pp. 117–37.
———. 1992c. 'Book Review: K Mathey (ed.), Housing Policy in the Socialist Third World, London: Mansell, 1990', *Housing Studies 7 (3)*, pp. 237–38.
Pugh, C. and S. Lewin. 1990. 'Women, Work, and Housing in the Soviet Union in Pre-Perestroika Times: Marxist Theory and Socialist Practice', *Netherlands Journal of Housing and Environmental Research 5 (4)*, pp. 339–57.
———. 1991. 'Housing, Gender and Family Policies in the Soviet Union Under Perestroika', *Netherlands Journal of Housing and Environmental Research 6 (1)*, pp. 47–55.
Ranibow, P. 1984. *The Foucault Reader.* Harmondsworth: Penguin.
Rondinelli, Dennis and Shabbir Cheema. 1988. *Urban Services in Developing Countries: Public and Private Roles in Urban Development.* Basingstoke: MacMillan.
Sharma, K. 1988. *Society and Politics in Sri Lanka.* New Delhi: South Asian Publishers.
Simonsen, Mario. 1988. 'Brazil', in Rudiger Dornbusch and F. Leslie Helmers (eds.), *The Open Economy: Tools for Policy Makers in Developing Countries.* Oxford: Oxford University Press and World Bank, pp. 285–307.
Strassman, Paul. 1976. 'Measuring the Employment Effects of Housing Policy in Developing Countries', *Economic and Cultural Change*, pp. 623–32.
———. 1978. *Housing and Building Technology in Developing Countries.* East Lansing: Michigan State University.
———. 1982. *The Transformation of Urban Housing: The Experience of Upgrading in Cartaqena.* Baltimore: Johns Hopkins and World Bank.
Stren, Richard and Rodney White. 1989. *African Cities in Crisis.* Boulder, CO: Westview Press.
Turner, J. 1967. 'Barriers and Channels for Housing Development in Modernizing Countries', *Journal of the American Institute of Planners 33 (3)*, pp. 167–81.
———. 1968. 'Housing Priorities, Settlement Patterns, and Urban Development in Modernizing Countries', *Journal of the American Institute of Planners 24 (6)*, pp. 354–63.
———. 1971. 'New View of the Housing Deficit', in D. Lewis (ed.), *The Growth of Cities.* London: Elek, pp. 43–61.
———. 1972a. 'The Re-education of a Professional', in J. Turner and R. Fichter (eds.), *Freedom to Build.* London: MacMillan, pp. 122–47.
———. 1972b. 'Housing as a Verb', in J. Turner and R. Fitchter (eds.), *Freedom to Build.* London: MacMillan, pp. 148–76.
———. 1976. *Housing by People: Towards Autonomy in Building.* London: Marion Boyars.
UNCHS (Habitat). 1987. *Global Report on Human Settlements.* Oxford: Oxford University Press/UNCHS.
———. 1990. *The Global Shelter Strategy for Shelter to the Year 2000.* Nairobi: UNCHS.
United Nations. 1992. *United Nations Development Program: Human Development Report, 1992.* Washington, D.C.: UNDP.
Valenca, Mario. 1992. 'The Inevitable Crisis of the Brazilian Housing Finance System', *Urban Studies 29 (1)*, pp. 39–56.
Woodring, M. 1984. *Evaluation of First Phase of Housing Guarantee Program.* Washington, D.C., Sri Lanka, USAID.

Woodfield, Anthony. 1989. *Housing and Economic Adjustment*. New York: Taylor and Francis.

World Bank. 1972. *Urbanization*. Washington, D.C.: World Bank.

———. 1974. *Housing*. Washington, D.C.: World Bank.

———. 1975. *Sites and Services Projects*. Washington, D.C.: World Bank.

———. 1989. *Sub-Saharan Africa: From Crisis to Sustainable Growth: A Long Term Perspective Study*. Washington, D.C.: World Bank.

———. 1990a. *World Development Report: Poverty*. Oxford: Oxford University Press and World Bank.

———. 1990b. *Report on Structural Adjustment Lending II: Policies for the Recovery of Growth*. Internal World Bank Paper, R90-57, IDA/R90-49, Washington, D.C.: World Bank.

———. 1991a. *World Development Report 1991: The Challenge of Development*. Oxford: Oxford University Press and World Bank.

———. 1991b. *Urban Policy and Economic Development: An Agenda for the 1990's*. Washington, D.C.: World Bank.

———. 1992. *Housing: Enabling Markets to Work*. Washington, D.C.: World Bank.

PART II

HOUSING UNDER HIGH LEVELS OF HUMAN DEVELOPMENT

Table 1.1 in Chapter 1 shows the Human Development Index for the four cases described in Part II. South Korea, Costa Rica, and Mexico are within ten points of the top of the index for all countries in the world, while Hong Kong ranks with industrial societies. In terms of life expectancy, literacy, and income the people in these countries are at or near the level of more industrialized societies. Furthermore, the GNP rank minus the HDI rank puts South Korea, Costa Rica, and Mexico well above where they would be expected to be just based on GNP. Mexico is 20 ranks and South Korea is nine ranks above where they would be expected to be on the basis of their GNP. All of these societies have put large amounts of resources into the social development for the good of their citizens. The descriptions in the case studies indicate a high-level of commitment to the improvement of housing in all three of these societies.

On comparing the HDI of 1970 with that of 1985, South Korea is third from the top in the amount of improvement (.285) during that period. Mexico is 17th (.189) and Hong Kong is 18th (.185) in improvement. Costa Rica was high on the Index in 1970 and consequently showed less improvement (.084) Not only are these societies high in social development when compared to all countries of the world, they are also high in the amount of improvement they have made since 1970.

Housing poverty in Hong Kong is described by Alan Smart in Chapter 3. The economic development of Hong Kong, with limited land, should have created housing poverty. Although the British colony does have very low-levels of space per individual, it has managed to rehouse 45 percent of its population in public housing since 1945. It has done this in a classic case of enablement. Faced with the possibility of using extension government controls and regulations to thwart the development of housing, the government of the British Crown colony used its extension controls to clear squatters, sell a major portion of the land to the private sector, and use the money thus obtained to rehouse the squatters. The motivation for this, Alan Smart argues, was to minimize political unrest over traditional squatter clearance for development (without resettlement) for fear of bringing the newly powerful Communist Party in China down on them. Whatever the motivation, the chapter describes how the government made it possible for millions of Hong

Kong residents to move into public housing without a major impact on their incomes.

South Korea has a long period from the 1930s to the present during which squatter settlements and poor housing were created. These settlements and other marginal housing areas are described by Jaesoon Cho and Jeonghee Park in Chapter 4. Their research describes the characteristics of the occupants of the 528 squatter settlements in the various cities. The government, in turn, has utilized a variety of schemes to try and eliminate squatter settlements, and other low-income or marginal housing areas. The phases are typical of the post-World War II process: demolition and renewal (1951–65), self-help upgrading (1966–72), rehabilitation and renewal (1973–83), urban housing renewal (1983 to present), and rehabilitation (1989 to present). Problems and limitations of each of these approaches are discussed in this chapter. All of them have only been partially effective. The 1983 to present program of urban housing renewal is typical of what Cedric Pugh has called enablement: developers and owners worked together to rehabilitate housing in areas which were under substantial pressure for development. Both the parties benefited from this cooperative approach. Renters, however, became politically active because they were left out of the benefits (and lost out on housing). The chapter documents support of Alan Smart's point about minimizing political unrest in Hong Kong by major resettlement of squatters. The early Korean programs of clearance and relocation to a distant site were stopped because of the negative reactions of the people who were affected.

Costa Rica, described in Chapter 5, is a special housing case. It received the 1987 World Habitat Award for a national housing program which surpassed its housing target, integrated low-income families into the system and developed a family bond system of mortgages which successfully brought housing to members of the society with the lowest incomes.

The chapter describes the special circumstances of this achievement. Although Costa Rica suffers from some of the problems of high urban migration, land scarcity, and proliferation of squatter and marginal housing, it has been able to largely contain housing poverty because the revolution of 1948 abolished the military and transferred those funds to welfare. It is a case study of how a serious housing problem can be handled using the construction industry, local community based organizations utilizing self-help, and a streamlined housing bureaucracy.

Mexico's housing poverty is described in detail in Chapter 6. Keith Pezzoli describes the post-World War II changes from rental to homeownership in Mexico, as well as economic expansion, population growth, and redistribution which is behind the shift. He describes the seven different types of housing in one of the largest economies in the Third World. The consequences for housing 'economics of austerity' as described by Cedric Pugh in Chapter 2 are even more clearly outlined in this chapter. The organization of Solidarity by the current President of Mexico is also presented in more detail. Unlike Cedric Pugh, Keith Pezzoli is much less optimistic about the ability of the current enablement to solve the problems of housing poverty in Mexico. A larger concern, he points out, is the environmental degradation associated with the current state of housing.

3

Hong Kong's Slums and Squatter Areas: A Developmental Perspective

Alan Smart

Hong Kong has been repeatedly discussed and dissected as one of the economic miracles of the modern era. This British colony is also seen as one of the few cities among the lesser developed countries (but now classed as a newly industrializing country) which has created a successful public housing program (Castells et al. 1988; Yeung and Drakakis-Smith 1982). This chapter will discuss the system of housing in Hong Kong, concentrating upon Hong Kong's slums and squatter areas. One of the main arguments of this analysis will be that one crucial support for Hong Kong's economic achievements has been the way in which it has coped with extremely high land costs and overcrowding while keeping the cost of labor relatively low (until recent years) and without creating high levels of social pathology. A major element of the response to these challenges has been the creation of a public housing program which now houses 2.63 million people—over 45 percent of the population.

This public housing program traces its origins to the clearance of Hong Kong's squatter areas, and it can be said that the standard interpretations of the shift from squatter clearance to squatter resettlement in 1954 are incorrect, and that an adequate explanation of this shift leads to new perspectives on Hong Kong's developmental pattern. One would agree with the observation of Rafferty (1989, p. 18) that:

> One of the mysteries and at the same time one of the achievements of the twentieth century is how Hong Kong came to achieve [its] high standard of living with such paucity of resources.

Hong Kong is one of a handful of former lesser developed countries that are now classed as newly industrializing countries and have been widely scrutinized for the secrets of their success. Annual income is now probably over US$ 10,000 per capita (Rafferty 1989, p. 17). Unemployment is consistently between 1 and 2 percent, salary and wage increases have averaged about 2.5 percent over the inflation, and real GDP growth was 7 percent in

1988, a decrease from 13.5 percent in 1987 (Yee 1989, p. 75). GDP real growth from 1961–76 was an average 8.9 percent or 6.4 percent per capita, and from 1976–79 averaged 12.5 percent. The continued growth up to 1992 has surprised many analysts, given the concerns raised by the imminent transfer of control of Hong Kong from Britain to China in 1997. Hong Kong's justly famous entrepreneurs have turned the threat into an opportunity by largely annexing the economy of the Pearl River Delta of Guangdong province in the People's Republic of China to the Hong Kong economy. Vogel (1989, p. 385) sees Hong Kong and Guangdong together as part of a 'Cantonese newly industrializing economy (NIE), centered in Hong Kong'. The largest portion of Hong Kong's production of manufactures for export, the basis of Hong Kong's economic miracle, has been transferred overseas, and most of it into China (Smart and Smart 1991; 1992).

Many explanations have been offered for Hong Kong's economic miracle, and no space is available here for a discussion of them in detail. One of the main arguments of this article, though, is that the role of the public housing program in this miracle has been seriously misunderstood. A re-examination of its historical origins, attempted subsequently in the context of a more general examination of Hong Kong's squatter areas and slums, raises serious questions about the influence of laisser-faire or non-interventionist economic policies allegedly preferred by Hong Kong's government. The public housing program is regularly identified as one of the main exceptions to what otherwise may be one of the least restrained capitalist societies in the world. However, it is usually interpreted as an example of a market failure, and the intervention inevitable. Research conducted in this field makes one put forward a stronger claim: that government intervention in the housing provision was prompted by a reluctance to dismantle already existing interventions in the land development process which were impeding private sector developments, and that market failure was not inevitable, but partially a product of a very interventionist government. One distinctive feature of Hong Kong is that all land is defined as crown land, and since the period prior to 1898, all development has been subject to detailed governmental scrutiny and approval.

In addition to this reinterpretation of Hong Kong's responses to the problems of squatter areas and slums, the contemporary character of low-income housing in Hong Kong will be described and the research that has been conducted on these topics will also be surveyed. To understand the present situation, however, it is necessary to first consider the past, and see how things got the way they are at present.

EXTENT AND CHARACTER OF SLUMS
AND SQUATTER AREAS IN HONG KONG

Hong Kong, with a population over 6 million in a land area of 1,049 sq. km., is one of the most densely populated cities in the world. The overall population density is about 4,400 per sq. km., but the rugged nature of the topography and the leased nature (from 1898 to 1997) of the New Territories have concentrated most of the growth into the area around the harbor. The population density in 14 percent of the territory which classifies as urban is nearly 26,000 per sq. km., and in 1971 Mongkok district had the highest density at 155,000 per sq. km. (Lee 1981). Its housing has always been extremely expensive in relation to average income.

One of the results of crowding and the high housing costs is that from its physical characteristics, a large proportion of its housing stock could be described as 'slums'. Even dual career professional households may live in a 300 sq. ft. apartment, and pay a significant proportion of their income in order to do so. Much of the public housing stock could have been described as government built slums when it was first constructed: the oldest public housing blocks are six-storey walkups with families placed in single room concrete cells with no private bathroom or kitchen facilities. These oldest blocks are being redeveloped, but even the latest public housing is spartan and cramped by Western standards. It can be argued, though, that the minimal standard for public housing was an important condition for the successes achieved by Hong Kong's public housing program, and thus part of the puzzle of Hong Kong's remarkable developmental achievements.

Many people in Hong Kong still live in abysmal housing conditions. Probably the worst are the 'caged men', a local term referring to bed-spaces for singles, the 'cage' suggested by the tendency of these tenants to erect wire coverings for their bed-spaces to prevent theft of their belongings. The average number of residents in one of the bed-space apartments is 38.3, and the average per capita living space is 1.8 sq. m. (19.4 sq. ft.). The ratio of residents to bathrooms is 18.7:1, and the ratio for toilets is 22.7:1. A government study located 102 bed-space apartments accommodating 3,903 singles. These figures do not include group elderly households which accommodated another 1,703 people but had slightly better accommodation (*South China Morning Post*—hereafter *SCMP*—15 January 1984, p. 10).

The government has estimated that a total of 260,000 additional living quarters were required for 367,000 households in order to provide minimally acceptable housing (Hong Kong Census Main Report 1981, p. 57). This estimate only included those inadequately housed at that time, and the new housing requirements to 1986 were estimated to be an additional 247,000 living quarters (Hong Kong Census Main Report 1981, p. 59). A study in 1977 found that 77 percent of the households in private tenement-style housing had to share facilities, and 90 percent of the households living in the prewar buildings were assessed as living in housing of poor standards (Ng 1981, p. 76).

The government has also become very concerned about illegal structures and extensions on private buildings (which are treated completely separately from squatter structures). The illegal structures are ubiquitous in Hong Kong, ranging from roof-top structures to covered verandas to filled-in airwells in the center of buildings. The ingenuity with which they are constructed is amazing. An estimate has been made that there are 50,000 illegal structures on private buildings which are used as dwellings, and that clearance would require rehousing for about 200,000 people (*SCMP*, 12 June 1984, p. 1). The procedures which have been suggested for dealing with the situation have come under considerable criticism (*SCMP*, 14 June 1984, p. 10; 28 June 1984, p. 15) and it remains to be seen whether or not the government can successfully eradicate this situation which has developed in response to the high rents and overcrowding of private housing without creating other housing problems. Even by 1988, nearly half of the living units were less than 40 sq. m. in size (Wong 1989, p. 235). This small size is hardly surprising, given that a boom in property prices in recent years has resulted in new apartments being priced at over US$ 350 per sq. ft., which means a price of US$ 175,000 for a 500 sq. ft. apartment.

The government has also decided to clear all squatter areas in the urban district by the end of the decade. However, this intention has been expressed many times in the last 30 years, and doubts have been expressed over whether the plan will really be completed, particularly since it involves clearing and rehousing squatters whose land is not required for development (*Hong Kong Standard*, 11 November 1985, p. 3). The trend for the population of squatter areas, though, is down with less than 300,000 people living in Hong Kong's squatter areas at present, compared to a peak of 750,000 in 1981, with little, if any, new construction of squatter dwellings.

The situation at present then is that all forms of housing are crowded, and private housing is expensive as well as congested. The spartan conditions of Hong Kong's public housing have contributed to its success by allowing its provision at a very high rate without requiring large government subsidies or resulting in government deficits. One of the main current government policies towards public housing is to make the program completely self-financing, which is resulting in some conflict as public housing rents are increasing quite rapidly (*SCMP*, 9 September 1984, p. 12). Squatter areas are gradually disappearing, and some squatter improvement projects are being instituted (partially to avoid fires which would require immediate rehousing). To understood how this situation developed, it will be necessary to look at some of the historical antecedents of current circumstances and policies. The history demonstrates an intimate relationship between Hong Kong's squatter areas, its slums, public housing, and its general developmental patterns.

RESEARCH ON HONG KONG'S SLUMS AND SQUATTER AREAS

There has been a remarkable amount of research on the low-income residential areas of Hong Kong, and this section can do no more than briefly survey this work, pointing out some of the main features, and paving the way for a discussion in the following sections.

The literature can be roughly divided into three main areas of concern, although many individual works straddle these divisions. First, there is research which is concerned with the documentation and explanation of the problems of these areas. Much of this work relates particularly to identifying social pathologies resulting from the high rates of crowding. Second, there is research directed towards examining and assessing government efforts to resolve some of the problems of slums and squatter areas. Third, there are studies devoted to the ethnographic description of social organization and nature of life in Hong Kong's slums and squatter areas.

A surprising amount of work in Hong Kong's congested residential areas was stimulated by controversial study of rats which linked overcrowding with pathological behaviors. Since the replication of such a study with human beings was considered unethical, researchers sought natural experiments which could duplicate to some degree the extreme conditions endured by the rats, and Hong Kong was the most commonly selected research site (see, for example, Millar 1980, Boyden 1981). The inability of these researchers to discover clear evidence of a relationship between residential density and psychological or behavioral problems seems to have engendered considerable frustration. The closest approach to identifying a clear effect of high density housing was the finding by Mitchell (1971) that when people had to share crowded housing units with unrelated people and lived on the higher floors of walk-up apartments, crowding led to considerably higher levels of stress and mental problems. Anderson (1972) argued that the absence of pathological effects was due to the utilization of Chinese culture and behavior to resolve some of the stresses that would otherwise be associated with high density. On a related subject, Golger (1972) found that mortality and morbidity rates in the squatter areas of Hong Kong were no higher than for Hong Kong on an average, although the rates of respiratory disease were lower and the rates for infectious diseases were higher. In much of the earlier work on squatter settlements, they were seen as problems (Dwyer 1965), while the general shift in academic studies has later begun to see them as a type of solution to the problems facing the urban poor (Mangin 1967). Indeed, there has been considerable research on the problems caused by the relocation of squatters (Fung 1968; Golger 1972; Lui 1984; Chui 1980; Smart 1992) and on life in government low-income housing (Sparks 1976; Ikels 1983; Lui 1984).

The second tendency in studies of Hong Kong's slums and squatter areas is to provide detailed considerations of the nature and organization of daily life, rather than just concentrating upon what are perceived as problems. A number of these studies have concentrated upon residents of squatter dwellings in the relatively rural New Territories (Aijmer 1975; Potter 1968; Blake 1981), or the communities living on boats in typhoon shelters (Anderson 1973; Ward 1954; Osgood 1975). Hayes (1983) has provided some important histories of the transformation of New Kowloon's villages into squatter areas, and Leeming (1977) has provided insights into a number of Hong Kong's squatter areas and dilapidated old tenement districts. Wong's (1972) work on residential associations has provided the much descriptive material on the low-income neighborhoods of Hong Kong, private, public, and illegal. Pryor (1973) and Drakakis-Smith (1973) include excellent descriptions of the appalling housing conditions in prewar housing. Kehl (1981b) and Smart (1986; 1992) conducted research and reported on long-term participant-observation in squatter areas.

The third grouping of studies which can be identified are those which concentrate upon interventions to try and solve some of the problems presented by slums and squatter settlements. One of the main concerns of these works are to explain the success of Hong Kong's public housing program, and why it came into being in a British colony priding itself upon a laissez-faire or a positive noninterventionist set of policies.

Squatting in the prewar period was not a serious problem, but difficulties of making land available for development were blamed on the illegal occupation of vacant land in the disorder following the occupation. At first, squatters were cleared with little or no provision for rehousing. A massive fire in Shekkipmei during Christmas in 1953, left 50,000 squatters homeless and provided the immediate stimulus for the subsequent interventions which eventually took the form of the public housing program. The Shekkipmei fire is a corner-stone of the first type of explanation of public housing program which sees it as an effort to improve public welfare in a situation of extreme deprivation when the private sector could not provide affordable housing and the prevailing conditions were a risk to public health and safety (Pryor 1973).

This public welfare view has been criticized by authors who feel that the government intervened in order to provide support to property developers. Drakakis-Smith (1981, p. 161) rejects the idea that the public housing program can be understood as a welfare measure (see also Mitchell 1972b, p. 118; Yeung and Drakakis-Smith 1982, p. 221). Rather, it is clear even from official statements that the primary concern was that squatters occupied land required for development, and that to resettle them instead of just removing them was politically expedient (Commissioner for Resettlement 1955, pp. 7, 30). One million squatters were resettled in 1971 on land equivalent to only 34 percent of the area previously occupied (Drakakis-Smith 1973, pp. 34). For Drakakis-Smith, the explanation of the squatter resettlement program is that it served to make land available for development by private enterprise and for public works (1981, p. 106). This explanation also accounts for the squatter areas which are not cleared: those on undevelopable land such as on steep hills, and those on the periphery of the built-up areas (Kehl 1981b, p. 13). Kehl (1981b) argued that the Hong Kong government attempts to maximize the production of land for the private sector. The portion of this newly available land used for public housing is minimized as much as is politically expedient. He further claims that:

> government intervention in housing through squatter resettlement creates the best conditions for the freest play of the market in private real estate (Kehl 1981b, p. 20).

A third type of explanation draws upon structuralist Marxism, and focuses particularly upon the contribution made by public housing to the reproduction of labor power, hence the subsidization of private industry. Lui (1984, p. 48) argues that in order to maintain its position in the world economy, Hong Kong has to keep its labor costs at a level which will allow it to remain competitive. Low wages threaten the reproduction, despite the subsidy of cheap imports from China (Schiffer 1991) and the state reacts to this by providing resources such as public housing to act as a social wage to subsidize workers and promote peaceful labor–management relations (Lui 1984, p. 57).

The conclusion drawn from the research on the history of Hong Kong's squatter areas and public housing program was that all of these explanations are inadequate, partly for logical reasons, but most importantly because they share a description of what happened which leaves out important factors, and the disagreement is primarily at the level of the interpretation of those facts (Smart 1989; 1992). A summary of those conclusions will be presented in the next section.

Once the squatter resettlement program began, it developed its own dynamic and became a much more general public housing program. Considerable credit for this has been given to Governor Murray Maclehose, who oversaw the largest expansion of the program (Castells et al. 1988). Considerable discussion of the public housing program has been conducted, but there is no room for reviewing this literature here (see Pryor 1973; Fung 1968; Li and Yu 1990).

INTERVENTIONS IN HONG KONG'S SLUMS AND SQUATTER AREAS

When the British regained control of Hong Kong from the Japanese in 1945, they were in possession of a demolished city with its population scattered in China, dead, or in dire poverty after surviving the occupation. In 1941, the population had dropped from nearly 2 million to 600,000. The chaos in China, however, meant that an influx of refugees rapidly swelled Hong Kong's numbers to over a million at the end of 1946, and 2 million by 1951 (Special Committee on Housing 1958). The number of squatters, rare before the war, had grown to 300,000 by 1949 (Wong 1978, p. 208). The number of people per domestic floor (tenement apartments, subdivided by partitions) was 9.05 in 1934 and rose to 16.5 in 1939 because of the war refugees from China, a figure which was reattained in 1949 and reached 18.144 in 1950. The ratio had risen to 19.597 by 1956 despite two years of public housing construction (Special Committee on Housing 1958).

In the previous section, three types of explanations of Hong Kong's public housing program have been discussed. Despite their differences, they share some common assumptions, presented as a description of the facts. This conventional wisdom is that Hong Kong was facing a critical housing problem after 1945 because of the inability of the private sector to profitably construct affordable housing for the large influx of low-income people. These conditions created problems for Hong Kong: threats to public health, large fires in squatter areas, barriers to development of the land which had been encroached upon by squatters, and the pressure on wages of high rents. Since the private sector was incapable of meeting the challenge, it was inevitable that the government would have to intervene, although this was postponed as much as possible because of the adherence to the philosophy of laisser-faire or positive noninterventionism. These accounts are common to each of the 15 explanations; they only disagree on the motivation that impelled government intervention through the creation of public housing.

However, after doing archival research, one tends to doubt the conventional description of these events. The account is not completely wrong. There was a massive housing problem that the private sector did not seem capable of solving. The Shekkipmei fire did act as an important stimulus for the resettlement program and the way that it was implemented was ultimately largely to the benefit of the government, property owners, and developers. However, these views tend to accept the housing problem as inevitable and that the only choices were whether or not the government would accept the responsibility of housing those the private sector could not, and how it would do so.

Such views leave out another alternative pointed out by legislative council members in a debate in 1947 (see Smart 1989). Instead of increasing its intervention in land administration and housing production, the government could have reduced its intervention which seems to have been blocking much potential development or channelling it into illegal forms in the squatter areas and former villages. Development did not occur to a large extent because the government held a central position in the development process, and did not simply make land available for development because of a large variety of controls and restrictions. It seems likely that a policy of allowing the private sector to build as it wished and charge what the market would bear could have been successful in producing more housing, although at great cost to the poor of Hong Kong and with considerable political risk to the government. A major piece of evidence for this assertion is that the private sector did, in fact, produce a great deal of such housing, but illegally, in the production of squatter dwellings for rent and for purchase (Smart 1986; 1992). Much of the squatting was illegal only because of the distinction between agricultural land and building land, and the control over construction given to the government by the building ordinances. Such illegal buildings can be seen as products of the private sector which overcame the impediments the legislative council members identified by going beyond the bounds of legality.

This argument suggests that rather than the private sector being unable to cope with the demand for housing and the government eventually being forced, for whichever reasons, to intervene, the state was already centrally involved in the land development process. Furthermore, it was involved in such a way so as to inhibit effective private responses to the postwar housing crisis.

Another element of the three rival explanations which is inadequate is their account of why squatter clearance became squatter resettlement. Squatter clearance without resettlement would make land available for development, and at a lower cost. There is no evidence that resettlement was necessary in order to reproduce labour power, since mortality rates were no higher in squatter areas. Moreover, statements by government officials make it clear that welfare issues were not the primary motive, although they were involved to a degree. There is a missing factor in the account, and what is missing is the active involvement of the squatters themselves.

The possibility that the actions of the squatters themselves may have been linked to the switch from squatter clearance to resettlement has not been considered, partly because of views like those of Dwyer (1965) which characterize Hong Kong's squatters as politically passive and apathetic. This may have been true at the time Dwyer was writing (although it was not the case in the early 1980s), but it misses important factors in the period when the resettlement program was initiated.

The potential for resistance by squatters, resistance which might result in political instability due to the tense relationship between Hong Kong, Britain, and the newly communist People's Republic of China, is the missing factor in the equation. Squatter clearance without rehousing could be difficult and was potentially a source of danger to the government functionaries carrying out the clearance and of disruption in a political system which was diplomatically threatened by the rise to power of the Chinese Communist Party. Thus, the mechanism which extended the program of squatter clearance to a public housing program was the anticipation by the government of the potential for and dangers of squatter resistance to clearance.

Once the squatter resettlement program was instituted, it took on its own dynamics. One result of this was its transformation into a general public housing program in 1963, so that between 1974–84, the proportion of housing units allocated to cleared squatters was usually less than a quarter of the total. Public housing is still being produced at a rapid rate, with a target of 30,000 units per year.

A relatively new component of the government's housing strategy is the homeownership scheme, where higher-quality units are sold to lower-middle-income families and public housing tenants. This program, intended to increase political stability by creating a sense of attachment and modeled upon Singapore's policies, housed 300,100 people by March 1988 (Wong 1989).

Another element of the public housing system are the temporary housing areas. They started as a form of 'core housing' where a basic framework, a roof, and services were produced by the government, but occupants were expected to finish the walls, etc., by themselves. The quality of this form of housing has gradually improved, but it has still been the general aim to make temporary housing areas unattractive in order to discourage squatting (Yan 1978, p. 18; Lui 1984, p. 75), since only those squatters who were not registered in a survey were eligible for this type of resettlement.

Government policies have had a critical influence on the character of Hong Kong's squatter areas. Unlike many other countries, Hong Kong has not yet regularized any squatter settlements. They remain in a limbo of illegality combined with toleration until the land is scheduled for development. Furthermore, one exception to the policy of toleration of already constructed squatter dwellings is that adding extensions or conducting significant renovations are considered grounds for demolition. Thus, the consolidation process by which many squatter dwellings are improved and eventually become a conventional part of the urban landscape is not possible in Hong Kong, and the government's policies are themselves to a large extent responsible for the poor conditions of housing in Hong Kong's squatter areas (Smart 1992).

In contrast to most of the other contributions to this volume, the influence of policies developed by the World Bank and other international agencies has not been addressed in this chapter. This omission is primarily because unlike most other Third World countries, the housing policies of international agencies have had little or no influence upon the Hong Kong government's actions. No projects have been supported by World Bank or other nonmarket funding (with the exception of refugee camps supported by the United Nations High Commission for Refugees, which are not addressed in this chapter), and there is no evidence of significant policy influence. If anything, the response has been in the opposite direction, as World Bank and United Nations studies attempt to account for Hong Kong's successes and explain why such policies would not be appropriate in other settings. Hong Kong has, for example, experimented with sites-and-services projects since the 1950s, and has persisted with the rapid production of high-rise public housing during periods when the World Bank criticized such projects as unsuitable and inefficient. Significantly, the new conventional wisdom of regularizing the tenure of squatter dwellings in order to support the self-help consolidation practices of squatters has never been implemented in Hong Kong, although there are proposals to do so for squatter areas in the nonurban parts of the New Territories.

Since 1982, there has been a small squatter upgrading program implemented in Hong Kong. The improvements are usually the provision of metered water and electricity supplies, improving garbage collection and drainage, installing public toilets, and creating firebreaks (Leung 1983). The major concerns seems to have been that, when in 1981, 35,000 people were made homeless because of squatter fires. The assistant director of housing noted that these squatter fires disrupt the clearance program for housing (*South China Morning Post*, 15 August 1982, p. 1). The program, unlike others sponsored and influenced by the World Bank, is not meant to transform squatter areas into safe and acceptable additions to the housing stock, but to serve as a holding operation until squatter areas are finally cleared.

Another important policy change has been that in 1985, when the system of toleration changed from one in which squatter dwellings were registered into one in which the squatter occupants were registered (Smart 1992). The result of this has been that an increasing proportion of squatter settlement residents are eligible only for temporary housing areas and not for permanent public housing.

In 1987, the Hong Kong government presented a long term housing strategy. This strategy represented a change of direction in which there would be more emphasis upon the promotion of homeownership and in encouraging public housing tenants to take advantage of the homeownership scheme in order to release public housing units from middle-class occupants for those in need of cheap rented accommodation (Wong 1989). This policy is accompanied by increased rents for public housing tenants with incomes above a certain threshold.

In private housing, two important policies are the legislation on rent controls, and the urban renewal program. Rent controls date back to 1921, but have progressively become less extensive. No rent controls apply to buildings constructed after 1981, or to new leases on postwar properties after 1983, or higher-priced dwellings (*Hong Kong Annual Report 1987*, pp. 160–61). The existence of rent controls has tended to encourage redevelopment of old properties. Various schemes have been adopted by the government to promote the redevelopment of tenement districts in an orderly and planned fashion. Bristow (1984, p. 230) concluded that most of these schemes have generally failed to promote comprehensive redevelopment and planning, because government policies have been more concerned with increasing government revenues than incurring expenses in order to improve the living environment. Redevelopment is occurring at a high rate, but in a piecemeal and uncoordinated fashion, and as it happens much of the rent-controlled housing stock is disappearing.

CONCLUSIONS

The current state of Hong Kong's low-income housing areas is the complicated outcome of rapidly expanding economy, a government which is more interventionist than it first appeared, a combination of scarce land and dense population which has kept housing costs very high, and the myriad individual decisions and strategies of the residents of these areas. Housing standards have clearly improved since 1945, and the improvement in per capita income has made the housing problem less of the availability of any kind of shelter and more of affordability of housing of minimally acceptable standards. Yet the level of crowding and housing quality are still remarkably low for a territory as wealthy as Hong Kong, and even the middle class commonly live in extremely cramped quarters.

Discussing the future is always a risky business, but it is probably more so in the case of Hong Kong, where control over the territory will be passed from Britain to China in only five years. It is safe to assume, though, that the future patterns will be, to a large extent, the outcome of developments within the economy and of the efforts of the government to maintain control over the urban areas and its revenues from the land development process. If Hong Kong continues its current evolution into the corporate command center for the Guangdong economy and an important international financial center, housing costs are likely to continue to push at the limits of affordability, and the spillover of Hong Kong's housing into China itself will become an important phenomenon. However, should the handover fail to preserve economic growth, property prices may collapse but Hong Kong's people will have less income with which to afford them.

There is no sign of Hong Kong's government loosening its controls over urban development in the run-up to 1997, nor in the period after when it becomes a Special Administrative Region of China. Squatter areas will probably continue to dwindle away, as the British attempt to hand over a Hong Kong with fewer eyesores. There are few signs to indicate that a considerable expansion in the provision of social services is at all likely, before or after 1997, but the partial democratization of the political system may result in some degree of movement in that direction.

REFERENCES

Aijmer, G. 1975. 'An Enquiry into Chinese Settlement Patterns: The Rural Squatters of Hong Kong', *Man 10(4)*, pp. 559–70.

Anderson, Eugene N. 1972. 'Some Chinese Methods of Dealing with Crowding', *Urban Anthropology 1*, pp. 141–50.

Anderson, Engene N. and **M. Anderson.** 1973. *Mountains and Water: Essays on the Cultural Ecology of South Coastal China.* Tapei: The Orient Cultural Service.

Blake, C.F. 1981. *Ethnic Groups and Social Change in Chinese Market Town.* Honolulu: The University Press of Hawaii.

Boyden, S. et al. 1981. *The Ecology of a City and its People.* Canberra: Australian National University Press.

Bristow, Roger. 1984. *Land-use Planning in Hong Kong.* Hong Kong: Oxford University Press.

Castells, Manuel, L. Goh, R. Kwok and **T. Kee.** 1988. *Economic Development and Housing Policy in the Asian Pacific Rim.* Berkeley: Institute of Urban and Regional Development, Monograph 37.

Chui, S.C. 1980. 'The Effects of Relocation on the Residents of Temporary Housing Areas in the Market Towns'. Unpublished B.A. dissertation, University of Hong Kong.

Commissioner for Resettlement. 1955. *Annual Report.* Hong Kong: Government Printer.
Drakakis-Smith, D.W. 1973. *Housing Provision in Hong Kong.* Hong Kong: Center of Asian Studies.
————. 1981. *Urbanization. Housing and the Development Process.* London: Croom Helm.
Dwyer, D.J. 1965. 'The Problems of In-migration and Squatter Settlement in Asian Cities', *Asian Studies 2*, pp. 145–69.
Fung, B.C.K. 1968. 'Diamond Hill Area: A Geographical Study of a Squatter Area'. Unpublished B.A. dissertation, University of Hong Kong.
Golger, O.J. 1972. *Squatters and Resettlement.* Hamburg: Institute of Asian Affairs.
Hayes, James W. 1983. *The Rural Communities of Hong Kong.* Hong Kong: Oxford University Press.
Hong Kong Annual Report. 1987. *Annual Report.* Hong Kong: Government Printer.
Hong Kong Census. 1981. *Main Report.* Hong Kong: Government Printer.
Hong Kong Standard. Various issues.
Ikels, Charlotte. 1983. *Aging and Adaptation: Chinese in Hong Kong and the United States.* Hamden: Archon Books.
Kehl, Frank. 1981a. 'Hong Kong Shantytowns'. Unpublished Ph. D. dissertation, Columbia University.
————. 1981b. 'John Stuart Mill's Other Island: Squatters, Real Estate and Hong Kong Government Policy'. Paper presented at the 1981 Conference of the American Anthropological Association.
Lee, P.L. Rance. 1981. 'High-density Effects in Urban Areas', in A. King and R. Lee (eds.), *Social Life and Development in Hong Kong.* Hong Kong: Chinese University Press, pp. 3–19.
Leeming, Frank. 1977. *Street Studies in Hong Kong.* Hong Kong: Oxford University Press.
Leung, W.T. 1983. 'Squatter Improvement in Hong Kong', *Annals of G.G.A.S.,* No. 11, University of Hong Kong.
Li, Si-ming and **Fu-lai Yu.** 1990 'The Redistributive Effects of Hong Kong's Public Housing Program 1976-86', *Urban Studies 27(1),* pp. 105–18.
Lui, T.L. 1984. 'Urban Protest in Hong Kong'. M. Phil. dissertation, University of Hong Kong.
Mangin, William. 1967. 'Latin American Squatter Settlements: A Problem and a Solution', *Latin American Research Review 2,* pp. 65–99.
Millar, S.E. 1980. *Health and Well-being in Relation to High Density Living in Hong Kong.* Canberra: Australian National University Press.
Mitchell, Robert E. 1971. 'Some Social Implications of High Density Housing', *American Sociological Review 36,* pp. 18–29.
————. 1972. *Housing: Urban Growth and Economic Development.* Taipei: Asian Folklore and Social Life Monographs No. 31.
Ng, Agnes. 1981. 'Hong Kong's Housing: Review of Needs and Provision', in John Jones (ed.), *The Common Welfare.* Hong Kong: Chinese University Press, pp. 69–82.
Osgood, C. 1975. *The Chinese: A Study of a Hong Kong Chinese Community.* Tucson: University of Arizona Press.
Potter, J. 1968. *Capitalism and the Chinese Peasant.* Berkeley: University of California Press.
Pryor, E.G. 1973. *Housing in Hong Kong.* Hong Kong: Oxford University Press.
————. 1981. 'Environmental Quality and Housing Policy in Hong Kong', in Victor Sit (ed.), *Urban Hong Kong.* Hong Kong: Summerson Eastern, pp. 202–12.
Rafferty, Kevin. 1989. *City on the Rocks.* Vancouver: Douglas and MacIntyre.
Schiffer, Jonathan. 1991. *International Journal of Urban and Regional Research 15(2),* pp. 603–30.
Smart, Alan. 1986. 'From Village to Squatter Area: The Historical Transformation of Diamond Hill', *Asian Journal of Public Administration 8,* pp. 24–63.

Smart, Alan. 1988. 'Old Huts and New Regulations: Changes in the Hong Kong Squatter Property Market', *International Journal of Urban and Regional Research 12*, pp. 303–7.

———. 1989a. 'Forgotten Obstacles, Neglected Forces: Explaining the Origins of Hong Kong Public Housing', *Environment and Planning D: Society and Space 7*, pp. 179–96.

———. 1989b. 'Extreme Case Comparison: Housing Provision and the State', *City & Society 3 (1)*, pp. 40–54.

———. 1992. *Making Room: Squatter Clearance in Hong Kong*. Hong Kong: Center of Asian Studies.

Smart, Alan and **Josephine Smart.** 1991. 'Personal Relations and Divergent Economies: A Case Study of Hong Kong Investment in South China', *International Journal of Urban and Regional Research 15*, pp. 216–33.

———. 1992. 'Capitalist Production in a Socialist Society: The Transfer of Manufacturing from Hong Kong to China', in F. Rothstein and M. Blim (eds.), *Anthropology and the Global Factory*. New York: Bergin & Garvey, pp. 216–33.

South China Morning Post. Various issues.

Sparks, D.W. 1976. 'The Teochiu: Ethnicity in Urban Hong Kong', *Journal of the Hong Kong Branch of the Royal Asiatic Society 16*, pp. 25–56.

Special Committee on Housing. 1958. *Final Report*. Hong Kong: Government Printer.

Vogel, Ezra. 1989. *One Step Ahead in China*. Cambridge: Harvard University Press.

Ward, Barbara. 1954. 'A Hong Kong Fishing Village', *Journal of Oriental Studies 1*, pp. 195–214.

Wong, A.K. 1972. *The Kaifon Associations and the Society of Hong Kong*. Taipei: Orient Cultural Service.

Wong, L.S.K. 1978. 'The Squatter Problem', in L. Wong (ed.), *Housing in Hong Kong*. Hong Kong: Heinnemann Educational Books, pp. 204–32.

———. 1989. 'Housing and the Residential Environment', in T. Tsim et al. (eds.), *The Other Hong Kong Report*. Hong Kong: Chinese University Press, pp. 229–44.

Yee, Albert H. 1989. *A People Misruled*. Hong Kong: API Press.

Yeung, Yue-man and **David Drakakis-Smith.** 1982. 'Public Housing in City States of Hong Kong and Singapore', in Taylor and Williams (eds.), *Planning Practice in Developing Countries*. Oxford: Pergamon Press, pp. 217–38.

4

Slums and Squatter Settlements in South Korea

Jaesoon Cho and Jeonghee Park

The ways that squatter areas of a city are formed and reproduced are closely related to the formation of the urban poor: change in society at large. The urban poor in Korea were formed through its particular historical experience. The process can be divided into three stages (KNHC 1983, 1989a, 1989b; KRIHS 1989a, 1989b, 1991). The first stage is from the late 1930s to 1960 when thousands of urban poor were formed for the first time during the Japan-governed period (1910–45), the 1945 Liberation and, the Korean War (1950–53). The second stage is the period after 1960 when Korean industrialization began. Many migrants from the rural areas rushed into the cities and became the urban poor. This stage can be viewed as 'the period of structural formation'. Industrialization encouraged migration from the rural areas and contributed to the expansion of the poor in the cities. The first stage can be seen as 'the period of primitive formation' through rapid social changes such as the colonial policy and the war.

In the third stage, since the mid-1980s, immigration from the rural areas almost stopped and the urban poor were produced within the city itself. This stage could be viewed as 'the period of structural reproduction' in the sense that urban poor of this period have different characteristics from the urban poor of the two previous periods.

Urban squatting in Seoul, like other large cities, has a long history although the scale was not that extensive in its early stages. Since the late 1930s, squatter settlements began to be formed in the national domain of the riverside and mountain area. An unexpected large group of returnees and refugees from neighboring countries and from North Korea have settled in their own houses without the consent of the city government since 1945. During the 1960s and 1970s, rapid economic development in urban areas pulled enormous numbers of people from rural areas to the metropolis. The influx of population from outside the city created an acute housing shortage (Ha 1991). From 1945 to the 1960s, Seoul experienced a rapid growth of population to over 1,500,000. The average annual growth rate of population of the 1960s was 11.4 percent. With the war and political/social disorder in this period urban structure and infrastructure were destroyed and there was overurbanization. The population grew constantly without construction of urban facilities. Korean industrialization since 1960 is characterized by export-driven industrialization. Many people from rural areas rushed into the city and most of them settled in the squatter areas which had existed before or were newly created. The national investment of this period was not concentrated on the consumption sector, which is for the reproduction of labor power, but on the accumulation of industrial capital. Thus, the quality of squatter areas was getting worse (Chang 1989). Housing policy in the First Five Year Plan (1962–67) stated that housing should mainly depend on the private sector due to the shortage of housing funds. Under this capitalistic housing mechanism, most urban housing poor could not participate in the ordinary housing market. But the developmental potential of the squatter areas has been gradually raised and the pressure for development from the outside has hardened since the 1980s. Thus, the struggle for housing through urban housing renewal began.

TYPES OF SQUATTER SETTLEMENTS

The squatter areas of Korea could be divided into four groups according to their formation process.

Illegal Self-generated Settlement

As many other countries have experienced the rapid changing process in industrial society, Korea has also experienced rapid social change aggravated by the Korean War. Most squatter areas of Korea before the 1960s belong to this type of settlement. Starting from Tomac village in the 1940s of the Japan-governed period, uncontrolled housing areas, called 'Hakkobang' and 'Panjajib', were extended through the Korean War. This type of settlement has gradually disappeared through clearance and relocation schemes. A large majority of the relocated poor went to other squatter areas or doubled up with relatives in Seoul (Ha 1991).

Government Designated Settlement

Being different from illegal self-generated settlement, this type provides the right to property. The origins of this type of settlement were the refugee settlements which were built after the Korean War. These were built by public sector financing and sold to individuals. The difference between the squatter areas of Seoul and other cities is in whether this type of settlement exists or not. This is not found in Seoul because of filtering up. Refugee settlements still remain in other cities.

High Density Blighted Area

These were once legal and standard housing areas, but turned into a super high density housing area by the influx of unmarried people like industrial workers and students. The most peculiar instance of them is the 'beehive' or 'henhouse', which is situated in and around the Guro industrial complex in Seoul. Several households live in houses which were built many years ago. This area is getting seriously blighted. The area is filled with substandard housing where habitable area per person is below the minimum standard. Residents of this area are employed lower-income workers *who expect to be the middle class in the future* (Park and Kim 1989).

Public Rental Housing Area

The citizens' flat program was inaugurated in Seoul in 1968. It was the first comprehensive program of the municipal government for on-site low-income households. Initially it was designed as a three year program for the construction of 2,000 units all over the cities. Four hundred and six buildings had been completed when one building collapsed killing 34 residents. This stopped the program. The areas in which the public rental housing was located have now become squatter areas.

CHARACTERISTICS OF SQUATTER SETTLEMENTS

Geographic Distribution

There are 528 squatter settlements in Korea (KNHC 1989b). About 20 percent of the settlements are in Seoul, over 50 percent in the five largest cities including Seoul and nearly 50 percent in the rest of the cities (Table 4.1). The settlements have had to be improved through redevelopment and/or renewal housing programs.

A city generally has several squatter settlements. The way in which the areas are distributed is smaller among cities. For instance, in the early stage in Seoul, squatter areas were mainly on the slopes of Namsan mountain and along the Hangang river. The expansion of the city boundary pushed them to the outskirts of the city. Then previous squatter areas in the central part of the city were redeveloped as districts of high-rise apartments for the middle-income households. This process has occurred in other cities as well.

Table 4.1: Demography of Squatter Settlements

Region	No. of Settlements	Housing	No. of Households
Seoul	103	54,351	121,750
Incheon	39	14,802	24,688
Kwongju	8	2,310	4,869
Taejeon	16	2,412	7,677
Pusan	66	30,926	54,532
Taegu	45	11,209	23,879
Kunggi	33	12,531	17,601
Kangwoen	19	4,452	6,288
Choongbuk	10	1,392	2,397
Choongnam	16	3,141	4,638
Cheonbuk	87	14,553	23,920
Cheonnam	27	4,714	7,617
Kyangbuk	18	2,891	4,383
Kyangnam	27	4,979	7,650
Cheju	14	2,077	4,546
Total	**528**	**166,740**	**316,435**

Source: Korea National Housing Corporation (1989b), *Housing Redevelopmental Strategies for the Low-Income Class*, p. 48.

Socioeconomic and Housing Characteristics of Households

Numerous studies have called attention to the problems and public policies for the households in the squatter settlements in Korea. However, they are quite limited in terms of regional coverage. Almost all of the studies uncovered the problems of the squatter settlements in Seoul, the capital of South Korea and its largest city, containing over 25 percent of the total population and about 50 percent of the squatter settlements of the country. An exception was a comprehensive nationwide survey carried out by the Korea Research Institute for Human Settlements in 1989. The sample of households was selected from the 21 squatter settlements in six cities: Seoul, Taegu, Seongnam, Cheongju, Mokpo, and Masan. One thousand fifty-five households were interviewed with a questionnaire during the period 20–30 September 1989. In this section we compare the results from the survey with the Korea Population and Housing Census Report (NBS 1987). According to the comparison there are some significant differences in the households and housing characteristics between the squatter settlements and households in all cities.

Sociodemographic Characteristics of Households

Household heads in the squatter settlements were relatively older than household heads overall. Over one-third of household heads in the squatter settlements were under 40 years of age, and about the same portion were over

50 years. The average years of education of the household head in the squatter settlements were relatively lower than for households in all cities. Nearly two out of five households in the squatter settlements had no more than six years of education. Household heads who finished over 12 years of education were quite few in the squatter settlements, while one-fifth of household heads in all urban areas attended some college.

Table 4.2: Sociodemographic Characteristics of Households

	Squatter Areas (%)	All cities (%)		Squatter Areas (%)	All cities (%)
Age			**Year of education**		
under 30	7.3	20.0	0	11.9	5.3
30–39	30.0	32.0	1–6	26.5	17.0
40–49	25.8	24.7	7–9	27.8	57.4
50–59	23.8	14.5	10–12	30.2	
60 and over	13.1	8.8	13 and over	3.6	20.3
Total	**100.0**	**100.0**	**Total**	**100.0**	**100.0**
Type of occupation			**Type of employment**		
Professional & technical workers	0.0	5.1	Employed	84.9	97.4
			Unemployed	15.1	2.6
Administrative & managerial workers	0.0	3.0	Total	100.0	100.0
Clerical & related workers	7.4	16.5	Average monthly household income	Won	$ (U.S)
Sales & related workers	23.5	27.8	Household income		
Production workers, transportation, equipment operators	51.7	43.7	in squatter settlements	409,000	545
No work	15.7	2.6	Household income of urban wage		
Others	2.3	1.6	earners	804,938	1,073
Total	**100.0**	**100.0**			

Source: Korea Research Institute for Human Settlements (1989b); National Bureau of Statistics (1987); National Statistical Office (1991).

The unemployment rate in the squatter settlements is about six times higher than that of whole urban areas. This is not surprising if age and years of education of the average household head are taken into consideration, i.e., the older or the less educated a person is, the harder it is to be employed. More than one out of every two household heads in the squatter settlements were production workers or transportation/equipment operators. About one-fourth were sales or service workers. There were no professional and technical workers, or administrative and managerial workers in the squatter settlements.

Average monthly income of households in the squatter settlements was 409,000 Won (approx. US $ 545). In 1989, the average monthly income of the urban wage earning households was 804,938 Won (US $ 1,078) (National Statistical Office [NSO] 1991). The average monthly household income in the squatter settlements was about one-half of the overall urban household income. About 45 percent of respondents had bank saving accounts for the expenses of home purchase and children's education.

Housing Characteristics in the Squatter Settlements

Over 50 percent of the respondents were renters, while about 46 percent were homeowners. One out of every four residents rented their dwellings with deposit, and about 3 out of 10 residents rented with monthly payment. The homeownership rate of the squatter settlements is a little higher than the rate for all urban households. Even though there were no differences in the total rate of rental between the two groups, residents in the squatter settlements had a lower rate of rental with a deposit and a higher rate of rental with monthly payments than the households in the cities.

The type of structure of dwellings in the squatter settlements was mostly a one-storey single-family type. Though quite a few respondents lived in multiplex dwellings, none lived in apartments. The structure type of the dwelling is related to the year it was built, as well as the building materials used for its construction. The major material of dwellings in the squatter areas were cement blocks which are inexpensive and usually used for temporary buildings. About 80 percent of dwellings in the squatter settlements were built before 1970 when apartments began to be built. Also, the area designated for urban housing renewal is restricted to housing with additions and alterations for the residents.

Nearly two out of five dwellings in the squatter settlements had one or two rooms with a mean of 3.5. The number of rooms per dwelling unit in the squatter settlements is less than in all cities (4.0). The average size of dwelling in the squatter settlements was 78.7 sq. m. while it was 82.3 sq. m. in urban areas.

Over half of the dwellings were shared by different households. Nearly one-third of the respondents lived together with more than three households. Overall, households in the squatter settlements were more likely to share with other households within one dwelling than households of all cities. The fact that the number of rooms per dwelling unit was relatively lower but the number of households occupied per dwelling was larger in the squatter settlements than in the whole cities could influence the lower number of rooms for each household in the squatter area. Over four out of five households lived in one or two rooms; below one-fifth in more than three rooms.

Table 4.3: Characteristics of Housing

	Squatter Areas (%)	All Cities (%)		Squatter Areas %	All Cities (%)
Homeownership type			**Structure type of dwelling**		
Homeowner	45.6	– 41.3	Single-family		
Rental	55.4	55.7	detached dwelling	92.3	76.3
Deposit	25.5	31.1	Multiplex	7.3	6.0
Monthly pay rent	29.9	– 24.6	apartment	0.0	12.8
Live-free	0.0	3.0	Building not intended		
			for human habitation	0.0	4.9
Total	**100.0**	**100.0**	**Total**	**100.0**	**100.0**
Building materials			**Built Year**		
Cement block		47.0	Before 1950	25.1	
Cement bricks		29.6	1950–1960	22.3	
Clay bricks		15.6	1961–1970	32.0	
Red bricks		1.9	1971–1980	15.3	
Woods		5.1	After 1981	5.3	
Others		0.8	**Total**	**100.0**	
Total		**100.0**			
Number of rooms per dwelling unit			**Number of households occupied per dwelling**		
1	12.6	3.0	1	45.1	53.8
2	26.1	16.2	2	23.6	24.6
3	23.2	28.1	3	15.3	11.8
4	15.4	22.1	over 4	16.0	9.8
5	7.7	12.6	**Total**	**100.0**	**100.0**
6	5.0	7.2	**Mean**		**2.3 (N)**
7	2.5	4.1			
over 8	8.0	6.7			
Total	**100.0**	100.0			
Mean	**3.5 (N)**	4.0 (N)			
Number of rooms per household			**The most needed space**		
1	39.6	38.7	Bedroom		65.9
2	43.0	31.3	Private toilet/shower room		17.2
3	12.7	18.7	Private kitchen/laundry		11.6
Over 4	4.7	11.3	Storage		5.3
Total	**100.0**	**100.0**	Total		**100.0**
Mean	**1.8 (N)**	**2.1 (N)**			

Source: Korea Research Institute for Human Settlements (1989b); National Bureau of Statistics (1987).

Less than 5 percent had more than four rooms in the squatter settlements. The average number of rooms per household is 1.8. Although the average number of rooms is a little higher in the whole cities (2.1), the difference is not very large. According to the type of homeownership, the number of rooms per household was not the same. Homeowners were more likely to use two or more than two rooms, while renters with deposits were likely to use one or two rooms, and renters with monthly payments mostly used one room in the squatter settlements.

A bedroom was the most needed space for 66 percent of the respondents. Private toilet or shower rooms were the second most needed space for 17 percent of the respondents, and a private kitchen or laundry space was so for 11 percent. The characteristics of housing in the squatter settlements in Korea can be summarized as follows. The homeownership rate in the squatter settlements was not lower than in the whole cities, but the rental with monthly payment was more common in the settlements. Almost all dwellings were one-storey single-family dwellings and were built more than 20 years ago. The number of rooms per dwelling unit in the settlements is a little less than in the cities. Moreover, the average size per dwelling is smaller than the cities. The number of households who are doubling up in the dwelling are larger in settlements and the number of rooms per household is lower. Rental households with monthly payments live mostly in one room.

Table 4.4: Other Housing Facilities

Other Housing Facilities	Squatter Areas (%)	All Cities (%)
Toilets		
Dwelling without toilets	29.34	NA
Private toilets	27.9	NA
Flush toilets	8.2	54.4
Piped water		
Dwelling without inside water connection	33.6	5.0
Heating facilities		
Coal briquette under floor	37.9	22.1
Piped coal briquette boiler	60.6	63.5
Piped oil boiler	1.1	4.5
Central heating	0.0	7.2
Piped gas boiler	0.0	0.6
Others	0.4	2.1

Source: Korea Research Institute for Human Settlements (1989b); National Bureau of Statistics (1987).

Nearly three out of 10 dwellings did not have toilet. About the same portion of households used their own private toilets. This implies that over seven out of 10 respondents shared toilets with other households. Flush toilets were not common in the squatter settlements (8.2 percent), while over 50 percent of urban households had a flush toilet even in 1985. About one-third of the dwellings did not have inside water connection in the squatter areas.

The shortage of inside water connections is more than six times higher in the squatter areas than in the general urban population. Almost all households in the squatter settlements (98.5 percent) used coal briquettes for heating. A piped coal briquette boiler was more popular than the coal briquette under floor.

Over 90 percent of respondents in the squatter areas had television sets, and nearly 80 percent had refrigerators. Over 70 percent had telephones and gas ranges while over one-third had washing machines. The higher percentages in the squatter areas are largely due to the difference in the time the survey was done. The survey was completed in 1989, but census data in all cities were collected in 1985.

Table 4.5: Durable Goods

Durable Goods	Squatter Areas (%)	All Cities (%)
TV	91.1	99.5
Refrigerator	79.1	78.7
Washing machine	35.9	33.7
Gas range	71.7	35.0
Telephone	74.6	56.3

Source: Korea Research Institute for Human Settlements (1989b); National Bureau of Statistics (1987).

Households in the squatter settlements strongly preferred housing policies calling for public rental housing program to policies for on-site improvement and housing renewal programs. Public rental housings were preferred by about 60 percent of residents in the squatter areas. On-site improvement program is the second best preference especially for squatters who own their homes. Housing renewal programs were the least preferred and more likely to be preferred by homeowners rather than renters.

Table 4.6: Preference of Housing Policies by Type of Homeownership (Percentage)

Housing Policies	Homeowners	Renters		Total
		Deposits	Monthly Pay	
Public rental housing	51.2	62.0	62.5	58.2
On-site improvement	44.9	37.1	35.3	39.4
Urban housing renewal	3.9	0.9	2.2	2.4
Total	100.0	100.0	100.0	100.0

Source: Korea Research Institute for Human Settlements (1989b).

GOVERNMENT POLICIES TOWARD SQUATTER SETTLEMENTS

During the 1945 Liberation and Korean War, a lot of houses were destroyed and there was an influx of rural immigrants and repatriates from overseas.

Consequently, most of largest cities in Korea had many illegal squatter areas. Government policy towards squatter areas was a problem solving approach in several cities including Seoul within a short period of time. At the risk of overgeneralization, past approaches can be depicted as having fallen into four broad phases (KNHC 1983, 1989a, 1989b; KRIHS 1989a, 1989b, 1991). The first, which persisted from 1951 to 1965 was 'Demolition and Removal'; the second, from 1966 to 1972, was 'Self-help Upgrading'; the third, from 1973 to 1983, could be called 'Rehabilitation'; and from 1980 onwards, 'Urban Renewal and Rehabilitation'.

Demolition and Removal (1951–65)

This approach was implemented to restore land to its original use which was illegally occupied during the 1950s and 1960s period of social disorder. It involved clearing the squatter areas in parks or green zones, restoring them to the original state and removing and resettling squatters to suburban areas. In the case of Seoul, the clearance was used to make settlements on the national or public domain and to move squatters there. It was also used to build rental apartments for the squatters. But in the former case, due to the isolation from the daily working place and insufficient infrastructure, the dissatisfactions of relocated squatter inhabitants were very high. In the latter case, rental apartments could not be continued to be provided because of lack of finances. This housing action contributed partially to demolition of the illegal housing which had caused the problem of urban environmental and aesthetic deterioration; restored the site to the original land use according to urban planning code; and improved the urban scenery (KNHC 1983). But by overall evaluation this housing action has resulted in the geographical expansion of low-income housing to the suburbs. As the city grew, these suburban settlements were designated as urban renewal districts. Consequently, the policy imposed a dual burden on the inhabitants.

Self-help Upgrading (1966–72)

This action used the housing of squatter areas as a resource by institutionally granting self-help improvement of illegal occupants. It was carried out in 1967 for the first time. The focus of this action toward illegal housing was as follows. The first step was to demolish the illegal houses which were well below the urban planning code and removing the occupants to newly developed residential complexes in other areas. The second was the legalization and upgrading of the illegal houses that were in good condition. The third alternative was to demolish the illegal houses and to build rental apartment units on the spot. The example of first action was Kwagju Residential Complex located in Kyunggi-Do near Seoul. It was planned to remove 278,000 inhabitants of the clearance areas to a site which was about ten thousand sq. m. But this plan was stopped after only 12,000 inhabitants moved to the residential complex by 1971. Most inhabitants of the relocation site moved back to Seoul or other large cities to seek a job. Moreover, since the facilities were not equipped with water supply, drainage, and paving, a serious trouble called 'The incidence of Kuangju' took place in 1971.

Legalization and upgrading were methods to sell national or public land to the inhabitants and to make them improve their housings by themselves first through administrative assistance, and then to legalize them. However, lack of financial ability of the inhabitants and the public financial investment required by this program prevented it from continuing even though it did contribute to improvement of housing quality. A large number of substandard houses were structurally improved through upgrading. But then it merely delayed the trend of deterioration. All these areas were designated residential renewal areas in 1970s. Legalization and upgrading was the program which showed that the housing environment could not be improved just by relaxing legal codes and encouraging the inhabitants' motivation to improve. There had to be public financial investment as well.

The third type of program involved building apartments for the lower-income groups. Its purpose was to increase the utilization of land use and rehouse the inhabitants. According to this program, Seoul city cleaned 1,367 substandard houses in 1967 and 15,840 houses in 1968 and provided rental apartments for the inhabitants (KNHC 1983). But the program was stopped when one of the public rental apartments, Wawoo apartment, was destroyed because of weak construction in 1971.

Rehabilitation and Renewal (1973–83)

Owing to the limitation of Self-help Upgrading on account of the public financial deficit and the change in housing needs according to the change in the structure of social strata, the policy toward squatter areas was changed through legislation of 'A Temporary Managerial Act for Rehabilitation'. Housing action was undertaken by the administration in which the housing renewal program was part of urban planning. Public financial aids were not sufficient to meet the minimum level needs. The main focus of this period was fund raising for these policies. In this period various renewal techniques based on many types of financial aid such as self-help renewal, AID loan renewal, and renewal consigned to private developer were used.

In the beginning, Seoul city sold the national and public dominion of

1,995,000 Pyoung (6,253,500 sq. m.) to the residents and used the money as a financial subsidy. Under this technique, the active participation of the residents was the most important factor for a successful execution. Since 1976, housing renewal seemed likely to be activated with the help of an AID loan. But since 1982, when the AID loan was stopped, it has been difficult to continue the program.

In order to mitigate the administrative burden, the medium-size developer was entrusted with executing the housing renewal project. This technique needed a tremendous amount of money for demolishing old housing and building new housing complexes which were different from the previous housing improvement renewal. Taking the residents into consideration, the community settlement areas in the suburban area, a settlement subsidy, and the right of living in public housing are all given. Even with these considerations, however, most of the low income residents could not purchase the rights to an apartment. So most benefits went to the middle class who could afford them. Since the projects of this period which cleared and rebuilt housing units were so costly, there was a large public outcry. From 1980 onwards, the rehabilitation technique has involved the alteration and repairment of housing.

Urban Housing Renewal (1983 to the present)

Economic expansion in Korea during the 1980s led to a rise in price of urban land and impacted the increasing developmental needs of squatter areas. While the most serious problems of previous housing renewal were the shortage of funds and the administrative burden on the municipal government body, this housing renewal technique of 1980s was the one that solved those problems. It contributed to the solution of squatter areas by creating a coalition of the residents and developers. This technique is characterized by a process in which the private developer participates in the residents' cooperation, which is the subject of the action, and manages the renewal action with business management principles, and seeks the maximization of profit. It encourages the developer and the residents to participate in the renewal action and makes tremendous developmental profits: developers gain from difference in prices between national domain land and other types of surrounding land, and the residents or owner gain developmental profit.

From 1983 to 1988, an average of 6,320 units were demolished and 7,452 units were constructed annually. This was a very large number of units in contrast to previous programs. On contrasting the success of activation of renewal, one observes that the conflict between the renter residents, who have been excluded from the benefits of the action, and the owner residents is deepened, and that the struggles for the right of existence of the renters have evoked a serious social problem.

Rehabilitation (1989 till the present)

Urban Housing Renewal since 1983 was severely constrained. Therefore the government designed a new urban renewal program which was initiated in 1989 with the object of improving living conditions in squatter areas. This program was devised for upgrading and improvement rather than for clearance or renewal with mass demolition (Ha 1991). Also public rental housing was constructed for the rental squatters.

CONCLUSIONS

Squatter settlements are areas clustered by substandard and/or illegal dwellings. In general, housing in these areas can be characterized as small, overcrowded, and substandard. There were over 500 squatter settlements with at least 162,000 substandard dwellings in 1991. The socioeconomic status of residents in the squatter areas is low in terms of occupation, education, and income. Low educational level, lack of work capabilities and family assets are usually the causes of poverty of the residents. However, most residents are hardworking and are oriented to social mobility. They have organized cooperative self-help activities to build community facilities as well as to help each other. These squatter settlements not only provide inexpensive shelters which low-income households can afford but also provide opportunities and information to low-income households so that they can adjust to urban life.

Various public policies such as medical aid, employment and housing are programed for residents in the squatter areas as well as low-income households. The impact of housing policies on the squatter settlements is tremendous. Housing policies have mainly focused on housing improvement, increase in quantity of housing, and facilitation of housing supply for homeownership. These programs resulted in improvement of housing qualities, decreases in substandard housing stocks as well as increases in overcrowdedness and rent prices for low-income families. The housing policies for squatter areas were usually pointed out to be dysfunctional to the residents, especially renters in the areas, and with their social networks destroyed they were expelled to new areas to start over again.

Since the squatters' housing needs and preferences on housing policies are different from other residents, it is necessary to collect census data on households and dwellings in the squatter settlements in order to know what they are like and what they want. Housing policies based on this data could consider all aspects of squatters' demands. Some studies have pointed out that housing policies must be turned to social housing programs such as housing allowance, housing subsidies, and public rental housings to provide a minimum standard of housing for the poor. Only public rental housing programs have been utilized since 1989. Stabilities of housing and land prices are necessary to protect rental as well as owner squatters. Rapid increases in rent and housing prices which have been experienced recently have produced a new phenomenon of social pathology. A squatter settlement contains whole lives of the squatters. While multidisciplinary approaches should be adopted to study squatter areas, subsequent research could shed light on how squatters' well-being could be improved.

REFERENCES

Chang, Sea H. 1989. 'Urbanization, State, and Urban Poor', in Hyngkook Kim (ed.), *Squatter Areas and Redevelopment*. Seoul: Nanam Publication Co., pp. 187–239.

Ha, Sang K. 1991. 'Shelter Strategies for the Urban Poor in Korea', in *Proceedings of International Conference on Housing Policies*. Seoul: Hunydai Research Institute for Economics and Society in Korea.

Korea Research Institute for Human Settlements. 1989a. *A Study on Low Income Housing Policy* (KRIHS Report no. 89-6). Seoul: Korea Research Institute for Human Settlement.

———. 1989b. *A Study on Policies for the Urban Poor* (KRIHS Report no. 89-22). Seoul: Korea Research Institute for Human Settlements.

———. 1991. *Evaluation of Urban Housing Renewal Program and Residential Environment Improvement Program* (KRIHS Report no. 91-22). Seoul: Korea Research Institute for Human Settlements.

Korea National Housing Corporation. 1983. *Housing Policy of Korea: The Impact of Housing Clearance and Redevelopment*. Seoul: Korea National Housing Corporation.

———. 1989a. *Housing Characteristics and Attitude toward Public Rental Housing among the Urban Poor* (KNHC Report no. 89-27). Seoul: Korea Research Institute for Human Settlements.

———. 1989b. *Housing Redevelopment Strategies for the Low-Income Class*. Seoul: Korea National Housing Corporation.

National Bureau of Statistics. 1987. *Korea Population Social Census Report, 1987*. Seoul: NBS.

National Statistical Office. 1991. *Annual Report on the Family Income and Expenditure Survey*. Seoul: National Statistical Office.

Park, Soo Y. and Yong Y. Kim. 1989. 'Marginal Characteristics of Residents in Squatter Areas', in Hyngkook Kim (ed.), *Squatter Areas and Redevelopment*. Seoul: Nanam Publication Co., pp. 106–36.

5

Housing in the Context of Sustainable Development: Problems, Policies and Practices in Costa Rica[*]

Jorge A. Gutierrez, Willem van Vliet,
Ernesto G. Arias, and Rosendo Pujol

The housing problems of the less industrialized countries have been well-documented. In almost all of these countries there are serious housing shortages. Large proportions of the existing housing stock are also of low quality and even those units are not affordable for many households. These problems are usually made worse by a deficient community infrastructure and inadequate services. In many large cities in the Third World, between 50 and 75 percent of the population now live in slums or squatter settlements (*Habitat* 1988–90; Van Vliet 1990).

The magnitude of their housing problems notwithstanding, housing typically is not the highest priority on the policy agenda of the less industrialized countries. In the overall schemes of national development, housing competes for finance and also for scarce materials and human resources with other concerns that are often considered to be more important. Housing is not usually seen as a productive investment. Cost recovery is very slow. For example, annual return on capital for recent construction in China was .5 percent, producing a period of 200 years for recuperating the investment, discounting maintenance, and depreciation costs (Chu and Kwok 1990). Hence, other objectives frequently take precedence. Industrial development, health care, and education are among the claims that compete with housing for national resources. However, it is the military expenditures that frequently represent a disproportionate share of the central government's budget.

Data recently published by the United Nations are revealing. They show military expenditures in countries worldwide relative to national outlays for health care and education. Although the figures indicate considerable varia-

* Work for this chapter was, in part, supported by the Center for International Research and Education Projects at University of Colorado, Boulder. This chapter is an expanded and revised version of the paper entitled 'In Defense of Housing', which appeared in *Habitat International*.

tion among countries, there is no pattern to suggest that the less industrialized world spends a smaller proportion of gross national product (GNP) on its military than does the more industrialized world. In fact, the data point in the opposite direction. Military expenditures in the more industrialized countries fluctuate around 6 percent of GNP.[1] In 1986–87, of the 53 Third World countries on which data are available, 29 (55 percent) spend 10 percent or more of their GNP on the military. Twenty percent of the less industrialized countries allocate in excess of one-fifth of their GNP to national defense (United Nations 1990, pp. 86–87).

Costa Rica stands out as a singular exception to this pattern. Following the revolution of 1948, the government redefined national security. It determined that the well-being of the population would be ensured better by investments in health care, education, and welfare than by investments in the military. Accordingly, the armed forces were disbanded, releasing considerable resources. However, in 1986–87, Costa Rica was third in the world, behind Bhutan and France, in health care expenditures. It also ranked among the top in expenditures on education. These investments have produced positive results. For example, compared to other countries in Central America, Costa Rica boasts of the highest literacy rate and the lowest infant mortality rate (IICA/FLASCO 1990).

In the area of housing as well, Costa Rica has made relatively large investments. However, Costa Rica also continues to face many of the problems that beset other countries in the Third World. For example, during the 1980–87 period, per capita GNP declined, debt service as a proportion of export earnings increased, annual inflation averaged 29 percent, and urbanization quickened (UNICEF 1990). Against this background, it is of interest to examine the Costa Rican housing experience. In this chapter we undertake such an assessment with a view to study the elements of housing policies and practices that may be transferable to other industrializing nations.

The rest of this chapter is organized into two main parts. Following a brief national background sketch, we first describe trends in basic housing conditions during the 1980s and review the National Housing Program implemented by the Arias administration (1986–90). Next, we emphasize the need for approaches that use low-cost construction materials and appropriate technologies, within a policy framework aimed at sustainable development, and review the innovative National Bamboo Project as a successful example of such an approach. The conclusion summarizes the accomplishments of the Housing Program, comments on factors that contributed to its success, and considers remaining challenges.

NATIONAL BACKGROUND[2]

Costa Rica is the second smallest country in Central America (51,000 km^2) and much of the land is not inhabitable. Overall population density is about 43 persons per sq. km. However, as Figure 5.1 shows, a large proportion of the population lives in the central valley which equals only 6 percent of the total land area. The country gained its independence from Spain in 1848. Following the Spanish conquest during the 1600s, the indigenous Indian population was decimated. At present, it represents less than 1 percent of the Costa Rican population and is scattered in 12 small reserves. The current population of 3.2 million (1992) is mostly of European descent. In the 1951–75 period, the population growth rate was among the highest in Latin America, averaging 3.3 percent per year. However, in the more recent decade, the annual growth rate has declined to around 2.8 percent as a result of dramatic decreases in the birth rate.

Notwithstanding the decrease in birth rate, the urban growth rate has accelerated to 4.4 percent (annual average, 1980–87). As a result, at present, one of Costa Rica's most pressing problems is that of urban sustainability. Today, 53.6 percent of the population live in urban areas, nearly 50 percent live in the Gran Area Metropolitana (GAM) which encompasses San Jose, the capital, and the next three largest province capitals in one continuous urban development (Salazar 1993). As a result of this urban sprawl, areas which could be built in the central valley are rapidly diminishing. In a related vein, rapidly increasing land costs are contributing to problems of housing affordability and the proliferation of *tugurios* (squatter settlements and marginal housing developments) in environmentally sensitive zones (OPAM 1983). Urban development thus presents a major challenge to the preservation of the natural resource systems necessary for the very sustainability of these population concentrations (Quesada 1990; Salazar 1993).

In socioeconomic terms, Costa Rica occupies an intermediate position in the Third World as measured by GNP per capita (US $ 1,760 in 1988). More meaningful than this average figure is the distribution of income. The top earning 20 percent of households take in 55 percent of all income; the share of the bottom 40 percent of households is just 12 percent of total earnings (UNICEF 1990, p. 77). These proportions show greater inequality than what is found in the more industrialized countries, but place Costa Rica in the middle of the less industrialized countries for which data are available.

BASIC HOUSING CONDITIONS AND TRENDS

The development and modernization of Costa Rica's basic community infrastructure has gradually evolved under various legislative actions. In

1941, Law Number 258 was responsible for the creation of the *Servicio Nacional de Electricidad* (National Electricity Service) which later became the *Instituto Costarricense de Electricidad* (National Institute of Energy and Communications) known today as the ICE. Some time later, the Water Law of 1942, provided the legal precedent for the *Instituto Nacional de Acueductos y Alcantarillados* (AYA, National Institute of Water and Sewer). The 1968 Urban Planning Law created the *Instituto Nacional de Viviendas y Urbanismo* (National Institute of Housing and Urbanization) or INVU. While INVU now concerns itself with both housing and urban growth, its initial focus was on the resolution of national housing problems, which were at the time more pressing than urban growth.

Broadly defined, housing includes the access it provides to basic community service. In this regard, Costa Rica is well-developed as a result of modernization efforts by AYA, ICE, and INVU. For example, in 1985, 93 percent of the total population had access to safe drinking water. In rural areas, this proportion was somewhat lower (82 percent), but much improved over the situation 10 years earlier, when it was only 56 percent. Similarly, in 1985, 95 percent of Costa Rica's population had access to sanitation services. In 1973, only 5.6 percent of dwellings were without bathing facilities and 1.5 percent were without cooking facilities; 29 percent lacked electric light, but the proportion has since been reduced.

However, as is the case in most pictures created from aggregate data, the national figures obscure important regional disparities. For example, in the mid-1970s, 75 percent of the national housing stock had indoor plumbing, including running water, 66 percent of all units were electrified, and 15 percent were connected to a sanitary sewer system (*Censo Nacional* 1973). However, in the San Jose Metropolitan Area these figures were much higher (93 percent, 96 percent, and 75 percent respectively), whereas they were much lower in the more outlying areas (Opam 1983; Booth 1974). In this regard, the Costa Rican situation conforms to the disparity between urban and rural housing conditions found in other less industrialized nations also. As is the case for most Third World countries, information on housing construction in Costa Rica is fragmented and incomplete. If data are collected, it is often on a local basis rather than nationwide basis. Further, much residential construction takes place in an irregular and piecemeal manner and without systematic monitoring. Building also occurs illegally, without legal title or permit and in contravention of prevailing building codes, zoning ordinances, and land use plans. As a result, the volume of officially authorized construction seriously underrepresents the number of units actually constructed. During the 1980s, officially authorized construction averaged 10,032 units per year. However, the number of households increased by

20,520 per year (U.N. Center for Human Settlements 1990, p. 53), producing a deficit for the decade of more than 100,000 units, not including the demolition of existing units and additional household formation resulting from marital dissolution.

Urbanization occurred hand-in-hand with an increase of poverty, an expansion of the *tugurios*, and inadequate housing. These developments had not been experienced previously in Costa Rica as in other Latin American countries. In 1974, the Ministry of the Economy estimated a deficit of 130,000 adequate units, affecting 1.3 million inhabitants, making this shortage of shelter one of the principal national problems (Biesanz 1979). By the end of that decade, it was estimated that approximately 250,000 *Ticos* (as Costa Ricans are known) lived in extremely inadequate housing conditions, i.e., housing with dirt floors, no running water, or structurally inadequate. This was particularly the case along the Pacific, Atlantic, and Northern regions (*La Nacion*, 26 May 1978, p. 14). In 1984, the National Institute of Housing and Urbanization (INVU) estimated that 33 percent of the existing stock was of substandard quality. An additional 12 percent was not in repairable condition. The total housing deficit (including irreparable units) was estimated at 122,321 dwellings (OPAM 1983). Due to its persistence and severity over nearly two decades, this problem of inadequate housing became a key campaign issue during the 1986 presidential elections, and a central policy concern of the Arias administration (1986–90).

The National Housing Program[3]

In 1986, the Arias administration proposed a four year National Housing Program. It aimed at providing 80,000 housing units by year 1990. In addition, its goal was to establish an institutional infrastructure that would support ongoing construction to meet the continuing demand. The government adopted a six-part strategy:

1. Classify and identify the target population to benefit from housing initiatives.
2. Restructure and reorganize the housing sector.
3. Redefine the functions of each housing institution in relation to the specific needs of the target groups.
4. Create a national financial system designed to ease access to credit and mortgages for low-income families.
5. Legislate to facilitate the urbanization process, construction of housing units and new settlements, especially for slum relocation.
6. Organize and mobilize the target groups to act cooperatively so that participation in self-help and shared construction program can be achieved.

Results of preliminary studies suggested that the Program be divided into three broad categories:

1. The traditional program was directed towards families with incomes that permit access to credit markets without need for other financial subsidy or support. A target of 40,000 units was assigned to meet the needs of these middle-income groups.

2. The slum eradication program was created to replace the dilapidated housing endemic to Costa Rica's inner urban slums, with improved housing units, physical infrastructure, and social services. The goal of 20,000 units would provide adequate housing for up to 50 percent of the families living in slums. This program was given national emergency status, a move that overcame the normal bureaucratic requirements, thereby permitting rapid implementation.

3. The rural housing program aimed to provide an additional 20,000 houses to families predominantly found in productive agricultural regions of the country. Although this program favored those rural households with some salaried income, appropriate credit facilities were established to allow rural families without such resources access to improved housing.

The strategic implementation of the Program developed three foci: the Housing Finance System, Institutional Reform, and Popular Participation. Next, we discuss each of these.

The Housing Finance System

Since the National Housing Program sought to target low-income families who could not afford to fund their own housing, a financial strategy was created that would transform their need into an effective demand for shelter. In this way, income groups traditionally excluded from the formal housing market could become fully integrated into it. This was to be achieved through a new financial system, funded by the reallocation of government funds, that aimed to realize the nation's productive potential for house construction. The National Housing Financial System was created in 1986, providing a structural, organizational, and operational framework to enable the National Housing Program to be carried out, and establishing the *Banco Hipotecario de la Vivienda* (BANHVI) whose role was to regulate and oversee this new financial system.

BANHVI (National Home Mortgage Bank) specializes in the provision of home mortgages. It is a secondary institution, that is, it centralizes resources and discounts mortgages through various types of financial intermediaries, rather than dealing with the public directly. Typically, these financial intermediaries are savings and loans organizations, credit and housing cooperatives or public commercial banks. The resources made available to BANHVI were divided between its two funding mechanisms: (1) FOSUVI, the National Housing Subsidy Fund (that deals with subsidized credits); and (2) FONAVI, the National Housing Fund (that deals with unsubsidized credits).

During 1986–90, FOSUVI received 3 percent of the central government's budgeted expenditures ($20 million) and a third of the finances for the family welfare budget ($20 million). FONAVI received its funding from various institutions including the *Caja Costarricense de Seguro Social* ($12 million); the US Agency for International Development ($50 million); the national lottery ($8.7 million); and the Savings and Loan system ($475,600). By 1990, an estimated 10.9 billion Costa Rican Colones ($9.5 million) had been channelled through these two arms, with FOSUVI funded projects receiving 66 percent of the total, and the remainder for FONAVI activities. On the other hand, BANHVI provided resources for both short-term bridging financing for construction firms and developers (thereby stimulating supply), and long-term mortgages to aid the process of house purchase (thereby enhancing demand). It was authorizing 1,500 mortgages per month by early 1990, of which 90 percent received a partial or total subsidy from either of the funding arms or financial intermediaries such as state banks, commercial banks, credit cooperatives and mutual associations.

Of particular importance to low-income families is the role of FOSUVI, a fund that directly meets the building material costs of housing provision through subsidies that are related to the cost of living. FOSUVI operates family bonds (*bono familiar*) which are nonnegotiable financial documents granted to selected families as a direct subsidy in conjunction with an ordinary mortgage. In effect, the bond is a financial credit that is tied to a second mortgage for a maximum of 25 years, but which is free from interest for the first 15 years. Families must apply for the bond through an authorized financial intermediary. The relative weight of the mortgage bonus decreases with the size of the family income. Thus a 100 percent subsidy is only approved for families whose monthly income falls below 14,400 Colones (or $130). Partial subsidies are distributed according to the income earning capacity of each family, which may vary between $130–$520. In all cases, eligibility is granted to families that are not already homeowners. Nationally, 80 percent of Costa Rican families qualify for FOSUVI support. To date, 35,000 bonds have been issued with the average value of the subsidy at 400,000 Colones ($3, 586).

Institutional Reorganization

Fundamental reform of all housing sector organizations was necessary in order to meet the target of 80,000 housing units in the space of four years. A newly created, but small-scale, Ministry of Housing and Human Settlements (MIVAH) took responsibility for coordinating activities and decision making. The traditional role of each entity, whether administrative, legal, or financial, was examined, adjusted, and resources were reallocated to enable the objectives of the Arias administration to be implemented. The result of this action was twofold: first, it optimized the work of programs and institutions, and second, it created new operating processes which acted innovatively, and with improved efficiency and effectiveness.

New guidelines were created for the two most important existing housing entities: the *Institutio Nacional de Vivienda v Urbanismo* (INVU), the *Institutio Mixto de Ayuda Social* (IMAS). New entities were also created to enlarge the operations of the Program in rural and urban areas, thereby complementing the activities of the traditional housing entities. These new entities are described here.

Along with INVU and IMAS, the *Comision Especial de Vivienda* (CEV) is the executive arm for housing of the Ministry of National Housing and Human Settlements. It undertook the task of slum improvements. In its first year, it implemented an immediate action plan that dealt with the most needy families living in conditions that were hazardous to health or were life threatening. The second year saw CEV consolidate its programs, such as those designed to rehabilitate poorly serviced settlements in situ, as well as relocating families to less seismically vulnerable areas. By March 1990, CEV had responded to the needs of 18,000 families. It has now reached an operational efficiency of 8,000 housing units annually. Of them, 70 percent are designated for squatters, 20 percent for grass-roots organizations, and 10 percent for emergency cases.

Fundacion de Vivienda Rural (FVR)

The FVR was created to provide much needed housing for agricultural workers in rural areas where a significant proportion of the housing deficit was recorded. It operated by co-opting existing organized groups (such as agricultural cooperatives) through which it channelled resources for housing. By the end of 1989, 3,818 houses had been built under this system. FVR has become one of the most efficient entities within the National Housing Program through its use of community organizations with a capacity to finance 1,600 mortgages annually, accounting for 20 percent of CEV-supported units. It also helps to retain cohesive communities in rural areas, thereby discouraging migration to the cities. FVR received substantial financial support from the Canadian government and BANHVI for the implementation of its objectives.

Fundacion Promotora de Vivienda (FUPROVI)

FUPROVI was created specifically to assist the organizational efforts of, and build units for, low-income families in urban areas. It has also made efforts to enhance community development. It provides financial credits for construction and home improvements. It also offers technical assistance and training, and facilitates the acquisition of tools and equipment. The aim of FUPROVI has been to finance bridging loans necessary for the working capital of small-scale urban housing projects. Once completed, an authorized financial intermediary approves a mortgage, and the bridging loan is reimbursed. Currently, FUPROVI assists 1,000 urban families per year. Furthermore, it promotes and facilitates self-build projects.

Participation

The new administration sought to encourage local participation as a way of mobilizing resources for local benefit. Families, already organized into construction groups, were encouraged to consolidate their activities and self-help efforts further, while those who were forming groups found that the National Housing Program aided their community actions and helped them achieve new goals and opportunities. The central tenet of this housing program clearly focused on assisting people to help themselves. Traditional construction firms, normally opposed to self-help construction options, have also endorsed and cooperated with organized groups when training was adequate. An accelerated pace of construction, qualitative improvements to materials and design, and reduced labor costs arising from the enhanced productivity of self-help are the principal advantages derived from this type of community participation.

Community based organizations were fundamental in the operation of the National Housing Program, since they led to cost savings and ensured that resources were channelled to areas of greatest need. In many instances, the organization of the people themselves proved to be of equal value to the construction of housing units. The Costa Rican cooperative movement, which unites a third of the economically active population, was crucial to the implementation of the housing programs. Nearly 40 percent of all mortgages financed through BANHVI were channelled through cooperatives, and the

Rural Housing program (FVR) relied almost entirely on cooperative organizations for funding and technical assistance. Furthermore, the success of cooperative involvement has served to attract established community based organizations, such as the nonprofit National Youth Movement, research and training centers, universities and small businesses. These organizations consolidate the role of grass-roots movements in the NHP and enrich assistance through the diversity of groups and people involved.

The strategy to attract greater private sector participation focused on two elements. The first was to stimulate private construction firms to provide housing other than for middle- to upper-income groups, by releasing substantial capital for projects directed solely at low-income families. Second, bureaucracy was reduced and the efficiency of the financial institutions responsible for credits and construction permits was optimized. By centralizing and streamlining these administrative procedures necessary for housing provision, a large volume of housing could be constructed on an annual basis, at a lower overall cost.

THE NATIONAL BAMBOO PROJECT

In Costa Rica, timber traditionally has had a prominent role as a construction material. This situation is entirely different from the rest of Latin America where adobe is predominant. However, rapid deforestation has made timber scarce and expensive, giving way to new construction materials such as masonry or precast concrete. Wooden houses dropped from 86 percent of total construction in 1963 to 60 percent in 1984. Together with the decline in usage of traditional materials, construction technology and labor skills have also diminished from the excellent levels which existed half a century ago.

The substitution of more complex construction technologies has produced three negative effects:

1. It has increased cost, because self-build is not possible and the materials are generally more expensive.
2. It has stimulated migration from rural areas to the cities where most of the massive construction programs have been developed.
3. The higher foreign component of the new materials has negatively affected the country's trade balance.

To overcome these negative effects it became necessary to stimulate massive construction programs in rural areas with low-cost materials and technologies appropriate for self-construction. Since wood is scarce, it was important to substitute it with a similar material—inexpensive, resistant, and accessible in rural areas. Bamboo satisfies all these requirements and the Costa Rican National Bamboo Project has been developed as a necessary and rational answer, introducing into the country a new, but well-proven building technology.[4] Funding for the Project has come primarily from the government of the Netherlands and the Central American Bank for Economic Integration (CABEI) ($117 million in total). It is estimated that by 1995 the program will have cultivated enough acreage of Bamboo Guadua to support the construction of 7,500 houses per year.

The project aims included:

1. The construction of 760 demonstration bamboo houses in 38 rural communities nationwide. These houses were to act as prototypes for a self-help construction program that aims to build 7,500 houses per year in the rural sector by 1995.

2. The cultivation of 700 hectares of Bambusa Guadua (Guadua Angustifolia) to provide the necessary material to supply this future program. This particular type of bamboo is favored for its length, straightness, thickness, and strength. Since the cultivated area is relatively small, plantations are located strategically across the nation in order to ensure a constant supply of raw materials to the different construction sites.

3. The education of over 1,000 professionals, technicians and family elders in methods of cultivation, production, and preservation of bamboo for use in construction.

There are five main benefits from the National Bamboo Project: reduction of building material costs; reduction of the need to use wood; diversification of agricultural production and stimulation of the local economy; establishment of small business enterprises to produce goods such as parcels and furniture; and use of structurally resilient materials and technology, a factor of significance in a country beset by frequent earthquakes.

Organizationally, the project attains these benefits through its programs for cultivation, research, construction, and education. When fully operationalized, the project's cultivation program will consist of several sites comprising some 700 hectares. This total area will yield enough building material for the projected construction objective of 7,500 units per year. The land belongs to several public institutions who have agreed on a future rational permanent harvesting program.

The research program is organized to study the physical and mechanical properties of bamboo, effectiveness of preservation techniques, and the structural capacity of the material for construction. In addition, research is being carried out in the areas of silviculture, construction management, and social organizations. The last evaluates different organizational schemes and their effects on workmanship quality, acceptance, motivation, and productivity of individuals and groups.

By diffusing the construction process to 38 rural communities, the National Bamboo Project has undertaken a large-scale education program to transfer this new construction technology to the rural sector. In each rural community, 20 individuals participate in the construction process guided by a previously trained technician. There is thus potential for villagers in rural areas to start small community businesses in the production of prefabricated elements/components for these new houses, thereby supplementing the traditional methods of income generation. Education is also critical in the sustained reproduction of bamboo to satisfy the requirements of the project in the future. Practical methods and basic silvicultural knowledge have been compiled in easy-to-understand manuals to be used by low-income rural families.

CONCLUSIONS

The achievements of Costa Rica's National Housing Program, 1989 World Habitat Award winner, can be summarized as follows:

1. Housing supply. The program surpassed the original target of 80,000 units by 5,821 homes. This represents a 43 percent increase in the volume of house construction when compared to the previous four year period. Just over 50 percent of all units constructed were directed towards those families with a monthly income of less than $420. In this respect, the National Housing Program has achieved its objectives of targeting the neediest of the poor. Schemes such as the National Bamboo Project, described in this chapter, fulfill an important function in this connection.

2. Financial consolidation. The integration of lower–middle income groups into the financial system permitted the release of funds for house construction and increased access to credit facilities, enabling 35,000 low-income housing units to be processed in the three years after 1986.

3. Mortgage disbursements. Just under two-thirds of all family mortgage bonuses (*bono familiar*) were effectively channelled to the poorest families, with 33.6 percent of total disbursements granted to families below the level of a minimum monthly salary (i.e., $140); and 3.7 percent to families between one and two minimum monthly salaries ($140–$280). The number of disbursements made annually increased rapidly over the

four year period with 9,856 being formalized in the first seven months of 1990.

These accomplishments reflect several factors. First, the national government combined clear and coherent policy directives with serious political commitment and real support. Second, grass-roots participation strengthened and facilitated the implementation of the Program, releasing human, technical, and material resources of the nation that would otherwise have remained unrealized. Of particular note was the proactive role of women in the construction and leadership of housing projects. Third, an equitable subsidy policy permitted access to credit and housing markets for previously excluded low-income families. Family need was turned into an effective demand by the increase in their real incomes brought about by the subsidy. Fourth, although housing objectives accorded a high priority, they were placed in a broader context of other salient policy goals. Increasingly central among them have become issues of sustainable development (Quesada and Solis 1990). The National Bamboo Project is an excellent example of how to meet housing needs in ways that are compatible with and support sustainable development.

Notwithstanding these positive outcomes, problems do remain. Critical among them is the low rate of cost recovery, estimated in 1992 by CEV at 50 percent of the investment. Given the need to recuperate funds lost owing to nonrepayment of loans, CEV now covers past program deficits from the total of current subsidies which are consequently much reduced. Another problem is that recipients of housing grants will often sell their lot and house at considerable profit, return to their rural area of origin, only to come back to the city some time later, once more eligible for subsidy. Furthermore, government will allocate funds to relocate spontaneous settlements, found in undesirable locations, which are subsequently recreated by other squatters in the same sites. These and other problems, also observed in other less industrialized countries, serve to remind us of the important financial and demographic challenges that attempt to replicate the Costa Rican experience.

NOTES

1. There are several notable exceptions, now rapidly decreasing as a result of the persisting economic recession and recent geopolitical changes.
2. Unless otherwise referenced, data in this section are taken from U.N. Center for Human Settlements (1990) and Tropical Research Center (1982).
3. The following discussion draws from two papers by Jorge Gutierrez: 'The National Housing

Program Costa Rica, 1986–90' and 'The National Bamboo Project of Costa Rica', presented at the International Conference on 'Housing through Support', Sri Lanka, 7–12 May, 1990, Building and Social Housing Foundation. Additional information was obtained in interviews, conducted in the Spring of 1992, with officials of BANHVI and the Ministry of Housing and Human Settlements.
4. The use of bamboo construction for low-income housing is already extensive in some countries in South America (e.g., Colombia and Ecuador).

REFERENCES

Biesanz, M.H., R. Biesanz and K.Z. de Biesanz. 1979. *The Costa Ricans*. San Jose, Costa Rica: Editorial Universidad Estatal a Distancia (available in English).

Booth, John A. 1974. *Caracteristicas Sociograficas de las Regiones Perifericas de Costa Rice*. San Jose, Costa Rica: IFAM/AITEC (Spanish only).

Censo Nacional (National Census). 1973. *Vivienda*. San Jose, Costa Rica: Officina del Censo (Spanish only).

Chu, David K.Y. and R. Yin-Wang Kwok. 1990. 'China', in William van Vliet (ed.), *International Handbook of Housing Policies and Practices*. Westport, CT: Greenwood Press, pp. 237-68.

Gutierrez, Jorge. 1990. 'The National Bamboo Project of Costa Rica'. Paper presented at the International Conference on Housing Through Support, Sri Lanka.

Hartchorn, G. (ed.). 1982. *Costa Rica: Country Environmental Profile, A Field Study*. San Jose: Tropical Science Center.

IICA/FLASCO. 1990. *Centro America Engraphicas*. San Jose. Instituto Interamericano de Cooperacion para La Agricultura and Facultad Latino Americana de Ciencias Sociales.

Nunley, R.E. 1990. *The Distribution of Population in Costa Rica*. Washington, D.C.: National Academy of Sciences, National Research Council (English).

OPAM. 1983. *Plan Regional Metropolitano GAM*. San Jose, Costa Rica: INVU (Spanish only).

Quesada-Mateo, C. 1990. *ECODES: Una Estrategia de Conservacion para el Desarrollo*. San Jose, Costa Rica: Minisdterio de Recursos Naturales, Energia y Minas (Spanish only).

Quesada-Mateo, C. and Vivienne Solis. 1990. 'Costa Rica's National Strategy for Sustainable Development: A Summary', *Futures*. Butterworth-Heinemann Ltd, pp. 396–416.

Salazar, R. 1993. *The Right to a Healthy Environment: Ecology and Sustainable Development*. San Jose, Costa Rica: Libro Libre (Spanish only).

Thiel, Bernando A. 1977. *Poblacion de Costa Rica y Origines des los Costanianes*. San Jose: Editorial Costa Rica.

United Nations Center for Human Settlements (Habitat). 1990. *Human Settlements Basic Statistics*. Nairobi: United Nations.

———. 1988–90. *Human Settlements Statistical Data Base* (HSDB. stat) Version 2.0.

United Nations Children's Fund (UNICEF). 1990. *The State of the World's Children 1990*. Oxford University Press.

Van Vliet, Willem (ed.). 1990. *International Handbook of Housing Policies and Practices*. Westport, CT: Greenwood Press.

Vargas, J. and G. Carvajal. 1988. 'El Surgimiento de un Espacio Urbano-metropolitano en el Valle Central de Costa Rica', in R. Fernandez and M. Lungo Ucles (eds.), *La Estructura de las Capitales Centroamericanas*. San Jose, C.R.: EDUCA, pp. 185–228.

6

Mexico's Urban Housing Environments: Economic and Ecological Challenges of the 1990s

Keith Pezzoli

Mexico is considered a relatively affluent country.[1] Its sustained economic growth from the 1940s to the 1970s made it one of the richest nations in Latin America. When ranked according to the value of manufacturing exports, Mexico is listed among the world's top ten developing countries (UNDP 1992). Its industrial base is larger than that of Belgium, Spain or Sweden (*Mexico Business Monthly*, 1992, p. 12). However, since the early 1980s, Mexico has been in the grip of an economic crisis. The 1980s are now looked back on as the lost decade—a period hammered by debt burdens, negative growth rates, austerity policies, net outflows of capital, and declining standards of living (Walton 1991). And there is concern that the 1990s may not turn out any better (Gilbert 1992).

Mexico's crisis is adversely impacting the form and production of low-income urban housing environments. This chapter presents the dimensions of this crisis and points to the interlocking socioeconomic and ecological challenges it gives rise to. The chapter begins by addressing two basic questions. First, what are the different types of urban housing environments in Mexico?[2] Second, what are the current unmet needs of the urban poor with regard to housing? Following this description, the chapter provides a historical analysis of trends in the production of housing environments, including hyperurbanization and the rise of megacities. With these trends in view, the impact of Mexico's recession and restructuring is specified—both in terms of political economy and ecology. The chapter ends with a critical and forward-looking evaluation of current housing research, policies, and strategies.

MEXICO'S URBAN HOUSING ENVIRONMENTS: TYPES, DIMENSIONS, AND CURRENT DEFICITS

Between 1940 and 1976, the dramatic expansion of Mexico's economy was based on import-substituting industrialization. During this period, most

Mexicans experienced improved socioeconomic conditions (Barry 1992, p. 94). Living standards rose as a large middle class of bureaucrats, professionals, and industrial workers grew to comprise nearly 30 percent of Mexican society. But as millions of people swelled the ranks of the nation's burgeoning cities, especially Mexico City, Guadalajara and, Monterrey, not everyone enjoyed the same benefits.

In 1977, the year after Mexico's first major economic crisis, the lowest strata comprising 40 percent of Mexico's population had less than 12 percent of the country's personal income (Barry 1992, p. 94). By 1980, according to a World Bank Report, Mexico had 'one of the worst profiles of income distribution of any nation on earth' (ibid.). The post-1982 crisis has aggravated long-term trends toward overall income concentration and the impoverishment of the poor majority. According to the 1990 census data, 19.3 percent of all workers (who reported income) earned less than the minimum salary; 36.7 percent earned between one and two times the minimum salary. Nearly two-thirds (63.2 percent) reported earnings of no greater than two times the minimum salary[3] (INEGI, XI Census of Population and Housing 1990) (see Table 6.1).

Table 6.1: Distribution of the Population Employed in Mexico by Sex according to Monthly Income, 1990

Monthly Income	Population Employed	%	Men	%	Women	%
Total	23,403,413	100	17,882,142	100	5,521,271	100
Do not receive income	1,690,126	7.2	1,536,812	8.6	153,314	2.8
Less than 1 × minimum salary	4,518,090	19.3	3,278,850	18.4	1,239,240	22.4
Between 1 × and 2 × minimum salary	8,588,579	36.7	6,228,595	34.8	2,359,984	42.7
Between 2 × and 3 × minimum salary	3,542,069	15.1	2,733,696	15.3	808,373	14.6
Between 3 × and 5 × minimum salary	2,283,543	9.8	1,827,792	10.2	455,751	8.3
More than 5 × minimum salary	1,780,769	7.6	1,505,454	8.4	275,315	5
Not specified	1,000,237	4.3	770,943	4.3	229,294	4.2

Source: INEGI, XI Censo Genral de Poblacion y Vivienda, 1990.

Due to the skewed distribution of income in Mexico, as well as rapid demographic growth, lack of mechanisms for low-income financing, and the inability of the economy to generate enough well-paying jobs, most urban families have not been able to purchase a housing unit in the formal (i.e., legally sanctioned) real estate market. Only the middle and the upper class have been able to do so, either in subsidized middle-class public housing or in private developments. The majority of the urban poor have constructed their own dwelling units in self-help settlements. Many other urban poor, either by choice or necessity, have resorted to renting, often in overcrowded and substandard units (Gilbert and Varley 1991).

In a recent study by the Research Center for Development (*Centro de Investigacion para el Desarrollo, A.C., CIDAC*), Mexico's housing market is divided into upper, middle, and lower segments. The upper segment is accessible to those who earn 10 times the minimum salary. Private developers targeting this income level have been able to realize profits from investments in housing. Until 1982, the functioning of the housing market for those with the highest incomes has been optimal in terms of supply and demand. Since 1982, times have been more difficult. Overall, the construction industry has floundered along with the rest of the economy (CIDAC 1991; Schteingart 1984; Business Monitor International Ltd. 1992).

The middle segment of the housing market is accessible to those who earn between 2.5 times and 10 times the minimum salary. By far, people in this income range have accrued the most benefits from publicly subsidized housing programs and lines of credit. Since the early 1980s, the most important programs along these lines have been FOVI (Fund for Banking Operations and Discounts to Housing) and INFONAVIT (National Institute for the Fund for Workers' Housing). FOVI targets those who have stable incomes of between three and ten times the minimum salary. INFONAVIT is a fund available to members of Mexico's labor unions.

The lowest segment of the housing market, which is the focus of this chapter, involves people who earn 2.5 times or less than the minimum salary. As noted above, most families fall in this category and thus are not able to purchase housing in the formal sector. In Mexico City, for example, 47 percent of the families lack the income necessary to purchase or rent a dwelling unit available in the formal real estate sector (CIDAC 1991, p. 29). This segment of the housing market is where most deficiencies in services are found. The 1990 census reports that 25.2 percent of all housing units do not have an indoor toilet, 20.6 percent lack potable water, 36.4 percent lack drainage, and 12.5 percent do not have electricity.[4]

The only significant government program that targets those in the lowest segment of the housing market is FONHAPO (Trust Fund for Popular Housing). FONHAPO received only 4 percent of the allocation of federal resources for housing programs from 1983–88, but it was responsible for approximately 15 percent of the housing starts over the same period. By comparison, FOVI had 50 percent of the resources and realized only 30 percent of the housing starts (CIDAC 1991, p. 99). The difference can be attributed to the type of assistance. Most of the FOVI resources went into the production of more costly finished housing units, whereas most FONHAPO funds went towards building *vivienda progressiva* (progressive housing,—a simple core structure that can be gradually expanded by the owner-occupant), and sites-and-services (projects in which beneficiaries get lots—equipped with access to water, drainage, and electricity—upon which they may build their own dwelling units from scratch) (see Figure 6.1).

Figure 6.1 FONHAPO, Allocation of Credits by Program

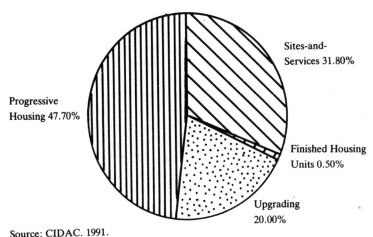

Progressive Housing 47.70%

Sites-and-Services 31.80%

Finished Housing Units 0.50%

Upgrading 20.00%

Source: CIDAC. 1991.

That FONHAPO receives less federal funding than FOVI in Mexico is a bias that can also be seen in the activity of large bilateral aid agencies. As Hardoy, Mitlan, and Satterthwaite (1992) point out, large bilateral aid agencies have given a low priority to infrastructure and improving shelter conditions for poorer groups. Where commitments have been made, they are marginal. For instance, 'despite the fact that during the 1980s, the World Bank's loan commitments to urban shelter, infrastructure, and services projects in Latin America were much the largest commitments of any agency to the region, these were estimated to represent little more than 2 percent of the total capital investments by sub-national governments in the region' (ibid., p. 166).

With few alternatives, then, most urban families must either construct their own dwelling units in self-help settlements or (by choice or necessity) resort to renting. The nomenclature describing self-help settlements varies (see Burgess 1985; Habitat 1983). Use of the term here includes three types of urban housing environments: (*1*) the officially sponsored sites-and-services and progressive housing projects described above, as well as (*2*) *colonias populares*—by far the most common type of housing environment, and (*3*) *colonias de paracaidistas*—settlements in formation by way of land invasion. Such invasions have become less common. In each of these three environments, houses are typically built by the initial owner-occupants. Over an extended period, the houses and neighborhood are upgraded. Although, on occasion, (more frequently in the case of invasions, less frequently in the case of incipient colonias populares) upgrading does not occur. On the contrary, the government eradicates the settlement in question. It is estimated that 65 percent of the two million housing units now standing in Mexico City were created by means of self-help (DDF 1986, p. 40).

Unlike sites-and-services or progressive housing settlements, *colonias populares* and *colonias de paracaidistas* begin their existence with an irregular land tenure status (i.e., the settlers do not possess, and must therefore mobilize themselves to obtain, legal title to the land they occupy). In terms of land use, roughly 50 percent of the surface area of Mexican cities is covered by *colonias populares* (Selby, et al. 1990, p. 16). As Castells (1983, p. 188) points out, this type of 'popular sector' housing is based on three interlinking elements: 'first, a considerable amount of work provided by the housing occupants themselves; second, the state's tolerance of the illegal status of most housing settlements; and third, investment by speculative private capital operating outside the legal limits through a variety of inter-mediaries.'

Two other types of housing environments have been occupied/created by the urban poor: (*1*) *vecindades* (inner-city apartment buildings), and (*2*) *ciudades perdidas* (translated as 'lost cities', meaning inner-city slums). The great majority of *vecindades* have one or two levels with a central patio; they were built before 1940 and are located in central parts of Mexico's larger cities. Most have between 20 to 50 units composed of either one or two small rooms; bath and washroom facilities are shared. Not all units in *vecindades* are low-income. In some cases, rents are relatively low because of rent control, but in others rents are higher (COPLAMAR 1982).

During the first few decades of this century, private sector *vecindades* housed most of the urban population. However, since 1940, the *vecindad* share of the total housing stock has greatly declined.[5] Investment in such rental units became unprofitable. In many cases, disinvestment and over-crowding have led to deplorable conditions (COPLAMAR 1982). As Gilbert and Varley (1991, p. 34) explain, 'growing numbers of people, a changing investment climate, a modified response by the state to housing and land issues, changing technological restrictions on urban growth, and changing tastes in accommodation and urban living were all producing a situation which encouraged the widespread shift from renting to legal or *de facto* home-ownership'.

Ciudades Perdidas first emerged as a significant feature of Mexico's urban landscape in the 1940s, around the same time that *vecindades* stopped keeping pace with demand for low-income, inner-city rental units. They are densely crowded slum sections, lacking potable water and drainage, located in various parts of the inner-city. 'The majority of the dwellers are persons of very minimal resources, who at times rent waste materials in order to construct their housing' COPLAMAR (1982, p. 28).

In sum, there are roughly seven types of housing environments in Mexico's urban milieu. The first two: (*1*) middle-class public housing, and (*2*) middle- and upper-class private developments, are not accessible to the great majority of city dwellers. Most urbanites have taken up residence in self-help settlements, including: (*3*) sites-and-services and progressive housing projects, (*4*) *colonias populares*, and (*5*) invasions. Many others live in (*6*) *vacindades*, or (*7*) *ciudades perdidas*. Table 6.2 gives crude estimates of the percentage that these categories contain of Mexico's total 1990 urban housing stock.

Table 6.2: Urban Housing Environments and Their Share of the Total Urban Housing Stock in Mexico, 1990

Type of Housing Environment	Percentage Share of Housing Stock
Higher-income housing	
Middle-class public housing	10
Upper- and middle-class private developments	15
Lower-income housing	
Vecindades and *Ciudades perdidas*	20
Colonias populares, sites-and-services,	
progressive housing and invasions	55
	100

Note: These numbers offer only the roughest aggregate estimations; the figures vary from one city to the next.

Sources: COPLAMAR (1982), pp. 28–30; INEGI, XI *Censo General de Poblacion y Vivienda* (1990); CIDAC (1991); Gilbert and Varley (1991); Selby et al. (1990).

That self-help housing production has helped families meet their basic needs for residential space in Mexico cannot be disputed. Indeed, in terms of housing policy, self-help settlement has gone from being viewed as a problem to be eradicated to a solution to be promoted. However, the self-help mechanisms by which the urban poor have historically gained access to land,

and gradually built and upgraded their dwellings and communities, have come under stress for both economic and environmental reasons. This is troubling because even while the systems were working, deficits continued to mount.

The National Housing Plan, published by the government in 1990, estimated the total urban and rural deficit to be 6.1 million housing units (see Table 6.3). To eradicate such a staggering deficit by the year 2000 would require an annual production of 610,000 housing units every year from 1990–2000 (assuming for the sake of illustration that the deficit does not get worse—i.e., that the annual increment in demand due to population growth will be met). Unfortunately, given the state of the economy and the austerity policies in place as part of Mexico's economic restructuring, there is no way that the deficit could be reduced so fast. Worse still, it is unlikely that supplies will soon begin to meet the additional increments of demand, much less the backlog of unmet needs.

Table 6.3: Deficit in Housing Units in Select Areas, 1990

Total deficit in housing units:	6,100,000
Mexico City	2,700,000
Monterrey	500,000
Guadalajara	500,000
Border states	1,200,000
Rural areas	1,200,000

Source: National Housing Plan (1990), cited in *Mexico Business Monthly*, May 1992, p. 12.

Demographers project that Mexico's population will increase by roughly 30 percent during the 1990s, rising from approximately 81 million in 1990 to 104 million in 2000. However, given the young age structure of the population (in 1990, over 80 percent of the population was under 40 years of age; 38 percent were under 15), the rate at which new households are forming is greater than the rate of total population increase. Whereas the total population is expected to increase by 30 percent, it is estimated that the population that will need housing (ages 20–49) will increase by 45 percent (*Mexico Business Monthly*, May 1992, p. 12).

Between 1980 and 1990, roughly 400,000 housing units were added to the total (formal and informal) stock every year, yet the housing deficit worsened. Considering the backlog of unmet needs, the annual demand for housing between 1990 and the year 2000 will be much higher than 400,000 units. As has already been noted, the capacity of the formal sector to meet this demand is limited. On an average, only 150,000 formal sector housing starts have been realized annually since 1988.[6] This sets up an unprecedented challenge, especially considering recent trends.

Access to Land, Housing Tenure, and Ecology: Historical Trends

In the three decades following World War II, the formation of self-help settlements—based largely on illegal and semilegal means of access to land—alleviated an otherwise critical housing shortage. In Mexico, there are three basic forms of illegal/semilegal land alienation. One is the illicit sale or cession of communal lands including *ejidos* and *tierras comunales*.[7] The second is the unauthorized subdivision of private lands, which violates urban planning laws and land use regulations. The third, and least common, is invasion—the occupation of land without or against the landowner's will. Legal forms of access to land for self-help construction have included the purchase of a plot in a sites-and-services scheme, or the purchase of a plot in any kind of existing legal settlement.[8]

That the bulk of Mexico's urban housing has been produced through such irregular (self-help) settlements during the 1950s, 1960s and 1970s is not unusual. As Gilbert and Varley (1991, p. 25) point out, during this period: 'Mexico was an archetypal Latin American society, its cities carefully divided into discrete social areas, affluent and attractive suburbs coexisting, albeit at a distance, with vast areas of poorly serviced unattractive low-income settlements'.

The expansion of self-help settlements has been dramatic. It is estimated, for example, that in 1947 only 2.3 percent of Mexico City's total housing stock was self-built. By 1952, this had risen to 22 percent and by 1975, over 50 percent of the metropolitan area's population lived in one or another variety of *colonia popular* (Connolly 1982, p. 150).

The local organization of *colonias populares* and their particular relationship to the state has been firmly integrated into the political system at large. Underlying the system of resource allocation by the government's dominant political party, the PRI (*Partido Revolucionario Institucional*), are strict but unwritten laws of exchange that demand votes and support through subordinated political participation. Castells (1983, p. 175) describes this arrangement as *urban populism*: 'a process of establishing political legitimacy on the basis of popular mobilization supported by and aimed at the delivery of land, housing and public services'. As Walton (1991, pp. 629–30) points out, rental housing has historically lacked such patrimonial advantages; consequently, it has received relatively little attention during the past several decades of rapid urbanization.

The rapid expansion of irregular settlements has happened in practically every large Mexican city. Consequently, there has been radical shift in the tenure of housing (see Table 6.4). During the 1940s, most of Mexico's people still lived in rural areas, and most city dwellers rented their habitation. Presently, the great majority of people (71.3 percent) live in urban areas, and most are homeowners.[9] As Walton (1991, p. 629) points out, this shift in tenure resulted from a number of economic and technological factors, 'but the single most important reason is a public policy that simultaneously depopulates the countryside (in support of commercial agriculture) and fosters urban home ownership via squatting or low-cost purchase of small plots and self-help construction'.

Table 6.4: Distribution of Housing Units in Mexico by Tenure, 1970 and 1990

Housing Tenure	1970		1990	
	Housing Units	%	Housing Units	%
Total:	8,286,369	100	16,035,233	100
Owned:	5,471,412	66	12,486,898	77.9
Rented:	2,814,957*	34	2,347,459	14.6
Other situation:	–	–	1,098,682	6.9
Not specified:	–	–	102,194	0.6

* Includes rental units plus all other types of dwelling units not classified as owned.
Source: *INEGI, Censos Generales de Poblacion y Vivienda*, 1970, 1990.

Of course, in order for irregular settlements to continue taking the edge off an otherwise critical housing shortage, the urban poor must continue to have access to land, be it through legal or illegal means. Yet, current research suggests that access to land for the urban poor is increasingly constrained. Ward and Macoloo (1992, p. 67) find that: 'access to land through invasion has declined as governments and landlords become more wary about the need to protect private property, and more efficient at doing so. Moreover, the *laissez-faire* attitude of many public authorities which prevailed in the past has been replaced by a greater willingness to intervene to control at least the excesses of illegal developers'.

The principal argument can be summed up as follows: Developers and speculators are consolidating control over unbuilt land supplies at urban fringes (Schteingart 1983; Dunkerley and Whitchead 1983). Consequently, the commodity nature of land is becoming more established. At the same time, the state is enforcing increasingly sophisticated administrative controls including zoning laws and land use regulations. Therefore the era of extensive availability of land for low-income settlements is coming to an end (Angel et al. 1983; Oberlander 1985; Habitat 1983; Doebele 1987).

It may be that the threat of land commodification as force undermining the capacity of informal, small-scale development has been exaggerated (see Ward and Macoloo 1992). What is certain, however, is that after a generation of hyper urban growth in Mexico,[10] the available supply of unbuilt land in the largest cities has become increasingly scarce and as a consequence, more actively contested among potential users. The hyperurbanization of Mexico City is an extreme case; it is a result of a historical pattern of concentrating resources and development opportunities in Mexico's largest cities. Along these lines, the 1990 Mexican census shows a total of 156,602 localities (i.e., distinct places of human settlement) throughout the entire country. Only 2,586 (1.7 percent) of these localities are urban, yet they contain 71.3 percent of the nation's entire population. At the other extreme, 154,016 (98.3 percent) of the localities are rural with only 28.7 percent of the country's total population (see Table 6.5).

Table 6.5: Distribution of Localities and Population in Mexico by Size of the Locality, 1970 and 1990

Size of Locality	1970				1990			
	Number of Localities	%	Population	%	Number of Localities	%	Population	%
(No. of individuals)								
Total	97,580	100	48,225,238	100	156,602	100	81,249,735	100
1–99	55,650	57	1,471,154	3.1	108,307	69.2	2,190,339	2.7
100–499	28,055	28.8	6,889,077	14.3	32,244	20.6	7,760,320	9.6
500–999	7,473	7.7	5,190,166	10.8	8,515	5.4	5,922,495	7.3
1000–2499	4,232	4.3	6,366,285	13.2	4,950	3.2	7,416,770	9.1
2500–4999	1,201	1.2	4,129,872	8.6	1,364	0.9	4,647,566	5.8
5000–9999	539	0.6	3,764,208	7.8	609	0.4	4,226,294	5.2
10000–19999	248	0.3	3,409,846	7.1	293	0.2	4,086,017	5
20000–49999	114	0.1	3,405,818	7.1	167	0.1	5,075,188	6.2
50000–99999	34	–	2,356,569	4.8	55	–	3,854,850	4.7
100000–499999	30	–	5,707,130	11.8	77	–	18,233,313	22.4
500000 & more	4	–	5,535,113	11.4	21	–	17,836,493	22

Source: Censos Generales de Poblacion y Vivienda, 1970, 1990, INEGI.

Forty-five percent of Mexico's urban population lives in cities of one million or more people. The nation's three largest cities: Mexico City, Guadalajara, and Monterrey, together account for nearly one-third of the country's total population. The excessive concentration of production in and around these three cities has created a serious imbalance in regional development. One of the results has been the unprecedented urban sprawl which in some places (most notably in Mexico City, but also in Guadalajara, Monterrey, and northern border cities) has reached the proportions of an ecological disaster.

Mexico City is the world's largest metropolis with a population of 20 million people growing at the rate of 700,000 per year (Cornelius and Craig, 1988, p. 52). It is situated in the Central Mexican Basin, a high plateau—nearly 6,800 feet above sea level—enclosed by mountains. The contained ecosystem of the Basin has become seriously degraded by urban and demographic growth, toxic output from industry and vehicles, extensive deforestation, desiccation of its lakes, and by the exploitation of materials for construction (Rivera 1987). Owing to its particular geography and subsoil conditions, Mexico City has chronic problems of air pollution and water supply (Carabias and Herrera 1986, p. 63). It has become increasingly cost-prohibitive to pump water up into the Valley from distant areas (Brown and Jacobson 1987). These concerns have prompted officials to contain the growth of the Capital.

The horizontal expansion of Mexico City is increasingly constrained. As a result, the city is experiencing a sort of 'urban implosion'—defined by the Center for Housing and Urban Studies (CENVI), as 'demographic densification combined with a restricted territorial expansion' (Connolly 1993: 69).[11] CENVI reports that Mexico City's urban implosion has led to the increased subdivision of lots, the proliferation of rooms for rent and overcrowding. As a response to the increasing demands for rental space, CENVI estimates that 35,000 rental units are added to Mexico City's informal housing stock each year. Most of these units are in the consolidated *colonias populares* of the city's periphery. This popular sector supply of rentals falls outside the auspices of government planning and the tax base; it is an unregulated supply without any codes that specify construction norms or health and safety standards.[12]

Despite such problems, Mexico's largest cities continue to attract both private investors and migrant workers from all over the country. Policies of decentralization have been attempted—but not to any great effect (Rodriguez 1987). It is estimated that over 1,000 people migrate to Mexico City every day—a dramatic fact illustrating the failure of attempts to improve conditions in rural areas. Indeed, on comparing Mexico's urban centers with its rural areas, one finds disparities on every indicator of economic opportunity and social well-being (Cornelius and Craig 1988).

In sum, conventional mechanisms of informal urban land development are increasingly constrained by socioeconomic, political, and ecological factors. Unfortunately, while the urban poor find it harder to gain access to land, the alternatives to irregular settlement are inadequate. The situation is aggravated by the impact of economic crisis, restructuring, and the politics of austerity.

The Impact of Economic Crisis, Restructuring and the Politics of Austerity: 1982–92

Considering the economic crisis and the chronic scarcity of resources facing governments, it has become conventional wisdom among housing specialists that 'the emphasis of public policy must shift from the housing construction process to the land delivery process, so that governments take responsibility for providing secure land and affordable infrastructure, while households or community groups take responsibility for building the shelter's structure' (Habitat 1983, p. 11). It is argued that these are the most urgent and intractable elements of the urban land and housing problems. Attention in Mexico is thus drawn to the advantages of land tenure regularization and to innovative forms of state intervention in the land market such as sites-and-services schemes (Azuela 1987; Malpezzi 1990; Payne 1989; Angel et al. 1983; Baross and Van Der Linden 1990).

This shift in policy is important. However, to leave the discussion at this level is inadequate. The urban poor's access to land depends on their capacities to pay for the land and infrastructure. At the same time, the question of expanding access must take into account environmental concerns (i.e., the regenerative capacities of the land itself, including the bioregion's air basin, watersheds, and other features necessary for ecological sustainability). This section of the chapter thus examines the impact of the economic crisis in terms of the availability of jobs, the minimum wage and cost of building materials, and the government's fiscal policy and level of public expenditures on housing. The next section puts the ecological dimension into focus.

From Import Substitution Industrialization to Export Led Industrialization

For a whole generation, Mexico based its development policy on import substitution industrialization (ISI). This urban biased, resource intensive model of development eventually produced many of the same problems that characterized the process elsewhere in Latin America: technological dependence, a balance of payments deficit, inefficient industries, hyperurbanization, environmental degradation, and the impoverishment of rural communities. Furthermore, by the end of the 1970s, it was obvious that formal sector job growth as a result of ISI did not keep pace with the growth in Mexico's economically active population. ISI as a development strategy came to be viewed as part of the problem; it has been abandoned in favor of export led industrialization.

In response to the debt burden, soaring inflation, and economic recession that took hold of the country in the early 1980s (see Table 6.5 for select details), President De la Madrid (1983–88) initiated an ambitious process of economic restructuring. President Carlos Salinas de Gortari has continued this process with an increasing emphasis on the privatization of the economy and trade liberalization that have aimed to strengthen Mexico's export industries. As a result, Mexico's economy began to experience economic growth in 1991, and the nation's international image has improved. However, as critics note, it is not certain that recent economic stability will endure, or that the benefits of this invigorated economy will eventually trickle down to the popular sectors.

Barry et al. (1992, p. 92) argue that the government's macroeconomic adjustment policies have been effective in certain respects, but at a high cost: 'reduced public-sector investment, layoffs of government employees, reduced social services, higher taxes on the working class, and the transferral of state enterprises, often at fire-sale prices, to the business elite'.[13] Austerity measures are reflected in new lending policies for housing investment. The Mexican government has shifted from funding urban projects directly, towards funding initiatives/projects aimed at strengthening the capacity of city and municipal governments to invest in and manage urban development. Hardoy et al. (1992) note that this shift is evident in the urban lending of the World Bank over the last decade. Recent World Bank activity in Mexico's housing sector supports this observation.

In 1992, the World Bank announced that it would loan Mexico 450 million dollars to help finance a 1.6 billion dollar Housing Market Development Project ($984 million will come from FOVI, and $160 million from homebuyer's down payments). As reported in the *Mexico Business Monthly* (August 1992), the project aims to expand the supply of mortgage finance for low-cost housing by assisting the government in four ways: '(*1*) removing regulatory barriers in order to lower housing costs and to encourage private builders and financiers to expand investment in housing...; (*2*) broadening the housing policy dialogue that addresses the government's medium-term housing strategy; (*3*) improving FOVI's mortgage instrument and its on-lending mechanisms so as to stimulate commercial bank interest in lending for low-cost housing; and (*4*) improving information on the housing market' (p. 14). However, in view of what has been happening with real income and price levels in Mexico, it is questionable how much this initiative will actually benefit the urban poor.

Table 6.6: Select Socioeconomic Indicators

GNP per capita	1989	$ 2,010 (US)
Per capita annual growth rate of GNP	1965–80	3.6%
	1980–1989	–1.5%
Total national debt as % of GNP	1989	51.0%
Debt service as % of exports		
of goods and services	1970	23.6%
	1989	39.6%
Percentage of total government		
expenditures on housing, social		
security, and welfare	1972	25.4%
	1990	13.0%
Annual rate of inflation	1980–89	72.7%
Earnings per employee annual growth rate	1970–80	1.2%
	1980–88	–5.2%
Unemployment	1990	18.0%
Minimum wage (daily rate)	1991, Nov.	U.S. $ 4.30
Decline in the purchasing power		
of the minimum wage	1982–92	72.0%
Annual rate of growth in value		
of manufacturing exports	1970–80	6.3%
	1980–88	19.1%

Sources: Barry (1992); Business Monitor International Ltd. (1992); Gonzalez de la Rocha and Escobar Latapi (1991); Mexico (1991); *Mexico Business Monthly*, 1992, p. 12.

Policies of macroeconomic restructuring implemented in Mexico since the early 1980s have had a major impact on the urban poor. Prices of food, water, energy, and housing have increased, while real wages have fallen (Gilbert 1992, p. 4). Between 1982 and 1992 the purchasing power of the minimum wage fell by 72 percent (Business Monitor International Ltd. 1992). Currency devaluations and reduced government backing for the demands of organized labor have contributed to the dramatic fall in real wages. The result has been a decline in the living standards of Mexico's poorest citizens.[14] The government justifies the decline by arguing that a reduced wage bill for the private sector will translate into greater competitiveness, higher employment, and greater production (Business Monitor International Ltd. 1992, p. 29). At the same time, the government argues that reduced wages will keep consumption pared to the bone, thus reducing both inflationary pressures and imports (ibid.). What impact has this had on housing? More specifically, how has the recession and politics of austerity impacted the form and production of low-income urban housing environments? Many good studies are available on this and several propositions can be put forward.

Based on an analysis of the cost of land, materials, and infrastructure, Glibert (1992) suggests that, overall, the recession has damaged housing standards. He cites evidence that the recession has negatively impacted housing tenure, housing densities, plot sizes, service and infrastructure provision, levels of rent, and frequency of eviction. At the same time, Gilbert (1992) cautions against overgeneralizations. Depending on local circumstances (e.g., the availability/tenure of land), cities have responded differently to the recession. Thus, it is with a broad brush that the following trends are noted.

The Expansion and Improvement of Self-help Settlements has Slowed Down while the Proportion of Renters to Homeowners has Risen

As De la Rocha, Gonzalez, and Escobar Latapi (1991, p. 11) point out, 'the expansion and improvement of the stock of popular housing has slowed as a direct consequence of the need to devote a larger part of household income to the satisfaction of more basic needs.' For instance, in 1981 one day's minimum wage could buy about 18 pounds of beans; by 1991 it could buy only 5.5 pounds (Barry 1992, p. 98). The magnitude of this ten year decline in purchasing power translates into a significantly diminished capacity to purchase building materials (see Ward and Macoloo 1992).[15] Thus, as Gilbert (1992) suggests, increased poverty will not necessarily translate into more self-help settlements. What is more likely, as in the case of Mexico City's 'urban implosion', is that increasing proportion of families will share or rent accommodation.

The Quality of Urban Housing Environments has Become More Uneven. In Some Cases, this has Undermined Prospects for Economic Growth

The expansion of self-built, single-family detached dwelling units as a driving force in urban sprawls has slowed down in many cities. This is not necessarily all that bad. Available land is often in short supply and alternative approaches to providing living space, such as affordable multifamily housing or rental accommodation, should be supported. The problem occurs when such alternatives are inadequate or substandard. This appears to be the case, a situation which exacerbates uneven development—i.e., the segregation of the city into a number of protected well-serviced upper-income sections on one side, and many more poorly serviced, increasingly overcrowded and unhealthy low-income housing environments on the other side.

As Barry (1992, p. 99) points out, deregulation, austerity measures, and privatization have cut bigger holes in the already tattered welfare net existing in Mexico. Facing a scarcity of resources, the government has opted to encourage private entrepreneurs to begin filling the large gaps in, among other areas, infrastructure and housing (Barry 1992, p. 99). For instance, the water distribution system in Mexico City has been opened to private investment and the government plans to overhaul the national legal structure to pave the way for similar investments elsewhere.[16] In his analysis of privatization along such lines, Gilbert (1992, p. 450) expresses the concern that 'it is likely to be the better-off who are provided with services and the poor who lose out'.

Private investment resources have flowed to parts of Mexico City, Monterrey, Guadalajara, and to other parts of northern border cities which have been undergoing a commercial real estate boom.[17] But the investment has not targeted the provision of housing or urban infrastructure. In Ciudad Juarez, for instance, there exists the largest concentration of *maquiladora* employment in Mexico. There is evidence that 'further maquiladora expansion has slowed, due in part to the lack of adequate urban (not industrial) infrastructure: prospective Japanese investors visiting in 1990 were negatively impressed by the city's inadequacy in providing low- and middle-income housing, public transportation, schools, and other urban amenities' (De la Rocha Gonzalez and Escobar Latapi 1991, p. 5).

In Mexico's Largest Cities, the Government has Stepped Up its Enforcement of a Politics of Containment, Often Based on Ecological Arguments

In Mexico, an emergent constraint on access to land has been the state's politics of containment: legal and institutional means aimed at controlling the horizontal expansion of irregular settlements on the basis of ecological arguments (Pezzoli 1991). As a part of this politics of containment, the government has stiffened its policy prohibiting land invasions and the formation of incipient colonias populares: evictions have increased (Gilbert and Varley 1991, p. 49). There is now a streamlined, usually well orchestrated, procedure for evictions. Pezzoli (1991) refers to the mechanism to conduct such evictions as the *desalojo machine*.[18] The *desalojo machine* includes the tools of eradication (e.g., sanitation trucks, walkie-talkies, horses, hammers, and guns), as well as the labor (e.g., police on foot and on horseback, clean up crews, and officials).

In Response to the Chronic Scarcity of Income and Resources, there has been a Heightening Activism of Civil Society

In many respects, the 1980s was indeed a lost decade for Mexico and the rest of Latin America. But there is more to the story. Throughout Latin America there has been heightening activism in civil society engendered by 'the utter inability of the modern production sectors to provide a sufficient livelihood for any but a minor fraction of the working population and a state whose repeated attempts at countervailing policies have proved ineffectual' (Friedmann 1986, p. 22). In the Mexican context, Foweraker and Craig (1988, p. 2) point out that, 'the proliferation of popular movements outside of (but also within) the traditional postrevolutionary, corporatist structures is one of the most significant developments in Mexican politics in the past twenty years'.

Some of the most powerful popular movements in Mexico, including CONAMUP (National Coordinator of Popular Urban Movements), and the Assembly of Barrios have focused their energy on the production of healthy housing environments for the urban poor. One of the most dramatic successes along these lines is the (re)construction of low cost housing in the downtown section of Mexico City following the 1985 earthquakes (Connolly 1990; Eckstein 1990; Ward 1990). Grass-roots groups with a focus on housing for the poor have had a significant impact on the political process in Mexico (Cornelius, Gentleman and Smith 1989). A large and growing literature documents the activities of such popular movements in response to urban crisis (Portes 1989; Diaz Barriga 1990; Coulomb and Duhau 1989).

One of the most significant characteristics of recent social movements is the depth of their critique, and the extent to which an alternative approach to development is sought (Walker 1990; Slater 1985). The critique stems from a view that the crisis in Mexico and throughout Latin America is not only economic and even less so only financial—it is a crisis in the mode of development with far reaching ecological, as well as social, ideological, and political dimensions (Sunkel and Giglo 1981; Sunkel 1985; Aguilar 1985; Friedmann 1987, 1992). In Mexico City, for instance, popular groups such as those working to build cooperative housing in El Molino (Suarez Pareyon 1987), or those engaged in promoting organic waste recycling systems and water reclamation projects in the ecological zone of Ajusco (Pezzoli 1991; Schteingart 1987; Mena 1987), recognize that the urban housing crisis goes beyond issues of land allocation and management into broader issues concerning livelihood opportunities, developmental sustainability, and ecological balance.

Confronted by critical social movements, and a serious erosion in the legitimacy citizens grant the government's dominant political party, the current administration in Mexico has generated new strategies to ameliorate the housing crisis in Mexico.

The National Development Plan (1988–94) and Current Housing Strategies

In his most recent state of the union address, President Carlos Salinas de Gortari acknowledged the enormous challenges people face living in the nation's burgeoning cities. One of the most pressing challenges, he said, is the need to create adequate housing. Salinas announced that housing 'constitutes a priority of my government'. On this point, he proclaimed that his administration 'will work to coordinate a system of cities that takes advantage of the economic potential—and of the availability of land, water, and, infrastructure—in the 80 most important population centers of the territory.'[19]

President Salinas' state of the union address reflects a shift that has been taking place in Mexico with regard to housing. This shift is evident in the housing element of the National Development Plan (NDP) for 1988–94.

In terms of resolving Mexico's housing crisis, the NDP spells out strategies that include: enhancing the urban poor's access to finance, institutional reform, support for self-help, support for the development of rental accommodation, and accelerated land tenure regularization. The NDP breaks new ground where it relates housing to the need to address the priority setting of national and municipal development goals. At this level, housing and ecology are considered together; housing is viewed as an integral component of the larger urban milieu which includes watersheds, air basins, sensitive lands, and ecosystems. While the housing crisis continues to be seen as rooted in economic conditions, it is also understood as part of a larger set of environmental problems that in some cases are reaching critical thresholds.

The NDP emphasizes the need to establish an urban–rural balance in the country. The strategy is: 'to channel economic activity towards places optimally suited in terms of resource availability, especially water; and to discourage the growth of overpopulated zones and of zones that have severe resource deficiencies' (Mexico 1989, p. 110). Overall, the NDP represents an important advance that links environment and development; this could ultimately have a significant impact on approaches to housing. However, what gets stated in the NDP and what happens in practice are not necessarily the same.

To implement the policies established to assist the country's poorest citizens, the NDP set up the National Solidarity Program (*PRONASOL: Programa Nacional de Solidaridad*). PRONASOL was started by President Salinas as soon as he took office in 1988. Its stated objective, as the centerpiece of the government's strategy 'to eradicate poverty', is to create and improve basic services and facilities, including housing, for citizens living in low-income urban neighborhoods as well as in the nation's poorest rural and indigenous communities

The Solidarity program gets its funds from sources made available after the renegotiation of the foreign debt; from the divestiture of public enterprises;[20] federal, state and municipal contributions; and from resources provided by beneficiary communities (Mexico 1991). The U.S. embassy estimated that more than 50 percent of the public sector's capital expenditures were channeled through PRONASOL in 1990 (Barry 1992, p. 99).

As the government describes it, 'Solidarity has adopted an innovative approach in that it encourages communities to take part in solving their most pressing problems. The priorities of the program in each community are thus determined by the beneficiaries themselves, who organize their own communities and elect their own representatives' (Mexico 1991, p. 101). Activities of the program involve support for housing construction, infrastructure projects, and public services, as well as job creation, health care, education, nutrition, and food distribution.

In his state of the nation address, President Salinas reported that great strides have been made: over 12 trillion pesos were budgeted for the construction of 150,000 housing units in 1991; and between 1989 and 1991, a total of 29 trillion pesos was budgeted, and 400,000 homes built (Mexico 1991, Tercer Informe). Salinas optimistically noted that such high figures are unprecedented, yet will be surpassed in the near future. Some housing specialists in Mexico are not so optimistic. Researchers at CIDAC (1991, p. 62), for instance, argue that, 'despite the recent increases in the production of housing and of financing made available by government institutions, the housing problem presents itself with ever greater force as a cumulative deficit that is now at the point of exploding'. In part, this is because most government support for housing has continued to favor the middle class which has a greater capacity to repay credits.

It may be that, as the heightening activism of civil society continues in Mexico, greater resources will be channeled to lower-income groups. This, at least, is what PRONASOL claims it aims to do. In terms of housing, this would mean greater support for the provision of rental accommodation and the type of housing actions undertaken by FONHAPO, including sites-and-service schemes, upgrading, and progressive housing. FONHAPO has acted as an external agent to facilitate self-help by providing credit to popular groups willing to sponsor it; approximately 110,000 progressive housing solutions and 75,000 serviced sites were reported to have been provided by this agency between 1983 and 1988 (Gibert and Varley 1991, p. 48).

In terms of the urban land problem, land tenure regularization and the creation of territorial reserves are emphasized as highest priorities in the National Development Plan (1988–94). Regarding land tenure regularization, the President reported that between 1989 and 1991 his administration had granted 1,200,000 title deeds to legalize as many lots in *colonias populares* throughout the country (Mexico 1991, Tercer Informe). Such large numbers of titles reflect the great emphasis the government has placed on regularization.

Gilbert and Varley (1991, p. 49) argue that the policy to create land reserves around the periphery of the largest cities represents a shift from the populist approach of politicians to the managerial approach favored by technicians. Such a shift, however, does not guarantee that land will be managed according to technical criteria. Indeed, Gilbert and Varley (1991) argue that the government continues to favor what is most politically expedient. In this respect, the PRONASOL social investment fund has been instrumental.

Critics argue that PRONASOL, which is supposed to be nonpartisan, has been used to bolster lagging support for the PRI, the government's dominant political party. Barry et al. (1992, p. 101) argue that as 'a manifestation of the government's neocorporatist strategy, PRONASOL has bypassed the old corporatist network and established new and innovative forms of PRI patronage and clientelism'. Furthermore, 'rather than tackling the deep structural problems leading to the skewed income and resource distribution in Mexico, PRONASOL is a compensatory program designed to pacify and provide temporary relief. An obvious problem with this strategy is that the funds to back this social investment fund are not built into the budget but come from the contingency fund created by the sale of state enterprises' (ibid., p. 102). As a result, areas of the greatest need are not necessarily PRONASOL's top priorities.

CONCLUSIONS

There is more than enough evidence to argue that Mexico's urban housing crisis will go from bad to worse during the 1990s. The nation faces profound socioeconomic, political and ecological problems in its urban and rural domains. At the same time, however, one can argue that the heightening activism of civil society has created a historic opportunity. It may be that critical social movements are generating the kind of social experimentation and social learning necessary to seriously begin improving living conditions for the urban poor in Mexico. This remains to be seen. What is clear is the nearly overwhelming magnitude of interlocking economic and ecological challenges confronting the Mexican people.

In terms of global urbanization, the World Commission on Environment and Development (WCED) points out that in 1940, only one person in 100 lived in a city of 1 million or more inhabitants. By 1980, one in 10 lived in such a city. In Mexico, nearly one out of every two urban dwellers (45 percent of the total urban population) live in a megacity of one million or more.

Between 1985 and the year 2000, Third World cities could grow by another three-quarters of a billion people. As the WCED (1987, p. 16) points out: 'This suggests that the developing world must, over the next few years, increase by 65 percent its capacity to produce and manage its urban infrastructure, services, and shelter merely to maintain today's often extremely inadequate conditions'.

The WCED observations accurately describe the situation facing Mexico. In absolute terms, Mexico is entering a period in which the need for public works and government assistance for housing the urban poor has never been greater. Yet, economic restructuring and the politics of austerity, at least in the near term, are likely to aggravate rather than diminish the chronic scarcity of income and resources among Mexico's poor majority. The ecological implications of this are cause for alarm. For instance, environmental degradation will increase as cities expand (or implode) without adequate facilities for sewage treatment, waste disposal, or policies to protect ecosystems (e.g., watersheds, wetlands, forests).

In view of such ecological problems, it is encouraging to reiterate that the NDP documented as a national priority, the need: 'to channel economic activity towards places optimally suited in terms of resource availability, especially water; and to discourage the growth of overpopulated zones and of zones that have severe resource deficiencies' (Mexico 1989, p. 110). Although it is not yet translated into effective practice, this linkage of environment and development is noteworthy.

In his analysis of the future of cities on the Pacific Rim, including Mexico City, Douglas (1989) examines the environment–development connection. From a forward-looking perspective, Douglas raises questions about the status of resources necessary to sustain the urban habitat, about employment for the urban labor force, and about financing the provisioning of infrastructure, and public goods and services. Such questions have direct relevance for, and must figure into, strategies to ameliorate the urban housing crisis.

Cities of the 1990s will be increasingly pressed to develop energy efficiency and to regenerate (sustain) their resource base including local ecosystems. This reality demands a new approach to the production of housing environments. Housing now has to be studied as a place for production and income/resource generation as well as a place for consumption and reproduction. Yet, as Gilbert (1992, p. 443) points out, 'it is surprising how little attention, both in terms of policy and research, has been directed into the whole issue of how housing can be used to generate income. Not only can space be used to earn rents but homes can also accommodate commercial and manufacturing activity'.

Mexico's urban housing crisis highlights the need for innovative approaches to development. One approach is to promote what Douglas (1987) refers to as *urban resource ecologies*: systems involving solar and biomass energy, water reclamation, composting, urban gardens, organic and inorganic resource recycling. As Douglas (1987, p. 46) notes: 'Cities will be increasingly pressed to renew themselves, provide food in their hinterlands, regenerate their resource base, and to recycle their own wastes. This may see an urban life that oddly revives the past—composting, vegetable gardens—while using the best of new technologies'. From this perspective, the challenge of the 1990s is to create housing environments that effectively link the need for job creation, life space, and ecological sustainability.

NOTES

1. According to the United Nations' Human Development Index, Mexico ranked 46 out of the 160 countries listed in 1990. This put Mexico in uppermost category of high human development, as opposed to medium or low development (UNDP 1992). In terms of GNP per capita, the World Bank divides all the world's countries into quintiles ranging from the poorest 20 percent up to richest 20 percent. In 1989, Mexico was in the upper fourth 20 percent (World Bank 1992).

2. The term environment is used here to broaden the discussion beyond building types. Besides the dwelling unit, housing *environments* include land and ecosystems, as well as infrastructure, services, and amenities. Overlaying this is a legal terrain (i.e., property law, tenure, etc.).

3. 4.3 percent of those with jobs did not specify their income level.

4. These figures refer to the total housing stock, urban and rural.

5. Gilbert and Varley (1991), p. 17 point out: 'Most rural people in Mexico have always housed themselves through self-help construction. In contrast, throughout the 19th century and up to the 1940s, Mexico's cities were dominated by tenants. Rental housing was not only the typical form of working-class accommodation but was also home for most of the middle class. Only the elite owned their own homes, usually in blocks close to the town's main square. There seems to be little real variation between cities. Reports of conditions in most Mexican cities are agreed that renting was dominant until the middle of this century'.

6. In 1987, a peak year, 300,000 housing starts were made, but most of it represented earthquake reconstruction (Business Monitor International Ltd. 1992).

7. *Ejidatarios* are peasants who occupy *ejidos*—landholdings that were distributed to landless peasants through agrarian reform after the Mexican Revolution. The term *ejido* refers to the land itself, and to the legal corporation, composed of *ejidatarios*, which own the land under important limitations (it cannot be sold, rented or mortgaged).

8. As Gilbert (1991, p. 229) points out, the extent by which each form of land alienation is practiced, varies considerably from city to city: In Mexico City, Guadalajara, and Puebla, there are few invasions and most new settlements are established either through ejidal subdivision or other kinds of illegal subdivision (COPEVI 1977; Azuela 1987; Gilbert and Ward 1985; Gilbert and Varley 1991; Mele 1986; Morfin and Sanchez 1984). In Monterrey, Tijuana, Chihuahua, and Durango, invasions have traditionally been much more important (Gilbert and Varley 1989; 1991 in ref. Hoenderdos and Verbeek 1989; Pozas Garza 1989).

9. Gilbert and Varley (1991, p. 29) point out that, in 1950, only three Mexican cities with more

that 100,000 inhabitants had a majority of owner-occupied homes. By 1980, the transformation was almost complete. Practically every large Mexican city had a predominance of owners, many cities with two-thirds of their households in that category.

10. Growing around 5 percent per annum, the population of many cities has doubled every fourteen years.

11. Cited in *La Jornada*, sec. *La Capital*, 10 August 1992, p. 29.

12. In the same study, CENVI notes that 46 percent of the population in Mexico City rent their habitation; of these roughly three-quarters use 56 percent of their household income for rent. CENVI also notes that upwards of 20 percent of all the public housing units in Mexico City are occupied by renters who are illegally subletting the space.

13. On the positive side, Barry, et al. (1992, pp. 92–93) argue that economic restructuring initiatives, debt renegotiations, and free trade discussions have created new interest in Mexico among foreign investors and lenders, and that this has contributed to capital flight repatriation. On the negative side, the same authors argue that 'this encouraging inflow of foreign capital had a dark side, since most of it went into indirect investment in the stock market and into services rather than into productive investment' (ibid.). At the same time, Barry, et al. (1992) point to the increasing concern about Mexico's deteriorating trade balance: 'As Mexico opened its borders to foreign trade, its domestic farm and industrial sectors found they could not compete against cheap imports and began shutting down production. Stagnant investment in production for the domestic market, then, is yet another sign of the economic malaise underlying the official optimism in Mexico' (p. 93).

14. This includes rural people, who as a result of the recession have increased the flow of rural to urban migration (Gilbert 1992, p. 438).

15. The demand for housing and construction materials and products in Mexico will increase if the FTA is approved. Tariffs will drop dramatically over a period of years and will make materials in products for the housing and construction industry less costly for Mexican companies to import from the U.S. (*Mexico Business Monthly*, 1992, p. 12).

16. Mexico City has over 2 million households and firms using water, yet only 1.2 million pay monthly bills. The government plans to do a water census in order to increase the number of paying accounts. Once the census is completed the government will invite private firms to take over the administration of separate water districts. It is hoped that the expected increases in the price of drinking water will encourage development of water recycling projects (*Mexico Business Monthly*, July 1991, p. 11).

17. Office rents in Mexico City's Bosque de las Lomas District, for instance, have risen from $10 (US)/sq ft to $40(US)/sq ft in less that five years (Business Monitor International 1992).

18. *Desalojo* is a conjugated form of the Spanish word *desalojar*, meaning to evict, to dislodge.

19. Tercer Informe, p. 43.

20. For example, the parastatal enterprise Telmex—Mexico's Telephone Company.

REFERENCES

Aguilar, A.M. 1985. 'Crisis and Development Strategies in Latin America', *Development and Peace 6*, pp. 17–32.

Angel, S., R. Archer, S. Tanphiphat and E. Wegelin (eds.). 1983. *Land for Housing the Poor*. Singapore: Select Books.

Azuela, A. 1987. 'Low-Income Settlements and the Law in Mexico City', *International Journal of Urban and Regional Research 11*, pp. 523–42.

Baross, P. and **J. Van Der Linden**. 1990. *The Transformation of Land Supply Systems in Third World Cities*. London: Avebury.

Barry, T. (ed.). 1992. *Mexico: A Country Guide*. Albuquerque: The Inter-Hemispheric Education Resource Center.

Brown, L.B. and **J.L. Jacobson**. 1987. *The Future of Urbanization: Facing the Ecological and Economic Constraints*, World Watch Paper No 77. Washington, D.C.: World Watch Institute.

Burgess, R. 1985. 'Problems in the Classification of Low-Income Neighborhoods in Latin America', *Third World Planning Review 7 (4)*, pp. 101–28.

Business Monitor International Ltd. 1992. *Mexico 1992: Annual Report on Government, Economy, Industry and Business, with Forecasts to 1993*. London: BMI Ltd.

Carabias, J. and **A. Herrera**. 1986. 'La ciudad y su ambiente', *Cuadernos Politicos 45* (January–March), pp. 56–69.

Castells, M. 1983. *The City and the Grassroots*. Los Angeles: University of California Press.

CIDAC (Centro de Investigacion para el Desarrollo, A.C.). 1991. *Vivienda y Estabilidad Politica: Alternativas para el Futuro*. Mexico City: Editorial Diana.

Coulomb, R. and **E. Duhau** (eds.). 1989. *Politicas Urbanas y Urbanizacion de la Politica*. Mexico City: Universidad Autonoma Metropolitana.

Connolly, P. 1982. 'Uncontrolled Settlements and Self-build: What Kind of Solution? The Mexico City Case', in P. Ward, *Self-help Housing: A Critique*. London: Mansell, pp. 141–74.

———. 1990. 'Housing and the State in Mexico', in G. Shidlo (ed.), *Housing Policy in Developing Countries*. London: Routledge, pp. 5–32.

———. 1993. 'The Go-Between: CENVI, A Habitat NGO in Mexico City', *Environment and Urbanization 5 (1)*, pp. 68–90.

COPEVI (Centro Operacional de Poblamiento y Vivienda). 1977. *Investigacion sobre la Vivienda*. Mexico: COPEVI.

COPLAMAR (Coordinacion General del Plan Nacional de Zonas Deprimidas y Grupos Marginados). 1982. *Vivienda: Necesidades Esenciales en Mexico (situacion actual y perspectivas al ano 2000)*. Mexico City: Siglo Veintiuno Editores.

Cornelius, W. and **A. Craig**. 1988. *Politics in Mexico: An Introduction and Overview*, Reprint Series 1, 2nd. ed. San Diego: Center for US-Mexican Studies, University of California.

Cornelius, W.A., J. Gentleman and **P.H. Smith** (eds.). *Mexico's Alternative Political Futures*, Monograph Series No. 30. San Diego: Center for U.S.–Mexican Studies.

DDF. 1986. *Programa de Integracion Social del Territorio: Belvederes, Tlalpan*.

De La Rocha, M. Gonzalez and **A. Escobar Laptapi** (eds.). 1991. *Social Responses to Mexico's Economic Crisis of the 1980s*. US-Mexico Contemporary Perspectives Series, 1. San Diego: Center for U.S.–Mexican Studies.

Díaz Barriga, M. 1990. 'Urban Politics in the Valley of Mexico: A Case Study of Urban Movements in the Ajusco Region of Mexico City, 1970 to 1987'. Ph. D. Dissertation, Stanford University, Department of Anthropology.

Doebele, William A. 1987. 'The Evolution of Concepts of Urban Land Tenure in Developing Countries', *Habitat International 11 (1)*, pp. 7–22.

Douglass, M. 1989. 'The Future of Cities on the Pacific Rim', in M.P. Smith (ed.), *Pacific Rim Cities in the World Economy*. Comparative Urban and Community Research Volume 2. New Brunswick (USA): Transaction Publishers, pp. 9–67.

Dunkerley, H. and **C. Whitehead** (eds.). 1983. *Urban Land Policy: Issues and Opportunities*. Washington, D.C.: World Bank.

Eckstein, S. 1990. 'Poor People verses the State and Capital: Autonomy of Successful Community Mobilization for Housing in Mexico City', *International Journal of Urban and Regional Research 14*, pp. 274–96.

Foweraker, J. and A. Craig (eds.). 1988. *Popular Movements and Political Change in Mexico*. Boulder: Lynne Rienner Publishers.

Friedmann, J. 1986. 'Planning in Latin America: From Technocratic Illusion to Open Democracy', in J. Friedmann, *Life Space and Economic Space: Essays in Third World Planning*, pp. 227–40.

———. 1987. *Planning in the Public Domain: From Knowledge to Action*. Princeton: Princeton University Press.

———. 1992. *Empowerment: The Politics of Alternative Development*. Cambridge, MA: Blackwell.

Gilbert, A. 1989. *Housing and Land in Urban Mexico*. Monograph Series 31. San Diego: Center for U.S.-Mexican Studies.

———. 1992. 'Third World Cities: Housing, Infrastructure and Servicing', *Urban Studies 29 (3 & 4)*, pp. 435–60.

Gilbert, A. and A. Varley. 1991. *Landlord and Tenant: Housing the Poor in Urban Mexico*. London: Routledge.

Gilbert, A. and P. Ward. 1985. *Housing the State and the Poor: Policy and Practice in Three Latin American Cities*. Cambridge: Cambridge University Press.

HABITAT. 1983. 'Land for Housing the Poor: Report of the United Nations Seminar of Experts on Land for Housing the Poor'. Thallberg and Stockholm, March.

Hoenderdos, W.H. and H.C.M. Verbeek. 1989. 'The Low-Income Housing Market in Mexico: Three Cities Compared', in A. Gilbert (ed.), *Housing and Land in Urban Mexico*, pp. 51–64.

Hardoy, Jorge E., Diana Mitlan and David Satterthwaite. 1992. *Environmental Problems in Third World Cities*. London: Earthscan Publications.

INEGI (Instituto Nacional de Estadistica Geografia E Informatica). 1991. *XI Censo General de Poblacion y Vivienda, 1990*, Mexico D.F.: INEGI.

Linn, J.F. 1983. *Cities in the Developing World: Policies for their Equitable and Efficient Growth*. A World Bank Publication, New York: Oxford University Press.

Mele, P. 1986. 'El Espacio Industrial entre la Ciudad y la Region', Documento de Investigacion No. 3, Instituto de Ciencias, Universidad Autonoma de Puebla.

Malpezzi, S. 1990. 'Urban Housing and Financial Markets: Some International Comparisons', *Urban Studies 27*, pp. 971–1022.

Mena, J. 1987. 'Technologia alternativa, transformacion de desechos y desarrollo urbano', *Estudios Demograficos y Urbanos 2 (3)*, Septiembre–Diciembre.

Mexico Business Monthly. 1922. *Mexico Business Month 1 (12)*. Mapelwood, N.J.: Kal Wagenheim.

MEXICO (Secretaria de Programacion y Presupuesto). 1989. *Plan Nacional de Desarroll: 1989–94*. Mexico City: SPP

MEXICO (Direccion General de Communicacion Social). 1991. *Mexican Agenda*. Mexico D.F.: Direccion de Publicaciones.

MEXICO (Direccion General de Communicacion Social). 1991. *Tercer Informe*. Mexico D.F.: Direccion de Publicaciones.

Morfin, G.A. and M. Sanchez. 1984. 'Controles Juridicos Psicosociales en la Produccion del Espacio Urbano para Sectores Populares en Guadalajara, *Encuentro 1*, pp. 115–41.

Oberlander, H.P. 1985. *Land the Central Human Settlement Issue*. Human Settlements Issue 7. Vancouver: University of British Columbia Press.

Payne, G. 1989. *Informal Housing and Land Subdivisions in Third World Cities: A Review of the Literature*. Oxford: CENDEP.

Pezzoli, K. 1991. 'Environmental Conflicts in the Urban Milieu: The Case of Mexico City', D. Goodman and M. Redclift (eds.), *Environment and Development in Latin America: The Politics of Sustainability*. New York: Manchester University Press, pp. 205–29.

Portes, A. 1989. 'Latin American Urbanization during the Years of the Crisis, in *Latin American Research Review 25*, pp. 7–44.

Pozas-Garza, M. 1989. 'Land Settlement by the Urban Poor in Monterrey', in A. Gilbert (ed.), *Housing and Land in Urban Mexico*, pp. 65–78.

Ramirez Saiz, J.M. 1990. 'Urban Struggles and their Political Consequences', in J. Foweraker and A. Craig (eds.), *Popular Movements and Political Change in Mexico*. Boulder: Lynne Riener Publishers, pp. 234–46.

Rivera, M. 1987. 'La Transformacion del Suelo Ejidal en Suelo Urbano. El Caso del Ejido de San Nicolas Totolapan', Tesis de Licenciado en Sociologia. Universidad Nacional Autonoma de Mexico. Mexico, D.F.

Rodriguez, V. 1987. 'The Politics of Decentralization in Mexico: Divergent Outcomes of Policy Implementation', Ph. D. Dissertation, University of California at Berkeley.

Schteingart, M. 1983. 'La Promocion Immobiliaro en el Area Metropolitana de la Ciudad de Mexico (1960–1980)', *Demografia y Economia XVII (53)*, pp. 453–70.

Schteingart, M. 1984. 'El Sector Imboliario y la Vivienda en la Crisis', *Comercio Exterior 34 (8)*, August.

———. 1987. 'Expansion urbana, conflictos sociales y deterio ambiental en la Ciudad de Mexico. El Caso del Ajusco', *Estudios Demograficos y urbanos 2 (3)*.

———. 1990. *Los Productores del Espacio Habitable: Estado, Empresa y Sociedad en la Ciudad de Mexico*. Mexico D.F.: El Colegio de Mexico.

Selby, H.A., A.D. Murphy and S.A. Lorenzen (with I. Cabrera, A. Castaneda and I. Ruiz Love). 1990. *The Mexican Urban Household: Organizing for Self-Defense*. Austin: University of Texas Press.

Slater, D. (ed.). 1985. *New Social Movements and the State in Latin America*. Amsterdam: CEDLA.

Suarez Pareyon, Alejandro. 1987. *El Programa de Vivienda del Molino: Una Experiencia Autogestiva de Urbanizacion Popular*. Mexico, D.F.: Centro de la Vivienda y Estudios Urbanos, A.C. (CENVI).

Sunkel, O. 1985. *America Latina y la Crisis Economica International: Ocho Tesis y una Propuesta*. Buenos Aires: Grupo Editor Latinamericano S.R.L.

Sunkel, O. and N. Gligo. 1981. '*Estilos de desarrollo y medio ambiente en la America Latina*. Mexico, FCE, Lecturas 36.

United Nations Development Program. 1992. *Human Development Report*. New York: Oxford University Press.

Walker, R.B.J. 1990. *One World Many Worlds: Struggles for a Just World Peace*. Boulder, Colorado: Lynne Rienner Publishers.

Walton, J. 1991. 'Review Article', *International Journal of Urban and Regional Research 15 (4)*, December, pp. 629–33.

Ward, P.M. 1990. *Mexico City: The Production and Reproduction of an Urban Environment*. London: Belhaven Press.

Ward, P.M. and G.C. Macoloo. 1992. 'Articulation Theory and Self-Help Housing Practice in the 1990s', *International Journal of Urban and Regional Research 16 (1)*, March, pp. 60–80.

World Bank. 1992. *World Development Report 1992: Development and the Environment*. New York: Oxford University Press.

World Commission on Environment and Development. 1987. *Our Common Future*. New York: Oxford University Press.

PART III

HOUSING UNDER MEDIUM LEVELS OF HUMAN DEVELOPMENT

An examination of Table 1.1 in Chapter 1 shows that the countries in this medium group are mixed in their HDI rank relative to GNP. Two countries, Brazil and Cuba, are just two ranks below their expected level based on GNP and three of them are several ranks above where they would be expected to be. China, especially, is 55 ranks above where its GNP would place it. Colombia and Thailand are each 22 ranks above the expected. It is hard to construct such a ranking for the Anglophone islands of the Caribbean. The HDI, on the average for the group, is similar to the other countries described in Part III. The case studies show that a very extensive effort has been made by these countries to deal with housing poverty. The chapter on China is perhaps an exception. It is much more critical of the efforts underway in that country to improve human development than the HDI suggests. Overall these countries are close to the top of the index.

An improvement calculation is not possible for all the countries in Part III. Brazil is eighth (.237) among all 110 countries for which information is available. It has an exceptionally high rate of improvement for a country in the medium index category. Thailand is in the top 30 percent (.170). This does not provide us with enough information on these countries as a group to draw many conclusions.

Housing poverty in the small island nations which were former colonies of Great Britain in the Caribbean are the subject of Chapter 7. Katharine Coit describes a situation where housing needs are greatest for female heads of families. With a capacity of good statistics, she estimates upwards of 75 percent of the housing to be of the self-help variety, with an estimated 20 percent, the result of squatting. These island societies have a history of slavery, large plantations, a colonial history, and an environment of hurricanes, volcanoes, and earthquakes. She reviews the many attempts to provide housing for low-income families in these island nations. Despite the extension of technical and economic assistance from the World Bank, USAID, and other governmental and nongovernmental organizations, the vagaries of local island politics appear to be the most important dimension of the housing problem. Political parties and political changes create a very unstable situation for the ongoing provision of housing for the poor. On the other hand, there appear to be adequate local community resources for the initiation and organization of low-income housing projects.

Chapter 8 on Brazil by Suzana Pasternak Taschner provides statistical and historical details on the emergence of slums and squatter settlements, shows how they have varied in development among the major urban centers, and then reviews the changes in the federal policy towards them over the years. She concludes with a detailed description of the changes which have occurred in Sao Paulo since the federal government's involvement in rehousing was eliminated in 1986. She describes changes similar to those in South Korea as discussed in Chapter 4: elimination of administrative regulations on land use, transfer, ownership, and elimination of municipal building codes. These were replaced by a dwellers' association which worked with local residents and contractors to rebuild and regularize neighborhoods. The land was held by the association and the houses were owned by the original occupant. Though successful, this shift leaves out the renters and turns the house into a marketable commodity. The result, because of the severe housing shortage, is a tremendous increase in the market value of the new housing.

Colombian housing problems, described in Chapter 9, parallel those of other Third World countries: rapid urbanization, insufficient jobs with insufficient wages, and a national housing policy indifferent to the needs of low-income urban residents. In addition to squatter settlements or spontaneous housing, John Betancur has described the 'Pirate Settlements' wherein speculators offer land to the urban poor (and not so poor) without following municipal regulations, i.e., without following the formal process of land subdivision and development. Consequently, the titles to these lands are suspect. The chapter describes the various attempts to control these two types of housing developments in Colombia utilizing various forms of international aid such as the Alliance for Progress or money from other foreign governments. Much of this type of aid resulted in housing for the moderate and middle classes.

In 1989, the government changed its housing policy. Building on the development of local collective associations of homeowners in the two types of settlements, it attempted to expropriate the land covered by these settlements, enact or perfect titles, legalize these settlements as 'social interest settlements', and provide housing subsidies for them through local taxation schemes. In order to carry out the process, the old national housing organization was replaced by the National Institute for Social Interest Housing and Urban Redevelopment. It combines the work of the national government, local muncipalities, the private sector, and the housing associations which have grown up in the settlements. These groups of organizations and institutions use self-help labor, progressive development, and minimum quality housing to carry out their objectives. Betancur discusses some of the possible outcomes of this, as yet untested, legislation.

Kosta Mathey concludes Chapter 10 on housing poverty in Cuba by stating '...the Cuban state has developed impressively imaginative and flexible housing strategies'. These strategies are clearly presented, as is the basis for carrying them out: through measures like overcoming poverty, elimination of land and property speculation, and removal of the insecurity of tenure. The collapse of COMECON in 1991 has brought these strategies to a halt, as favorable trade relations with eastern European countries are no longer possible.

The most important strategy for reducing the level of housing poverty in Cuba, according to Mathey, was of the microbrigades. Made up of the staff of work units, the brigades built houses for each other when they were underutilized in the workplace. These were disbanded after a very successful decade because they did not provide housing for nonworking members of society. They were reintroduced in even larger numbers in 1988 with the proviso that 40 percent of their housing production would go to those outside the work unit. Social microbrigades were also developed with teams from local neighborhoods. They used volunteers and also employed the locally unemployed, giving them both jobs and a way to learn the trade (training was built into the process). The descriptions of the reduction in housing poverty in Cuba contrast radically with the descriptions in other chapters of increasing levels of housing poverty.

The chapter on Thailand is really about the primate city of Bangkok. Housing 60 percent of the population of the country, Bangkok is 20 times as large as the next sized city. Housing poverty in Bangkok is either the most backward or the most advanced says Kioe Sheng Yap, depending upon your perspective. He describes a city (and a country) where the government policy is nonintervention in both public and private land use disputes. Consequently, about 13 percent of the households are considered to be slum or informal squatter settlements. Most of these households are on private land or land owned by large government bureaus. They suffer from problems of poor housing construction, crowding, lack of road access, stagnant water, disease, drugs, AIDS, and threat of fire. Most of all, they are threatened by eviction. In the last decade, only seven settlements out of 1,500 have had land-sharing, a concept developed in Bangkok; 200 settlements have been evicted. The National Housing Authority has not been very effective, but the government has not been extensively involved in most of the other policies reported in these chapters such as clearance and relocation, sites-and-services and slum upgrading. The changes have been left to be worked out by the market and the Thai culture. For a brief period in the late 1980s there was a shift in the market provision of low-income housing with the result that 55 percent of the metro population could afford a house. That window has now been partially closed, but it affords a picture of a country that has reached levels of economic growth which are high enough to create a housing market for over half of the population.

The People's Republic of China, described in Chapter 12, forms an important part of global housing poverty because it contains such a large proportion of the population of the planet. On-Kwok Lai's description of the changes in government housing policy since the rise to power of the Chinese Communist Party in 1949 indicates the extent to which China has wrestled with the same housing problems as other Third World countries. The increased urbanization of the 1950s, as immigrants from the rural areas crowded into the cities, and the old treaty port cities of the coast grew in size, was met with Stalinist type solutions: control the movement of people; empty out the cities. The consequences of that policy, as in Cuba, led to the deterioration of much of the urban housing stock in the major cities and the creation of housing poverty.

Ideologically a new element in the mix was the Maoist emphasis upon lack of material goods, including housing, as a condition necessary for the continuation of the revolution. In fact, the emphasis upon production in the socialist development model, at the expense of (housing) consumption, led to minimal investment by the central government in housing. This also increased housing poverty. Additionally, the *highly centralized production hierarchy* reduced the ability of the local government to deal with land use issues in a way that could reduce housing poverty. The latest phase has seen an increase in urbanization, especially in the new economic zones, and a contradictory policy of both a planned economy and limited free enterprise.

7

Politics and Housing Strategies in the Anglophone Caribbean

Katharine Coit

The triple inheritance of slavery, colonialism, and a plantation economy has had a major impact on the social and economic situation in the Caribbean. Housing and urban development are good examples of this triple influence. Slavery and the colonial society exaggerated inequality by keeping a large portion of the society in extreme poverty long after slavery was abolished. Under slavery the African roots of the captured populations had been cut off. As far as housing was concerned the slaves were forced to live in shacks designed if not built by their masters. Traditional forms and building techniques were generally lost. The plantation system contributed to the concentration of all the good arable lands in large estates, a situation which still exists in the present day. In Dominica, for instance, in 1960 over half the agricultural land belonged to 67 estates. Six families owned 20 of the large estates and foreign investors owned most of the others.

A look at the historical background and the economic setting helps us understand why the housing tends to be small, simply built, and of simple rough material. Formerly, the slave huts were built to be moved easily and even presently, as ownership of housing is distinct from ownership of land, one can still see houses being transported on trucks or on rollers.

The tropical climate also influences the Caribbean dwelling style as it permits many activities to be performed outside. The home is made of house and garden, the latter being used for washing, preparing food, play and entertaining, and for cooking when there is no separate kitchen house. In urban areas overcrowding reduces this outside dwelling space as more houses are added to accommodate family or newcomers causing people to live in what was once just considered sleeping space.

The Caribbean is situated in a zone that is prone to hurricanes, earthquakes, and volcanic eruptions. The hurricanes are a persistent danger to buildings and crops. In the areas in the path of a hurricane, economic production is halted while the inhabitants rebuild their homes and industries and replant their crops.

Until recently, the bulk of the population—descendants of the slaves—were agricultural workers on sugar-cane plantations or small peasants. As in most Third World cities, rural–urban migration has been a major trend. The dwindling sugar estates no longer employ many workers and the small peasant holdings of the post-slave period are not large enough to support the rapidly growing population. As elsewhere in the Third World, rural–urban migration of mostly unskilled workers has added extra pressure to the low-cost housing of the swelling cities causing much overcrowding.

The towns and cities of the Caribbean have traditionally had slave quarters or yards where the slaves, who worked in urban industry, were housed in shacks. These areas have grown and multiplied and become the overcrowded slums and shanty towns of the modern Caribbean. The other major source of low-cost housing has been the 'captured land' or the areas squatted on which the households build their own dwelling.

Independence from Great Britain has resulted in the area being made up of small to tiny island states with few resources. Each island has one major urban center comprising one-fourth to one-third of the island's population. This center tends to concentrate all the urban functions—administrative, commercial, and industrial.

THE MAIN CHARACTERISTICS OF THE SLUMS
AND SQUATTER SETTLEMENTS

Because such a large percent of the population of the Caribbean have low incomes due to low wages, high unemployment, and high underemployment there is a large percentage of the population that cannot afford formal housing. In Jamaica, 60 or 70 percent of housing is built by the informal sector (Francis-Hinds and Jones 1989). In the eastern Caribbean, 75 percent of the population cannot pay for housing of the formal market (Ishmael 1991) in keeping with the planning regulations.

Traditionally, in the Caribbean, a couple lives under a separate roof although they may share the same outside space. This tendency has carried on into today's slums and squatter settlements where there is a preference for owner occupancy of separate single-storey dwellings, however tiny they may be.

The traditional Caribbean 'chattel houses' (the name given to the huts of the slaves) are usually owner built, by the household itself or by a friend or relative with some building skills. The land is often leased. The older run-down houses in the cities are rented or squatted by low-income households and split up for multihousehold usage. It is not uncommon for many households to share the same kitchen and toilet. Where there are two or three rooms, one may be rented out for a little income.

Squatting has existed in the Caribbean ever since the 19th century when the newly freed slaves took over crown lands to settle and farm away from their former masters' estates. Today most towns and cities have extensive squatter communities but few statistics exist giving the extent of this phenomenon. In Jamaica, squatting is estimated to provide about 20 percent of the housing. Squatters usually capture government land on the periphery of cities and towns in the hope that political allies will support them and permit them to stay. The areas which are squatted are often on steep slopes or in danger of flooding or of landslides and are of less interest to commercial builders. Squatting is highest during periods of crisis, for example after hurricanes or in periods of economic crisis.

In contrast to South America, squatting in the Caribbean is done individually rather than in organized invasions. At first, the houses are rudimentary but they are improved gradually. Rooms are added and cement blocks replace boards or sheets of galvanized iron. Squatters face difficulties in obtaining potable water, drainage systems, latrines, roads, electricity, and other infrastructure. Schools and shops are often far. On the other hand a study in Jamaica shows some positive aspects of squatting. 'In a buoyant squatter community almost every house or yard has its income generating projects. Householders may buy and sell goods...rear small animals, cook food for sale, or scavenging for raw materials to sell or process further....The buoyancy of the squatter communities often resides in the freeing up of meager cash resources previously absorbed by rent and in the existence of space within which these resources can be put to use in income generating projects' (Francis-Hinds and Jose 1989).

The pattern of family life has a direct impact on the housing situation. There is a marked tendency for late marriages of informal cohabitation. The majority of children are born out of wedlock. There are thus a large number of female heads of household. In Kingston, Jamaica, for instance, 40 percent of the low-income households are headed by single women (McLeod 1988). Generally these women only get very aleatory support from the fathers of the children and have very uncertain incomes. They accumulate difficulties in obtaining decent housing because not only do they have the children to look after making it difficult for them to work, but when they do work they have the lowest paid jobs as they tend to have the least education. Furthermore, they have more difficulty in obtaining loans for housing and they rarely have skills in construction.

Housing is often treated by the authorities as though it were a technical question and perhaps a financial one with no relation to politics. This, of course, is false. There are many direct and indirect ways in which housing is closely tied to politics. Whether the government makes serious attempts to improve the quality and quantity of low cost housing is of major importance. The income group that the government tries to help is another major political factor.

In Trinidad and Tobago, squatting became a political issue on a national scale in the 1970s first, because of the hillside settlements and the problems of deforestation, erosion, pollution, and flood damage and second, because adding infrastructure and services after the squatters have settled is so costly (Glenn, Labossiere and Wolfe 1992). In 1977, the government promised large-scale regularization but this policy took a long time to be implemented and did not have a major impact on squatting in the 1980s. More recently, a new attempt at squatter regulation has been undertaken which will be discussed subsequently (Glenn, Labossiere and Wolfe 1992).

In Jamaica, there is a phenomenon known as 'political tribalism' where members of one political party dominate an area and all other residents and businesses are terrorized by the violence and leave. In this way there are areas in central Kingston which are nearly a hundred and look as though a war or a hurricane hit them. The low-income victims of 'political tribalism' tend to squat on the edge of the town.

In Dominica, the housing policy was totally transformed with the change of government in 1980. The former Labor Party had created a Housing Development Corporation (HDC) which serviced lots and built low cost housing. When the Freedom government was elected they disbanded the HDC and pulled the government out from most of its involvement in low cost housing. Between 1980 and 1986, only 225 low cost houses were built, 105 of which were in the works before they took office. According to World Bank statistics, more than half of the public investment in housing in Dominica during this period went to help the middle classes. The Prime Minister herself has said 'it was not the role of the government to house the poor' (Coit 1988, p. 5).

There are two political tendencies in the Caribbean which have a negative impact on housing, the first is the 'spoils system', that is, upon being elected the victorious party tends to fire the government employees and even disband whole units (i.e., the Urban Development Corporation [UDC] in Jamaica and the HDC in Dominica) in order to rid the administration of followers of the other camp. The other tendency is to provide jobs and services for one's own followers and neglect the rest of the population.

STRATEGIES OF COMMUNITY BASED ORGANIZATIONS AND NON-GOVERNMENTAL ORGANIZATIONS

Collective efforts of the population to improve housing are initiated by community based organizations, local and international NGOs. They include self-help projects, building skills improvement, cooperatives, credit unions, and the 'sou-sou' or 'partner' system (an informal method of organizing savings).

An example of a very effective housing program organized by the community itself was that of the Giraudel, Eggleston Reconstruction Committee in a village of Dominica in the Windward Islands. This community was severely hit by hurricane David in 1979 and most of the houses were flattened; many people were living in very makeshift, patched up shacks for years afterwards. A local church committee decided to create a housing reconstruction group. They knew the limited resources of many of the poorly housed and realized that the only affordable housing could be built by self-help with soft loans to pay for the building material. What they needed most were the initial funds to provide the loans. With the help of a Belgian priest they were able to obtain a grant for \$ 600.000EC (or US\$ 222.222) from a Dutch NGO (CEBEMO). This money was to allow 100 needy households to obtain a loan of \$ 6,000 EC for the purchase of the building material. The committee provided simple plan for a house 12 ft. by 20 ft. which could be changed by the future owner if he wished. The committee members took care of the administrative details and organized the buying of materials. The heads of the household never saw the money but signed for the material received and were to pay back at no interest in installments they had agreed upon. A team of villagers provided the skilled and unskilled labor to put up the houses. Fifty-five houses were reconstructed in this manner in a village of 172 households at a price people could afford. This is a very high ratio of successful renovation.

Squatter upgrading projects have also been undertaken by local committees and NGOs. The Construction Resource Development Center (CRDC), a local NGO, helped the people of Highlight View, a squatted zone in Kingston, Jamaica to work collectively at community projects such as building a community center, providing day-dare facilities, and building retaining walls to prevent soil erosion on the steep slopes of their neighborhood. The CRDC has also helped Highlight View negotiate with the National Water Commission to obtain stand pipes for the area. Until then, the squatters had had to use a river situated way below their houses. A collection system was set up by the community to pay for this service.

Another strategy of the CRDC has been to encourage people in poor housing to be trained in basic construction skills and in techniques for building safer, hurricane resistant houses. They helped set up the Women's Construction Collective, a nonprofit organization, whose role is to train women to be construction workers, a field in which previously there were very few women. Once trained, the women are helped by the WCC to find construction jobs. From 1983 to 1989, 120 women were trained by the WCC. It now runs a repair and maintenance business, a carpentry shop and also accepts construction work.

A recent effort to improve housing for women in Kingston has been the creation of the St. Peter Claver Women's Housing Co-op. The members are low-income working women with severe housing problems. With help from the Canadian International Development Agency (CIDA) they were able to raise enough money to buy and rehabilitate several large old houses which were to be shared by the members. The women, who had usually been living in run-down areas, sharing kitchens and outdoor toilets with many families would now be housed much better. They would get two rooms with an indoor toilet and kitchen to be shared with only one other member. Only women can be members of the co-op. They can live with their husbands or boyfriends but if the couple separates it is the woman with the children who will keep the home rather than the man. The women are required to understand the functioning of a co-op before joining it to ensure that the members are committed to the cooperative idea. The group requires that all future applicants attend five general meetings, pass an oral test and be interviewed before being accepted (Francis-Hinds and Jones 1989). Living in the co-ops is seen by the women not only as a means to a better home but also as a way to fulfill themselves. They have other projects in common such as day-care for the children and cooperative food purchasing.

One of the scarce resources necessary to improve housing is credit. Access to loans from formal banking institutions is often denied to poor people for lack of equity. In many of the Caribbean islands a system for raising money called 'sou-sou' or 'partner', much like the African 'tantines', is used. A group of people agree to each pool a certain amount of money every week. Every so often, there is a lottery and one of the partners takes all of the money. All the partners continue to contribute until each one has been able to draw the money. A 'partner' is often organized so that each of its members will be able to buy a plot of land or build a house. There is mutual support for the building or repairing of the house as well as for financing it.

STRATEGIES OF GOVERNMENT
AND INTERNATIONAL ORGANIZATIONS

Faced with a drastic need of low-cost housing which the formal housing market could never begin to fulfil, most governments of the region have developed programs to address the question. The World Bank and other international organizations have often helped develop the programs. The programs range from government housing schemes, sites-and-services, slum upgrading, house repair programs, and housing financing. An evaluation of some of these programs suggests that the type of program and the efficiency (or lack of it) of the administration do not fully explain their relative success or failure. Other factors are related to local politics, state of the economy, and the international aid organizations.

A program that has sometimes been used in Grenada and in St. Vincent is a house repair program which provides building material loans at very low interest rates for improving housing. This program was quite successful under the revolutionary impetus of the New Jewel government in Grenada because enthusiastic local committees implemented the program; they decided who the most needy households were, how much material was necessary, and organized collective self-help groups to do the rebuilding. Recently these programs have not been as successful. For one thing, tests are not used and it is claimed that the material does not reach those most in need (Ishmael 1991). Politicians are known to take advantage of these programs for electioneering purposes. As with any program which is poorly administered and without proper monitoring, even potentially good programs can be derailed because of the 'pork barrel' or corruption.

Many of the Urban Development Corporations have been accused of ineffectiveness, 'poor debt collection mechanisms, process of land distribution, lack of clearly defined policy and overall poor management practices' (Ishmael 1991, personal communication). There is certainly some justification for this criticism. Indeed, these are problems typical of many bureaucracies in both Third World and developed countries. It should be realized, however, that this type of criticism is often used to hide more unavowable reasons for abolishing whole programs or departments.

Jamaica offers a good example of how this type of argument was used for terminating a program. In 1970, the World Bank started cooperating with the Jamaican government on a low-income housing program. The Minister of Housing adopted the recommendations of a study that proposed 'sites-and-services' projects as the most appropriate type of housing for households in the lower-income bracket. A task force was set up within the ministry which worked with World Bank experts to provide 6,000 serviced lots with community facilities and land for industrial complexes to provide employment. The World Bank also made funds available for mortgages at 8 percent interest for 25 years (Isaacs 1992).

The same task force also prepared programs to upgrade three squatter communities of a total of 2,750 households. They were to provide roads and footpaths, storm water drainage, individual water supply connections, electricity, community facilities, and, most important, security of land tenure. The Dutch government and USAID became involved in funding these upgrading programs. At the start, there were only a few people who had experimented with this sort of a project and the institutional backing was weak. The sites-and-services unit grew from eight to 100 people between 1974 and 1980. With time they developed a 'cadre of professionals skilled in all aspects of Sites and Services and Upgrading capable of holding their own anywhere in the world' (Isaacs 1989, personal communication). The role of the World Bank does not seem to have been entirely neutral. In spite of high inflation, the programs were progressing well. However, citing the cause of inefficiency, the World Bank decided to withdraw its support of the program in early 1979. The self-help element was eliminated and contractors used to enclose 120 sq. ft. of shelter after which the Bank's involvement was terminated.

A World Bank evaluation of these projects suggests that there had been 'early wrinkles that were ironed out as the team grew and became more experienced' (Isaacs 1989, p. 203). Among the many reasons for the significant cost overruns identified by the Bank's Project Completion Report were:

- Unresolved details in the early planning stage, both physical and social, that were carried into the implementation.
- Implementation during a period of deflation. (The Jamaican dollar was repeatedly devalued causing severe inflation of building materials.)
- Early institutional weakness (Isaacs 1989, pp. 189-210).

Nadine Isaacs writes of this Report: 'The analysis of these weaknesses in the Report, particularly the institutional weaknesses are contradictory and encouraged the politically astute mind to speculate on what motivated the Bank to abandon the project when it did (1979)' (Isaacs 1989, p. 205). The same World Bank Report said, 'By 1978, however, the unit was operating rather well, and was called upon to implement other projects financed by other international assistance agencies, USAID and the Dutch government' (Isaacs 1989, p. 205). It should be noted that towards the end of the 1970s, the Manley government, facing a grave deficit of foreign currency, had at first tried to apply the IMF stabilization program and had then tried to defy it. The World Bank's withdrawal from the sites-and-services projects coincides with the period in which Manley was resisting the IMF proposals. This case also indicates the impact of international politics and economics on housing policy.

In the mid-1970s, another agent, the Urban Development Corporation, charged with responsibility for land assembly, planning, construction of infrastructure, promoting secondary development, etc., was given the additional responsibility for providing housing for the lower-income workers in the tourist industry in Ochos Rios—an important tourist center. The incomes of the target group for this housing were just above those of the poorest households but below those of the middle-income group. It included a large percentage of households which had one or more persons earning the minimum wage (30 Jamaican dollars a week in 1976). It was a policy of the government to attempt to provide the hotel and tourist workers with decent affordable housing, as the unhappy and unhealthy state of workers in this industry was thought to have a negative impact on their attitude towards tourists. These projects were also to prevent further squatting. Because of the limited resources of the homeowners and the limitations on the financial support offered by the Inter American Development Bank (IADB), it was obvious that the only way to satisfy these requirements was to provide a core house or a serviced lot for the future owner(s) to build on. In Ochos Rios, the UDC chose to combine two different types of lots. One consisted of a shell of a house, which left the work of subdividing and adding extensions to the household. The reason for choosing this type of program was to avoid opposition from local authorities who were afraid of an unsightly low-income settlement in a tourist center. However, as the cost of the shells for a large number of potential owners was too much, a second type was prepared that would be more affordable for lower-income groups. It consisted of serviced lots with sanitary cores on which the homeowner was to build the rest of the house. Eight prototypes were built in order to experiment with building methods, to reduce costs, iron out technical bugs, and to ascertain if the houses were acceptable to the future occupants. In this case both types were well received by the target group but there was:

> implacable hostility on the part of local politicians and leading citizens to the core-plus-add-on units (which were) seen as a threat to bring a slum-like environment to the heart of Ochos Rios or as an attempt to impose substandard and old fashioned conditions on the working people of the area. In the circumstance, the attempt to produce a housing solution for the lower end of the income group specified by the IADB had to be abandoned and work was concentrated on the [Shell] Units (UDC 1981, personal interview).

The UDC was even asked to hide the project behind a wall, which it did at considerable expense. However, once the project was finished, the town found the houses so attractive that they asked the UDC to take away the wall (Gregory-Jones and Taylor 1992). The cost of the shell units escalated considerably due to delays in the decision making system in a period of very high inflation. In spite of all these problems they were sold at a price that met the needs of the top level of the target group (12,700 Jamaican dollars in 1979).

In 1980, the election of the conservative Seaga government caused a total disruption of the housing policy. The government was very suspicious of the sites-and-services project unit 'which was regarded as a "hot bed of socialist ideology" and the sites and services approach nothing short of a "communist conspiracy" ' (Issacs 1989, p. 204). A large majority of the employees were supporters of the Manley government and although they were highly professional, the majority of the unit was fired. Their skills in sites-and-services and upgrading acquired with some difficulty were lost to the government. The upgrading programs of USAID continued but eventually ran aground.

While rejecting the name and concept of sites-and-services, the Seaga government developed, ironically, what they called the starter home approach which has a striking similarity to the program they abolished in everything except in name. Seven years later, the National Shelter Sector Strategy Report, prepared for the IYSH in Nairobi, recognized sites-and-services as part of government policy for the very low-income earners.

The disruption caused by the change in government was not limited to firing employees and changing the names of policies. Some projects that were underway were left to wrack and ruin. The one in Kingston, in which the infrastructure had already been put in place and some of the shelters and a school had already been built, was torn down and replaced by sites for factories. The justification was that it was a poor location for people to live in. On the contrary, senior planners considered it a very good place for housing and many people were happy to live nearby. The result was an extraordinary waste of scarce funds for low-income housing. It is surprising to agents of the UDC that the World Bank tolerates such a waste of its funds which are usually hard to come by (Gregory-Jones and Taylor 1992).

A major problem for low- and middle-income households is the difficulty in obtaining mortgages at a reasonable interest rate. In most Caribbean countries, banks have limited funds available for mortgages and their equity requirements are strict. In Jamaica, the National Housing Trust (NHT) was founded by government in 1976 to provide funds for a variety of housing solutions. To finance this fund the NHT required employers to contribute 5 percent of the wage of each employee and the employees to contribute 2 percent of their salary. The employee's contribution was refundable after seven years at 3 percent interest if the employee had not used the money as equity for a loan. The objectives of the NHT were to add to and improve the country's existing supply of housing by:

a) promoting housing projects to such extent as may from time to time be approved by the Minister;

b) making available loans to contributors to assist in the purchase, building, maintenance, repair or improvement of houses; and

c) encouraging and stimulating improved methods of production of houses (George and Whittle 1992, p. 39).

Seven different housing solutions were proposed to the contributors:

* scheme units
* build on own land
* open market
* home improvement

* serviced lots
* mortgage certificates
* group financing

The NHT has had increasing difficulties during the macroeconomic situation causing the price of housing to rise at a greater rate than other consumer goods because of the high level of imported material required. It rose more rapidly than the income level of Jamaicans which in constant dollars has been decreasing. It has had to shift to a higher-income group of beneficiaries over the last 12 years—a situation which has caused certain criticism. It has been able to maintain as its beneficiaries households in income groups in proportion to the income groups of the contributors. If any group is overrepresented it is the next to lowest-income group and not the highest-income group it has been accused of supporting (George and Whittle 1992). Another criticism aimed at the NHT from those who believe in IMF liberalism is that:

NHT interest rates distort the market place by introducing imbalances. These imbalances lead to inefficiency in the allocation of funds and funds are attracted by the cheaper cost of NHT loans (Klak 1992, p. 73).

George and Whittle agree that there is some truth in this criticism and believe that the interest rates should go up for the higher level beneficiaries but they object strenuously to the elimination of housing subsidies for the lower-income beneficiaries.

For a low-income person...a subsidy on housing should be seen as no different from a subsidy offered to the 'productive' sector. Furthermore, many low-income contributors cannot *even now* afford the heavily subsidized loans *even if interest rates were at zero*. It may well be that even *higher* subsidies are necessary for the truly low-income households (George and Whittle 1992, p. 43).

The debate on the appropriateness of housing subsidies is an indication of the impact of IMF and World Bank policy in Jamaica. Subsidies in other social sectors such as health and education have been reduced as a result and there is much fear that the housing sector will undergo the same fate.

Quite a few of the countries in the Caribbean have programs that attempt to regulate squatter settlements by providing land tenure, infrastructure, and services where in return the squatters agree to pay for the land and the services received. In Trinidad and Tobago, having promised large-scale regularization of squatter settlements in 1977, the government finally introduced legislation to this effect in 1981 and in 1986. It was modified again in 1989, as the first legislation had several weaknesses, one of the main ones being that it dealt with individuals and not the whole community (Glenn, Labossiere and Wolfe 1992). The 1989 legislation was designed 'to encourage community involvement and self-help in the ongoing development of an established squatter community' (p. 7). Tenure was granted and the physical infrastructure upgraded wherever it was deemed possible in return for long-term or short-term leases of the land. The latest legislation is an improvement over the others. However, the Canadian team studying its implementation has indicated that there are still problems that come under the following headings:

a) *legal impediments* to the acquisition of the land;
b) *planning standards* that are too demanding;
c) *community resources* which need to be supported by the government in the form of material and equipment;
d) *political will*: If squatter regularization is to be effective, the difficulties being experienced with the present program will have to be resolved, and this will require major governmental commitment (Glenn, Labossiere and Wolfe 1992, p. 14).

Political will, that is, the energy political leaders put into solving a problem, is, indeed, a major factor in achieving results.

CONCLUSION: THE FUTURE OF THESE SETTLEMENTS

These strategies consist very often of putting a finger in a small hole at one end of a dike that is caving in at the other end. Improvements are made in some parts of a town while at the same time many more zones become run-down and overcrowded and the other terrain not suited for habitation is squatted. The few actions taken are swallowed up by the enormity of the problem. Improving housing conditions is a battle against the present trends.

Not enough attention is paid to the roots of the problem which is not only a question of housing but is, of course, related to more general societal problems: poverty, unemployment, very low wages, etc. Strategies which do not deal with the whole society will only work as stop-gaps. Housing cannot be improved as long as the economic situation of a population is being undermined by local and international factors. On the other hand, improvement of housing should coincide with efforts of economic development and should even become part of the efforts.

While poverty is the fundamental cause of poor housing, more immediate causes are both of a local and an international nature. If basically slums and squatter settlements are the result of a formal housing market that excludes a large percentage of the population, or in other words, an insolvent demand for decent housing, there are many other factors involved: the high price of land and construction, inefficient or inappropriate planning regulations and building codes, scarce credit, severe inflation, an exorbitant foreign debt causing devaluation, and scarcity of cheap construction material. Above all, is a lack of commitment on the part of the leaders to deal with these obstacles.

The government strategies that have discussed have often been effective but they only reach a small part of the poorly housed population. Institutions for financing housing similar to the National Housing Trust in Jamaica need to be created or enlarged and their credit open to nonsalaried people. Major government commitment to programs of upgrading squatter settlements and urban slums and providing low cost serviced lots for new buildings for the lowest-income bracket is needed. Local organizations should be encouraged to address the question as part of an economic development program. Technical assistance and affordable materials should be provided. Very often, government policies are related to 'port barrel' politics and serve a narrow clientele at the expense of the poorest groups. Destructive actions, such as 'political tribalism' need to be vigorously denounced.

The international economic situation of these small island states has a direct impact on the local housing market and in particular, their obligation to abide by the rigid dictates of the International Monetary Fund concerning housing subsidies and state run Urban Development Corporations. Rather than oblige the weaker states to swallow a medicine which the larger states are not ready to take concerning subsidies for certain sectors of the society, the international community should develop strategies whereby the improvement of housing and the urban environment contributes to the economic development and the well-being of low-income communities. The international lending institutions should lead the way and open up low cost credit to the economically weakest households by making loans available for local NGOs who will be responsible for overseeing the repayment. The industrialized countries should lead the way by providing this sort of loan and developing policy to eliminate homelessness and slums. Housing will remain a serious social problem until the international community and the governments transform their attitude and treat it as a major concern.

REFERENCES

Coit, K. 1988. *Housing and Development in the Lesser Antilles.* Human Settlements and Socio-Cultural Environments Series No. 40. New York: UNESCO.

Francis-Hinds, S. and J. Jones. 1989. *Initiatives in Low Income Housing: A Resource Manual.* Kingston: The Association of Development Agencies.

Glenn, J., R. Labossiere, and J. Wolfe. 1992. 'Squatter Regularization: Problems and Prospects'. Paper presented at the 5th Conference on Housing, Montreal.

Gregory-Jones, David and Alicia Taylor. 1992. Interviews with UDC staff (April).

George, Vincent and Shelley Whittle. 1992. *Jamaica's NHT: Its Attempt at Addressing Housing Affordability and a Brief Comment on Environmental Impact.* Kingston: Roneo.

Isaacs, Nadine. 1989. 'The History of Sites and Services and Squatter Upgrading in Jamaica', *Housing and Finance.* Kingston: The Building Societies Association of Jamaica.

————. 1992. Personal interview (April).

Ishmael, Len. 1991. 'Urbanization Dynamics in the Eastern Caribbean', *Cities 9(4),* pp. 371-89.

Klak. 1992. In V. George and S. Whittle, *Jamaica's NHT: Its Attempt at Addressing Housing Affordability and a Brief Comment on Environmental Impact.* Kingston: Roneo.

McLeod, Ruth. 1988. *Shelter Experiences of Female Heads of Household in Kingston* (draft). Kingston: UNCHS.

UDC. 1981. *Fern Grove Housing Scheme* (February). Kingston: United Development Corporation.

8

Squatter Settlements and Slums in Brazil: Twenty Years of Research and Policy

Suzana Pasternak Taschner

Brazilian economic growth, since the 1950s, has been based on industrial expansion, with a lesser growth of agricultural activities. In the 1930s, the federal government started a policy of transferring resources from the agro-exporter sector to the industrial sector. It also started to govern the capital/work relationship. From this time on the cities, especially in the Southeast–South region, became the industry seats. The Brazilian industrial complex, located on the Rio–Sao Paulo axis, started to receive increasing amounts of population. The urbanization ratio increased from 36.2 percent in 1950 to 75.5 percent in 1991. Population projections indicate that by the year 2,000 the Brazilian population living in urban areas should reach 136 million people or 80 percent of the total population.

It is worth mentioning that until the 1970s the Brazilian population grew at quite high rates: around 3.96 percent per year between 1950 and 1970. In the 1970s, the overall populational growth rate dropped to 2.48 percent per year, a 15 percent drop. In the 1980s, the strong reduction of fertility reduced the populational growth rate to 1.89 percent annually between 1980 and 1991, a 24 percent drop. Forecasts of 170 million Brazilians in 1990 did not come true and the total number of people reached only 146 million. However, this growth was entirely urban. The rural population has decreased in absolute numbers since 1980. Between 1980 and 1991, this decrease reached 2.6 million. Thus, both the increment of 25.8 million Brazilians in 1970 and 1989, and the increment of 27.1 million between 1980 and 1991 were entirely urban.

Until 1980, this growth was not only urban but it was also concentrated in cities with over 500,000 inhabitants, and, especially in the metropolitan regions: between 1970 and 1980, 41 percent of the total increase of the Brazilian population was located in the nine Brazilian metropolitan regions. Sao Paulo, in the southeast of Brazil, grew by 2.6 million people (17.2 percent of the Brazilian growth during the period) in the 1970s.

The 1980s show a diversion in metropolitan growth. The urban growth rate is still higher than the total rate (2.96 percent), but it is lower than the previous decade (4.44 percent). The share of the metropolitan growth in the total drops dramatically. Instead of 41 percent achieved in the 1970s, only 28.8 percent of the 27 million new Brazilians lived in the metropolis between 1980 and 1981. For the first time we see in Brazil the phenomenon of metropolitan deconcentration, already known in South America and in Europe.

Both slums (*corticos*) and squatter settlements (*favelas*) in Brazil, are an urban metropolitan issue. According to the data from the 1980[1] Census, almost 80 percent of the squatter population is concentrated in the metropolitan regions. There are also squatter settlements in smaller cities: according to the Brazilian Institute of Geography and Statistics (IBGE), out of the 126 Brazilian municipalities that presented squatter settlements in 1980, 40 had an urban population below 50,000 inhabitants. They were found especially in the states of Ninas Gerais (southeast) and Rio Grande do Sul (south). Poverty and the associated ways of living appear primarily in large cities.

According to IBGE data, 2.25 million Brazilians lived in squatter settlements in 1980, i.e., about 2.8 percent of the urban population and 1.9 percent of the total population. After adjusting the possible underestimation in the IBGE data, the number of squatters in 1980 increased to 3.04 million, representing 3.8 percent of the urban population and 2.6 percent of the total Brazilian population. Information for 1991 is not yet available. It is thought that this percentage has increased, considering the economic crisis that permeated the 1980s. The low performance of the Brazilian economy was translated into an annual decrease of –0.5 percent per inhabitant in the gross domestic product (GDP) between 1981 and 1990. The performance did not improve in 1991 and 1992 and the total GDP dropped by –1.08 from January to September 1992, with a sharper drop in the processing industry where it reached –11.10 percent. Minimum wage lost 46 percent of its real value in the 1980s and the income concentration is amazing: 7 percent of the wealthy population held 14.8 percent of the national income in 1990. The deterioration of the monetary basis is translated into an accrued inflation of 1150 percent during the year of 1992, which corrodes the currency, wages, and purchasing power.

POPULAR HOUSING FORMS

The forms of popular housing prevailing for low-income groups in Brazil vary according to the city and the period of time. For every local and each period a specific housing type dominated which also influenced the urban design. Three basic historic types are the most important: slums (tenements), squatter settlements (illegal occupation of lands) and 'peripheric low-income housing tracts'.

In Rio de Janeiro and Sao Paulo, the first manifestations of massive lack of housing can be found as early as the second half of the last century, and they lasted until around the 1930s. They correspond to the beginning of urbanization and industrialization, of great transformations in the economic, political, and cultural structures, as well as of the spatial structures. Among them are the abolition of slavery (1888), consequent expansion of paid work, the emergence of large markets and trade posts, decadence of the coffee-based economy, the implementation of industry, and a new political definition, with the abolition of the Empire and the proclamation of the Republic (1889). At the same time an accelerated growth of the Southeast cities occurred. Rio de Janeiro, for instance, had 235,000 inhabitants in 1870, which by 1890 had already increased to 522,000 (4.07 percent rate per year). Sao Paulo was smaller, and grew with more intensity one decade later: in 1872 it had 31,000 inhabitants and in 1890, 65,000, but it reached 240,000 in 1900 and 579,000 in 1920 (6.26 percent rate per year in these 48 years).

A large number of freed slaves as well as foreign immigrants arrived in the city looking for housing and jobs; especially jobs close to downtown. In the beginning of the century, the urban structure was characterized by the agglomeration of activities and people around the downtown area. Gradually these spaces became commercial, industrial, and residential areas. It was in this central area that the first tenements for the poor population were established.[2] For Rio de Janeiro, Vaz (1985) estimates that during this period 20 to 25 percent of the population lived in these inadequate tenements with reduced spaces, poor infrastructures, overcrowdedness, and sanitary services in common. In Sao Paulo, estimates indicate about 20 percent of the municipality population lived in slums during the 1930s.

Urban reforms in Rio de Janeiro during the first decade of this century, with the opening of broad avenues, and central urban renovation, expelled violently the dwellers from the downtown slums. According to Pfeiffer and Vaz (1992), the remodelling of the city of Rio de Janeiro by its Mayor, Pereira Passos, (considered a tropical Haussmann) in 1904–06, led to the demolition of about 550 old buildings. The subsequent relocation of the poor population to the hills, typical of Rio de Janeiro's topography, marked the beginning of the acceleration of the squatter process in Rio de Janeiro.

Although Sao Paulo's downtown was also subject to the beautifying and sanitizing plans, its spatial structure was more affected by the decision, in the 1930s, for a specific choice of public transportation and urban structure. In the second half of the 1930s, two plans for the remodelling of the urban roads appeared: the Light Project (1927) and the Avenues Plan (1930). Each of them was based on a different concept of the city. The Light Project (Light was the company that supplied electrical power to the city) proposed a system of collective transportation by tramways, a moderate extension of rails and even a presubway project, with tramways running by underground tunnels in a 5 km radius from the historical center of the downtown. This would have resulted in a denser city, and in conserving population strata of different purchasing power around the center. At this point in 1914, the gross demographic density of the urbanized area of the municipality was 110 inhabitants per hectare. The Avenues Plan, proposed by the city Mayor, Prestes Maia, intended to renovate the central area and to expand the urban network with nonestablished limits, through highway axes and privileged transportation by bus.

The choice of the Avenues Plan and the opening of new roads provided access to areas that were not inhabited until then. This expansion of the urban network was associated with population growth, better transportation (there was a great increase in number of urban buses), and the action of real estate developers. The result was the dividing of the peripheral lands of the area at an impressive speed, the populist interventions of the federal government in the Tenants' Law, freezing rents, and discouraging investment in housing. This combination of variables made the urbanized network of Sao Paulo extend by means of the tripod—peripheral allotment—homeownership—self-help construction. According to Lagenest (1962), approximately 18 percent of the Sao Paulo population lived in these popular type of rented houses. The decades of 1940s and 1950s were marked by an incredible expansion of the city towards the periphery; continuing at a slightly less intensive rate until the 1980s. By 1991, the gross demographic density of the municipality of Sao Paulo was lower than in 1914: 63 inhabitants per hectare.

Therefore, for the two largest Brazilian cities, the first mass housing for the poor populations was the slum. In Rio de Janeiro, illegal squattering of lands in the hills, frequently tolerated and even encouraged, was the next alternative. In the decade of 1910, the Rio press already pointed out the proliferation of squatter settlements.[3] In Sao Paulo, the prevailing alternative until mid-1975 was the construction of private houses in peripheric allotments. Although these allotments were frequently irregular in relation to municipal laws, the land was legally commercialized and these were not squatters.

One cannot affirm that there were no squatter settlements in Sao Paulo. Apparently the first squatter settlements in Sao Paulo appeared in the 1940s. Research done by the now extinct Division of Statistics and Documentation of the City of Sao Paulo shows that in 1950, there was a squatter settlement in the eastern region with 245 people and one in the western region with 1,000 people, in addition to others such as the one in Vila Prudente which still exists. But the phenomenon of squatter settlements was not fully developed in Sao Paulo until the second half of 1970s.

Belo Horizonte is the third largest metropolis of the southern region. In 1991, the Belo Horizonte metropolitan region had 3.48 million inhabitants, with 2.05 living in its central municipal core. The issue of squatter settlements dates from the city's construction. Implemented in 1895 to become the political and administrative center of the state of Minas Gerais, it already had two squatter areas with approximately 3,000 people two years before its inauguration (Guimaraes 1992, p. 2). Just as what happened later in Brasilia, squatting was a consequence of not providing a place to house the employees in charge of its construction. The civil construction workers were seen as temporary but they did not leave when the city was completed.

Then, repeating the stages undergone earlier by Rio de Janeiro and Sao Paulo, little by little the *favelas* were expelled to the periphery. The accelerated growth of the population, starting in the 1940s, was accompanied by the growth in the number of *favelas*, which started to occupy more and more distant areas close to the neighboring municipalities. The percentage of squatters in the municipal population increased: in 1950, it was estimated at 7.1 percent but by 1991, it reached almost 20 percent or approximately 400,000 squatters. Although there are peripheral developments in Belo Horizonte, the *favela* has always been the prevailing choice of housing for the poor population there, and this provided the municipality with a pioneering experience in interventions.

In Salvador, the largest metropolitan region in the northeastern region comprising 2.06 million of the 2.47 million inhabitants in the region in 1991, the housing history is different from the history of Belo Horizonte. Salvador is one of the oldest cities in Brazil and its capital was built during the Colonial period. By 1940, with the decay of the agro-exporting economy there was a high rate of rural immigration and a huge demand for housing in the city. Its population increased from 298,000 inhabitants in 1940 to 417,000 in 1950. Prior to that there was a predominance in the housing system, of the emphytheusis of lands and rent of houses, especially for the medium- and low-income population that occupied the slums in the degraded central areas. The city had inherited an ancient land system called the emphytheusis[4] wherein the actual land remained in the hands of a few large owners who blocked the sale of land in the land market (Gordilho 1992). This factor led to organized collective land occupations in Salvador in the 1940s. Between 1946 and 1950, there were 26 invasions occupying around 253 hectares. The land squatting system continues to this date, both through programed collective squattering and by individual and gradual invasions. In 1990, according to Gordilho (1992) there were 357 squattered settlements in Salvador occupying an area of 1,473 hectares with an estimated population of 591 people or 30 percent of the municipal population.

Housing has been one of the main problems of Brasilia since the beginning of construction of this new city. The Nucleo Bandeirante, then called Free City, was planned to house the workers constructing this entirely planned and completely isolated new capital in the Brazilian central plateau. This settlement, in accordance with the original plan, was to be extinguished upon Brasilia's inauguration.

Already by the end of 1958, when the constructions of new buildings in the Free City were banned, the squatters and illegal constructions proliferated, and besides the building site camps, they became housing alternatives for the workers that came to the city (Jaccoud 1991, p. 147).

In the face of growing resistance to the removal of the local populace to the satellite cities, the establishment and urbanization of the Free City was decided in 1960. This urbanization and the creation of the satellite cities were insufficient to house the workers who came to the city looking for job opportunities.

In contrast with the temporary character of the worksite camps and squatterings, the satellite cities were an official initiative, with a special focus, and their implementation follows certain plans and designs (Resende 1991, p. 218).

The creation of these centers was anticipated by official city planners but was to be implemented at a further stage when the Pilot Plan population had already reached the established limit of 500,000 to 700,000 inhabitants. However, the lesson of Belo Horizonte had not been absorbed. Similar to what had happened there, the population of those who built the city remained there, creating the same problem of how and where to house them. In 1958, prior to the inauguration of Brasilia and in addition to the urbanization of Free City, now called Nucleo Bandeirante, the satellite city of Taguatinga was built to absorb squatters in the Pilot Plan urban network. In 1959, Sobradinho, another satellite city was created, and in 1961, the satellite city of Gama came into being. Ceilandia was created in 1971 with the same idea of absorbing squatters. Its name also reveals the same as it is derived from the acronym CEI: Campanha de Erradicacao de Invasoes (Squattering Eradication Campaign).

The satellite cities did not prevent the appearance of new squatter settlements (*favelas*). One example is the Vila Parano with almost 40,000 inhabitants in 1989, which originated from a camp of workers who built the Brasilia Lake dam in 1957 (Paviani 1988). Another *favela*, Vila Planalto, situated strategically between the Planalto Palace (Government seat) and the Alvorada Palace (President's living quarters) with less population, shows the hard face of the fight for land in a city planned by urbanistic rationality.

Housing for the poor strata in Brasilia was located in the periphery, in the satellite cities. The Pilot Plan, which included infrastructure, green areas, and good living conditions, remained in the hands of the most privileged social layers. Although there are a few *favelas* in the central areas, besides Vila Paranoa and Vila Planalto, e.g., Vila dos Carroceiros, Areal, and 110 Norte, it is likely that they will be removed since they are not very populated. In the satellite cities the infrastructure is deficient and the subdivision of lots with the rent of several units in the same lot, forming a real slum, is the most frequent housing alternative. The population of the satellite cities grows faster than that of the Pilot Plan: they represented 65 percent of the federal district population in 1970 and in 1991 they reached approximately 75 percent.

To sum it up, one can see that in the various Brazilian cities like Rio de Janeiro, Sao Paulo, Belo Horizonte, Salvador, and Brasilia, the housing types of the poor population show a specific evolution. Rio de Janeiro, Sao Paulo, and Salvador present slums in the beginning of the century. In Rio, *favelas* appear after the slums as a hegemonic housing way for the poor. In Sao Paulo, peripheral developments prevail and *favelas* have grown in the last 20 years. In Salvador, conditions connected to the land structure and rural immigration made the city the 'locus' of the first large organized collective squatting in the 1940s. Belo Horizonte and Brasilia, both planned cities, expel their poor to the periphery: Belo Horizonte in a spontaneous way by means of *favelas* and Brasilia in an organized way, through the construction of satellite cities. An additional but constant feature in large Brazilian cities is housing segregation. It is a result of both the real estate market that makes land in urbanized areas inaccessible for the low-income population and of the action of government as clearly evidenced in the case of Brasilia.

MAIN CHARACTERISTICS:
EXTENT AND PATTERN IN BRAZIL

Squatter Settlements

Data from 1980 with the underestimation introduced by IBGE, show a total of 1,780,000 squatters in the nine Brazilian metropolitan regions (Belem, in the north; Fortaleza, Recife, and Salvador in the northeast; Belo Horizonte,

Rio de Janeiro, and Sao Paulo, in the southeast; and Curitiba and Porto Alegre in the south). As already mentioned, 80 percent of the Brazilian squatter population was concentrated in the metropolitan regions. This means that, in 1980, 5.6 percent of the urban population of the Brazilian metropoles lived in *favelas*. The percentages are higher in Fortaleza, where they reached 11.4 percent and lower in Curitiba, with 1.5 percent. In the northern and northeastern regions, the entire squatter population is concentrated in metropoles. There is no record of squatting in smaller cities. In the southeastern and southern metropoles, although the weight of the metropolitan squatters in the total number of squatters in each state is always above 70 percent, the phenomenon of *favela* has already been reproduced at many places in the urban network. This is especially true for the most dynamic cities such as Campinas. It is a highly industrialized municipality in the state of Sao Paulo with a population of approximately 850,000. In 1991, it had over 6 percent of its urban population living in *favelas*. Cubatao, an industrial center in the Baixada Santista, had almost 20 percent of its urban population living in *favelas* in 1980.

These percentages should be higher for 1992. The 1980s' crisis impoverished the Brazilian society with a strong impact on all aspects of urban life. Even the underestimated data from IBGE indicate, for Sao Paulo, a growth in the squatter population of 6.2 percent annually,[5] compared to a total growth of 1 percent for the total population during the same period.

In the municipality of Sao Paulo, the existence of a *favela* file, which is periodically updated, permits a better estimate and characterization of both domiciles and population. In 1987, 1,592 squatter settlements were computed with over 150,000 domiciles and a population of 812,800 people. This figure is higher than the figure presented by IBGE in 1991: 629 squatter settlements with an estimated population of 647,200 people and 142,800 domiciles. The estimated population projected for 1991 of those living in *favelas* was 1,071,000 people; 11.3 percent of the local population in 1805 settlements.

If we accept the veracity of the population figures given in the municipal file, there is clear evidence of the deterioration of the quality of life in the largest Brazilian industrial metropolis: the Sao Paulo population increased by 987,000 people between 1980 and 1991. The squatter population, during the same period, increased by approximately 600,000. About 60 percent of the population growth in Sao Paulo is due to the increase in the number of squatters. Until the 1970s, the city was one of the few Latin American capitals without *favelas*. In 1973, only 1.09 percent of the population lived in this type of a settlement. In 1987, this figure reached 8.92 percent and in 1991, it was over 11 percent. Table 8.1 shows that the absolute number of people in Sao Paulo living in *favelas* is higher than that of Rio's.

The highest increment in the number of *favelas* occurred in the 1970s when 823 *favelas* appeared; 52 percent of the total stock of *favelas* in the municipality in 1987. During the 1980s, until December 1987, there were 353 new *favelas* formed in the urban network; 22 percent of the total of the 1,592 squatter settlements filed in 1987. Between 1987 and 1991, new squatter settlements were noticed around the periphery of the city in addition to the densification of the existing *favelas*.

Table 8.1: Growth of the Squatter Population in the Municipalities of Sao Paulo and Rio de Janeiro

Year	Rio de Janeiro Population			Sao Paulo Population		
	Squatter	*Total*	*%*	*Squatter*	*Total*	*%*
1950	169,305	2,336,000	7.2	–	2,198,096	
1960	335,063	3,307,167	10.1	–	3,666,701	
1970	554,277	4,285,738	13.0	–	5,924,615	
1973	595,974	4,513,369	13.2	71,840	6,590,826	1.1
1975	625,500	4,671,800	13.4	117,237	7,327,312	1.6
1980	705,874	5,090,700	13.8	439,721	8,493,226	5.2
1987	844,706	5,245,921	16.1	812,764	9,108,854	8.9
1991	935,979	5,336,176	17.5	1,071,288	9,480,427	11.3

Source: Veras and Taschner (1990).

The enormous growth of the *favelas* in the municipality of Sao Paulo did not occur evenly throughout the city. They grew mainly in the southern zone of the municipality. In 1973, the southern quadrant held 29 percent of the squatter domiciles. In 1987, it held 48 percent. Half of Sao Paulo's *favelas* are located on the banks of the reservoirs that supply water to the city. This puts public health at risk, since the squatters throw their wastes directly into the reservoir or into the brooks that supply water to it. Systems for quality control of the municipal water network have had numerous problems in the last few years. In addition to increasing water chlorination to prevent enteric diseases, they can hardly control algae proliferation since it grows enormously with the accumulation of organic material. Thirty percent of city dwellers who drink water coming from the Guarapiranga dam are forced to live with the strangest tastes, depending on the algae and the algicide used: BHC, mildew, clay, etc.

If, on the one hand, the increase of the squatter population in Sao Paulo is staggering, on the other hand, one cannot deny that there has been a relative improvement in living conditions: built area per domicile grew on average from 16.2 sq m in 1973 to 28.9 sq m in 1987. The percentage of domiciles with dirt floors decreased from 46.3 percent to 7.4 percent. Surface per inhabitant increased from 3.9 sq m in 1973 to 5.7 sq m in 1987. The change in the profile of the prevailing construction type is amazing. In 1973, 1.3 percent were in masonry and in 1980 the figure was 2.4 percent. But by 1987, 50.5 percent of the squatter houses had external walls made of brick or concrete blocks. Houses replaced the shacks, evidencing the most visible qualitative change in the squatter dwellings. The increase of 48.1 percentage points in masonry domiciles in the 1980s, reflects higher investment by dwellers in their houses. The fear of removals decreased significantly with a shift flexibility of the housing policies in handling squatters and the action of social groups in their struggle for housing. Upgrading settlements whenever possible became the prevailing policy. Together with greater awareness, both on the part of the dweller and of the public branches, the *favela* is no longer temporary housing. It is likely that a *favela* dweller has already perceived that it will be a long-term domicile or even a definitive one.

The programs of *favelas* upgrading, in force since 1979 in the municipality of Sao Paulo, resulted in 98 percent of the squatter dwellings being connected to the public electric power network (compared to 65 percent in 1980), 72.5 percent having suitable garbage disposal and 92 percent having access to public water supply. On the other hand, the lack of basic sanitation did not improve very much with 56 percent of the dwellings disposing of their sewage outdoors and/or directly into brooks and reservoirs. Although the percentage of squatter domiciles connected to the public sewer network has grown from less than 1 percent in 1973 to 19.3 percent in 1987, the enormous mass of domiciles that dispose of the domestic sewages directly into the soil or into the water system is frightening—there are over 110,000 dwellings.

It would be an exaggeration to say that a process that has been called urban spoliation has decreased. Poverty is still present. But squatters' living conditions have doubtlessly improved since they now have access to electric power, water at minimum tariffs, and garbage collection.

The *favela* appears to be the physical expression of the urban contradictions of a poor society, where the little wealth it has is concentrated in the hands of a few. It is the last housing resource for over one million people in the largest South American metropolis. In 1949, surveys conducted in the few *favelas* existing at the time pointed out that 'they were not an agglomeration of bums, but of poor workers'. The squatter population is that part of the urban poverty of Sao Paulo which chose to live in a *favela* as a feasible survival strategy. In demographic terms, their population is younger than the municipality population as a whole: 46 percent of the squatters are less than 14 years old, while the proportion of young people for the municipality is 32 percent. In 1980, 57.3 percent of the active family heads worked in the secondary sector, especially in the processing industry. In 1987, accompanying the tertiary trend in the city, 47 percent of family heads were employed in trade and services.

The relationship between squatting and migration holds, but the growth of *favelas* is greater and it is not due exclusively to migration flows. The large majority of family heads are migrants (87 percent in 1987) but not recent ones: around 35 percent had previous housing experience in the city before living in a *favela*. In 1980, 28 percent came from rented houses; in 1987 this percentage increased.

Average family income in 1987 was 3.85 minimum wages (standard deviation of 2.63). Average income in 1973 was 1.2 the minimum wages and, in 1980, 2.2 times the minimum wages.[6] Even considering the minimum wage purchasing power drop (approximately 60 percent between 1977 and 1987), family income in 1987 is almost 17 percent above that of 1980.

How does one explain this apparent wealth of squatters? Population segments that previously had access to leasing houses or to buying lots in the periphery faced difficulties in 1980. They were left with the alternative of occupying a squattered lot. Medium-income strata were displaced to the periphery and tenants became squatters. Physical routes that express new trajectories of inequality.

Although *favelas* are currently an old phenomenon in Rio de Janeiro, data about the characteristics of these settlements and a socioeconomic profile of their residents are still missing. IBGE official data only divulged the number of settlements, their distribution in the metropolitan area and the total population, and total of domiciles inside each *favela*. The only agency that tried to collect regular data on *favelas* was Instituto de Planejamento do Rio de Janeiro (IPLAN-RIO) (Valladares and Ribeiro 1992). In 1981, by means of airphotographs the agency counted 460 settlements. This is a surprising figure since the 1980 census of the preceding year had counted only 192 *favelas*. As in Sao Paulo, the difference of counting criteria can be responsible for the disparity of information: the census only computes settlements above 50 domiciles, while IPLAN-RIO used the limit of 20 units. The census usually computes several continuous settlements as one settlement while IPLAN-RIO considers each *favela* individually. Population estimates also differ, but not so strongly: the estimate from IPLAN-RIO (used in Table 8.1) reports a total of 705,874 squatters or 13.8 percent of the municipal population in 1980. The census estimates 628 squatters or 12.3 percent of the population. The interpretation of the 1970s changes depending upon the estimates which are taken to be correct. According to IBGE figures, for the first time in several decades the squatter population grew at a lower rate than the total population: 1.08 percent annually compared to 1.74 percent

(Valladares and Ribeiro 1992). However, if the census figures are correct, how does one explain the partial removal of some *favelas* and the total removal of 80 between 1962 and 1978? In addition, during the 1970s a strong peripherization took place and many more of the poor population of Rio de Janeiro occupied the suburbs and satellite cities located at Baixada Fluminense. They used a process equivalent to that used in Sao Paulo decades before: self-help building of private houses in illegal peripheral low-income housing tracts. At the same time the *favelas* in the municipalities of the metropolitan region of Rio de Janeiro increased in number: 41 were added in 1970 and 66 in 1980 which represents an increase of 61 percent.

In 1991, IPLAN-RIO updated its counting, adding 545 *favelas*, or 85 new settlements in a ten year period. These data point out that 59 percent of the Rio de Janeiro *favelas* already existed before 1960, 22 percent appeared between 1961 and 1981, and 19 percent between 1981 and 1991. In population terms, the squatter population in Rio grew at a 2.6 percent rate yearly between 1980 and 1991, while the population of Rio de Janeiro as a whole increased at an annual rate of 0.43 percent.

These data seem to indicate a revival in the growth of the squatter population in the central municipality of the metropolitan region. According to data from IPLAN-RIO, in addition to the 85 new *favelas*, 69 of the existing ones expanded, 198 became denser and 167 both expanded and became denser. Only 26 (4.8 percent) remained as they were.

According to Valladares and Ribeiro (1992) this renewed takeoff of the *favelas* results from a combination of factors: the mushrooming of new *favelas*, the physical expansion of the existing *favelas*, and last, but not least, the densification of the already consolidated settlements. These three movements indicate the self-reproduction of *favelas* under different forms: the creation of new settlements or the expansion of the existing ones occurs because of the pressure of the land market inside the *favelas*, both due to the arrival of new poor people and the need to house the second and even the third generation of squatters. We can see side by side with the peripherization of Rio *favelas*, a verticalization of the oldest ones, where buildings with four to six stories appear, often for rent.

It is rather interesting to compare the housing routes of the poor in Sao Paulo and Rio de Janeiro. 1970 marks the greatest increment of *favelas* in Sao Paulo and the smallest in Rio. In the 1980s, both in Sao Paulo and Rio, the total population grew at a lower intensity (1 percent for Sao Paulo and 0.43 percent for Rio), but their squatter populations were largely responsible for the total population growth: 60 percent of the population differential between 1980 and 1991 was absorbed by the squatter population in Sao Paulo and 94 percent by the squatter population in Rio!

Favelas when compared with other alternatives are better located and equipped. Pauperization, as well as the downgrading process of low-medium class sectors brought new social groups to the *favela*. In the long-term perspective, this modified the traditional profile of the *favela* residents. What seemed to be a simple expression of socio-spatial segregation became a complex and intricate reality.

On Slums

The concept of slum does not have a consensus among the technicians who work on this subject. But different sources attribute to the slum a character that emphasizes poor housing; or a tenement where crowding and cohabitation can be found. The slum census, scheduled by the Sao Paulo local authorities for 1993 will use this operational definition. It will try not to lose sight of the endless range of poor tenements and go beyond the classic figure of the deteriorated old great house subdivided into a tenement with insufficient or common sanitary facilities, or a row of rooms along a sideroad with one single access to the street which was typical of slums that were built specifically for such a purpose.

Using the strict concept of derelict housing or a tenement with common sanitary facilities, information from the demographic census of 1980, revealed a total of approximately 182,000 domiciles (a domicile is defined here as the room[s] occupied by a household). This represents 10.03 percent of the municipality's housing stock. This figure, according to the strict operational definition, underestimates the phenomenon because many buildings designed or adapted to be slums present units with a room and private sanitary facilities without losing their characteristics of precariousness and crowding that defined slum housing.

Some estimates of the percentage of population living in slums in Sao Paulo are as follows: Lagenest (1961) estimated that in 1961, 18 percent of the city's population lived in slums concentrated in the downtown. In 1975, the Welfare Department studying the phenomenon based on Property Income data estimated that 9.3 percent of the population lived in slums (Sao Paulo Municipio 1975). The most recent estimates mentioned in the Immediate Action Plan for the Housing and Urban Development Secretary (Sao Paulo Municipio 1989) that 28 percent of the population in Sao Paulo lived in slum tenements. This amounts to around 3 million inhabitants who are distributed among 820,000 families occupying around 88,000 buildings. Although the 1989 study tried to estimate the entire population living in tenements, the disparity between the various estimates indicates that the phenomenon, unlike the information on *favelas*, is little researched and even less known.

Contrary to what happened at the beginning of the century, the poor tenements are no longer located mainly in the central zones with good infrastructure and close to the workplace. Data from the 1980 census showed that 23 percent of the tenements with common sanitary facilities were located in the central and interior belts of the municipality while 60 percent were located in the peripheral and external belt. This information shows the remarkable presence of the slums in the periphery. As mentioned in previous studies (Bonduki and Rolnik 1979; Pasternak and Mautner 1992; Kowarick and Ant 1985) the self-builder frequently builds a row of cubicles served by a single bathroom on the land left after the building is finished. These housing 'arrangements' which show the working class itself providing housing to its poorer members, explain the shocking proportion of more than one-third of the domiciles rented in the peripheric belt using a collective bathroom.

The situation of the tenants living in the peripheral fringes of the city is disturbing. Very often they pay relatively high rents for rooms in unhealthy houses with no infrastructure, and in badly equipped illegal developments with deficient public transportation. When the basic infrastructure begins to be implemented, or when 'the city arrives to the periphery', as pertinently put by Bogus (1980), they are very often the first to leave since they are not able to bear the increases in rent.

Although the presentation of comprehensive and reliable quantitative data for the municipality of Sao Paulo is problematic, the following conclusions can be drawn:

1. The proportion of the population living in this type of housing is increasing. The comparison of data of one room rented dwelling with collective use of bathroom between 1970 and 1980 showed an increase of 3.0 percent;

2. Even in the historical center there are indications that the population living in the classic slums of old, subdivided great houses increased in the 1980s;

3. The increase of children mortality rates in the central areas, with total coverage of water and sewers networks and due mainly to pneumonia is very often associated with bad living conditions;

4. Data from the Finance Secretary for 1985 showed that about 54 percent of the tenements were located at the city's intermediate belt and there are indications that this type of housing is moving towards the periphery.

What are the population characteristics of the residents of slum housing?

From the population viewpoint, it is a heterogenous group, consisting mainly of people working in the tertiary sector. There are also industry workers, daily workers that work in the vicinity of the slum, preferring to save transportation costs (Veras 1992, p. 114).

The most recent survey about a segment of the slum population in Sao Paulo was the pilot survey of the Pari section, in a central neighborhood of the municipality of Sao Paulo. Pari subdistrict has 275 hectares with a population of 21,900 people according to the preliminary data of the 1991 demographic census. That is a gross demographic density of 79.6 inhabitants per hectare. The subdistrict has been losing its resident population since 1960 when it had over 34,000 inhabitants. In 1970, it had a little more than 30,000 and in 1980, 27,700. The survey, conducted in June 1991, showed the existence of 101 slums. This was less than expected since there were over 200 in 1982. It is a rather poor urban zone, but it is under a gentrification process: many slums have become small apparel industry shops usually controlled by Korean immigrants.[7]

Pari has always been a poor neighborhood. It contains historic slums built before 1940. This is very different from Campos Eliseos, another neighborhood whose present slums are a result of the decay of this part of the urban network. It was the residence of the bourgeoisie in the 1920s. Today Pari has 2,221 people in its 101 slums representing 10.14 percent of the subdistrict population. They are joined by 849 households resulting in an average of 8.5 households per slum and 23 individuals per slum. The so-called comfort indicators show an average of 2.7 people per occupied room, 9.6 individuals per sanitary facility, and 10.3 individuals per shower. Around 71 percent of the households are core families of two to four people.

In relation to age structure, 32 percent are children up to 14 years of age. It is young population where only 11 percent are over 46 years of age. It is also a population with low levels of schooling as 9.3 percent of the people are illiterate. The level of open unemployment of the Pari slum population is similar to the municipality population as a whole, i.e., ten percent. Contrary to the idea that workers who live in slums make a living by working independently in the formal economy with lesser jobs, is the fact that 60 percent of them are registered workers. They walk to their working places; a fact that shows the importance of the house location. A surprising datum is the permanence of the family heads in this type of housing: 27 percent have always lived in slums since they arrived in Sao Paulo and 35 percent have lived in slums for over five years. It is worth mentioning that the large majority of family heads are migrants from the Brazilian northeast.

The average expenditure per household living in the Pari slums, including rent, water, and light, is 1.5 times the minimum wages (see note 6). The ownership of the housing is varied. There are owners who have built housing just for this purpose (especially in the periphery); there are those who adapted the property to this purpose; and there those who received the property as an inheritance under the express condition of not demolishing it. In many of the latter cases the neighborhood deteriorated and the heir did not want to occupy the house but could not demolish it. Room rental appears as a profitable choice. This category also includes owners who do not invest in the property because they do not have the capital required to change its use (the area is zoned so as not to allow verticalization). There are also those owners who collect some income by renting rooms while they wait for the land to become more valuable and then demolish it to build a skyscraper.

The slum itself is illegal only when it violates the sanitation code which regulates ventilation, lighting, size of rooms, and number of sanitary facilities, sinks, and showers (one bathroom and one toilet each for 20 people). It is forbidden to cook unless it is in a room designed for this activity with a minimum area of 7 sq. m. The slum first appeared with regulations in the first construction code of the municipality of Sao Paulo in 1886. The next construction code, named Artur Saboya (1921 and reviewed in 1934), contains an article where it is mentioned that infected and/or unhealthy slums shall not be permitted and should be rebuilt in accordance with the provisions related to multiple housing of the 'apartment class'. It accepts slums that are in accordance with the local laws. It does not permit the subdividing of large houses into tenements. The Construction Code of 1975, however, ignores the slums. It regulates only boarding houses and other types of family type housings where people remain for longer periods than in hotels.

One can perceive that the relationship between the slums and the law is ambiguous: slums do exist and frequently are not in agreement with the sanitation code. The local legislation ignored them until 1991 when the City Council through Law Number 10928 (8 January) tried to establish minimum housing conditions for the slums. The new regulations are similar to what had been done by the codes issued at the end of the last century. The alterations of the local law in Sao Paulo, with regard to slums and squatter settlements, reflect the change in the type of intervention proposed in the 1980s.

For Rio de Janeiro, there is information about collective housings from the middle of the last century to 1920. As the *favela* is the symbol of housing poverty in the 20th century, slums are the symbol of housing poverty in old Rio. The sanitary services regulations of the federal government, in a publication issued on 8 March 1904, characterize unhealthy housings of collective nature as *avenidas*, inns, slums, hostels, lodges, tenements, boarding houses and hotels (Vaz 1985). The important point in this work is to characterize the permanent nature of this type of housing: slums, inns, tenements, and *avenidas*.

Inns were a succession of rooms or small houses along a pateo/corridor with sanitary facilities (when they existed) at the back or in the corridor. Slums, in the beginning, were deteriorated inns. Later on, the name was generalized to include tenements in bad conditions.

The old *senzala* or slave quarters, present a remarkable analogy with the inns: a succession of rooms in row, with access only through one side, communicating by means of a passageway or veranda:

> The comparison of plans points out to so many similarities, that the only difference is the position of the key in the lock: in the *senzala*, the door is locked from the outside, in the inn, from the inside. This is an architectural symbol of the difference in the social relationships or production, at two different times: in the first, the worker belongs to the master who protects him at night for a new working journey; in the second, the worker is his own master, and uses the condition of being a free man—selling his working force—for which he protects himself until the new working journey (Vaz 1985, p. 71).

The *avenida* was an improved inn with water and sewers system. Very often complete little houses were aligned along the *avenida* corridor. In the first legislation related to this matter, in the mid-1880s, certain sanitation parameters were established for the *avenidas*, e.g., water-closets should follow the proportion of one for 35 inhabitants. In 1896, local regulations demanded that each little house should have its own privy, tank, and kitchen.

Tenements were houses divided internally into the largest possible number of divisions. As to the evolution of these types of housing in the city of Rio de Janeiro, the authors are unanimous in stating that until 1855, the inns expanded freely, both downtown and near the port. When the end of the century came closer, the press and reports of sanitation experts made the first accusations which induced public authorities to try to regulate collective housing. Finally, it was forbidden to build them and in the beginning of the century, the urban renewal undergone by Rio de Janeiro eradicated the majority of the inns and tenements.

In quantitative terms, data from Pimentel (Vaz 1985) point to 642 slums in 1969, which would represent 3.1 percent of the housing stock in Rio, with 9,671 rooms and/or little houses, sheltering 21,900 inhabitants or about 9.6 percent of the city's population. In 1881, slums reached the number of 1,331 or about 40 percent of the total of buildings, with 18,866 rooms and/or little houses and 46,700 dwellers or approximately 9 percent of the total population. In 1910, the only datum is of 3,145 slums, with estimates that they sheltered 25 to 30 percent of the population of Rio. In 1920, the effects of the slum clearance are reflected in the number and type of collective housing: slums drop to 2,967. Inns, where poverty was exposed outdoors, practically disappeared. Slums in tenements covered 90 percent of rented collective housings.

The poor population, suffering from the effects of the urbanistic legislation that governed both the constructions downtown and in the periphery, occupied the nongoverned space par excellence—the *favela*. Dialectically, the control over the space generated its own denial.

After 1920, there is no information about rented collective housings in Rio de Janeiro. There are indications of a reversal of the peripheral pattern in force in the 1970s when the poor population occupied the Baixada Fluminense. Recent data from Light Electric Supply Company, indicate a population growth in the central area of Rio de Janeiro (Pfeiffer and Vaz 1992). Light's surveys show a population consisting of a small minority of middle class young members (artists, students, intellectuals,) and a large segment of low-income groups. In addition, the homeless also occupied the central areas.

Urban renewal, connected with historic revitalization projects, started very shyly. One of the best known projects is the 'Cultural Corridor'. The recommendations connected to protection of the historical buildings, however, are more at the level of discourse than at the intervention practice level.

Two contradictory trends live together in the central area of Rio de Janeiro: the valorization and recovery of historical buildings, and the decay that will be followed by a growing number of slums and of homeless people.

STRATEGIES TO AMELIORATE THE CONDITIONS IN THESE SETTLEMENTS AND THEIR CRITIQUES

Policies related to population housing in Brazil, and especially those related to squatter settlements and slums were highly centralized at the federal level until 1984. It is not that local interventions did not exist. They have always existed, but until the extinction of the B.N.H. (Banco Nacional da Habitaao—National Housing Bank) in November 1986, they did not have the same relevance. After that date, autonomous and local solutions prevail. This article will outline the interventions at the federal level since the so-called populist time until the disarticulation of the national housing system during the New Republic (after the military government). Then it will detail the local solutions for some metropoles with special emphasis on Sao Paulo.

Policies at the Federal Level

One of the first interventions in popular housing in Brazil was in 1946 when the Popular House Foundation was implemented. The housing issue had not yet achieved the status of a crisis: that would only happen by the 1960s. From its foundation to its extinction in the early 1960s, this Foundation built only 4,879 houses in 12 states of the Federation. On the other hand, local governments were aware of the growth in the number of *favelas* and they had the illusion that they would be able to suppress spontaneous occupations of urban spaces by means of regulations and laws. In 1947, a Squatter Settlement Extinction Commission was created in Rio de Janeiro. The first census in the *favelas* of this city, held in January 1948, indicated almost 139,000 squatters. By July 1950, they amounted to 169,000 or 7.1 percent of the Rio population. In 1955, the Squatter Extinction Committee of Belo Horizonte completed a file of 35,000 dwellers of *favelas* (7.4 percent of the municipality's population). In 1951, the local authorities of Porto Alegre, located at the far south of the country, counted 56 squatter settlements that housed 54,000 people. Even in Sao Paulo, where the *favelas* became a problem only by the 1970s, 141 settlements had been identified in 1957 with approximately 8,500 shacks and a population of approximately 50,000 people (1.8 percent of the municipality population) (FINEP-GAP 1985).

Once the existence of this amount of squatter population in the major Brazilian cities became evident, the federal government in September 1956, issued the *Favelas* Law. Through this law several municipalities were able to get credit lines for services with a view to improve squatter housing conditions. This is the case of the Social 21 Service Against 'Mocambo', in Recife, of the Popular Housing Department of the Federal District (DHP, Rio de Janeiro), and of Cruzada Sao Sebastiao which resulted from an agreement between the Catholic Church and the Municipality of Rio de Janeiro in 1955.

Until 1960, an overview of the actions taken, especially in Rio de Janeiro, clearly shows the lack of a defined line of action with regard to the *favelas*. On the one hand Cruzada Sao Sebastiao tended to urbanize the existing *favelas*. Between 1955 and 1960, it conducted upgrading at the level of basic services in 12 *favelas*, executed 51 lighting network projects, completely upgraded one *favela* and partially upgraded another one, built the Cruzada at Praia do Pinto—the first and only experience of lodging inside the *favela* itself—, and intervened before the administration against the eviction of three *favelas* in the city (Valladares 1978, p. 23).

On the other hand, local authorities prepared through the *Favelas* Law a project to transfer the squatters to temporary quarters while masonry houses were being built. These houses were first planned on the same location but this idea was abandoned later on. Around 8,000 people were transferred to lodgings called '*Parques Proletarios* (Proletarian Parks)' and some of them were able to obtain housing in the popular buildings of Pedregulho and Gavea.

The most remarkable achievement during this period, called populist period (1945–64), was the construction by DHP of the Pedregulho Complex with 328 units. In quantitative terms it represents housing for only 1,700 people. However, as an architectural design it is a benchmark. Its author, Affonso Reidy, incorporated in a masterly way the main design characteristics of Le Corbusier's rationalism to the solution of housing estate for the poor strata: construction on piles, a corridor street, large openings for light and ventilation, standardization of construction elements with pure lines, etc. Two years later, the DHP itself tried to extend the Pedregulho experiment to the building of a new housing complex in Gavea. However, the execution was incomplete and the design was mutilated in 1982 when it was crossed by a highway. The Gavea complex was granted to the dwellers of Proletarian Park number one.

Both Cruzada Sao Sebastiao and DHP showed the ambiguity of the *favelas* eradication policies. In the Cruzada action, the maintenance of the dwellers in their location prevailed and the upgrading experience was started. During the DHP action, the removal of the squatters to Proletarian Park and the building of complexes were the most frequent. During the Kubitscheck government (1956–61), little attention was given to the popular housing issue. The Goal Plan emphasized the installation of the automotive industry in the state of Sao Paulo and the progression towards the West through the construction of Brasilia. In the large urban centers the housing crisis became deeper, worsened by the intensive urbanization and the huge rural exodus.

By the end of the 1960s, external factors influenced and significantly altered the understanding of the housing issue. The Cuban Revolution in 1959 and Fidel Castro's urban reform found an echo in the impoverished urban masses of Latin American metropoles. In order to fight the possible repercussion of these measures in other points of Latin America, the United States of America expedited loan grant funds of popular housings through the Agency for International Development. Abrams (1964, p. 131) comments that 'with the promise of aid of 20 billion dollars to the Latin American countries for a 10 year period, funds started to be granted at a pace that had never been achieved before'.

The importance of eradication of the precarious housing in the Latin American continent is emphasized by the United States Congress. In 1962, it recognized the 'relationship between housing and the stability of the underdeveloped free countries in the world' (Abrams 1964, p. 132). Housing was no longer only a problem, but became strategic for the protection of Western democracy.

During the same year, the government of the State of Guanabara (corresponding now to the municipality of Rio de Janeiro) created COHAB-GB—the Housing Company of Guanabara—to start squatter settlement eradication programs with funds from United States Agency for International Development (USAID). The policy now has nothing in common with Cruzada Sao Sebastiao. The elimination of *favelas* and transference of their population to housing estates at other sites is emphasized. There is a similarity to the popular housing department. The difference lies in the typology of housing complex. Those financed by USAID consist of detached houses with 30 to 47 sq m areas at 30–40 km from the southern zone *favelas* where the originally removed people had lived. Vila Kennedy, Vila Alianca, and Vila Esperanca also show the change in the intervention scale: they consist of 7,720 units with a population of approximately 39,000 people. Later on in 1966, the Alliance for Progress analyzed the social problems caused by placing squatters in suburban ghettos far from their work locations and concluded that: 'Time has come to reconsider the thesis that the intensive construction of inexpensive houses is the best solution for the housing problems in Latin America' (Serran 1976, p. 151).

With the beginning of the military government (1964–1984), the intensive production of houses for sale was emphasized. The implementation of the Housing Financing System (SFS) had the purpose of boosting the civilian construction industry and absorbing a significant number of nonqualified workers and softening the impact on employment caused by the inflation control. The housing issue had its focus changed: provision of employment was the goal with the production of suitable housing as a politically desirable by-product.

Specifically in relation to *favelas*, the beginning of the military period was characterized by an authoritarian attitude, removing squatter settlements compulsorily and with the aid of public security forces. Valladares (1978, p. 39) supplies the order of magnitude for the removals just in the municipality of Rio de Janeiro. Between 1962 and 1974, 80 *favelas* were removed, with 26,193 shacks destroyed and 139,218 dwellers displaced from their houses on the hills of Rio.

It is strongly evidenced in the available literature that SFH was unable to meet fully the housing needs of the Brazilian population, especially the poor. However, the construction of 4.8 million units, 25.8 percent of the increment in the Brazilian housing stock between 1964 and 1986 cannot be ignored. Out of these 4.8 million, a quarter were produced as public promotion by the COHAB's, for the population with incomes up to five minimum wages per month. Both the popular houses and those designed for the commercial market were abundantly subsidized. According to Arrectche (1990), the World Bank estimated that in 1985 the credit subsidy for borrowers with income below 5 minimum wages, was 112 dollars per year. It should be kept in mind that the houses built by COHABs were not specifically designed for squatters as the Gavea and Pedregulho buildings while the USAID housing complexes were.

By mid-1970s, SFH reversed the tradition of building houses to sell and created two new programs, Programa de Financiamento de Lotes Urbanizados (PROFILURB) and Programa de Erradicacao de Sub-Habitacao (PROMORAR); the later dedicated specifically to *favela* dwellers. PROFILURB, which stands for the Site and Services Financing Program, was created in June 1975. It allowed low-income workers to acquire a plot of land served by basic infrastructure: lighting, water, and sewers. PROMORAR, implemented in June 1979, proposed the eradication of *favelas* by replacing the shacks with masonry houses in the same area and regularizing the land-ownership. It is the only program at federal level that makes possible the permanence of the population in the previously occupied area. The units were delivered in plots of land measuring 75 sq m and occupying 25 sq m surface, with a multipurpose room and a bathroom, and the possibility of expansion.

In the 1980s, the economic crisis in Brazil evidenced the frailty of the SFH. The System counted upon funds from the Guarantee Fund for Service Time (FGTS), a type of unemployment insurance, and resources from savings accounts. The crisis increased unemployment which increased drafts on both FGTS and savings. By 1984, there was a drop of 35 percent in savings in the National Housing Bank (BNH). In an effort to decrease costs and maintain its activity SFH created the 'Joao de Barro' program in 1984 which provides for self-help and mutual help construction.

At that time local and state governments started to implement their own solutions. In Goias, the state Governor promoted the construction of 1,000 houses in one single Sunday in October 1983 by collective work. Mutual help experiments started later in Parana and Sao Paulo.

During the first years of the New Republic, 50 percent of BNH borrowers had their loan installments in arrears. The federal government started a structure in parallel for the poor population through the Special Community Action Secretary (SEAC) which started a series of clientelistic programs. The State was fragmented and the public powers were duplicated. In November 1986, the BNH was officially extinguished with an estimated deficit of 20 billion dollars.

Since 1984, the federal government has had little influence in the *favela* eradication policy. Its last important intervention was the upgrading plan for Favelas da Mare, in the municipality of Rio de Janeiro in 1985. It was supposed to serve 75,000 people and has never been completed. The number of financings of social interest units reflects the institutional and financial confusion of the federal agency. In 1980, 284,000 units were financed. The number dropped to 44,000 in 1986 and 15,000 in 1991 (through Federal Savings Bank) which received BNH's estate.

Summarizing the federal action then, during the populist period, it was ambiguous: during the first half of the military period it was authoritarian, advising the removal of *favelas* and the transference of their dwellers to periphery housing estates; after 1975, it was more flexible providing differentiated programs and allowing squatter settlement upgrading. After 1984, it was confused, clientelistic, and disorganized. The final coup came in 1988 with the new constitution. It made the federal government lose resources to unstructured states and municipalities, configurating an unsystematic way to transmit responsibilities.

At this time it is impossible to talk about policies related to squatter settlements and slums in Brazil. Each municipality has operated in a specific way. In general, very little has been done. One exception is the municipality of Sao Paulo where, since the 1960s, the intervention in precarious housing, especially in *favelas*, has been with its own resources. SFH resources helped to build housing estates. COHAB-SP built approximately 120,000 units: 90 percent after 1980, approximately 5,000 PROMORAR units between 1980 and 1984, when the program was extinguished.

Policies at the Municipality Level: The Case of Sao Paulo

For the analysis of the local policy related to *favelas* and slums in the municipality of Sao Paulo, the last 30 years were divided into five periods. In each one we discuss the type of analysis the problem underwent, the solutions found, and the problems and reactions created by these interventions. This analysis scheme has already been used by Taschner (1986) and was enriched by the reading of Patton (1980). Analysis here should be understood in the light of the prevailing ideas, concepts, and hegemonic theories in each period of time. Solutions found are the actions effectively executed in response to the problems and theories. Reactions are the new problems detected, which redefine theories and actions. Figure 8.1 summarizes this analytic schema.

The first basic type of intervention in squatter settlements was the removal and reinstallation of the settlement. This was a policy in force in the 1960s under the influence of the idea that the *favela* was a den of vice, diseases,

Figure 8.1: Summary of the Intervention Policies in *Favelas* and Slums in Sao Paulo

Period	Analysis (Rationale)	Solution (Action)	Problems (Reaction)
1960–70	*Favela* as a city 'disease', a lair of crimes. Squatters as a marginalized group, 'lumpen'. Slums as the space of disorder, in the decaying central areas. Slum-dwellers as sub-employees of the tertiary sector.	Extirpation from the urban network; removal and reinstallation of squatters in housing estates. There were no interventions in slums, theoretically subject to the Sanitary Code.	Distance between working and living locations, increasing transportation cost and making it difficult for the women to contribute to the family income—income reduction—return to the *favela*.
70–79	*Favela* as a 'springboard' to the city, a time required for integration. Squatters as migrants. Slum as a space of segregation and social exclusion. Slum-dwellers as workers registered in the tertiary sector.	Temporary Housing Village—projects viewing to shorten the time required to remain in the *favela*. Social work and professional training in the temporary shelters. Attempts to measure the problem in slums (1975 survey).	*Theoretical:* social integration is not assured. *Empirical:* squatters are not recent migrants and the *favela* is not their first dwelling. In 1980 and 1987, 39% and 34% of family heads had different housing experiences, arriving to the *favela* by 'descendent filtration'.
80–85	*Favela* as the physical expression of urban contradictions. Perception of permanence of *favelas*. Squatters as workers. Slums: detailing of typology. Perception of the existence of 'periphery slums'.	1. Large scale construction (COHABs) 2. Tolerance with squatterings. 3. Attempts to solve the land problem. 4. Upgrading and rehabilitation of *favelas*. 5. Self-help housing programs (beginning: 223 units ready, 4,471 in the agenda in Dec./85)	1. In the case of PROFAVELA: high costs, lack of people participation. 2. In the case of PROMORAR: poor construction quality, clientelism. 3. In the upgrading of *favelas* in general; if, on the one hand, the certainty of permanence makes the squatter invest (50.5% of masonry houses in 1987, compared to 2.4% in 1980), permissivity induces new squatterings and a speculative market is created in the *favelas*.
86–88	Need to recover lands for the 1986 real estate boom. Squatters as poor who should be	Removal of *favelas* located at prime sites, building of popular housing estates by the private initiative, in exchange for grants from the public	Interconnected operations were simply a trick against restrictions of land occupation and of the zoning law to increase real state

86–88	segregated. Removal from the urban center, verticalization and demolition of deteriorated houses. Partnership with free enterprize.	authorities (interconnected operations).	profits. Policy at the time was more at discourse level than at action level.
89–92	1. Squatters and slum-dwellers as poor who should be integrated into the urban network. Trial to incorporate the 'illegal city'. 2. Perception of the impossibility of the state to solve the housing problem alone, but with technical and financial assistance, the people are able to improve housing and achieve their own houses. Failure of the state as a provider. Continuation of homeownership policy. 3. Participative planning and decentralization of the decision making policy. 4. Segregation as an item to avoid. 5. Introduction of the environmental hazard concept. 6. Introduction of the concept of property's social function with restriction to its full right. 7. Attempt to increase the supply of urban land.	1. Debureaucratization and simplification of the construction standards (New Building Code). 2. Organization of the population, choosing dwellers' movements as privileged interlocutors. 3. Building of houses and infrastructure by co-managed mutual-help housing. 4. Upgrading of *favelas*, with priority for those with environmental hazards caused by geomorphological problems. 5. Grant of the right of real use of the land for *favelas* in public lands (Bill no. 51/91, still at the City Council). 6. Interventions in slums. Pilot projects of condemnations and new constructions, establishing dwellers in the central area. 7. Continuation of the partnership with the private sector, through interconnected operations. 8. Continuation of the construction of new housing estates (appr. 33,000, part of them started by the previous government). 9. Use of the tax over land to increase the supply of parcels.	1. Transformation of popular movements into political machines. Community associations create an 'urban coronelism'. 2. Continuity of formation of new *favelas* and densification of the existing ones. 3. Increase of the speculative market in upgraded *favelas*. 4. The differentiated urbanization standard and the identification of *favelas* with a criminal environment does not reduce the segregation of their dwellers. 5. Slowness in the process of co-managed mutual help construction (only 10,000 houses). 6. Theoretical discussions about collective work: overexploitation for the labour force or simple production of goods? 7. Insufficient cost appropriation, both for direct and indirect costs.

crimes, social disorganization, and criminals. This pathology, the argument went, would be extinguished with the elimination of the settlement and the removal of the squatters to suitable units. The removal, in Sao Paulo, never reached the violence of Rio de Janeiro. Although the removal was frequent in 1960, no quantitative data can be found. Between 1971 and 1979, approximately 4,000 families, representing over 19,000 squatters, were removed from their shacks (little more than 6 percent of the squatter population in 1978–79).

The results of the removal policy, both in Sao Paulo and Rio de Janeiro, were not very encouraging. The housing estates to which the squatters were removed were usually located on peripheric lands with difficult access by transportation in order to keep land costs down:

a) longer distance from service centers hinders the women's contribution to the family income, since they have no opportunity to use their free time for paid jobs;

b) transportation costs increase, burdening the household budget even more.

As a consequence of this, the purchasing power decreases, making buying or monthly rent for the house difficult. This situation led to an increasing indebtment and return to the *favela*. It became clear in the 1970s, based on the analysis of the attempts to remove squatters to traditional housing estates (Valladares 1978; Rush 1974; Blanck 1980; Bank 1986; among others), and evidenced by the abandonment and sale of apartments and return to the *favela*, that the removal would only be a competent resource in emergency situations.

Thus in the 1970–79 period, instead of relocating the squatters to a specific permanent site they were taken to the so-called temporary housing villages, which existed in Rio de Janeiro since the mid-1940s under the name of Proletarian Parks. Theoretical statements that supported these types of intervention were inspired by the formulations of the social integration school of functionalistic sociology. They emphasized the idea that the *favela* was the first housing alternative for the migrants, a springboard into the city, a stage required for integration to urban life. At the temporary housing villages, the basic concern was to shorten the compulsory time for which the immigrant would stay in the *favela* by supplying some basic structure, professional guidance, and formal schooling. Therefore, the temporary shelters, forecast to provide one year of housing, had schools to teach adults and to form manpower for the trade and the industry. It was expected that after this period the family would be ready to be integrated in the housing and job market.

Critics of this project were numerous. In addition to the implicit and false assumption of social integration, empirical data very soon evidenced that the squatters were by no means recent immigrants and had not always first lived in a *favela*. The *favelas* were growing more due to impoverishment than to immigration. Dwellers of *favelas* were not installed immediately in the shack where they lived. They moved in the urban space, in a 'downwards route', within the process of valorization of urban lands and impoverishment of the working class, from the central areas to the periphery, from masonry houses to the squatter settlement shacks (Pasternak Taschner 1986).

The perception by the end of the 1970s that the *favela* was here to stay, and that the squatters were workers, the majority of whom were employed by the industries of Sao Paulo, raised the need to look for new solutions. The failure, both of the violent removal plans and of the well-meaning temporary shelters for integration into urban life, could be measured: in the removals, the sale of the houses where they had been moved to and the return to the *favelas* was a constant. Temporary shelters became permanent. The assumption of social integration in a society with the Brazilian characteristics presents serious limitations: in addition to the requirements of schooling and professional qualification, the capability of the Sao Paulo system to include the workforce in the dynamic poles of the economy was limited.

The awareness that the *favela* did not represent a disturbance of the system, but the physical expression of its contradictions, appeared in the 1980-85 period. This led to an operational dilemma—how to determine the intervention problem? If the reasons for squatting are found in the contradictions of the very system that generated it, how can an action plan be prepared which is not a total rupture of the existing system?

Certain sectors of society believed that large-scale construction, prefabrication, industrialization, and rationalization of the construction could promote a decrease in the cost of housing, which would in turn make it affordable to all. Cooperation, self-help and mutual help, private initiative, and community development were the instruments that would allow for the problems of the *favelas* to be overcome. This approach arose from the need of the Brazilian middle class to transmit to the squatters certain concept of society: the idea that their daily life could be improved by their own effort and community help within the system in force.

This type of thinking led to the construction of a large quantity of housing units with more modern technologies—at the Itaquera housing complex, in the periphery of the municipality of Sao Paulo, using both the light prefabricated system with metallic shapes of the 'outnord' type, and structural masonry—and a higher tolerance with the squatting and even, paradoxically, the search of suitable and legal standards for illegal settlements. This no longer entailed violence of removals or the benevolent understanding of

V.H.P. The chosen solutions were the mass construction of popular houses (four to five of the 90,570 housings built by COHAB–SP until 1985, were built between 1980 and 1985) and the *favelas* upgrading.

Thus, projects of installation of sanitary infrastructure (water and sewers), electricity, and garbage collection were created for the settlements. The regularization of the land-ownership was still unknown, but the infrastructure installation seemed to indicate acceptance of the permanence of the squatters. In Sao Paulo, by the end of 1979, Programa de Abastecimento de Aqua para Habitacoes Sub-Normais (PRO-AGUA) was started, proposing the expansion of the water network to the *favelas* by means of domicile connection whenever possible or by means of collective tap, when the urban design, with narrow alleys did not allow for the passage of piping. The program of electrification of *favelas*—Programa de Electrificacao de Favelas (PRO-LUZ), was also started in 1979 and by 1987, they had installed electric power in all squatter houses in Sao Paulo. Both the water and the lighting programs were included in what was called compensatory policies and squatters were charged only the minimum tariff regardless of the real consumption.

Starting in 1981, a more ambitious upgrading program was also implemented—Programa de Urbanizacao de Favelas (PROFAVELA). This program not only provided for the installation of infrastructure but also services of education and health, as well as financing, highly subsidized, of the improvement or building of new housing units. PROFAVELA served 24 *favelas*, benefitting approximately 9,000 people, although, in the current ideology, community development and popular participation were the prevailing ideas at the end of the military dictatorship. The involvement of the population in the reurbanization work had been forecast but this did not happen. In addition, extremely high indirect costs, quite high direct costs (the urbanization cost forecast was US$ 350 per family, which was exceeded), caused the project to be abandoned in 1984. Another factor that worsened the quality and increased the cost of PROFAVELA was the pressure from contractors looking for work. The authorities split the building sites, worsening the work organization and burdening it with the utilization of more intermediates.

Another project, PROMORAR, within the Housing Financing System (implemented in June 1979) proposed the eradication of the *favelas*, by replacing the shacks with embryo units of a multipurpose room and kitchen, in the same area, and regularization of the land-ownership. In Sao Paulo, until 1986, 11 PROMORAR housing complexes were built, with 5,000 units. The maximum price of the PROMORAR unit, measuring 25 sq m was US$ 1,800, amortized by the family. Community equipment was subsidized. According to the initial project, the installment was not to go beyond 10 percent of the minimum wage.

In the specific case of Sao Paulo, PROMORAR, in addition to serving only a minimum part of the demand, showed itself as an experiment with considerable technical-constructive problems (Pasternak Taschner 1986).

In 1980, the popular movements for housing exploded. These movements claimed, in addition to ownership of the land, government help to build houses by self-help and mutual help. The Housing Financing System created in 1984, the Joao de Barro Program which provided for the use of the dweller's own manpower. In Sao Paulo, the housing provision program, specific for squatters, supplied sites-and-services and financing of material for the embryo-house, together with technical assistance for self-help construction. In 1985, when the new Mayor took office, only 223 houses were ready and almost 3,000 in progress. At the time, it was only an experimental program, but it had huge repercussions.

The critics of *favelas* upgrading programs claim that the certainty of permanence stimulates new invasions, the densification of old settlements, and brings a simulacrum of the legal real estate market, both in relation to the land and to the buildings. In reality, in 1987, 4.3 percent of the total squatter families declared that they had paid for their plot of land. Prices varied greatly as a consequence of the site where the *favela* was located, and the services with which it was supplied. A dweller of Campo Limpo, at the south end of the municipality, paid three minimum wages for a 100 sq m lot in 1983. In 1987, an interviewee from Vila Prudente (east zone and more central) declared that he paid 38 minimum wages for an equivalent piece of land (Veras and Taschner 1990). In relation to houses, real estate transactions are somewhat similar to the formal market: sales are made upon a downpayment, installments and a fee (purchasing guarantee). In the best structured *favelas* the dwellers association operates as the 'notary'—it is through the association that transactions are conducted, in addition to the license for expansion and remodelling and even license to invade a piece of land in the settlement. This service is usually remunerated by a percentage that ranges from one to three percent of the transaction value.

In the southern zone of Sao Paulo, in February 1987, a squatter asked for 25 minimum wages for a masonry house with one room, kitchen, and bathroom. For the same house, he had paid in July 1985, an amount of 15 minimum wages (see note 6).

The dwellers associations, by means of the control of sales of the licenses for expansion and remodelling, and access to the land, 'were involved in a complex game of interests exposed to corruption, and were very often characterized as legitimate representatives of the poor strata' (Guimaraes

1992, p. 11). The testimony of a squatter from Jaguare (west zone of Sao Paulo), illustrates the clientelism in force:

> My husband went to a meeting in order to be able to get this place, there, with the Directory. He had to beg, pray and kneel before them because they didn't want to let us build the shack here, by no means....(Pasternak Taschner 1982, p. 388).

In the case of Maria das Neves, after having lived for two years with a relative in the same *favela*, her lobby power was enough. In many cases, family connections or bribes are instruments needed to support this emerging clientelism.

Although the precariousness of the information about prices of lots and houses suggests prudence, the trade of houses and plots of land in *favelas* seems to be increasing. There is value where before there was nothing, and the intervention of the authorities increased the speculation processes that had already arisen due to the scarcity of housings.

To the critics of the self-help and mutual help programs who condemn the low productivity of the work under this system and consider it an exploitation of the labour force, the supporters of this policy reply:

a) self-help housing, willy-nilly, can be kept within the worker's salary. The work progress/budget follows the pace of the user's disbursement capability;

b) the Brazilian urban peripheries have been built by self-help construction. It is better to institutionalize the process, thus ensuring technical assistance that improves the quality of the product and reduces the worker's wear;

c) considering the problem's scale, it is impossible to think only about finished units;

d) the unit design has more suitable features for the living family than the inflexible plans for housing estates.

Finally, the ideas of John Turner and the World Bank were recovered in Sao Paulo in the mid-1980s.

In relation to slums, until the 1980s, the intervention occurred at the level of sanitary legislation (the first, dated 1886). In 1975, the authorities tried to identify the incidence of slums in the urban network and characterize their population. In 1983, the Municipal Housing Plan proposed to intervene in spot experiments. In reality, very little was accomplished except for assistance to dwellers in relation to individualization of lighting bills. As the unit price of the kilowatt rose according to the electric power consumption, a collective bill was more burdensome than meters installed by domicile and individualization of the payment. In 1985, the acknowledgement of slums as a housing problem led the city hall to make an effort and conduct surveys about their form. It was found that the dilapidated rental housings were not a phenomenon exclusive to the deteriorated urban center, but that it was also spread throughout the fringes (Veras 1992; Pasternak and Mautner 1992).

In January 1986, a new municipal government took office, the first to be directly elected by the people since 1964. Supported by conservative forces and by large sectors of the middle class, fearing the increasing urban violence, and attributing it partially to compromises with the poor population strata, this government started once more to discuss the removal of *favelas*, especially in areas close to the wealthiest neighborhoods. The prevailing rationale was that the squatters were poor and should be segregated, and the space of the better located *favelas* should be considered as lands to be recovered to house the middle classes. In 1986, as an effect of the Cruzado Plan which froze prices, a real estate boom occurred.

The housing plan of the 1986–89 government remained more at the level of discourse than action. Two *favelas* located in prime areas were removed. The proposed renovation scheme for the center, with a slum clearance and eviction of their population, has never been implemented. The most interesting contribution of the period was the partnership with the private initiative for the eradication of *favelas*, by offering central urban sites in exchange for the construction of houses for squatters. The interconnected operations made it possible for a contractor to build more than the area permitted by the Zoning Law in exchange for the donation of houses for squatters to the city hall. This law created an enormous polemic at the time, strongly condemned by the leftists who saw in it only a trick against the restrictions of site occupation to increase real estate gains. The same leftists, however, on reaching the public office in 1989, made ample use of the interconnected operations.

In 1989, a municipal government connected to the Workers Party (PT), committed to the popular movements and union struggles, took office. The prevailing lines of thought showed this commitment. The city outline prepared by government technicians and their assistants showed the existence of a huge illegal city which housed the poor strata. Three hundred and fifty thousand units were estimated as illegal in relation to the zoning law and the construction code in force (14 percent of the housing units in the municipality). Seventy-four percent of these illegal units presented areas up to 125 sq m. Adding up the houses in squatter settlements, slums, and the illegal developments in the periphery, approximately 65 percent of the real city was illegal. It was also deemed necessary to integrate this illegal city. Although poverty is the major cause behind it, it was argued that elitist construction standards and regulations led to the illegality. One of the proposals executed was the simplification of the construction code and the debureaucratization of procedures related to building licenses. The approval of a construction plan by the local authorities took 120 days, in addition to requiring a fee of US$ 1.00 per sq m to be authorized. In a country where the minimum wage is historically US$ 60, this cost is burdensome. Time for approval of a development was approximately 19 months, counting state and municipality approvals. It would be reduced to six months. The liberal ideas of Hermando de Soto (1990), were being practiced by a leftist administration.

Urban segregation appears as an item to be avoided. The right to the city belongs to all. This statement led to a first concrete attempt to maintain the permanence of the population that lived in downtown slums, and to go beyond the spot assistance provided to them during the period from 1983 to 1986. The basic idea of intervention in the slums was to respect the desire of the inhabitants to live downtown. These are pilot projects still on a small-scale and they comply with the following dynamics:

a) Use of the partnership with the owner of the house transformed in the slum, who assigns it and is paid with part of the new building to be constructed. As multiple purpose buildings have been privileged (with storeys at ground level and four to five storeys of apartments), very often the property's owner is paid in storeys. The City Hall buys the property and mortgages it. This money is used to start the building work that will allow the permanence of the dwellers in the location. Up to the end of 1992, six slums were the target of this type of intervention, which involves only the lot where the building was located.

b) Large size intervention, in areas from 5,000 to 10,000 sq m. *Due to the scale*, these are operations of urban renewal and they involve condemnations, use of empty lots, and reformulation of underused buildings. Some projects are underway. Among others, are the construction of a building on the site of an abandoned movie theater in Mooca (central zone, east sector) where 111 families were housed and the construction of three buildings with five to six storeys at Rua Celso Garcia, in Bras, a project that will house 182 families, in a concept of recovery of the entire block with stores and community hall, children day care center, maintenance of an old house of eclectic architecture to be used as a cultural center for the neighborhood, and an internal pateo surrounded by small apartments with 32 sq m of useful area (56 sq m total area).

In all, 22 slum reconstruction projects were in progress by the end of 1992. The project cost was around US$ 11,500 per family and 95 percent of this cost represented the cost of construction. The projects transfer the subsidy to the dweller. Nothing was made as social rent. The principle that has been stated by the so-called Progressives in Brazil was that the private owned house will reinforce the society's conservative character, transforming the worker into a small property owner. This argument is strongly inspired by Engels, who qualifies the idea of a private house as petit bourgeois, and as a factor that will tie the population to the soil, preventing it from freely selling its working force.

The technicians of Mayor Luiza Erundina's administration (1989–92) seemed to agree more with Saunders (1990) who legitimates the right to live in a privately owned house, and believes that workers are perfectly able to differentiate the ownership of consumption goods from the cartelized ownership of thousands of shares of companies. According to the Superintendent of Popular Housing during this administration:

all evidences show that the aspiration of owning a house is not only legitimate, that is, it is not the result of propaganda and enforcement of consumption standards by the current system, but it means a previous condition required for the workers to be able to conquer a better quality of urban life (BONDUKI 1992, p. 142).

Therefore, houseownership was ensured in the projects for slums and *favelas*. In the case of *favelas*, the problems connected to land squatting are more difficult to solve. It has been petitioned to the local authorities that the real right of use be granted to the dwellers associations. This would make real an idea of collective land-ownership and private ownership of the housing unit. The unconditional right to land-ownership is currently a strong obstacle to the obtainment of housing. One of the proposals for the solution of the housing problem involves the increase of land supply. This includes the progressive taxation of empty lots, as a stimulus to sell them.

In addition to keeping the privately owned house policy, the perception of the failure of the state as a provider and its inability to independently solve the housing problems, together with the reinforcement of the idea of the people's participation and the choice of organized movements as privileged interlocutors, made mutual help, co-managed by the City Hall and dwellers associations, the prevailing policy during the period.

Approximately 14,000 units were built by 84 dwellers associations. To critics who claim that self-managed mutual help work is inefficient, slow, and anachronistic from the technological viewpoint, its upholders claim that they not only modify the relationship between the civil construction and the state, eliminating intermediates, but also unveil the ideology of incompetence, which divides the society between those who lead it, because they have the knowledge and those who execute, because they know nothing.

Popular movements, strengthened after the democratic opening in the 1980s, demanded the removal of intermediates and the participation of the end user in the decision making process. Proposals of self-construction, both individually and by mutual help, were only one-step ahead. Public officers had only to ensure resources and land. Self-help construction, criticized by the traditional leftists as overwork which would be reflected in the decrease of the cost of labour force reproduction, and would thereby increase its exploitation even more, was seen by the 'new left' as domestic production, with the dweller as an individual producer of goods and not as a seller of his labour force to the capitalist. It creates a use value entirely appropriated by him and this is potentially a commodity. The critics of the 'new left' now criticise spontaneous self-help housing because it stimulates individuality. Contrary to this fact, mutual help housing is undeniably a generator of a large part of the Third World urban peripheries, where the effort is rationalized and productivity increased. But above all in importance is the self-managed collective work where in addition to cost reduction, 'the organization to build becomes a self-management and collective organization school' (Bonduki 1992, p. 164).

On the issue of the upgrading of the *favelas,* the following happened in the year 1990. Twenty-six thousand families in 50 *favelas* were served with infrastructure services: paving, redivision of the soil, water system, sewers system, drainage, and opening of access roads. At the same time, 3,500 families in 70 *favelas* executed or are executing small improvements as well as collective work (Sao Paulo Municipality 1992, p. 12). The concept of environmental hazard was introduced into the *favelas* upgrading. In this case it is the geomorphological risk for its inhabitants: earth sliding, washout or floods. These three hazard types were classified according to their urgency: imminent risk (500 housings with 2,710 people), short-term risk (7,000 houses with 37,000 people) and medium- and long-term risk (17,255 houses with 93,990 people). Adding them up gives a total of 133,700 people who are under life risk and/or loss of their property while 40,000 were under imminent or on the short-term risk. Over 25,000 people have already been removed with many of them sent to housing estates.

These 133,700 people represented 16 percent of the squatters. It is worth mentioning that 50 percent of the *favelas* in Sao Paulo are located at the banks of rivers or reservoirs, 30 percent in sites with steep slopes, and 25 percent in lands which are already strongly eroded. What can be done? Remove 1 million squatters? How and where to? Sao Paulo municipality estimated the cost of removing each family as 10,000 dollars. The removal of the entire squatter population will require approximately 10 billion dollars. According to the City Hall, the upgrading of all *favelas* will cost a little less than $1.3

billion. The current *Favelas* Upgrading Program is primarily to implement infrastructure works: water, sewers, drainage, and slope bracing, in addition to land regularization. This last item is on hold at the City Council. It proposes the granting of real use for 90 years to 138 *favelas* with 26,000 families located in lands belonging to the City Hall.

Upgrading seems to be a way to be followed as a cure for the existing problem. However, this cure has its own repercussions. Unfortunately, with the upgrading, the real estate submarket consolidates in the *favela*. Both land and houses become consumption goods and the price soars. The perfect solution will be housing and land for all. Is this a utopia?

CONCLUSION: BEYOND THE 1990s

The reduction of the Brazilian *metropoles'* growth rate relieves, to a certain extent, the pressures for housing in large centers. However, from the viewpoint of urban structuralism, the repetition of the 'peripheric growth pattern' in middle-size cities in the state of Sao Paulo and the consequent formation of a poverty belt shows that the reversion of the segregating standard, characteristic of Brazilian cities, will not occur in the short term. *Favelas*, slums, and peripheric areas deprived of services will be seen in Brazilian cities during the next millennium.

As an emerging practice, one can already detect:

a) Growing commodification in the social relationships of housing production, both in squattered land and in private lands (Pasternak Taschner 1992).

b) The moving of the middle classes to the periphery, and even the construction, by these social layers, of illegal houses, outside of the building code and the zoning law.

c) The increase of the poor tenements, both in the low-income housing tracts in the peripheric belts and in the squatter settlements. In Rocinha (the biggest *favela* in Rio de Janeiro) there are three to four storey buildings with rented rooms; real slums in squatted land.

d) The invasion of Rio squatter settlements by drug trafficking. If, on the one hand, this fact once more associates squatters with criminals, on the other hand, it makes possible the measurement of the wealth of Rio hills. Parabolic antennae, cellular telephones are usual in Pavao-Pavaozin-ho, Santa Marta, and other *favelas* in Rio. Traffickers buy the silence of the working population through fear and by providing them with benefits. They employ youngsters to deliver cocaine to their clients. They provide justice instead of the public branches: on a famous Sunday when the population of the hills came down to the beach, mugging and scaring the people away, very few drugs were sold. On the following day, the traffickers declared that they would watch the hills so that such a situation would not occur again. A sad destiny for a place where drug trafficking lords ensure public safety.

A new type of illegal allotment has emerged in Sao Paulo. The zoning law of 1972 established high level requirements to approve a land development plan. Its intention was to prevent disorderly growth and ensure suitable allotments. Until 1981, when popular developments were allowed with lesser requirements, only six land developments were approved in the municipality. Its horizontal expansion was done through the proliferation of clandestine allotments. In 1979, a federal law was enacted which declared that clandestine developers were criminals, and regulated works, projects, and free areas. In addition, it linked the lot purchasing and sale to the approval of the development and made it possible for the buyer to pay the installments in court, if the development was illegal.

The strictness of the regulation, the amount of investments and delay in the approval of projects, (approximately 19 months) discouraged the supply of lots. But in 1989, illegal developments reappeared under a new guise: though the developer did not exist anymore, he eventually appeared in the form of a technical advisor. The dwellers associations arose instead, and bought and developed the land, without the previous authorization of the public officers. The old developer found his new function: he performed the intermediation between the associations and the land sellers. Dwellers, generally tenants, paid for the land in six months and chose to divide it without the bureaucratic ritual because of the costs and delays involved. The public officers, especially in the 1989–92 governments who were committed to the popular movements, were put in a quandary: if it was easy to criminalize a developer, the same cannot be said about an association. In addition, this type of process has serious political repercussions at the political base.

After 10 years, the supply of lots for sale has increased, but not as planned and desired by the public officers and the technicians.

From the viewpoint of public policies, the Brazilian government and society face a difficult challenge. The expected rebirth of economic growth and the reintegration of the country into the world economy will certainly help to solve many of these problems.

NOTES

1. IBGE's definition of squatter settlements (*favelas*) takes into consideration and computes only the settlements with at least 51 domiciles, occupying or having occupied until recently, plots of land owned by others (either public or private), laid out, generally, in a disorganized and dense way, and in their majority, lacking essential public services (IBGE—Operational basis. Sectors and Work Zones Limitation Manual GR—7.01). Therefore, it introduced two types of underestimations, which are difficult to correct:
    *   in relation to the presented number of squatter domiciles, since it excludes smaller settlements;
    *   in relation to the possible municipalities that may present settlements with less than 50 units and which do not even appear in the list of municipalities with *favelas*.

    The second type of underestimation is impossible to be corrected, unless by means of collection of local information from all the municipalities in Brazil. In the first, in some municipalities that have filed the *favelas*, one can measure the underestimation introduced by IBGE's definition through data comparison. Obviously the underestimation will vary enormously from municipality to municipality, since it depends on the structure of the squatter settlements in each of them, directly connected to the size of lands available for squattering. In Sao Paulo, for instance, there are a large number of *favelas* with few domiciles. IBGE's underestimation of the squatter population in the city of Sao Paulo was 24 percent in 1980 and 37 percent in 1987.

2. The word 'slum' (*cortico*, in Portuguese) means literally 'beehive'. Although they already existed in the 18th century with their Spanish name—corridor houses—, the word slum was found in documents of the mid-19th century. Another name for these precarious rented houses in Rio de Janeiro is 'pig's head'. This was the name of a famous slum in Rio, similar to lair, and the antithesis of the hygienic houses recommended in the beginning of the century.

3. The word *favela* originated from a bush with oleagionus seeds, found in the northern backwoods. By the end of the 19th century, soldiers returning from Canudos (rebellion in the backwoods of Bahia, centered around a fanatic who instituted an autonomous government which was decimated by the federal troops in 1897), did not have anywhere to live and started to occupy, in Rio de Janeiro, the hills of Providencia and Santo Antonio, behind the barracks. It was said that tents grew like bushes (*favelas*) in the backwoods, resulting in the name.

4. 'Emphyteusis' is a legal instrument which was used to divide land during the colonial times. It consists of the real right on the part of the tenant-in-fee of planting and using fully, perpetually, the property of others upon payment, without, however, removing from the property's owner the ownership. It is a type of rent.

5. Until the time this article was written, we were able to obtain only the gross data of the squatter settlements by the 1991 Census for the municipality of Sao Paulo.

6. Minimum wage in Brazil has been historically around US $ 60.

7. The result of the pilot survey of the Pari slums was presented in the seminar 'Urban Policies and Slums in Sao Paulo: Yesterday and Today' on 8 December 1992, at Pontificia Universidade Catolica 9 (PUC-SP), and promoted by the Urban Studies and Survey Center of the Sociology Department.

REFERENCES

Abrams, C. 1964. *Habitaao: desenvolvimento e urbanizacao* (Housing: Development and Upgrading). Rio de Janeiro: Editor O. Cruzeiro.

Arretche, M. 1990. 'Intervencao do Estato e setor privado: o modelo brasileiro de poltica habitacional' (State Intervention and Private Sector: The Brazilian Housing Policy Model), *Espaco e Debates 31*, pp. 21–36.

Bank, G.A. 1986. 'Poverty, Politics and the Shaping of Urban Space: a Brazilian Example', *International Journal of Urban and Regional Research 10(4)*, pp. 522–40.

Blanck, G. 1980. Bras de Pina. 'Experiencia de urbanizacao de favela' (Squatter Settlement Upgrading Experience), in L. Valladares (ed.), *Housing in Question*. Rio de Janeiro, Zahar, pp. 93–124.

Bogus, L. 1980. 'Vila do Encontro: a cidade chega a periferia' (Vila do Encontro: The City Arrives to the Periphery). Master's thesis presented to the Social Sciences Department, PUC- SP.

Bonduki, N. 1992. *Habitacao e auto-gestao* (Housing and Self-management). Building Utopy Territories: Rio de Janeiro, FASE.

Bonduki, N. and R. Rolnik. 1979. *Periferias* (Peripheries). Cadernos PRODEUR 2, Sao Paulo, FUPAM and FAU-USP.

FINEP. 1988. *Inventario da acaao governamental— Complementacao* (Governmental Action Analysis—Supplementation) 1984/1986. Rio de Janeiro.

FINEP-GAP. 1985. *Inventario da acao governamental* (Governmental Action Analysis). Rio de Janeiro.

Gordilho, A. 1992. 'Novas formas de habitar velhas estruturas' (New Housing Forms, Old Structures). Paper presented at the XVI Annual Meeting of ANPOCS (National Association of Post Graduation and Research in Social Sciences), Caxambu, Minas Gerais, 20–23 October.

Guimaraes, B.M. 1992. 'Favelas em Belo Horizonte: Tendencias e desafios' (Squatter Settlements in Belo Horizonte: Trends and Challenges). Paper presented at the XVI Annual Meeting of ANPOCS (National Association of Post Graduation and Research in Social Sciences), Caxambu, Minas Gerais, 20–23 October.

Jaccoud, L. 1991. 'Lutas sociais: populismo e democracia: 1960/1964' (Social Struggles: Populism and Democracy: 1960/1964), in A. Paviani, *Popular Movements in Brasilia*. Brasilia, Editora Universidade de Brasilia, pp. 145–68.

Kowarick, L. and C. Ant. 1985. 'Cortios: cem anos de promiscuidade' (Slums: One Hundred Years of Promiscuity), *Revista Novos Estudos CEBRAP 1(2)*, pp. 33-46.

Lagenest, B.D.E. 1962. 'Os corticos de Sao Paulo' (Slums in Sao Paulo). *Revista Anhembi 139*, pp. 503-23. Sao Paulo, June.

Pasternak Taschner, S. 1982. 'Moradia da pobreza: habitaao sem saude (The Housing of Poverty: Housing without Health)'. Ph.D. thesis presented to the Public Health School, University of Sao Paulo.

———. 1986. 'Squatter Settlements: The Facts and the Policies'. Paper presented in the International Research Conference on Housing Policy, Gavle, Sweden and later published in *Espaco e Debates* 18, pp. 79–112.

———. 1990. 'Habitaao e demografia intra-urbana em Sao Paulo' (Intraurban Housing and Demography in Sao Paulo), *Revista Brasileira de estudos populacionais 7 (1)*, pp. 7–34, January/June.

———. 1992. 'Changes in the process of Self-Help Housing Production in Sao Paulo', in K. Mathey (ed.), *Beyond Self-Help*. London: Mansell, pp. 145-56.

Pasternak Taschner, S. and **Y. Mautner**. 1992. 'Habitacao da Pobreza' (The Housing of Poverty). Cadernos PRODEUR 5, Sao Paulo, FUPAM and FAU-USP.

Patton, C. and **E.K. Palmer**. 1980. 'Evolution of the Third World Shelter Policies', in C. Patton (ed.), *Spontaneous Shelter*. Philadelphia: Temple University Press, pp. 3–24.

Paviani, A. 1988. *Brasilia: A Metrople Em Crise* (Brasilia: Metropolis in Crisis). Brasilia. Editora Universidade de Brasilia.

Pfeiffer, P. and **L.F. Vaz**. 1992. 'El area central de Rio de Janeiro: entre marginacion y valorizacion', *Anuario sobre Renovacion Urbana*, 1992 (Jahrbuch Stadterneuerung).

Queiroz Ribeiro, L.C. and **L. Correa Do Lago**. 1991. 'Transformaao das metroploes brasileiras: algumas hipoteses de pesquisa' (Transformation of Brazilian Metropoles: Some Research Hypotheses), Caxambu, Minas Gerais. Paper presented at the XVth Annual Meeting of ANPOCS, October.

Resende, M. 1991. 'Movimento de moradores: a experiencia dos inquilinos de Ceilandia' (Movement of Dwellers: The Experience of Ceilandia Tenants), in A. Paviani, (ed.), *Popular Movements in Brasilia*. Brasilia: Editora Universidade de Brasilia, pp. 209–30.

Rush, B.S. 1974. 'From Favela to Conjunto: The Experience of Squatters Removed to Low Cost Housing in Rio de Janeiro', Brazil. Cambridge (mimeo.).

Sao Paulo, Municipio. 1975. Secretaria do Bem Estar Social. *Diagnostico sobre o fenomeno cortico no Municipio do Sao Paulo* (Diagnosis on Slums [Tenements] in the Municipality of Sao Paulo). Sao Paulo: SEBES.

———. 1989. Housing and Urban Development Secretary. *Diagnostico sobre o fenomeno do cortico no municipio de Sao Paulo* (Diagnosis on the Slum Phenomenon in the Municipality of Sao Paulo). Sao Paulo: SABES-HABI.

———. 1989. Housing and Urban Development Secretary. 'Programa de Acao Imediata' (Immediate Action Program) (mimeo.).

———. 1992. Housing and Urban Development Secretary. *Urbanizacao de favelas em Sao Paulo: uma experiencia de recuperacao ambiental* (Upgrading of 'Favelas' in Sao Paulo: An Experience of Environmental Recovery).

Saunders, P. 1990. *A Nation of Home Owners*. London: Unwin Hyman Ltd.

Serran, J.R. 1976. *O IAB e a politica habitacional* (IAB and the Housing Policy) (1954–1975). Sao Paulo, Schema.

Soto, H. de. 1990. *The Other Path*. New York: Perennial Library.

Valladares, C. 1978. *Passa-se uma casa* (House Available). Rio de Janeiro, Zahaı.

Valladares, C. and **R. Ribeiro**. 1992. 'The Return of Favela. Recent Changes in Intrametropolitan Rio'. Paper presented in the meeting of ISA-RC 21, Los Angeles, April 23–25.

Vaz, L.F. 1985. 'Contribuicao ao estudo da producao e transformacao do espaco da habitacao popular. As habitacocos colctivas no Rio de Janeiro antigo' (Contribution to the Study of Production and Transformation of the Space of Popular Housing. The slums in Ancient Rio de Janeiro). Master's dissertation presented to the Graduate Programme in Regional and Urban Planning, Federal University of Rio de Janeiro.

Veras, M.P.B. 1992. 'Corticos em Sao Paulo: velhas e novas formas de pobreza e de segregacao social (Slums in Sao Paulo: Old and New Forms of Poverty and of Social Segregation)', in L.M. Bogus and L.E. Wanderlely (eds.), *The Struggle for the City in Sao Paulo*. Sao Paulo: Cortez, pp. 81–126.

Veras, M.P.B. and **S. Pasternak Taschner**. 1990. 'Evolucao e mudancas das favelas paulistanas (Evolution and Changes of 'Favelas' in Sao Paulo)', *Espaco e Debates 31*, pp. 52–71.

9

Spontaneous Settlements in Colombia: From Opposition to Reluctant Acceptance to... Again Opposition

John J. Betancur

Housing production in Colombia has been highly segmented by income. While the formal construction industry has predominantly served the well-to-do, low-to-moderate income groups have been housing themselves on a self-help/mutual help basis within the framework of the so-called 'informal economy'. The government, in fact, has acted so as to create a demand for the private construction industry—usually through subcontracting of publicly subsidized moderate-to-middle-income settlements. In contrast, it has given minimal assistance to the poor for the purpose of controlling self-help construction activity and gaining their political support. At the same time, public policy has reinforced and indeed institutionalized the resulting urban segmentation (Reig 1976; Molina and Mondragón 1976; Murillo and Ungar 1978).

Displaced from the countryside by political violence and capital penetration, peasants were forced into the cities within a very short period of time. In contrast to developed countries where urbanization was accompanied by a dynamic, large process of industrialization, Colombian cities have had a foreign-dependent, incipient, endemic industry, unable to employ even one-fourth of the immigrants. As the cores of a peripheral economic dependency, such cities were dominated by housing and settlement standards affordable only to people with at least well-paid, steady jobs.

Struggling against all odds, immigrants have been producing their own jobs and satisfying a large proportion of their needs—housing included. Moreover, their spontaneous settlements have subsidized the economy by keeping demands on wages at a minimal level and by producing a high proportion of the urban infrastructure on largely self-help, low-cash terms. They have saved billions of pesos. Yet, their contribution has been underestimated, their settlements have been opposed, and their extreme condition of need has been abused through political manipulation, co-optation of self-help efforts, and neglect.

As a result of opposition and neglect and the lack of meaningful job opportunities, spontaneous settlements stand today as a testimony to both the ability of the poor to find solutions—no matter how incipient—for their problems, and the inability of governments and the private sector to meaningfully contribute to these monumental efforts. These solutions, then, have trapped the poor in highly segregated areas with minimal infrastructure and inadequate services. They, in fact, have become a dead-end for a huge proportion of the urban poor in Colombian cities.

This chapter examines policy responses to spontaneous settlement in Colombia. It argues that policy has been dominated by efforts to prevent, manipulate and, most recently, legalize them, while appropriating some limited elements for public housing schemes and policies. The chapter also surveys the contribution of spontaneous settlements to Colombian cities. It claims that not only have they provided lower-income groups with a solution, but have become an extremely valuable source of inspiration for housing policies. Finally, we indicate that without creative intervention to add on to such efforts, these solutions, while being the only housing alternatives for the urban poor in Colombia, will continue denying their residents the proper opportunities for advancement, and will barely continue guaranteeing their class reproduction.

HOUSING THE POOR IN COLOMBIAN CITIES: THE ROLE OF SPONTANEOUS SETTLEMENTS

As in most underdeveloped countries, the lowest economic sectors of Colombian cities have been forced to take care of themselves[1] on highly alienating terms. Displaced by the process of capitalist transformation of the countryside, most of them have been crowding in cities, particularly those centralizing economic activity. Meanwhile, extremely limited opportunities in such cities denied them decent jobs in the formal sector leaving them with no other alternative but to engage in self-help activities for the satisfaction of their own needs.

Housing construction became the core of this effort. It grouped immigrants together around the satisfaction of their subsistence needs. Combining their main resource, labor power, with recycled materials and some cash, groups of the poor managed to develop entire neighborhoods[2] and engage in self-employment ventures. The absence of steady, livable incomes, and self-help housing, no matter how incipient, provided them with an alternative to rental housing and its associated cash demands—utilities, rent, etc. A house made them part of a group with shared needs, provided them with some self-employment opportunities, and facilitated service exchanges and organizing for development of institutions. It gave them a foothold in the city from which to work.

Self-help settlement, however, did not come easy: the urban poor had to fight every inch of the way to get land, build homes, obtain services, and defend their settlements against landowners, government[3], and even other settlers. Largely designed by the urban poor, spontaneous settlements thus became both their main mechanism of urbanization and the basis of their reproduction. At the same time, they reflected the meager living conditions of squatters in the cities of Colombia.

Forms and Importance of Spontaneous Settlement

Spontaneous settlements have taken two main forms in Colombia:[4] pirate settlements and invasions or land take-overs.

Pirate settlements are areas of self-development established in violation of urbanization procedures and requirements. Owners of unimproved lands, usually located outside the urban perimeter, are engaged in illegal sub-division and sale of lots for housing construction. Purchasers then became responsible for making the necessary improvements and installing services while building their individual units. As a result of these violations, pur-chasers of such lots have imperfect titles to the land. Even after many years, most of these settlements lack proper public services and have incipient infrastructures. They are considered illegal and classified as such by local authorities.

Invasions or **land take-overs** result from invasion of private and public lands for self-help housing. Occupants lack titles to these lands. Improve-ments in such areas can be challenged by the legal owners as violation of property rights. Hence, **invasions** have more difficulties than **pirate settle-ments** in getting infrastructure, public services, and facilities. **Invasions** have two distinct forms: they can take place in public spaces that, by definition, should be kept free of any structures (e.g., parks, rights-of-way, or underneath bridges), or they can occupy publicly or privately-owned unimproved lands, often neglected by the owners or reserved for future development.

The importance of these settlements can be illustrated by their size.[5] In Bogotá, according to Vernez, 45.3 percent of the families, or 47.7 percent of the population lived in pirate settlements in 1970. An additional 1.1 percent of total families lived in invasions (Vernez 1973). An estimated 40 percent of the housing stock in that city had been produced through **pirate settlement** (Vernez and Valenzuela 1972). The Planning Department of Bogotá reported that 59 percent of the population lived in **pirate settlements** occupying 38.4 percent of the total built area of the city (Losada Lora and Gómez Buendía

1976, p. 12). Finally, Reig (1976) estimated that between 1960–1974, 27.4 percent of total housing units in the city had been built clandestinely.

Meanwhile, in 1968, local authorities in Medellín[6] counted 80 illegal settlements with nearly 200,000 residents (Campo 1977, p. 133) within the urban perimeter. Six of them were **invasions** and the rest were pirate urbanizations. Estimates of these and other cities suggest that nearly half of the population of large cities in Colombia lives in these two types of settlements.

POLICY EFFORTS

Policies related to spontaneous settlement have ranged from opposition, through initiatives at upgrading and legalizing irreversible situations, to schemes appropriating elements of this form of settlement. Underlying these policies were processes and conditions that local municipalities had little control of and this made policies largely ineffective. A brief discussion of these issues with some reference to the underlying forces follows.

Efforts at Opposing or Regulating Spontaneous Settlement

As in any underdeveloped country, urbanization in Colombia has been sudden, massive, and highly chaotic. While in 1938, 69 percent of the population lived in the countryside, by 1973, 64 percent was urban. In other words, within 35 years the population went from predominantly rural to predominantly urban. The urban proportion in 1986 was 67 percent. As a result, urban centers went from small administrative and commercial towns to large metropolises in a matter of decades. Totally unprepared for this change, cities only started developing comprehensive plans in the late 1940s and early 1950s and have been unable to control or rationalize growth.[7]

The four largest Colombian cities started growing at a fast pace at the beginning of this century, particularly in the 1920s. This growth was characterized by three separate trends: first was the expansion of the old urban core; second, the suburbanization of the upper-income groups; and third, the development of low-income settlements, mostly in rural lands, outside the established urban perimeter. Low-income settlements were usually the result of the illegal subdivision of rural lands and their sale by the lot without any improvements on the land.

The initial reaction to these changes consisted of initiatives towards maintaining the human scale and ordered environment of the traditional town. Such initiatives were introduced by local authorities. They aimed at ridding the city of the 'terrible conditions, often amounting to a public threat, of these settlements' (Vergara y Vergara, 1936, pp. 118–19)—not to say from the poor and their self-help urbanization. Policies included the establishment of urban perimeters to limit expansion (since 1910), zoning regulations (since the 1940s), urbanization procedures (since the 1900s), and urban plans (a few since the 1920s, but most since the 1940s).

Urban perimeters were never respected by pirate developers.[8] Their speculative activities and the prohibitive costs of urban locations for immigrants resulted in the illegal urbanization of noncontiguous rural land. Meanwhile, authorities went along with the violation of established perimeters by periodically adjusting them to include de facto additions.[9]

Zoning was an explicit effort to control pirate development. Trying to prevent the encircling of their neighborhoods or land by the urban poor, local elites pressured local authorities into enacting strict **zoning** laws. These laws stratified cities by use, economic activity and socioeconomic level (Planeación Metropolitana de Medellín 1985, p. 39; Campo 1977). As a result, stratification was institutionalized since the 1940s and the location of settlements of the poor was largely dictated by such regulations.

Urbanization Procedures are particularly relevant for this analysis because they determine the characteristics required from settlements. They include licenses, public services and amenities, open spaces, and housing conditions. Most of them were based on middle-income housing standards, making development of low-income housing cost-prohibitive. Many analysts have indeed attributed spontaneous settlement to these regulations. At the same time, enforcement was hampered by a combination of difficulties in the application of sanctions[10] and an attitude of neglect, permissiveness or selective intervention on the part of local authorities.

In 1968, the national government enacted law 66 of 1968 to regulate urbanization, construction, inspection, and credit. According to this law, developers were required to register with the Superintendencia Bancaria, the national agency regulating banking activity, and to obtain a license for each project they undertook. Violation of these requirements was punishable by cash penalties and intervention of projects (receivership) by the national housing agency, Instituto de Crédito Territorial or ICT. Compliance, however, has been limited and the impact of this law on preventing further pirate development has been minimal for three main reasons: the process was extremely complex and cumbersome; sanctions were relatively modest; and enforcement was extremely limited and highly arbitrary. Moreover, one of the agencies responsible for implementation of this law, ICT, has been accused of being the main pirate developer in the country.[11]

GOVERNMENT INTERVENTION IN THE REGULATION
AND IMPROVEMENT OF SETTLEMENTS

As **pirate settlements** and **invasions** expanded beyond control, local governments decided to intervene. Initially, they issued regulations and provisions outlawing such settlements. They also intervened on numerous occasions to oppose construction, to discourage or bring down illegally built dwellings, and to relocate settlements. This latter form of intervention was particularly strong in **invasions** and was highly resented by settlers.

Residents also resented the neglect of their settlements by the government in contrast to the high attention paid to middle- and upper-income areas. Arguing the illegal status of settlements, public authorities denied them infrastructure and services. Overtime, however, politicians and political parties patronized settlements in exchange for votes and political support.[12] As part of this, they managed to provide assistance with the establishment of some institutions (schools and health centers in particular), the provision of basic services, and street development.

The main mechanism of government intervention in spontaneous settlements were the Community Action Boards or JACs[13] (Juntas de Acción Communal). Created in 1959 for development of public services at the local level, on a self-help basis, JACs became the official vehicles of government assistance to these communities. JACs provided labor and government entities provided materials, direction, and technical assistance. Once established, JACs replaced spontaneous community development[14] efforts and became arms of local administrations and politicians. As such, they were instrumental in penetrating and controlling settlements. Not only were JACs extremely effective as a system of co-optation, but they were a very cheap and convenient way for production of local infrastructure and public services. Through JACs, communities could also be made responsible for resolving their own development problems. Finally, JACs cooperated with the government to incrementally force residents to pay for public services and comply with established regulations (Betancur 1986). In this way, residents—as represented by JACs—often became instruments of their own displacement because many people could no longer afford living in the 'improved' settlements.[15]

GOVERNMENT ALTERNATIVES
FOR HOUSING THE URBAN POOR

In 1929, the government enacted a legislation requiring that municipalities invest 2 percent of their budgets in so-called workers' housing. Individual municipalities set the terms and many of them ended up building housing for their own employees.

In 1939, the government created ICT, for production of low-income housing. ICT followed the orthodox line of opposition to spontaneous settlement and development of public, subsidized housing for private owner-ship. Total combined housing production by ICT and municipalities between 1928 and 1950 amounted to a meager 3,500 dwellings. Annual production by ICT increased to 1,000 in 1951–52 and to nearly 3,000 in 1953–54. Large infusions of foreign finance capital as part of the Alliance for Progress resulted in nearly 85,000 dwellings between 1960–64. Production then decreased to less than 2,500 units in 1965 and reached an average of 10,000 in the following years up to 1971.

Most of this housing was built by the private sector on contract with ICT. In spite of a loan structure of subsidized interest rates, predominantly moderate and middle-income groups with steady incomes benefited from ICT's programs.

In 1970, in an effort to boost the construction industry, the government introduced UPACs (units of acquisitive power) or index linked savings and loans. Private funds tied to this system became the predominant source of housing loans. Only middle- and upper-income buyers and private developers of commercial space could afford such loans.

Meanwhile, ICT continued operating under the fixed interest rate system with differential rates for different types of housing schemes—or solutions as ICT called them. Interest rates skyrocketed, forcing ICT to increase its rates for new projects. Land and building prices also rose dramatically in response to the construction boom set off by the UPAC system. Under these conditions, the costs of housing increased much beyond the possibilities of a majority of the population and illegal housing became the only feasible alternative for them.

During the 1970s, ICT resorted to cofinancing schemes with the private sector. These arrangements proved very expensive and a large proportion of housing subsidies actually went to private developers. In spite of subsidized mortgages, the resulting units were so expensive that only moderate and middle-income households could afford them.

The government of Betancur (1982–86) responded with a substantial increase in the public housing budget and boosted production to a peak of nearly 123,000 units for the period 1982–84. The index-linked UPAC system was also reformed to require the investment of half of its receipts in low-income housing. In spite of a public commitment to the continuation of Betancur's program, succeeding governments were unable to maintain this level of funding and housing production declined again.

Finally, a chronic problem of collection of loan payments left ICT with a $20 billion total in unpaid claims by the end of 1983.[16]

CHANGES IN PERCEPTION
OF SPONTANEOUS SETTLEMENT

Acceleration of rural to urban migration and massive spontaneous settlement in the 1950s and 1960s made opposition to this form of settlement impractical and largely symbolic. Public policies, meanwhile, continued insisting on established schemes of urbanization. A series of political events and practical concerns progressively changed attitudes and policies.

On the political front, the US government moved in the early 1960s to defuse social unrest in Latin America and prevent a repeat of the Cuban revolution in other countries. Loans were, thus, made available under the Alliance for Progress for low-income community development programs. In order to make housing affordable to low-income families, a series of experimental projects of combined self-help and private contract development were undertaken. Developments such as Ciudad Kennedy in Bogota (80,000 people) and Villa Socorro in Medellín (12,000 people) combining self-help and formal construction became international showcases. Within this spirit of reform, ICT adopted schemes of self-help in at least half of its projects boosting housing production to unexpected levels and being able to reach lower-income groups.

The spirit of reform expanded to research and policy. Analysts claimed that spontaneous settlements were indeed a solution to the problem of housing the poor (Mangin 1967; Turner 1967 and 1968). The Colombian government itself started exploring schemes which appropriated elements of spontaneous settlement while maintaining urbanization codes and regulations. Flexible procedures (normas mínimas) allowing for incremental development of dwellings while regulating the activities of self-builders, owners of land, and housing organizations were enacted in large cities since the 1970s. ICT adopted schemes such as loans for self-built dwellings, site-and-service units, and minimal and intermediate dwellings.

On the practical front, in spite of subsidies, adoption of self-help, and other housing and payment schemes, only a low proportion of the poor were able to afford public housing. The rest had to continue engaging in outlawed development forms. Pressure mounted to give a free hand to pirate developers, to give land to the poor and let them build their dwellings, to legalize and upgrade existing spontaneous settlements, and to use public subsidies for those most in need (Arango 1986; Gauhan 1975; Vernez 1973). Meanwhile, recent governments became increasingly reluctant to engage in large efforts of public housing such as those of the Betancur government. Finally, strong populist pressures in the mid-to-late 1980s and a highly explosive political environment forced the government to enact a new constitution and to engage in urban reform.

As a result, in 1989 an urban reform package was passed with strong provisions regarding the legalization and upgrading of spontaneous settlements. The urban reform provided legal and financial mechanisms but the government has been moving very slowly with implementation, settlers are being asked to pay for a costly process of legalizing their properties,[17] and the law has a limited applicability to properties covered by Law 200 of 1936.[18] Preliminary results are discouraging and only a strong commitment on the part of the government to the removal of initial difficulties will profit from the great potential of this reform.

The Urban Reform of 1989 and Subsequent Legislation and Policies Related to Spontaneous Settlement.[19]

Four elements of the legislation are particularly relevant to these settlements, namely the expropriation or voluntary alienation of private property, enactment or perfection of individual land titles, legalization of social interest settlement, and housing subsidies.

Land Expropriation

The Colombian constitution states that property has a social function and, hence, implies certain obligations. Based on this, the 1989 urban reform contains key provisions allowing for land expropriation. It authorizes municipalities and other entities to acquire property either through voluntary alienation or through expropriation for a series of uses including public services, social interest housing, future development, social infrastructure, public works, legalization of titles in illegal settlements, and reallocation of settlements from high risk areas.

Lands can be expropriated without indemnization when owners promote or tolerate their occupation for construction of housing in violation of land use regulations, sanitary or **urban perimeters**, licenses, and other requirements. Expropriation should be initiated by the respective municipalities and excludes improvements or dwellings of the social interest type.[20] This provision applies to **pirate settlements**.

As far as **invasions** are concerned, the law orders national public entities to turn fiscal property owned by them over to illegal occupants at no cost to the latter, provided that the property had been used for social interest housing and that it had been occupied before 28 July 1988. This provision excludes public spaces and facilities, fiscal property reserved for health and educational uses, and property in unhealthy or high risk areas. Meanwhile, starting 1 January 1990, property can be obtained by 'prescription'[21] in the case of social interest housing after three or five years, depending on the form of occupation of the land—by pirate subdivision or **invasion**. Properties owned by municipalities or JACs cannot be acquired by 'prescription'.

In short, all lands illegally occupied by social interest housing can be expropriated with or without indemnization, depending on the case.[22] Since only a few of them would qualify for indemnization, according to the terms of the law, expropriation seems the obvious course of action for local municipalities. The complexity, backlog, delays resulting from appeals, length and cost of the legal process, and the details of actual implementation are not totally clear at this point and could take years to develop, hence preventing or delaying implementation.[23]

Enactment and Perfection of Titles

Occupants of social interest housing in illegal settlements have to initiate a court process to claim legal title to the property they occupy or to perfect imperfect titles. They can do it individually or in groups.[24] They do not need to include the name of the title holder in the demand but are responsible for providing the proper information on the property so that the registrar can produce the necessary documentation. In the case of expropriation without indemnization, occupants do not have to pay any balance owed to the owner. In fact, they can demand restitution of the amounts already paid by them with interest. Municipalities are responsible for carrying out these action on behalf of the occupants and for investing the amounts recovered from the owners in improvements and services of the expropriated property. States may establish sliding scales for registration and other property transfer taxes for the purpose of social interest housing.

In order to facilitate the proper registration and extension of titles, the law waived a series of requirements including income tax return, proof of military service, payment of national taxes, construction or urbanization licenses, deeds, and other taxes.

Purchasers of owner-occupied social interest housing are not obliged to make any payments to sellers so long as they fail to provide the water, sewer, electricity, streets, and other services required by the local municipality.

Meanwhile, in the absence of a legal title, the law authorizes lending institutions to accept as a guarantee on loans, improvements carried out by applicants on land they have occupied as social interest housing during a period of no less than five years.

Legalization of Illegal Settlements

City councils may delegate legalization of settlements (incorporation into the **urban perimeter** and upgrading) to mayors. The law authorizes individuals or groups to request and obtain all public services upon proof of habitation and instructs the proper authorities to give priority to social interest housing units. Service provision is conditionally based on technical feasibility and payment of connection costs by the user. For social interest housing units, connection costs will be billed after installation and will be paid in terms convenient to the user.[25]

It is the responsibility of communities—through their representative JACs—and municipalities to provide services, infrastructure, and other improvements required for legalization of settlements. To finance this work, cities use allocations from their regular budgets along with proceeds from two national taxes created by the law and ceded to them by the national government, namely the **Contribution to Local Development** and the **Tax on Socioeconomic Stratification**. The former is a tax on urban land rent resulting from social or public improvements. It is charged to owners of real estate property in municipalities of 100,000 or more people at the time of realization of land rent.[26] The latter is a tax on the owners of middle- to upper-income housing also in municipalities of 100,000 people or more.[27] Finally, cities can issue urban reform bonds for this purpose. Such bonds will not be guaranteed by the national government.

Housing Subsidies

Law 03 of 15 January 1991 established a housing subsidy in money or in kind[28] for households with monthly incomes of four or less minimum wages. The subsidy can be used for the acquisition of unurbanized or urbanized lots, basic housing units, used dwellings, minimum dwellings, productive dwellings, for housing solutions resulting from improvements and rehabilitation or from legalization of titles, and for the various rural housing solutions. If the recipient of the subsidy transfers the dwelling to other parties or moves out before the fifth anniversary, the subsidy should be returned to the government. The subsidy will also be returned in case of false information in the application.

Any qualified household can apply for the subsidy. Applicants should indicate the amount and nature of resources available for the solution they will apply the subsidy to.[29] Applications are ordered on the basis of available resources and membership in a housing organization.[30]

The maximum amount of subsidies is 15 minimum monthly wages per household, with individual solutions receiving up to 12 and collective solutions up to 15 minimum monthly wages per solution. For solutions resulting in rehab and improvement of existing units or from legalization of titles, the amount of subsidy will be determined on a project by project basis—consisting of up to 75 percent of the cost but not exceeding 15 minimum monthly wages.

Subsidies are distributed by ICT and Cajas de Compensación Familiar in municipalities of more than 15,000 people and by the Caja de Crédito Agrario in municipalities with less than 15,000 people.

Eligibility for application of subsidies is determined by ICT on the basis of cost, licenses, and characteristics. Solutions should not exceed the maximum prices indicated earlier.

Prohibition of Future Invasions or Pirate Settlements

While establishing provisions for legalization of spontaneous settlements, urban reform includes other provisions outlawing any future developments of this type.

Besides ordering the expropriation of lands and the reimbursement of payments to purchasers when owners engage in illegal urbanization, the law establishes cash penalties for developers operating without a license or in violation of established regulations. Furthermore, it authorizes police intervention to stop their projects and instructs authorities to disconnect public services to the sites unless people live there on a permanent basis. Similar penalties are established for the use of real estate for purposes other than those stipulated in licenses or for establishments operating without a license.

The reform orders the demolition of buildings constructed without a license or in violation of established regulations as well as those portions of buildings not covered by or built in violation of the license. It also includes cash penalties for occupation or closing of public areas without the proper permits. The urban reform law authorizes the use of police to remove occupants of illegally occupied lands when their owners or representatives do not do it themselves as determined by Law 57 of 1905. Removal is permitted only when occupation has just started or is about to happen, implies a risk for anybody, or takes place against established regulations. In these cases, local authorities may order demolition of all built structures and other necessary actions to restore the property to its previous condition. Owners are required to carry out this work. Otherwise, local authorities will conduct it and bill owners for the total cost plus an additional 10 percent for administrative costs.

The law orders local authorities to inventory and relocate settlements currently in unhealthy or risky areas and to make sure that such lands are not resettled. Land and improvements can be expropriated or voluntarily alienated through procedures indicated earlier and can be traded for other property. In case of refusal, settlers can be forcefully removed from the site and the settlement razed.

It is clear then that any future urban settlement has to either proceed according to established regulations or face expropriation and demolition. Similarly, any illegal construction can be stopped and demolished and the owners penalized. Meanwhile, the law provides for an alternative in the form of a more flexible, subsidized process of urbanization for development of social interest housing and settlement.

'NEW' ALTERNATIVE SOCIAL INTEREST SETTLEMENT SOLUTIONS

The urban reform and ensuing legislation promote flexible housing schemes—some of which had been progressively introduced since the 1960s, as mentioned earlier, while adding a few reinforcing elements. In fact, the law incorporates alternative housing solutions ranging from self-building, through combined self-help and privately developed schemes, to finished dwellings. It provides for subsidies and other mechanisms to guarantee an adequate availability of land and other required elements at costs lower than those available in the market. Besides the household subsidy already described, it calls for cities to make the necessary service installations and provide infrastructure and social services in social interest settlements.

It calls for expropriation and acquisition of land for development and upgrading of settlements, land banks, organized community participation in the development and improvement of settlements, research and development of new schemes including alternative construction techniques and materials, establishment of centers for provision of construction materials and tools at reasonable prices and terms, and development of people's housing organizations.

Finally, it instructs INURBE—National Institute of Social Interest Housing and Urban Reform, formerly ICT—to preside over these activities, to work with municipalities, the private sector, and housing organizations in such efforts. The mandate is to give priority to joint projects with municipalities and housing organizations of the poor, while only exceptionally engaging in direct development of INURBE's own projects. This is a dramatic change in the direction of the agency which, with the exception of the 1970s, had traditionally emphasized direct development.

For coordination and implementation of these efforts, Law 03 of 1991 created the social interest housing system and made the changes in the structure of INURBE. The system operates as a mechanism of coordination of all entities involved in provision of social interest housing. It is divided into the subsystems of promotion and implementation, technical assistance and social organization, and financing. The Ministry of Economic Development is charged with the responsibility of coordinating the system and developing policies and plans. Municipalities are instructed to coordinate the local system and to create a social interest housing fund.[31]

INURBE is responsible for promotion of social interest housing and implementation of urban reform.

CONCLUDING COMMENTS

As the previous pages indicate, in Colombia, housing policies related to spontaneous settlement have come a long way from the initial attitude of total opposition and neglect. In fact, they seem to imply the impossibility of the system—government and private sector included—to provide a better alternative. At the same time, however, policy efforts and practice bear multiple contradictions. Forced by circumstances, the government has assumed a contradictory attitude of opposition and permissiveness. Real opposition was impractical, politically unfeasible, and potentially explosive.

Looking backwards, we can identify an overall policy of legal opposition and practical permissiveness, accompanied by indirect mechanisms of penetration, intervention, and control of illegal, *de facto* situations. Legal, public opposition helped maintain the foundations of private property and the formal market system. Permissiveness allowed for solutions within the possibilities of the population and prevented potentially explosive confrontations between the government and the population. Meanwhile, mechanisms such as JACs and *clientelismo* gave the government extremely effective tools for manipulation of deprivation and social control.

The next piece of this policy was a comprehensive program of amnesty and legalization *after the fact*. This is what the urban reform and other previous pieces of legislation provided. Had the government engaged in long-term thinking, it would not have been able to come up with such a clever incremental design. The force of the circumstances and the needs of maintaining law and order produced this outcome through trial and error but more importantly through accommodation and struggle by the multiple interests involved. The urban reform itself brought together a series of elements that had been progressively introduced and that were largely imposed by illegal developers on the urban poor in the absence of any other real alternatives.

Interestingly enough, while providing for legalization of illegal settlements, the reform reintroduced and strengthened the principles of opposition to spontaneous settlement and imposition of private property and market terms. This opposition could be viewed as a commitment on the part of the system to provide a decent settlement for all citizens. Unfortunately, this is not the ultimate rationale. Spontaneous settlements operate on the elimination of costs that make housing cost-prohibitive for large sectors of the urban poor in underdeveloped, peripheral countries.[32] They also operate on deprivation and the flexible combinations of labor, cash, and recyclable materials, as well as on informal systems of mutual help and individual transactions. While integrating some of these elements and adding some subsidies, the alternatives provided by the reform, add back many of these costs, replace informal with formal transactions, and eliminate much of the flexibility. Subsidies are largely absorbed by the additional costs and profits of industries involved in market production. The formula for prioritizing applications puts those with more resources at the top, while pushing those with less to the bottom. In short, the reform operates on the full guarantee of private property, protection of the formal construction industry, and the requirement of infrastructure and other improvements, largely developed in market terms. Self-help labor, progressive development, and minimum quality housing are elements taken from spontaneous settlement schemes. These elements are appropriated here for the purpose of making the system feasible and guaranteeing private property.

The reform also takes the national government out of the business of direct housing development while putting much of the responsibility on municipalities, housing organizations of the poor, the private sector, and the poor themselves. Funding for improvement and future development of social interest settlements comes largely from owners of real estate property. Lands currently occupied by settlements are expropriated without indemnization. Upgrading depends on government resources in combination with forced labor extracted from residents of settlements. Subsidies can be applied to a variety of housing solutions from upgrading to the acquisition of privately-produced units.

Under these circumstances, three main hypothetical results are advanced here:

1. Conditions for the urban poor in spontaneous settlements are not likely to improve much in the near future. In fact, based on the historical pace of implementation of reforms in Colombia, the additional costs of legal processes, potential challenges, the political muscle of affected interests, and the number of cases involved, expropriation and perfection or enactment of titles may become a nightmare or a practical impossibility. Furthermore, residents of these settlements may view the process with suspicion particularly if they are forced to pay anything, as the case of

Modellín, mentioned earlier, suggests. Upgrading is even more complicated. Municipalities have been involved in this effort since the 1960s. Yet, the results have been disappointing. Residents are fed up with the system of forced labor and the replacement of their own solutions with often poorer government installations. Upgrading includes a series of additional costs that residents have avoided or cannot afford. Finally, housing subsidies are too low to make a dent in the problem, are now spread too thin,[33] and are allocated to the better-off among applicants. In the best of cases, residents may achieve title to the land, but continue living in the same downgraded conditions they live in today.

2. Development of new settlements has slowed down. If the reform is properly implemented, it will most likely discourage further development. Overcrowding or homelessness will increase unless new loopholes are found in the law to continue or come up with new forms of spontaneous settlement. In fact, established provisions will substantially slow down or prevent pirate development because the owners of unimproved land will be unwilling to take the risks of expropriation and cash penalties. The prices determined by the legislation for social interest dwellings are extremely low, and can only buy outlawed settlements. Alternatively, the government will have to enact new regulations close to those of spontaneous settlements or beef up subsidies to include the costs that the urban poor cannot afford. Otherwise, loopholes may be found in the law or permissiveness may continue to allow for further spontaneous settlement.

3. In spite of this, the reform is a big step ahead in that it accepts the need for the government to upgrade settlements; to work with organizations of the poor; to give more flexibility to subsidies; to build on the social function of private property, particularly land; to coordinate the activities of players involved in the production of social interest housing; to allow for more flexible schemes of housing production and settlement; and to stop prosecution of residents of existing settlements, while extending protection to their possessions. Short of decent jobs and other opportunities allowing the poor to buy decent settlement, more efforts are needed to decommodify housing; to encourage creative solutions such as self-provision of services—rather than razing them and hooking all settlements to monopolistic local public systems; to desegregate the settlements of the poor; to increase local economic opportunities; to prevent manipulation of their needs and co-optation of their organizational efforts; to form real partnerships with settlements; in short, to work with people around the solution of their problems rather than trying to force them into generic schemes and consumption forms they cannot afford.

How much of this is feasible within the current development level and conditions of countries like Colombia is difficult to determine. Perhaps we need to revise this as part of the effort. What is very clear is the need to push this groundwork to its full potential and to take the necessary measures towards its implementation. Initial evidence from spontaneous settlements recently visited by the author in Medellín suggests that initial efforts at legalization have failed, that upgrading continues largely along the previous lines, and that authorities are more concerned about stopping further spontaneous settlements than about providing decent alternatives for the urban poor.

NOTES

1. Most analysts concede that a large majority of the urban population in Colombia cannot afford commercial housing (Vernez 1973; Murillo and Unga 1978; Jaramillo 1980; Soto Sierra 1981). In the metropolitan area of Medellín, for instance, 80 percent of the population received 49.3 percent of total income, compared to the upper 20 percent which received 50.7 percent. Similarly, 75.6 percent of all dwellings in this area are classified as medium-low or lower-income (Planeación Metropolitana de Medellín 1985, p. 73).

2. Individual housing construction has been largely a family project. Many descriptions of this process and spontaneous or squatter settlement are available in the literature and we refer the reader to them (Mangin 1967; Turner 1967 and 1968; Vernez 1973; Serna, Betancur, and Londoño 1981). Neighbors, coworkers, members of extended families, friends, parishioners, or others assist families with the main tasks. The settlement as a whole, its layout, defense, development of infrastructure and services, however, are usually a collective undertaking.

3. Many descriptions of this struggle are available in the literature (Campo 1977; Janssen 1984; Santana 1981; Serna, Betancur and Londoño 1981). Confronted with problems of titles and multiple forms of exploitation in the countryside, Colombian peasants have been involved in a never-ending struggle for land, whose most dramatic illustration was La Violencia of the 1950s and the ensuing guerrilla warfare and other more recent efforts. Displaced to the cities, peasants continued this fight through the struggle for a roof, a job, education, and so on (Betancur 1986; Campo 1977).

.4. Generic descriptions of squatter settlements are available in the literature and have been already mentioned. Each country, however, has its own, distinct versions of these settlements. Their possibility, form, and development are closely tied to the structure, legislation, and history of the specific country.

5. Even though this paper focuses on squatter settlements, it is important to mention here that self-help housing extends beyond them. A large proportion of middle-income families use self-help methods and tactics to escape the high costs of housing developed along government-established regulations. In Bogota, an estimated 65 to 70 percent of total dwellings have been illegally developed and such an estimate can be comfortably applied to the other large cities of the country (Foro 1985). Our discussion, hence, can be extended to apply to all illegally developed housing. This analysis, however, strictly addresses squatters settlements.

6. Medellín was the second largest city of Colombia at the time.

7. The City of Bogota grew at an annual rate of 7.4 percent between 1950–60 and at 7.3 percent between 1960–1970. During this period, only 11 other cities in the world grew at higher rates (Davis 1969). Since 1970, the city has been expanding at a rate of 6.8 percent per year,

still one of the largest in the world. Between 1938–51, the metropolitan area of Medellín grew at a yearly rate of 6.76 percent and between 1951–64 at 6.66 percent. The rates for the periods 1964–73 and 1973–85 were 4.58 and 3.1 percent respectively. The other two largest Colombian cities, Cali and Barranquilla, grew at comparable rates.

8. **Pirate settlements** were facilitated by illegal land speculation. Owners of rural land in the periphery of urban cores were engaged in the sale of unimproved, small lots for housing construction. Given the location and unimproved condition of the land, prices were as low as they could possibly be. Immigrants used proceeds from the sale of a piece of land or a harvest back in the countryside to buy these lots. Others paid by installments. Transactions were imperfect because they violated established urbanization procedures. Besides, land was used for a purpose other than the one determined by its location (Losada Lora and Gomez Buendía 1976). When questioned about their activity, sellers argued that they were selling the land for cultivation and that use of the lots for housing was beyond their control. Soon after the purchase of a lot, buyers engaged in the progressive construction of housing.

9. Many of these speculators were involved in local politics or were able to buy their way. Furthermore, authorities often assumed a permissive attitude to avoid further conflicts with immigrants or because they could not offer an alternative housing solution to the urban poor.

10. Loopholes in the law often prevented its implementation as people could always argue otherwise or as they could delay for ever the process of enforcement.

11. A 1972 national study of so-called subnormal settlements (or settlements not complying with existing regulations) identified 198 projects developed by ICT that fell under this category (out of a total of 2,136 subnormal settlements identified). Hence, 10 percent of subnormal settlements had been developed by the national housing agency of the government (Campo 1977, p. 175). The same agency has followed many of the practices of pirate developers: it has developed projects outside established urban perimeters; it has built housing for the poor in steep lands with high risks for residents; it has acquired lands without previously determining their conditions for settlement; it has developed settlements far away from the rest of the city reinforcing the discontinuity between the city and peripheral settlements; finally, through these activities it has contributed to the valorization of rural land and has facilitated the urbanization of previously inaccessible private areas. It is certainly a big irony that Law 66 of 1968 assigned this agency the responsibility of inspection and supervision of private urbanization activities!

12. This process has been called **clientelismo** in Colombia. Individual politicians or political parties managed to gain the trust of local leaders, supported specific projects in the settlements, or became their official protectors, in exchange for political support (e.g., votes, attendance to rallies, signing of petitions, and so on). In turn, residents welcomed this help to gain legitimacy for their settlements. Besides, need was such that any help made a significant difference. Over the years, residents learned to manipulate this situation and systematically turned to elected politicians for support. **Clientelismo** operated as a system of mutual obligations in which support was paid with support. In the long run, the system became a political machine: local leaders were co-opted through jobs in the public sector, assistance in obtaining licenses to operate small businesses, scholarships for their children, and so on. Meanwhile, politicians or parties gained the monopoly of their settlements.

13. These boards institutionalized a rural tradition of collective action and self-help at the local level, known as **convites. Convites** were gatherings of neighbors for development projects of general benefit such as a small bridge, a school, or a road. They were also used to assist members of the group in situations of extreme need. Spontaneous versions of JACs existed in urban settlements as early as the 1940s. This concept was combined with community development schemes introduced in Colombia by international missions and experimented

with as pacifiers of the countryside and for development of infrastructure and services at the community level (Betancur 1986, pp. 112–31).

14. Since public resources were only channelled through JACs, spontaneous organizations controlled by local communities were forced to fold. Some communities viewed this as a co-optation of their own organization and resisted JACs. In the long run, however, most communities acceded to the JAC structure. As entities regulated by the government, JACs became highly politicized and played into the hands of politicians along the **clientelismo** lines mentioned earlier. This was largely the end of the locally controlled, independent organization in these settlements.

15. The extremely low incomes of immigrants prevented them from entering into any forms of housing consumption with high and steady cash demands. Spontaneous settlements were built to maximize the use of labor while minimizing the need for cash. Public services were usually obtained on an unpaid basis either through use of local streams and latrines, or through illegal connection of dwellings to public electricity poles. Once services were legally connected through the intervention of JACs, residents had to pay for installation and use. JACs were also used to introduce numbering of houses with the subsequent registration in the local tax system and the collection of real estate taxes. These improvements increased the need for cash making settlements unaffordable for many residents.

16. The potentially explosive impact of foreclosures and evictions along with the intervention of politicians on behalf of settlements and individuals under the **clientelismo** scheme described earlier tied the hands of the agency. Local JACs often worked with politicians to prevent eviction and ICT was unable to enforce loan payments (Betancur 1986, pp. 180–88).

17. In Medellín, for instance, residents have to pay for the costs of legalization or perfection of titles. Costs include surveys of land, development of maps identifying each of the lots, license permits, land assessments, and legal fees associated with the transfer of titles to the municipality and from this to the landholder. Residents have to also pay taxes on land improvements in case they exceed 700,000 pesos. If the municipality has to acquire the land from the legal owners for some reason, residents may be required to pay for it. Residents of two settlements indicated that they had gained possession or had already paid for the land and the improvements and that they did not owe anything to anybody.

18. According to our interviews of public functionaires in Medellín during the summer of 1993, settlements qualifying for legalization under this law do not qualify under the urban reform. As a result, the majority of spontaneous settlements in the city do not qualify for legalization through the reform but through Law 200. At the same time, however, mechanisms created by the former are being extended to the legalizations of the latter. These include waivers on some taxes and requirements, and the processing of large areas under a single process. An additional issue is that titles become the patrimony of the family and, hence, cannot be transferred without the consent of all members—children need to have reached majority age to sign for themselves or an additional legal process including a curator is required.

19. This section includes only those elements of the urban reform and other recent legislation related to squatter settlements.

20. These are dwellings priced at a maximum of 100 minimum monthly wages for cities of 100,000 people or less at the time of acquisition, 120 wages for cities of more than 100,000 and less than 500,000 people, and 135 for cities of over 500,000 people.

21. Previous to this law, property could be obtained by 'prescription' or loss of ownership after 10 and 20 years of occupation by an invader.

22. The only cases in which indemnization seems to be justified are **invasions** in which owners acted as the law required or **pirate settlements** not tolerated or promoted by the legal owner of the land—there were cases in which family members or legal managers acted without the consent of the owners, in their absence, or after they died (Betancur 1986, pp. 153–62).

Loopholes or other allegations, however, may allow many owners to contest expropriation of their lands without indemnization.

23. Based on the implementation of previous legislation and all the tools available to lawyers, it is realistic to expect challenges, delays, and obstructions to the implementation of these provisions.

24. Occupants of the same track of land can raise a single claim against the legal title holder.

25. In Colombia, the cost of public utilities varies from neighborhood to neighborhood based on the socioeconomic stratum of the neighborhood, with lower-strata neighborhoods paying less and higher ones more.

26. This tax consists of a third of the estimated rent. The estimated rent will be the difference between the assessment before improvements and a final assessment at the time of sale or public registration or the enactment of a new lease or contract. Local councils in municipalities of less than 100,000 people will determine whether or not to charge this tax. Social interest, minimum size dwellings and housing rehabilitation projects increasing the density of occupation are exempt from this tax.

27. This tax will be based on classifications established by each municipality on the basis of the characteristics and locations of housing as well as on stratification as determined by the National Department of Statistics (DANE). It will range from one to five per 1000 annually of the tax assessment of the property. Local councils will determine the rates for each stratum and will establish any exemptions.

28. In kind, subsidies consist of land, construction materials, and public services.

29. Applicants should have at least 5 percent of the cost of that solution in kind or money. In kind, contributions include land, construction materials, labor, and savings or retirement funds.

30. For individual projects applications are ordered on the basis of the percentage resulting from dividing the amount of the subsidy plus the amount contributed by the applicant by the total cost of the proposed solution. For ties, the order will be based on the date of the application. Applicant contributions exceeding 30 percent of the cost will be treated as equal. For collective projects, the ordering will be based on the amount of additional credit per solution required, with those requiring less having a priority over those requiring more.

31. The fund consists of appropriations demanded by law; at least 5 percent of the municipal budget; penalties from illegal urbanization, illegal use of real estate, and illegal occupation of public use areas and facilities; a portion of the contribution to local development tax, donations, ejidos, abandoned real estate property, transfers from other public entities, and proceeds from its own activities.

32. These costs include acquisition—or invasion—of unimproved lands, elimination of costs associated with property transactions, licenses, and other urban regulations, self-help, incremental building, and nonpayment of services and infrastructure.

33. While subsidies were used previously for development of new settlements, under the new legislation they can be applied to spontaneous settlements as well as to the acquisition of new housing.

REFERENCES

Arango, Carlos. 1986. *La Lucha por la Vivienda en Colombia.* Bogota: Ediciones Eco.

Betancur, John J. 1986. 'Domination Through Community Development: A New-Hegelian Perspective'. Ph.D. Dissertation, University of Illinois at Chicago.

Campo, Urbano. 1977. *La Urbanización en Colombia*. Bogota: Biblioteca Marxista Colombiana.

Davis, K. 1969. *World Urbanization, 1950–70*. Vol. I. Berkeley: University of California, Institute of International Studies.

Foro Nacional por Colombia. 1985. 'Documentos del Foro'. Paper presented to the Primer Congreso Unitario de Vivienda Popular. Bogota. 17–19 August.

Gauhan, Timothy. 1975. 'Some Economic and Political Characteristics of the Low-Income Housing Market in Bogota, Colombia and their Implications for Public Policy Alternatives'. Program of Development Studies Paper No. 64. Houston: Rice University.

Janssen, Roel. 1984. *Vivienda y Luchas Populares en Bogota*. Bogota: Ediciones Tercer Mundo.

Jaramillo, Samuel. 1980. *Producción de Vivienda y Capitalismo Dependiente: El Caso de Bogota*. Bogota: Editorial Dintel.

Losada Lora, Rodrigo and **Hernando Gómez Buendía**. 1976. *La Tierra en el Mercado Pirata de Bogota*. Bogota: Fedesarrollo.

Mangin, William. 1967. 'Latin American Squatter Settlements: A Problem and a Solution'. *Latin American Research Review 2(3)*, pp. 65–98.

Molina, Humberto and **Luz Angela Mondragón**. 1976. 'Política de Vivienda del Estado Colombiano', in CIAP, CID, CPU, *EL Problema de la Vivienda en Colombia*. Bogota: CIAD, CID, CPU.

Murillo, Gabriel and **Elizabeth Ungar**. 1978. *Política, Vivienda Popular y el Proceso de Toma de Decisiones en Colombia*. Bogota: Uniandes.

Planeación Metropolitana de Medellín. 1985. *Plan de Desarrollo Metropolitano del Valle de Aburrá*. Medellín, Planeación Metropolitana.

Reig, Martin. 1976. 'La Proyección de la Coexistencia de Formas de Producción de Vivienda sobre la Morfología Urbana: El Caso de Bogota', in CIAP, CID, and CPU, *El Problema de la Vivienda en Colombia*, Vol. VII. Bogota: SIAP, CID, and CPU.

Santana, Pedro. 1981. 'Movimientos Populares y Reivindicaciones Urbanas', *La Problemática Urbana Hoy en Colombia*. Bogota: Centro de Investigación y Educación Popular, Serie Teoría y Sociedad.

Serna, Albalucía, John J. Betancur and **Patricia Londoño**. 1981. *Composición Social y Mobilización Política en Barrios Populares de Medellín*. Medellín: Universidad de Antioquia.

Soto Sierra, Pedro Javier. 1981. 'Un Nuevo Enfoque en las Soluciones Habitacionales para Sectores de Muy Bajos Ingresos', in Pedro Santana (ed.), *La Vivienda Popular en Colombia*. Bogota: Centro de Investigación y Educación Popular, pp. 127–59.

Turner, John. 1967. 'Barriers and Channels for Housing Development in Modernizing Countries', *Journal of the American Institute of Planners 33(3)*, pp. 167–81.

———. 1968. 'Housing Priorities, Settlement Patterns, and Urban Development in Modernizing Countries', *Journal of the American Institute of Planners 34(6)*, pp. 354–63.

Vergara y Vergara, Julio C. 1936. 'El Desarrollo Urbano de la Capital y las Obras del Cuarto Centenario', *Registro Municipal VI*, pp. 7–19. Bogota.

Vernez, George and **Jaime Valenzuela**. 1972. 'La Estructura del Mercado de la Vivienda en Bogota y la Magnitud de la Actividad Constructora Popular', *Economía Colombiana 93*, pp. 8–21.

Vernez, George. 1973. *Bogota's Pirate Settlements: An Opportunity for Metropolitan Development*. Berkeley: University of California at Berkeley.

10

Informal and Substandard Housing in Revolutionary Cuba

Kosta Mathey

URBANIZATION AND ANTIURBANIZATION

Like all Latin American States, Cuba has a severe housing problem. The situation is nevertheless different in many aspects. There are, for example, no pavement dwellers, and the proportion of people living in slums and squatter settlements is just a fraction of what we are accustomed to find in typical Third World cities. In Cuba, different qualities of accommodation do not necessarily represent a social segregation too, since income differentials are not very big in the first place, and generally speaking, housing access does not depend on the rules of the market. Already the Moncada program of 1953, a kind of manifesto outlining the priorities of the Cuban revolution, established the right of every family to a home; this principle has also been included in the constitution of 1976. Because shelter is considered a social good, the different policies chosen to combat the housing problem imply a collective effort, rather than leaving it to the individual alone (Rey, no date, p. 1).

In the Third World, the problem of deficient housing supply is closely linked to urbanization processes and demographic growth. Also in Cuba before 1959, almost all infrastructure and other productive investment was concentrated in the capital city, which attracted a large number of migrants, and helped, together with high reproduction rates, to turn Havana into a typical primate city several times bigger than the next largest city. After the victory of the revolution, a more balanced regional development and distribution of population over the national territory was attempted. This implied the extension of social infrastructure and housing provision to small towns and the countryside, and concentration of investment in provincial centers, such as Villa Clara, Holguin and Las Tunas. where accelerated urbanization processes were experienced as a consequence. The strategy of making only very little investment available to the capital was successful and reduced Havana's dominant position in almost all sectors, as Table 10.1 illustrates. This is a unique case in Latin America.

However, in respect to housing provision, the price for this success was high: lack of repairs and maintenance over the last 30 years was responsible for the serious deterioration of Havana's existing housing stock. The situation would have been even more dramatic, if not some 100,000 Habaneros had left the country during the massive exodus in 1981, and if the general population growth rate had not gone down to levels even below those in many industrialized countries due to a social policy providing excellent educational and employment opportunities, and a social security system better than elsewhere in Latin America (Catasus et al., 1988).

Table 10.1: Reduction of Havana's Primacy in Relation to the Rest of the Country between 1959 and 1984

Population	from 21%[*] to 19%
Buildings	from 55% to 30%
Non-sugar industries	from 70% to 36%
Importation	from 90% to 39%
Hospital beds	from 61% to 39%
Doctors	from 63% to 30%
University students	from 80% to 36%

[*] 23% according to Estevez (1985, p. 7).
Source: Instituto Nacional de la Vivienda (1987, p. 9).

SLUMS AND SQUATTER SETTLEMENTS

Housing stress is expressed by a number of different phenomena in Cuba. Apart from general conditions of overcrowding which propel self-help solutions in the form of *barbacoas* (second floors inserted into rooms with a high ceiling) and *casetas en azoteas* (rooftop huts), problems are perceived in the existence of *barrios insalubres* (improvised or squatter settlements), *cuarterias* (subdivided older inner-city tenements) and *ciudadelas*, also known as *solares*, *casas de vicinidad* (slums). The bottom end of the list is filled by the *albergues* (emergency shelters) in the urban areas. In the countryside, the persistence of *bohios* (one-room thatched huts, often without a floor) is generally accepted to be part of the housing problem.

Barbacoas are a particularity in the older parts of Havana. There the tall ground floors were originally built to accommodate shops and warehouses. Also the rooms in the first and second floor, which formerly accommodated the owners of the enterprise, had high ceilings. Unlike the capitalist capitals abroad, once freed from their original use there is no economic pressure for modernization to install shops, or to convert warehouses into offices. This permitted the use for housing. To accommodate relatives and growing families the occupants very often inserted a second floor into existing rooms, thus creating maisonette type dwellings. Existing tall windows were partly bricked up and replaced by smaller ones, which is visible from outside and modifies the original facade. What is worse, however, is the lack of ventilation inside the rooms given the typically hot climate, and the additional load on floors which aggravates the weakness of the structures due to deterioration, and frequently leads to the collapse of whole buildings (Autorenkollektiv 1987, p. 31; Coyula 1986, p. 186).

Casetas en azoteas: Older multistorey buildings, most of which are in Havana, have flat and usually accessible roofs. To satisfy the same needs which made people build *barbacoas*, there developed the fashion to construct huts on top of existing buildings. There was no private landlord to object, and the authorities turned a blind eye on it since they would have been responsible to provide alternative accommodation. Again, where the original structure had already been *overcharged* from *barbacoas* or weakened through decay, there was a hazard of buildings collapsing. In Havana's peripheral residential areas and in other towns most houses built since the 1930s have flat roofs, too, following the architectural models fashionable in the United States at that time (Martin & Rodriguez 1992), However, since these more recent structures are normally sound, and in order to use existing infrastructure (water and electricity lines, sewers) more intensively, the construction of *casetas en azoteas* and second floors is now being encouraged by the authorities. A special section on the recent housing legislation deals with this issue (Cuba 1984; Davalos 1990, pp. 72–74)

Barrios insalubres are neighborhoods of illegally built huts and houses, comparable to squatter settlements in other developing countries. Many of them still date from the time before the revolution, when they were much more common. Although most of the existing *barrios insalubres* had disappeared in the first years after 1959, some new ones have also been formed, particularly in Santiago de Cuba, the country's second largest city with a surrounding poor and mountainous countryside that profited the least from the general decentralization programs. More recent statistics list 416 *barrios insalubres*, all 61 of which are in Havana, with a total population of 300,000 (Hamberg 1990, p. 52).[1] Most *barrios* have consolidated over time and contain a considerable proportion of comfortable and spacious residences— much unlike the majority of squatter settlements abroad. This development became possible because the residents were not threatened by forceful removal, the authorities even extended many social services (schools, family doctors) and public transport to these areas. In Havana, for example, a study about the quality of *barrios insalubres* was conducted in 1983. It came to the conclusion that 28 out of the 61 recognized *barrios insalubres* should be exempted from that category, since their consolidation has advanced so far that they could be considered a regular part of the city pattern. Also, in the remainder 33 *barrios* demolition seemed advisable only partially, while a certain proportion if the existing dwellings were well-worth saving or upgrading (Coyula 1986, p. 193).

Cuarterias are a common name for subdivided tenements in mansions of old Habana, built as boarding houses in the first half of this century. In Centro Habana, particularly the blocks close to the University, some of them were originally constructed as *casas de huespedes* (private student hosiels; Leinauer et al. 1992). This type of accommodation not only tends to be run-down to the extreme, but also lacks private facilities. The number of *cuarterias* declined by 139,507 (8.2 percent) between 1970 and 1981, with less than 5 percent of the capital's population living in them in the 1980s (Luzon 1988, p. 72).

Ciudadelas (also: *solares, casas de vicinidad*) are a modified version of the former servants' quarters in the rear part of colonial mansions. In post-colonial times these adopted the forms of long corridors of one-room dwellings with collective sanitary facilities at the end, quite similar to many inner-city slums in other Latin American metropolis (Leinauer et al. 1992).

More than 60,000 families are reported to live either in *cuarterias* or *ciudadelas*—60 percent of them concentrated in the capital (Rodriguez 1985, p. 5). The National Housing Institute's policy is to make the demolition of these places without exception a priority.[2] This is an indication that housing conditions tend to be much worse here than in most *barrios insalubres*.

Albergues are often converted industrial buildings or structures offered as interim shelter to those who became homeless after the collapse of their previous homes or through other mishaps. They usually provide dormitory accommodation; and often several families share one room. As shown in a Cuban documentary at the 1990 Havana film festival, many of the people are forced to stay in this transitory and often disgraceful situation for several years until alternative accommodation can be found. In total, some 17,000 families, or 45,000 people, were reported to be living in *albergues* in 1985 (Garcilaso and Vigil, no date, p. 12).[3] Most of them were located in Havana.

Bohios are traditional self-built huts in the countryside, usually consisting of only one room, with a thatched roof, and often lack a solid floor. Over the first 30 years of the revolution, *bohios* have been considered a symbol of backwardness, which ought to be overcome better today than tomorrow, and replaced by modern standard houses (sometimes even in the form of multi-storey prefabricated blocks of flats). However, in spite of recurrent promises by Fidel Castro and other politicians to get the problem under control within a few years, the absolute number of *bohios*[4] has in fact increased again (to a number of 355,000 according to Hamberg 1990, p. 52) rather than diminished. But also the perception of the problem has changed: apartment blocks are no longer viewed as an adequate solution in the rural context;

instead privacy and cultural identity, both of which are offered in the traditional *bohio*, have been accepted as necessary qualities of modern housing solutions in the countryside. A reinterpretation of the *bohio* concept is, for example, now being attempted in new rural mountain settlements as part of the Plan Turquino (Gonzalez 1992).[5]

Much of the described housing problem has been inherited from the prerevolutionary period, when the situation was similar as in other countries of the region at the time. In 1959, some 700,000 units, or 50 percent of the entire national housing stock, was considered to be substandard (Hamberg 1990, p. 37). Thirty percent lived in slums (Moser 1985, p. 18); 6 percent of Havana's population stayed in squatter settlements (Hamberg 1986, p. 588). Even if the old housing stock has deteriorated on the whole, the worst conditions have been removed step-by-step, both in relative terms and in absolute numbers (see Table 10.2).

Table 10.2: Evolution in the Composition of Housing Stock in Cuba

	1970#	1970[*]	1980[*]
	units	percent	percent
Houses	1,200,000	63.5	66.9
Flats	188,000	9.8	14.9
Cuarterias	254,000	12.9	4.7
Bohios	258,000	13.5	13.3
Improvised dwellings	2,500	0.1	0.1
Others		0.2	0.1

Sources: # Unpublished notes by Hans Harms from a study trip in 1981 (number of improvised dwellings added with a question mark); [*] Rodreguez (1985, p. 10).

CUBAN HOUSING POLICY AS AN ISSUE FOR RESEARCH

Research interest in Cuban housing problems and policies differs in its orientation probably more than it does in other countries: National institutions were primarily interested in creating a reliable data base to improve overall planning and administration (CEE 1983; Quintero 1987; Rodriguez 1985), or in technical investigations to increase productivity of housing production and to reduce building failures (i.e., Choy et al. 1984; Lapidus 1985; Naredo et al. 1987; Ortega 1987b).[6] The underlying social concept can be characterized as one of consensus. On the other hand, for foreign researchers from the First World, the starting point was more likely a critical analysis of housing policies in the capitalist world, where social conflict was the key concept to explain the residential circumstances of the masses and the positive or negative changes over time. Hence, their primary interest was to find alternatives to certain disappointing developments in capitalist societies; their implicit or explicit approach was comparative research. From eastern Europe no research related to Cuban housing and spatial planning has become known internationally.[7]

During the period of the cold war, not many Western researchers had the opportunity to visit the country and do research. But from the mid-1980s onwards, more academics from Western Europe and the US entered the country and were met with professional interest by local colleagues and institutions. From this new situation evolved a number of joint research projects and a wider coverage of Cuban housing and planning issues abroad.[8] The topics, which first attracted attention, included the classical Marxist theme of overcoming the imbalance between the town and countryside and urbanization control, areas where the outcome of the Cuban socialist government was most spectacular (Acosta and Hardoy 1971; Susman 1974, 1987; Morse 1977; Barkin 1978a, b; Eckstein 1978; Edwards 1979; Luzon 1988; Bahr & Mertins 1989).

Specific research on housing started in the mid-1970s with attempts to understand the Cuban system of housing provision as a whole (Schuman 1975; Mace 1979; Pena 1982; Hamberg 1985, 1986, 1988, 1990; Castex 1986; Bjorklund 1986, 1989) before selected aspects were analyzed more in depth. The most researched single issue must have been on the so-called microbrigades, which had been created in the early 1970s on a workplace basis using the underused labor force to construct new staff housing (Segre 1979, 1984). In the late 1980s, the concept was extended to renew run-down existing dwellings with neighborhood assistance, both in the city cores and in the *barrios insalubres* (Mathey 1988, 1989a–c; Hoffmann and Stumpler 1992). In a comparative perspective, the organization of the construction industry by Wells (1986), and the aspect of self-help housing were analyzed by Mathey (1992a, b). Wider issues of urban renewal and slum upgrading entered the agenda around 1990 after ambiguous experiences in this field had fuelled the international debate (Nickel 1989; Leinauer et al. 1992; Dirsch and Konrad 1992).

SLUM IMPROVEMENT AND ERADICATION POLICIES

Immediately after the victory of the Cuban revolution first, measures were taken to improve housing conditions of the worst accommodated citizens. Some of the measures aimed at improving the physical situation, but providing better homes for more than a third of the country's population is impossible from one day to the other. Therefore the immediate and most effective assistance was primarily of a nonphysical nature directed to stop material exploitation by unscrupulous landlords and to remove fear from evictions. Security of tenure was guaranteed. Occupants of unserviced lots (subdivisions) were authorized to withhold rent payment until services were installed. The 1960 urban reform law removed the basis for real estate speculation. It transferred the control over *cuarterias* to the state, without compensating the landlords, and the tenants' payments were credited towards the later purchase of better accommodation. In 1967, the residents of *cuarterias* were eventually granted free leases for their accommodation after it became evident that good standard housing could not be offered to all those who were even within a medium-term period (Hamberg 1986, p. 621).

It was one of the promises of the revolution to eliminate all *barrios insalubres*, but not without providing better housing to its inhabitants. This marks a sharp contrast to the bulldozing practice common in other Third World countries at the time, where the evicted dwellers found themselves pushed back to square one and forced to start the squatting circle again in a different settlement. In Havana, the postrevolutionary departure of large parts of the bourgeoisie heading abroad[9] created a basic stock of vacant housing, which provided the authorities[10] with some space for manoeuvre: in 1961–62, nearly 20,000 units were redistributed, of which over 10,000 went to the residents of former *cuarterias* (Hamberg 1986, p. 595).

The first construction program to house residents of *barrios insalubres* and other slums (often referred to as *focos insalubres*, including *ciudadelas* and *cuarterias*) was a self-help housing scheme. It started in 1960 in Santiago de Cuba[11] and provided new homes to 3,400 families formerly living in slums, which were destroyed after vacating. The participating families also received some financial aid and employment. At the end of 1961, this initial program was stopped because the renewed concentration of socially stigmatized families in one neighborhood was considered politically undesirable, and because the self-help labor provided by the target group without professional training was estimated to be highly inefficient (Aguero 1977, p. 6; Cuba 1973, p. 162; Schuman 1975, p. 6; Autorenkollektiv 1987, p. 15). In the following years new projects were to provide housing built by the state.[12] In the countryside, however, self-help programs were periodically revitalized, with the culmination of a national design competition for rural self-help housing in 1981.

In the 1970s, the state housing program (executed by the Ministry of Construction) was complemented by new scheme which was known as microbrigades. The idea of the microbrigades was first put forward in public by Fidel Castro during one of his long and famous speeches in the year 1970.[13] The workers within an office, a factory or any other productive unit should be given an opportunity to build houses for themselves and for their colleagues. For this purpose some of them were to be released from their normal work duties and integrated into building brigades, while their colleagues, who stayed behind, guaranteed to maintain the previous level of productivity in the unit. In that period, the US trade embargo had interrupted the supply of raw material and spare parts resulting in decreased production and over-staffing of many work centers. Thus, the microbrigades presented a possibility of making productive use of the otherwise idle labor force. The *Microbrigadistas* (the members of a microbrigade) continued to receive their regular salary from their permanent employer. All dwellings constructed by a microbrigade were then distributed amongst the workers of the base work unit—whether brigadistas or not—according to the housing need and work merits. By the year 1978, more than 1,100 teams had been formed by some 30,000 brigadistas, having completed 82,000 dwellings.[14] Complete satellite cities around the capital were built by the microbrigades: typical examples are Alta Habana, Reparto Electrico, San Augustin, Cotorro and Alamar[15]— the last designed to house some 150,000 people.

Despite the recognized achievements of the microbrigades, the movement almost came to a standstill by the late 1970s. There was more than one single and evident reason for this halt, and it is evident that the ongoing in-stitutionalization and restructuring of the national economy played a major role in this. In particular, it was argued that the predominantly artisan building technology applied by the microbrigades was not very efficient, and that both the quality of the product and the productivity of the process could be raised by relying more on industrialized systems—which in turn would require a skilled labor force and not the laymen of microbrigades. Another criticism concerns the selective distribution mechanism of the microbrigade-houses, excluding some of the people with the greatest housing need, namely people without employment (including old age pensioners, single mothers, etc., many of them living in slums and *barrios insalubres*) and certain key professions with staff shortages (education, health, etc.). Also the work centers themselves became increasingly reluctant to release their workers to join a microbrigade once certain earlier production problems, which had frequently caused overstaffing, were largely overcome. Last but not least, a new economic and management system, which had been introduced in the second half of the 1970s requested the self-financing of these enterprises and called for a more economical and product oriented use of the employed labor force (Azicri 1988, pp. 137-38). In respect to housing production, it was planned that the gap which the dissolved microbrigades left behind would be filled by additional, and more efficient, state brigades.

The expected increase in the output of houses built directly by the state did not materialize for various reasons. It seemed that the possible productivity gains through industrialization had been overestimated, an experience also shared by most European countries. In addition to this structural limitation, the newly formed state brigades were not primarily used for housing construction, but diverted to nonresidential projects which had a higher political priority. At the same time as the state sector housing output (which includes the microbrigades) dropped, the housing demand increased because the generation born during the 1960s baby boom reached the marrying age in the 1980s: between 1958 and 1988, the country's population had increased by 58 percent (Cuba 1989, p. 9). The increasing housing deficit built up considerable popular pressure and dissatisfaction; the politicians recognized the need to attribute a much higher priority to housing issues than in the past.

A logical response to the tightening situation was a revival of the previous successful microbrigade movement. This was suggested by Fidel Castro in a speech in 1986. In 1988, the number of microbrigadistas had risen to almost 38,000 (in 10,000 brigades), exceeding their number at any time before in the 1970s. Three thousand dwellings had already been finished in less than two years, and another 25,000 were under construction in 1989. In addition, the microbrigades also constructed a similar volume of social infrastructure and services. Although the old microbrigade concept of the 1970s was taken up, it was not copied point by point. In Havana, which was once again the principal arena of the program, the explicit goal was to start 'a radical transformation of the capital', a statement hinting at the new urban planning and architectural emphasis to be followed. Similarly as in Europe, the euphoria for large-scale housing development in the urban periphery had passed. The need for urban repair and conservation, particularly of historic neighborhoods, had been recognized and resulted in various reconstruction and infill projects.

The biggest difference in today's microbrigades as compared to the previous practice, is their explicit social responsibility: only 60 percent (50 percent before 1989) of all the dwellings they produce go to the brigadistas and their colleagues in the unit's workplace; the remainder is offered to the *poder popular* for distribution among those members of the community who need a house but are not connected with any microbrigade. This means that a great number of dwellings become available to rehouse those in the most urgent need, like those living in *cuarterias* and *ciudadelas*. In addition to housing, the microbrigades simultaneously provide urgently needed buildings for community facilities.

A recent variation of the microbrigade concept is that of the 'social microbrigades', which were introduced at the end of 1987. The main difference of these from the ordinary microbrigades is that the workers do not belong to the same work center, but they all live in the same neighborhood—

the one in which the microbrigade is operating. The main activity performed by this type of microbrigade is the repair or renovation of the existing housing stock and urban infrastructure, including the transformation of *cuarterias* and the renewal of *ciudadelas*. Previously, the maintenance of the housing stock was the responsibility of municipal repair enterprises (*empresas*), which were directed by the *poder popular*. However, the poor performance of these units was notorious for a number of reasons, and demanded more efficient solutions. One of the first social microbrigades was started on an experimental basis in Centro Habana, where the concentration of substandard dwellings called for attention. Another main field of activity for socials microbrigades are the *barrios insalubres*, where sometimes even new constructions are carried out in addition to upgrading and repair, particularly when dwellings are of such a very poor quality that replacing them with new houses is more economical than repairing them. Examples include the barrio La Guinera in Havana, or the settlement Van-Van in Santiago de Cuba.

Because the social microbrigades are not linked to an existing work center where the labor force is recruited, unemployed people from within the neighborhood are incorporated, particularly young adults and housewives, and given a renumerated job. Those without previous professional training can learn a building trade as a part of the job (two or three hours training per day) while they receive a regular income as untrained workers.[16] Old age pensioners, who have worked in the building trades before, join as trainers.[17] Apart from the paid members working full time, the social microbrigades also incorporate voluntary workers, who are either neighbors joining the unit during their free time, or individuals given paid leave from their regular work center.

It seems important to note that the social microbrigades perform several functions at a time: apart from addressing the housing problem through upgrading and maintaining the urban fabric, they also provide jobs for the increasing number of mostly unemployed youth. As a supplementary advantage it has also been pointed out that the residents may take greater care of the houses they live in, and that they will be better equipped to carry out future maintenance jobs by themselves once they have participated in renovating or rebuilding a house.

Outside the areas where social microbrigades have been established, individual houseowners in the consolidated *barrios* may obtain assistance from the local authorities and the housing department if they want to improve their houses. They will obtain the necessary quantities of building materials, although they may have to wait for it for extended periods, and tools and machinery like concrete mixers can be hired from state outlets. Even state employed professional artisans may be hired for jobs which require special skills, like for electrical installations, casting a concrete slab, or welding iron gates. Credits are available to pay for materials and assistance, but not for the owner's own labor input (Cuba 1989, p. 9).

The functioning of this and all other housing programs, including the very promising start of the social microbrigade movement, was abruptly interrupted in 1991 for transportation problems and for acute lack of cement. This was a direct consequence of the collapse of eastern European regimes, which were Cuba's major trading partners (granting more or less fair terms of trade), and from where mineral oil, the fuel used in cement production, had been imported at extremely favorable conditions. Faced with the new situation the authorities are trying to at least enable the most necessary repairs and to maintain the status quo of the housing stock with the limited supply of building materials available. Alternatives are sought by exploiting local building materials and intermediate building technologies, namely in the form of soil-cement (Navarro Campos et al. 1991; Cuba 1991), but to proceed from research and development to large-scale application of these technologies may take years. In the present situation where priority is put on maintenance rather than new construction, the emphasis has now shifted from collective self-help solutions (in form of the microbrigades) to individual self-help efforts, since the existing housing stock is best looked after by the people who actually live in it. This new policy coincides with a general trend for political decentralization, and the recent introduction of the *concejos populares*, semi-autonomous government units at the neighborhood level. They will be responsible for coordinating such maintenance and upgrading activities and for allocating scarce building materials while being directly accountable to the neighborhood for the decisions they take.

WILL THE *BARRIOS INSALUBRES* DISAPPEAR IN CUBA?

The achievements of the Cuban state in improving the residential circumstances are impressive. This is particularly true if one looks at housing not only in terms of completed housing units (the number's game), but strategies to overcome the underlying causes of the housing problem, which is poverty, land and property speculation, and insecure tenure. Some countries have a large stock of empty houses coupled with large-scale homelessness. This is certainly not the case in Cuba. Furthermore, it is noteworthy that even the badly housed are still satisfied with other basic needs, including food, work, health care, education, clothing as much as the rest of the population—which helps to avoid secondary effects of substandard housing, such as illness, hunger, criminality, fear or psychological disorders.

Officially the plan to overcome all substandard housing conditions such as *cuarterias*, *ciudadelas*, and *barrios insalubres* until the year 2000 still stands (Cuba 1989, p. 20). However, the actual economically difficult period obliges the Cuban state to cut its traditionally very generous budget for social expenditure drastically. Housing as a high volume, long-term investment tends to be affected by such measures sooner than other sectors of the economy, in capitalist and socialist economies alike (Mathey 1991b, p. 14). Therefore the goal to solve the problem of substandard housing may not be very realistic in the short-term. On the other hand, it must be recognized that the housing and living situation of Cuban citizens is significantly better in comparison to other Latin American countries except for the richest few percent. Therefore solving the housing problem is a question of definition to certain extent, and acceptable standards tend to be moving all the time. A substandard home in Cuba might fit as upper-working class accommodation in another place. In the past, the Cuban state has developed impressively imaginative and flexible housing strategies. The current decentralization policy, which can be interpreted as an expression of the central state's increasing difficulties to guarantee welfare to everybody, also incorporates new chances of grass-roots democracy by short-cutting bureaucratic hurdles, one of the recurrent problems of real socialism in the past.

NOTES

1. For 1990, 60 *barrios* and 100 focos *insalubres* together with some 17,000 houses were listed for Havana, according to Perez (1990, p. 12).
2. '*Priorizar la transformacion de cuarterias y ciudadelas para su total erradicacion*' (Instituto Nacional de la Vivienda, 1987, p. 19).
3. A much lower figure, about 6,000 was given more recently by Hamberg (1990, p. 52).
4. In relative terms they represent a stable share as the overall housing stock grew at the same rate (Luzon 1988, p. 72).
5. The Plan Turquino was started in 1988 with the objective of reversing the out-migration from the less developed mountain region in the eastern parts of Cuba. One important element of it is the construction of houses and preparation of arable land by army recruits. After their service the same people are offered to stay in the same new village under attractive conditions.
6. One of the exceptions from this observation is a paper by Nisia Aguero Benitez (1977) which was written for a seminar of the 'Expertos Latinoamericanos y Africanos sobre Asentamientos Humanos Marginados' in Jalapa, Veracruz-Mejico, and published in 1988 in Colombia. It provided a central source of reference for many foreign essays written thereafter.
7. One exemption is a technical research on earth construction conducted by the University (HAB) of Weimar, German Democratic Republic, shortly before unification with West Germany.
8. In Germany with the University of Kassel 1985 (Mathey 1992a, b), University of Marburg

1986 (Nickel 1989), Technical University of Hamburg 1987 (Autorenkollektiv 1987; Zschaebitz and Lesta 1988, 1990), Technical University Berlin, 1992 (Leinauer et al. 1992).

9. Approximately 600,000 Cubans, 10 per cent of the island's 1959 population, left the country between 1959 and 1973 (Azicri 1988, p. 133).

10. The Direccion de Viviendas Urbanas del Ministerio de Obras Publicas, which was created in 1961, was the authority responsible for dealing with the *barrios insalubres* in the first years (Autorenkollektiv 1987, p. 14).

11. One of the new settlements built by the ex-squatters is Nueva Vista Allegre in Santiago de Cuba with 600 dwellings.

12. The most important examples of such development include the Unidad Vecinal no. 1 in Habana del Este with 1,306 dwellings, or the repartos Capri and Embil.

13. 26 July 1970. In the following month, the workers of the cement factory 'Jose Merceron', in Santiago de Cuba, organized the first microbrigade. Later, in another speech to the National Conference of Basic Industries in December 1970, Castro expanded further on the envisaged working modalities he proposed for the microbrigades.

14. In 1971, already 444 microbrigades had been formed by 12,715 workers. In 1972, the number had risen to 1,073 brigades and 28,178 workers; and in 1975, there were 1,150 microbrigades and more than 30,000 workers. In that year the demand for building materials by the microbrigadistas exceeded the available supply (Ortega 1987a, pp. 22 and 36; Segre 1984, p. 356).

15. In Alamar, the people were also involved to a certain extent in the urban administration, and not only in executing the works. The population had already reached 30,000 (7,700 flats) in 1978, and social infrastructure provision started to get better. Local factory jobs were created particularly for female workers (Ortega 1987a, p. 23).

16. The same salary, which amounts to 148 pesos per month, is received by the housewives.

17. They receive their preretirement salaries (typically between 203 and 233 pesos) in addition to their pension.

REFERENCES

Acosta, Maruja and **Jorge E. Hardoy**. 1971. *Reforma urbana en Cuba revolucionaria.* Caracas: Sintesis.

Aguero Benitez, Nisia. 1977. La vivienda: experiencia de la revolucion Cubana. Reunion de Expertos Laninoamericanos y Africanos sobre Asentamientos Humanos Marginados in Jalapa, Veracruz-Mexico, Vol. 1, pp. 1-22, edn. 9.

Autorenkollektiv des Instituto Politecnico Jose Antonio Echeverria. 1987. *Nuevas tendencias en la polftica habitacional y la produccion de viviendas en Cuba.* Panorama de su desarrollo. Arbeitsbereich Stadtebau Band 27. Hamburg: Technical University.

Azicri, Max. 1988. *Cuba. Politics, Economics and Society.* London: Francis Pinter.

Bahr, Jurgen and **Gunter Mertins**. 1989. 'Regionalpolitik undentwicklung in Kuba 1959-1989', *Geographische Rundschau 41(1)*, pp. 4–13.

Barkin, David. 1978a. 'Cuba: evolucion de las relaciones entre el campo y la ciudad', *Comerciocterior 28(2)*, pp. 135–43.

———. 1978b. 'Confronting the Separation of Town and Country in Cuba', in William Tabb and Harry Sawers, *Marxism and the Metropolis. New Perspectives in Urban Economy.* New York: Oxford University Press, pp. 317–37.

Bjorklund, Eva. 1986. 'Housing Policies in Developing Countries, the Cuban Experience'. International Conference on Housing Policy, SIB Gavle Sweden, 10-13 June 1986.

Bjorklund, Eva. 1989. 'Good Housing for Everybody. An Original and Promising Approach to a Difficult Question'. International Conference on Thirty Years of the Cuban Revolution. Halifax.

Castex, Patrick. 1986. *La politique de production—distribution di logement a Cuba*. David et Goliath: Le combat inegal entre la propriete individuelle. Paris: GRET.

Catasus, S., A. Farns, F. Gonzelez, R. Grove, R. Hernandez and B. Morejon. 1988. *Cuban Women: Changing Roles and Population Trends*. Geneva: International Labour Office, p. 125.

CEE. 1983. *Censo de viviendas construfdas por la poplacion 1981–83*. La Havana: Comite Estadal de Estadisticas.

Choy Lopez, Jose Antonio, Julia Leoon Lacher and Bartelemy Alvarez (Empresa de Proyectos 15 MICON). 1984. Algunas Consideraciones sobre la creacion de una base documental para la construccion de viviendas por esfuerzo proio. Ponencia. XI seminario de vienda y Urbanismo La Habana: MICONS.

Coyula, Mario. 1985. 'Cuba: Housing, Urban Renovation, and Popular Power', *Trialog 6*, Darmstadt, pp. 35–39.

———. 1986. 'Vivienda, renovacion urbana y poder popular: algunas consideracionessobre la Habana', in International Conference 1985, Urban Renewal and Housing for Low-Income Groups in Metropolitan Areas 2. Hamburg-Harburg: TUHH, FSP 6, pp. 181–222.

———. 1986. 'Al reencuentro de la ciudad perdida', *Arquitectura y Urbanismo 91(1)*, pp. 50–59. Shorter version 1992, 'Uber die Kunst, verlorengegangene Stadtqualitaten wiederzufinden', *Trialog 33*, pp. 27–33.

Cuba (JUCEPLAN). 1973. 'La construction de viviendas y centros comunales en Cuba', *Economia y Desarrollo 9* (Sept./Oct.), pp. 159–75. Also published in *Revista Interamericana de Plaificacion 8(28–9)*, pp. 135–47.

Cuba. 1984. 'Ley 48: Ley General de la Vivienda', *Gazeta Oficial de la Republica de Cuba 22*, La Habana, pp. 101–22.

———. 1989. Cuba—'Politica habitacional y su financiamiento', in VI reunion del comite technico de ALIDE, Asociacion Latinoamericano de Instituciones Financieras de Desarrollo La Habana (Government Planning Document).

Cuba (Comision Tecnica parqa el Desarrollo y Aplicacion de Suelos Estabilizados). 1991. Instruccion Tecnica IT-01-91 to IT- 16-91. La Habana: INV, MICONS, MINAZ, MINAGRI, CECAT, IPF. 16 leaflets, Government of Cuba.

Davalos, Rodolfo. 1990. *La nueva Ley General de la Vivienda*. La Habana: Editorial de cinecias Sociales.

Dirsch, Rosa Maria Josef Konrad. 1992. 'Privatsanierung versus Denkmalschutz–ein losbarer Konflikt?' *Trialog 33*, pp. 39–42.

Eckstein, Susan. 1978. 'Las ciudades en la Cuba socialista', *Revista Mexicana de Sociologia 40 (1)*, pp. 155–80.

Edwards, Michael. 1979. 'Urban and Rural Planning', in J. Griffiths and Peter Griffiths (eds.), *Cuba: the Second Decade*. London: Writers and Readers, pp. 110–20.

Esteves Curbelo, Reynaldo. 'The Cuban Experience'. Seminar on Planning for Settlements in Rural Regions—The Case of Spontaneous Settlements. Nairobi: UNCHS, 11–20 November.

Garcilaso de la Vega, Marta and Teresa Vigil. No date. 'Consideraciones para la definicion de una politica de vivienda en Cuba' (mimeo.), p. 14.

Gonzalez, Dania. 1992. 'Der Plan Turquino. Ein Programm zur Verbesserung der Wohn–und Lebensbedingungen in den Bergregionen Cubas', *Trialog 33*, pp. 43–45.

Hamberg, Jill. 1985: *Under Construction. Housing Policy in Revolutionary Cuba*. New York: Center for Cuban Studies, Report no. 36.

Hamberg, Jill. 1986. 'The Dynamics of Cuban Housing Policy', in Bratt et al., *Critical Perspectives on Housing*. Philadelphia: Temple University Press, pp. 586–624.

———. 1988. 'Some Critical Issues in Cuban Housing Provision and the Changes Brought about by the Ley General de la V', in International Seminar, Autoconstruccion, Construccion por Esfuerzo Porpio, y Autogestion en la Produccion de Viviendas en America Latina Kassel: GHK, FB 12.

———. 1990. 'Cuba', in Kosta Mathey, *Housing Policies in the Socialist Third World*. London: Mansell, pp. 35–70.

Hoffmann, Dirk and Uta Stumpler. 1992. 'Erfahrungen mit dem Modell des Wohnungsbaus und der Stadtteilsanierung durch Microbrigaden', *Trialog 33*, Darmstadt, pp. 21–26.

Instituto Nacional de la Vivienda. 1987. 'La vivienda en Cuba: politica y desarrollo'. Conferencia Internacional Sobre vienda y Urbanismo, La Habana, February.

Leinauer, Irma, Kathrin Wolff, Birgit Hunkenschroer, Stephan Heerde and Markus Stilo. 1992. 'Cayo Hueso. Erneuerung eines Barrios in La Habana', *Trialog 33*, pp. 34–38.

Lapidus Mandel, Luis. 1985. 'Participation, Self-Help Housing and the Choice of Technology', *Trialog 6*, Darmstadt, 41 S.

Luzon, Jose. 1988. 'Housing in Socialist Cuba: An Analysis Using Cuban Census of Population and Housing', *Cuban Studies 18*, pp. 65–83.

Mace, Rodney. 1979. 'Housing', in John Griffiths and Peter Griffiths (eds.), *Cuba: The Second Decade*. London: Writers and Readers, pp. 121–30.

Martin, Maria Elena and Eduardo Luis Rodriguez. 1992. 'Architektur der Stadt Havanna im 20. Jahrhundert. Notizen und Bilder', *Trialog 33*, pp. 9–13.

Mathey, Kosta. 1988. 'Microbrigadas—A Cuban Interpretation of Self-Help Housing', *Trialog 18*, pp. 24–30.

———. 1989a. 'Recent Trends in Cuban Housing Policies', *Bulletin of Latin American Research 8(1)*, pp. 8–12.

———. 1989b. 'Microbrigadas in Cuba. An Unconventional Response to the Housing Problem in a Latin American State', *Habitat International 12(4)*, pp. 55–62.

———. 1989c. 'Microbrigadas: A Collective Form of Self-Help Housing', *The Netherlands Journal of Housing and Environmental Research 4 (1)*, pp. 67–84.

———. 1991a. 'Periodo Especial: wie Cuba die wirtschaftliche Krise okologisch zu uberstehen versucht', *Trialog 28*, pp. 53–54.

———. 1991b. 'Socialist Housing: Some Key Issues', in K. Mathey (ed.), *Housing Policies in the Socialist Third World*. London & New York: Mansell.

———. 1992a. 'Self-Help Housing Policies and Practices in Cuba', in K. Mathey (ed.), *Beyond Self-Help Housing*. London & New York: Mansell; Munchen: Profil, pp. 1–14; pp. 181–216.

———. 1992b. 'Kommodifizierung, soziale Integration udn Wohnqualitat. Fragen zum Selbsthilfe-Wohnungsbau in Cuba und Ergebnisse aus einem Forschungsprojekt', *Trialog 33*, pp. 14–20.

Morse, Richard. 1977. 'Cuba', in R. Morse (ed.), *The Urban Development of Latin America*. Stanford: Stanford University Press, pp. 77–93.

Moser, Christine. 1985. Havana—Stadt ohne Slums—Ila Info. 88, pp. 18–20.

Naredo M., Teresa and Jose L. Bermudez. 1987. Technicas constructivas para la vivienda de esfuerzo propio. Conferencia Internacional sobre la Vivienda y el Urbanismo. Comission La Habana, pp. 264–75.

Navarro Campos, Nelson et al. 1991. Suelo Cemento. Fundamentos para su aplicacion en Cuba. La Habana: Instituto Nacional de la Vivienda.

Nickel, Annegret. 1989. 'Die Altstadt von La Habana. Wohnsituation und Konzepte der Altstadterneuerung', *Geographische Rundschau 41 (1)*, pp. 14–21.

Ortega Morales, Lourdes et al. 1987a. 'Nevas tendencias en la Politica Habitacional y la

Producion de Viviendas en Cuba. panorama de su Desarollo', in Harms, Hans und Zschabitz, Ulrike, Arbeitsbereich Stadtebau, Objektbezogene Stadtplanung im Forschung 27. Hamburg. TUHH. 206 S.

Ortega Morales, Lourdes et al. 1987b. Technologia y construccion de viviendas por iniciativa de la poblacion en zonas de renovacion. Conferencia Internacional sobre la Vivienda y el Urbanismo, Comision I La Habana, pp. 154–64.

Pena, Alquimia. 1982. 'La vivienda en Cuba revolucionaria', in Emilio Pradilla Cobos (ed.), *Ensayos sobre el problema de la vivienda en America Latina*. Mexico ciudad: Universidad Autonoma Metropolitana Unidad Xochimilco.

Perez, Mayra. 1990. consideraciones para abordar la problematica de la vivienda en Ciudad de La Habana. Boletin Informativo (del Centro de Documentacion, poder popular de la Habana) 7, pp. 11-17.

Quintero Hierrezuelo, Miguel. 1987. La construccion de viviendas por esfuerzo propio y requerimientos urbanisticos. Conferencia Internacional sobre la Vivienda y el Urbanismo, Comision 3 La Habana, pp. 107–48.

Rey, Gina. no date. *Vienda y desarrollo integral en Cuba*. La Habana: Grupo por eo Desarollo Integral de la Capital.

Rodriguez, Maria L. 1985. La tipologia de la vivienda y su distribucion en el sistema de asentamientos. I Jornada Cientifica Internacioanl sobre Planificacion Regional y Urbana, Nov. 1985, Juceplan La Habana.

Schuman, Tony. 1975. 'Housing: We Don't have the Right to Wait', *Cuba Review 5(1)*, pp. 3–22.

Segre, Roberto. 1979. 'La vivienda en Cuba: Republica y revolucion', in Concurso 13 de Marzo, Premio Insayo La Habana: Universidad de La Habana, 240 S.

———. 1984. 'Architecture in the Revolution', in C. Reinhard Hatch (ed.), *The Scope of Social Architecture*. New York: Van Nostrand, pp. 348–60.

Susman, Paul. 1974. 'Cuban Development: From Dualism to Integration', *Antipode 6(3)*, pp. 10–29.

———. 1987. 'Spatial Equality in Cuba', *International Journal of Urban and Regional Research 11 (2)*, pp. 218–42.

Vega Vega, Juan 1986. Comentarios a la Ley General de la vivienda. La Habana: Editorial de Ciencias Sociales. 288 S.

Wells, Jill. 1986. 'Conclusions in the Light of the Development of Construction Resources in Cuba', in Jill Wells, *The Construction Industry in Developing Countries: Alternative Strategies for Development*. London: Croom Helm, pp. 150–77.

Zimbalist, Andrew and Susan Eckstein. 1987. 'Patterns of Cuban Development: The First Twenty-Five Years', in A. Zimbalist (ed.), *Cuba's Socialist Economy Toward the 1990s*. Boulder: Lynne Rienner, pp. 7–24.

Zschaebitz, Ulrike and Francisco Lesta. 1988. 'Construccion por esfuerzo propio en la ciudad de la Habana: lementos para una tipologia', in Arbeitsbereich Stadtebau, FSP 6, TU Hamburg Harburg, Hamburg: TUHH, University Report.

———. 1990. Actas de Atares. mimeo, Hamburg: TUHH, FSP 1-07. 119 S, Unpublished University Report.

11

Slums and Squatter Settlements in Thailand

Kioe Sheng Yap

Bangkok is a clear example of a primate city. According to the preliminary results of the 1990 Population and Housing census (National Statistical Office [NSO] N.d., p. 24), the Bangkok Metropolitan Area (BMA) had a population of 5,876,000 persons. Because of the rapid economic and demographic growth, Bangkok's urbanized area now extends far beyond the BMA into the adjacent provinces of Nonthaburi, Pathum Thani, Samut Prakan, Samut Sakhon and Nakhon Pathom. The 1990 Population and Housing census estimates the population of the Bangkok Metropolitan Region (BMR) at 8.5 million inhabitants (NSO N.d., pp. 38–42). Its population is more than 20 times that of Thailand's second city, Nakhon Ratchasima; about 60 percent of the country's urban population live in Bangkok. Given the predominance of Bangkok, urban research, of which the results are available in English, has focused almost exclusively on Bangkok and this chapter deals with the slums and squatter settlements of Bangkok only.

SLUMS AND SQUATTER SETTLEMENTS

Bangkok is the political, economic, financial, sociocultural and educational centre of Thailand. National economic growth, which reached levels of over 10 percent per annum in the past years, is concentrated in and around Bangkok. Foreign investors are attracted by low wages, lenient regulations, a submissive labor force, and tax concessions. As a result, industries mushroom in the urban fringe, particularly along the roads to the north and the southeast. Employment opportunities in industrial and service sectors attract labor from all over the country to Bangkok. The 1988 per capita household income in the BMR was Baht 28,098 against Baht 12,766 for Thailand as a whole and Baht 7,867 for the northeastern region (Thailand Development Research Institute [TDRI] N.d., pp. 12–13). Some migrants come to work for only part of the year and return to their villages when needed on the farm. Others come for a couple of years to earn sufficient money to make a larger investment back home. Many come to stay. Most families in Bangkok, whether they stay for short or long periods, face enormous problems finding affordable housing and have to often live in informal settlements.

In most cities of developing countries, informal settlements are squatter settlements, built on vacant land without the agreement of the landowner and/or permission from the authorities. In Bangkok, pure squatter settlements form only 16 percent of the informal settlements. They house approximately 225 persons and are mainly situated on land along the *klong* (waterways) owned by the Royal Irrigation Department or on land along the railway lines owned by the State Railways of Thailand. The majority of the informal settlements in Bangkok are land-rental slums. Unfortunately, the term 'slums' usually refers to both land-rental slums and squatter settlements.

Bangkok's growth is mostly unplanned. The Highway Department constructs the primary roads; the BMA is supposed to build the secondary roads, but it is often unable to do so due to lack of funds. In negotiation with owners of adjacent plots, landowners and developers connect their plots to the nearest primary road by means of narrow roads (*soi*) along the boundaries of their land, in the most economical way and with no regard for the public interest, to occupy as little as possible of the land parcels. The outcome is a haphazard network of narrow, often dead-end, roads which are not interconnected. The situation is further complicated by a large number of irrigation and transportation canals. As a result, many plots of land cannot be easily developed because of their inaccessibility and, therefore, have a relatively low value. As long as the value of the land is low, owners often allow low-income families to occupy it at a nominal rent or even free of charge. The low-income family and the landowner may sign a contract which allows the family to occupy the land and build its house, but stipulates that the landowner can terminate the lease on 30 days' notice. Furthermore, the renter has no right to stay on the land after the lease has been terminated and is not entitled to claim any compensation from the landowner (Yamklinfung 1973, p. 25). Security of tenure is consequently rather low; nevertheless, many informal settlements have been in existence in Bangkok for several decades.

Table 11.1: Informal Settlements and their Population in
the Bangkok Metropolitan Region in 1988

Province	Settlements	Dwellings	Households	Population
Bangkok (BMA)	1,032	129,033	177,593	852,500
Nonthaburi	88	6,929	9,941	48,000
Samut Prakan	278	28,849	36,063	173,000
Pathum Thani	44	3,818	5,167	25,000
Total BMR	1,442	168,629	228,764	1,098,500

Source: NHA Survey (1988).

According to the most recent data (Table 11.1) of the National Housing Authority (NHA), 1.1 million persons or 13 percent of the population of the Bangkok Metropolitan Region live in informal settlements.

The NHA distinguishes three types of informal settlements: settlements on private land (63 percent), settlements on public land (25 percent) and settlements on land with a mixed, i.e., public–private ownership (11 percent); for 1 percent of the slum land, the landowner is not known. The *wat* (temples) and the Crown Property Bureau are the major public slum landowners in Bangkok with 189 and 101 parcels of land with slums respectively. The Royal Irrigation Department is an important owner of land with squatter settlements. In only 46 percent of the cases, the landowner and the slum-dwellers have signed a contract; these settlements can be called pure land-rental slums. In 21 percent of the cases, there is no contract; this category includes pure squatter settlements and settlements where the landowner accepts the slum on his land, but does not formalize the arrangement. In the remaining settlements, the contract has expired, some settlers have a contract and others do not, or no information is available. Land-renting slum-dwellers may for their part rent out their house or one or more rooms to other households. Households build their house in between the slum houses; if they do not pay rent to the landowner, they can be considered squatters. Within a single informal settlement there are often land-renting households and house-renting or room-renting households as well as squatters.

Situated in the flood-plain of the Chao Phraya river on swamps and marshlands which were formerly rice paddy fields, Bangkok is regularly flooded by rain and river water in the monsoon season. This situation is aggravated by land subsidence due to the extraction of groundwater and the indiscriminate filling of drainage canals. To prevent flooding of their plots and houses, most landowners raise the level of the land with earth, but the cost is high and unused land usually remains unfilled. Such parcels of unfilled land are the prime sites for informal settlements. Because the land for informal settlements is low, most slum houses are built on posts. In some slums there is stagnant water under the houses throughout the year, creating very unsanitary conditions (Yamklinfung 1973, p. 21). Most slum-dwellers have to build their own houses out of wood, corrugated iron sheets, and waste materials. They use a cesspool under their toilet from where the sewage soaks into the subsoil and pollutes the land and the water under the houses. The stagnant water and the inadequate infrastructure create poor living conditions in the slums. Children suffer from respiratory problems, heart and kidney diseases, and malnutrition. Some slums have a high rate of drug addiction which is nowadays often accompanied by a high incidence of AIDS due to the sharing of contaminated needles. Because slums houses are built of wood and because slums have, almost by definition, poor access to the public road, slum-dwellers tend to be very concerned about the risk of fires, as these can spread quickly and often block the only exit from the settlement.

Slums and squatter settlements provide affordable housing for the low-income population of Bangkok, but not all slum-dwellers are poor and not all poor live in slums and squatter settlements. As Table 11.2 shows, the population of 30 randomly selected slums in Bangkok have a higher income than the population of the Bangkok Metropolitan Administration as a whole. Almost 30 percent of the slum households earn Baht 10,000 or more per month and could thus easily afford a private sector low-cost house. One has to conclude that in Bangkok, plagued by traffic jams and long commuting times, location is more important than housing quality for many people. Preliminary data from a survey of low-income rental housing in Bangkok presently conducted by the author indicate that most house-renters in slums and squatter settlements have a lower monthly household income (average income Baht 7,030; median income Baht 5,400) than houseowners in slums and squatter settlements (average income Baht 8,884; median income Baht 7,000).

Table 11.2: Total Monthly Household Income in the
Bangkok Metropolitan Area (1988) and in 30 Slums (1991)

| Monthly Household Income | BMA | | Slums | |
(in Baht)	%	Cum. %	%	Cum. %
0,000–1,999	7.3	7.8	5.8	5.8
2,000–3,999	21.7	29.0	17.5	23.3
4,000–5,999	21.5	50.5	19.1	42.5
6,000–7,999	14.8	64.3	17.3	59.7
8,000–9,999	9.2	74.5	11.7	71.4
10,000 and more	25.5	100.0	28.6	100.0

When land prices increase, a landowner may decide to develop or sell his land. To avoid a direct confrontation with the slum-dwellers, he may stop collecting rent to signal his intention to terminate the lease contract. It can take several more years before he actually tells the slum-dwellers to leave and this gives the slum-dwellers the time to prepare for the eviction. With the same desire to avoid a conflict, many slum communities accept that their stay on the land is temporary and agree to leave when told to by the landowner. If a community does not accept the eviction order, a fire may raze the mainly wooden houses. The contract between the slum-dwellers and the landowner stipulates that the lease is terminated if a fire destroys the houses. Moreover, the regulations of the BMA state that structures destroyed by fire cannot be rebuilt within 45 days, to allow officials to look into the cause of the fire. A fire is, therefore, a blessing for a landowner who wants to evict slum-dwellers from his property. Slum-dwellers who return to the site to rebuild their houses become virtual squatters on the land they rented and occupied for years.

Table 11.3: Distance of Slum Housing to the Center of Bangkok

Distance	1974	1984	1988
00–05 km	69,738	69,906	63,907
06–10 km	42,296	46,031	40,654
11–20 km	23,091	36,581	47,718
21–30 km	4,015	6,370	15,398
> 30 km	186	1,257	2,961
Total	139,326	160,145	170,638

Source: PADCO/LIF (1990, p. 125).

Between 1984 and 1988, as Table 11.3 shows, slum housing declined by 11,376 housing units in the area within 10 km of the city centre. During the same period, a considerable number of slum housing units emerged in the suburban areas beyond 11 km from the city centre. The average distance from the slums to the centre of Bangkok increased from 8.74 km (in 1984) to 9.97 km (in 1988, excluding Pathum Thani which was not surveyed in 1984). Two factors explain this development. As more and more slum-dwellers are being evicted and more and more slums are being demolished in the central areas of the city without being replaced by any formal low-income housing, slum-dwellers are forced to seek other locations even further away from the center. On the other hand, new investments have generated many employment opportunities in the urban fringe. These opportunities have attracted many low-income households. Given the lack of affordable formal housing in the areas, households often find shelter in informal settlements. The number of informal settlements in the province of Samut Prakan almost doubled between 1984 and 1988. Whether the families who now settle in the slums of Samut Prakan and Pathum Thani are those evicted from slums in the city center is difficult to determine. The slums in the central parts of Bangkok are populated mainly by families who find employment in the service sector and small-scale industry, while the suburban factories tend to employ single young men and women. There are indications that as slum-dwellers from the center of Bangkok cannot move too far away from their job opportunities, they resettle in existing slums in between the slum housing thereby increasing the densities.

RESEARCH

Over the years, researchers have conducted considerable number of studies on slums and squatter settlements in Bangkok. Many of these studies were initiated by public agencies; they were policy- and problem-oriented in nature; their results were documented in reports with a limited distribution and are, therefore, hard to find. Moreover, institutions like the National Housing Authority, Chulalongkorn University, Thammasat University and the National Institute for Development Administration (NIDA) which carried out a large portion of this research, published the results in articles, books, and reports in Thai and these are, therefore, not easily accessible to foreigners. Research on slums and squatter settlements in other towns of Thailand is extremely limited (Vorratnchaiphan 1988, p. 9). Consequently, this section deals exclusively with research on slums and squatter settlements in Bangkok for which publications in English are available.

In the early 1970s, the United Nations Children Fund (UNICEF) increased its attention for the living conditions of mothers and children in urban areas and in collaboration with local research institutes it commissioned several studies of slums in Bangkok (e.g., Yamklinfung 1973). The findings of these studies were summarized and synthesized by Morell and Morell (1972). In 1976, Angel, Benjamin and De Goede (1977) of the Division of Human Settlements Development at the Asian Institute of Technology (AIT) in Bangkok prepared a paper for the Vancouver conference describing the low-income housing delivery system in Bangkok. They distinguished several housing subsystems including a squatter housing subsystem consisting of three types: pure squatter settlements, land-rental settlements and boat houses. Over the years, staff and students of AIT conducted extensive research and published reports and articles about slums and squatter settlements (Pornchokchai 1984; Chin 1987; Panroj 1987; Yap 1989). An important publication produced by the Human Settlements Division was *Land for Housing the Poor* (Angel, Archer, Tanphiphat and Wegelin 1983) with articles on slum evictions (Boonyabancha 1983) and land supply (Tanphiphat 1983).

In 1986, Korff published *Bangkok: Urban System and Everyday Life* which deals with the socioeconomic aspects of a slum settlement in Bangkok. The base-line survey for many studies of slums and squatter settlements in Bangkok has been *1020 Bangkok Slums: Evidence, Analysis, Critics*. For this study, Pornchokchai (1984) inventorized the slums and squatter settlements of Bangkok, Nonthaburi and Samut Prakan and recorded their age, location, land-ownership (public, private, mixed), legal status (slum or squatter settlement), the distance from the city center, the number of households, the percentage of house-renting households, the eviction pressure, the presence of a community committee, and whether the settlements had been upgraded. In 1988, the NHA updated this data base. It found almost 1,500 slum and squatter settlements (including settlements which existed in 1984, but had not been identified by Pornchokchai) and recorded settlement characteristics such as the landowner, the size of the area, the legal status and rent collection, and the availability of infrastructure. Some results of the survey were published by Yap (1992) and have been used in this chapter. In 1990, the Bangkok Metropolitan Administration (BMA) updated the information (BMA 1990).

In the 1980s, Angel and Boonyabancha (then of the NHA) studied evictions and developed the land sharing concept which was implemented in several slums in Bangkok. Several articles and reports on the land sharing experiences in Bangkok, in particular the Sengki land sharing project, were published (Angel and Chirathamkijkul 1983; UNCHS 1986; Boonyabancha 1985; Angel and Boonyabancha 1988; Panroj and Yap 1989). In 1986, Angel became the team leader of the land management study; Angel, Dowall, Pornchokchai and others published the results of the study in a two volume report, *'The Land and Housing Markets of Bangkok: Strategies for Public Sector Participation'* (PADCO/NHA 1987) and in several articles (e.g., Angel and Pornchokchai 1987). In 1993, Yap, De Wanderler and Khanaiklang completed a study of the low-income rental housing in the Bangkok Metropolitan Area which covered rental housing by the public and the private sector as well as rental housing in slums and squatter settlements. The NHA, and particularly its Center for Housing and Human Settlements Studies, has produced many short reports on slums and squatter settlements in Bangkok, but they have had only a limited distribution.

Similarly, nongovernmental organizations have published reports and studies about their activities in slums of Bangkok like Klong Toey (Boonyabancha, Niyom, Patpui, Suksumake and Maier 1988). Several studies have also been conducted on women and slums. Shahand, Tekie and Weber (1986) published *The Role of Women in Slum Improvement: A Comparative Study of the Squatter Settlements at Klong Toey and Wat Yai Sri Suphan in Bangkok*. In 1987, Thorbek (1987) published *Voices from the City: Women of Bangkok*, a case study of women's daily lives in slum settlements in Bangkok. Green (1990) wrote an M.Sc. thesis entitled 'Psychological Impacts of Slum Eviction: Women in Bangkok'.

IMPROVEMENT STRATEGIES

The initial objective of the National Housing Authority which was established in 1973, was to construct walk-up apartments for the resettlement of evicted slum-dwellers. Its First Five Year Plan (1976–80) proposed the construction of 120,000 housing units, predominantly walk-up apartments. In 1978, the government canceled the Plan, as it proved to be overambitious and unaffordable. The NHA developed a new plan which called for the construction of 5,600 walk-up apartments, the development of 19,160 plots in sites-and-services schemes and the upgrading of slums for 26,000 households, with only a limited subsidy. In 1980–81, the plan was also abandoned (Wonghanchao 1987, pp. 175–94). When the government decided to further reduce its subsidies, the NHA changed its policy again and started to build middle-income housing for profit which it could use to finance its low-income housing programs. However, this plan has not been very successful as NHA housing competes poorly with the private sector.

The NHA manages several low-income rental housing estates and sites-and-services schemes in and around Bangkok. The Authority's housing estates are mainly made up of four storey walk-up apartment buildings consisting of one-room units with attached bathroom/toilet. Rents range from Baht 400–800 per month, while economic rents are around Baht 1,500 per month. As a result, there is considerable subletting of units. The NHA has launched four sites-and-services schemes in Bangkok, but these have also not been very successful as they have not reached the target groups (NHA 1991, p. 6). One of the major problems which the NHA faces is the acquisition of land for its housing projects. The high land prices in Bangkok and the procedure which it needs to follow to obtain approval for a land purchase make it impossible for the NHA to compete with the private sector land buyers. The impact of the NHA slum improvements program on the housing conditions in Bangkok's slums is limited (Table 11.4). The NHA upgraded 132 slums (NHA 1991, pp. 78–89). The main problem for the NHA is that it cannot improve a slum unless the landowners agree and many landowners fear that upgrading will give the slums and squatter settlements a permanent character. Upgrading is also not a guarantee against eviction: 13 settlements which had been upgraded by 1984 had been evicted by 1988.

Table 11.4: Number of Slums Upgraded by the NHA (1978–91)

Year	Slums	Households	Year	Slums	Households
1978	10	4656	1985	–	–
1979	21	4769	1986	13	4970
1980	17	5112	1987	14	4516
1981	12	5077	1988	4	2150
1982	11	7847	1989	2	400
1983	21	10011	1990	4	810
1984	–	–	1991	3	630
			Total	132	50,948

Source: NHA (1991, pp. 78–89).

While most slums-dwellers still agree to vacate the land after an eviction, nongovernmental organizations have been able to persuade an increasing number of slum communities not to give up their land so easily. Emphasizing the right of the urban poor to live in the city, they have introduced an innovative approach called land sharing. This is an arrangement by which a plot of land occupied by slum-dwellers is partitioned into two parts: one part is leased or sold to the slum community to rehouse its members; the other part is returned to the landowner, who can develop it to the best possible advantage. Land sharing can be justified by two principles: the right of the slum-dwellers to live in the city and the right of the slum-dwellers to share in the increased land value, but these principles do not seem to play a role in Bangkok. The landowner's acceptance of land sharing is often either an act of charity and merit-making, or it is a peaceful way to resolve a potentially embarrassing conflict between the landowner and slum-dwellers.

Land sharing requires that both parties accept less than everything, that they give up a part of the land in exchange for a workable arrangement on the remaining part. For the slum-dwellers, this means the removal of the eviction threat and a secure land tenure arrangement which may lead to adequate infrastructure and permanent housing. For landowners, it means recovering part of the land for development rather than becoming engaged in a possibly costly and ultimately unsuccessful tug-of-war with the slum dwellers lasting an unforeseeable period of time. It should be noted that there are 1,500 slum and squatter settlements in the Bangkok Metropolitan Region. Only seven slum communities have reached a land sharing agreement, two have acquired the freehold title to their land and three land sharing projects are still under implementation (Table 11.5). Two hundred slum communities were evicted between 1974 and 1986.

Table 11.5: The Slum Community's Land Before and After Land Sharing

Slum	Original Slum Area	Area after Land Sharing	Percentage of Land for Slum Community
Wat Ladbuakaw	1.60 ha	0.32 ha	20
Klong Toey	na	na	na
Manangkasila	1.75 ha	0.67 ha	38
Rama IV	8.50 ha	2.40 ha	28
Sam Yod	.95 ha	0.65 ha	68
Soi Sengki	1.10 ha	0.60 ha	55
Inthamara 10	.30 ha	0.10 ha	65

Land sharing is not a panacea for slum evictions. The slum houses on the landowner's portion of the land have to be demolished and rebuilt on the community's land in between the existing houses. This may be impossible if the density is already high. As a result, the entire slum may have to be demolished and the settlement reconstructed. The land area may be so small that it is impossible to resettle the entire community on the portion of land acquired by the slum-dwellers unless walk-up apartment buildings are constructed. However, slum-dwellers may not like the idea of living in an apartment as it limits their income generating activities, while the housing costs may also be prohibitive. Ultimately, land sharing may only be possible if some of the original families leave the settlement, with or without compensation, before the agreement on land sharing is reached. Many of the better-off families may not be too unhappy to see the usually poorer families leave, as it will give them more land and make the project financially more feasible (Panroj 1987, pp. 7–28).

Some slum-dwellers are reluctant to fight an eviction, even if there is a potential for land sharing. Houseowners and families who lived in a settlement for a long time are more inclined to resist eviction than renters and families who have settled recently (Panroj 1989, p. 68). The community has to weigh the costs of resisting eviction against those of leaving, with or without compensation. A landowner may offer money as compensation for the eviction, but if he fails to persuade the slum-dwellers to leave, he may threaten them with violence. The community risks arson, the harassment of its leaders, arrest, and fines. It needs to organize itself in order to be recognized as a negotiating partner, but few communities are able to do so without outside support. As a blanket solution to eviction, land sharing ignores the heterogeneity of the slum population. A slum houses land renters, house renters and squatters, who do not operate in the same housing market. It has households at different income levels which can afford different types of housing; some may be able to buy a plot in the scheme or even own land or a house on the urban fringe, while others may be too poor to take part in the project. Many households may leave the settlement even after land sharing (Table 11.6). They may move to other slums, thereby contributing to further densification of the already dense slums of Bangkok, or they may be forced to move to the urban fringe.

Table 11.6: Number of Households Before and After Land Sharing

	Original Number of Households	Households Remaining after Land Sharing	Percentage of Households Remaining
Wat Ladbuakaw	300	67	22
Klong Toey	1780	1080	61
Manangkasila	500	198	40
Rama TV	1000	850	85
Sam Yod	210	192	91
Soi Sengki	216	198	92
Inthamara 10	85	70	82

Given the very high land prices, a landowner may nowadays offer up to Baht 10,000 per household if it is prepared to vacate his land immediately. More and more slum communities initially resist such a buy out and ask for a higher compensation. Some have succeeded in bargaining compensation of Baht 40,000 per household, enough to buy land on the urban fringe, although not in a good location. Such a sum is also insufficient to construct a house, but it is an option for slum communities which are threatened with eviction when land sharing is not possible. The NHA has a large resettlement site for evicted slum-dwellers in Rom Klao in the east of Bangkok where slum-dwellers can buy a plot of land of 72 to 112 sq m. The area is, however, far from the centers of employment and residents have to travel several hours to get to their work. Many households, therefore, leave the site and return to slums in Bangkok.

Some slum communities under the threat of eviction have found land for themselves in what they consider suitable locations and at affordable prices. A slum eviction and resettlement which received considerable publicity and became an example for many other slum communities under the threat of eviction was the *Rachadapisek* slum resettlement. Thirty years ago, the site of the slum was a tract of rough agricultural land which belonged to the State Railways of Thailand (SRT). As the SRT had no immediate use for the land, squatters began to settle there. In 1986, after the construction of *Rachadapisek* Road, the SRT leased the land to a developer to construct a commercial centre, but the squatters formed a community association and made it clear to the developer that they were not willing to give up their houses unless an alternative site was provided. The developer sent police and demolition squads, and the community organized demonstrations. Eventually, the developer and the Metropolitan Waterworks Authority paid Baht 3.9 million and 1 million to buy a plot of land which some families had identified in the northeast of Bangkok. In February 1988, around 120 families left *Rachadapisek* Road with support from NGOs for the new site where they were given plots of 52 to 60 sq m. The residents called their new settlement *Suwan Prasid*. Later, other evicted slum communities settled nearby in *Suwan Prasid* 2 and *Suwan Prasid* 3. This type of resettlement project is becoming more and more common in Bangkok. It is usually a direct agreement between the landowners and/or the developer, and the slum community with support from an NGO; the National Housing Authority only plays a marginal role. However, resettlement in the urban fringe is not a solution for many slum-dwellers and normally only a portion of the original slum community settles at the new site and stays.

In the late 1980s, private developers moved into the low-cost housing market, producing large numbers of complete land-and-housing units in the outlying suburbs. The units were selling for less than Baht 250,000 and many of the houses cost Baht 175,000–200,000, with an average down payment of Baht 50,000 and monthly repayments of Baht 1,750 on a 15 year mortgage loan bearing 11.75 percent interest per annum. Although unaffordable for the lowest-income groups, the houses made an important contribution to the housing stock in Bangkok. In 1980, households which could afford the then least expensive private sector house (i.e., households earning at least Baht 10,000 per month) formed 15 percent of the Bangkok population; in other words, private sector housing was unaffordable for 85 percent of the city's population. In 1987, the private sector was producing housing units which required a monthly payment of Baht 1,500 and, therefore, were affordable to households with a total income of Baht 6,000 per month. Such households formed 55 percent of the population of the city (Angel and Chuated 1987).

The 1987 low cost houses differ markedly from those constructed in 1980. The plot and the floor area are smaller than those of 1980; the 1987 houses are almost exclusively row houses and the projects are located further away from the center of the city. Moreover, with the banking system experiencing a high liquidity, the Government Housing Bank offered mortgage loans at 11.75 percent which forced commercial banks to lower their rates from an average of 16 percent in 1980. Local finance and insurance companies also began to compete in the mortgage loan market. Building material prices were relatively low, partly due to low oil prices. The saturation of the local middle-income and high-income housing market forced down the private sector market. The strong overall economic performance of Thailand increased incomes, especially in Bangkok. At present (1992), construction costs have changed again. The arrival of new industry from Japan, Korea, Taiwan, and Singapore; and of capital from Hong Kong has increased the demand for offices and high-income housing. This has resulted in a boom in the construction of office buildings and condominiums, which has pushed up the land and building material prices. It seems likely that the down market trend in house construction was only a temporary phenomenon. A new development is the construction of low cost condominiums offering one-room apartments with toilet/bathroom for Baht 250,000 and more.

Whereas in the 1970s and early 1980s, the World Bank tried rather unsuccessfully to introduce slum and squatter settlement regularization and upgrading programmes in Bangkok, the success of the private sector to produce low-cost housing has made Bangkok the primary example for the effectiveness of recommendations by the World Bank and the US Agency for International Development (USAID) to deregulate the housing market. The World Bank frequently points at the performance of the Government Housing Bank and its successful effort to reduce the interest rates for housing loans in the country, even those of the commercial banks. In Bangkok, the role of the government in low-income housing, in particular through the National Housing Authority (and often in cooperation with NGOs), is limited to the resettlement of slum-dwellers who are evicted by public and private landowners, the production of middle-income housing in joint ventures with the private sector and the construction of housing for government personnel such as staff of the police and the armed forces. At the same time, non-governmental organizations are actively involved in the physical and social improvement of the living conditions of the slum-dwellers, but the scale of the operations is rather small.

CONCLUSIONS

In several Asian countries, governments are now providing protection of sorts to the residents of informal settlements. Policies range from granting *de jure* security of tenure by regularizing the unauthorized settlements, to giving a form of *de facto* security of tenure by issuing stay orders at the time of evictions. Research has shown that an increase in the security of tenure is an incentive for the dwellers to improve their housing conditions. Both the NHA and some slum-dweller federations have been proposing similar policies for Bangkok, although the coverage of their proposals differs. The NHA wants to be able to improve land-rental slums regardless of the views of the owner of the land; the slum-dweller federations want the government to expropriate all slum land and to sell it to the slum-dwellers at subsidized rates. However, the government is unlikely to adopt such a policy in view of their generally accepted attitude of nonintervention in private land-rental agreements. It is also doubtful whether such a policy would improve the conditions of the slum-dwellers. One argument widely raised against a policy to provide protection for residents of unauthorized settlements is that it is tantamount to inviting other people to occupy vacant land without permission from the owner or the authorities. The opposite argument applies in the case of Bangkok: it would dissuade landowners from renting out vacant land on a temporary basis to low-income households in search of affordable accommodation, and it would encourage current slum landowners to evict the slum-dwellers before such a policy takes effect. This would be truly disastrous for the slum population. In fact, any attempt by the authorities to improve the living conditions of the slum-dwellers by granting them a more permanent right to the land they occupy might result in such a reaction by the landowners.

The implication is that improvements in the living conditions in the Bangkok slums can only be initiated by the landowners themselves. If the major slum landowner is prepared to work together with the slum communities to improve living conditions in the slum settlements, even if only on a temporary basis, this would help many low-income households. The Crown Property Bureau, the major single slum landowner in Bangkok, has announced that it plans to improve the conditions of the slums on its land. The Bureau Director has said that he would put on hold the idea of making full commercial use of the Bureau's assets and concentrate instead on developing the quality of life of people living on its land by helping the slum community to become self-employed and self-sufficient (*Bangkok Post*, 3 September 1990; *Nation*, 24 October 1990; *Bangkok Post*, 5 November 1990). The chances that such a policy could be adopted by many slum landowners are, however, small. The State Railways of Thailand and the Treasury Department, two major landowners and two major slum landowners, have been urged to make better (i.e., more commercial) use of their property (*Bangkok Post*, 27 June 1991; 26 July 1991). The only alternative policy left for the government is, paradoxically, to ensure that the low-income housing delivery subsystem, which provides slum lands for rent at affordable rates and in suitable locations, is preserved because it is in the interest of the low-income population.

REFERENCES

Angel, Shlomo, Raymon W. Archer, Sidhijai Tanphiphat and Emiel A. Wegelin (eds.). 1983. *Land for Housing the Poor*. Singapore: Select Books.

Angel, S., S. Benjamin and K.H. De Goede. 1977. 'The Low-Income Housing System in Bangkok', *Ekistics 44 (261)*, pp. 79–84.

Angel, Shlomo and Somsook Boonyabancha. 1988. 'Land Sharing as an Alternative to Eviction: The Bangkok Experience', *Third World Planning Review 10 (2)*, pp. 107–27.

Angel, Shlomo and Thipparat Chirathamkijkul. 1983. 'Slum Reconstruction: Land Sharing as an Alternative to Eviction in Bangkok', in Shlomo Angel, Raymon W. Archer, Sidhijai Tanphiphat and Emiel A. Wegelin (eds.), *Land for Housing the Poor*. Singapore: Select Books, pp. 430–60.

Angel, Shlomo and Sureeporn Chuated. 1987. 'The Down-Market Trend in Housing Production in Bangkok'. Technical Report 3, Asian Institute of Technology, Bangkok.

Angel, Shlomo and Sopon Pornchokchai. 1987. 'Bangkok Slum Lands: Policy Implications of Recent Findings', Technical Report 5.

Bangkok Metropolitan Administration. 1990. *Congested Community Survey Bangkok*. Bangkok: Bangkok Metropolitan Administration and UNICEF.

Boonyabancha, Somsook. 1983. 'The Causes and Effects of Slum Eviction in Bangkok', in Shlomo Angel, Raymon W. Archer, Sidhijai Tanphiphat and Emiel A. Wegelin (eds.), *Land for Housing the Poor*. Singapore: Select Books, pp. 254–80.

Boonyabancha, S., P. Niyom, S. Patpui, K. Suksumake and Fr. S. Maier. 1988. *Struggle to*

Stay: A Case Study of People in Slum Klong Toey Fighting for Their Home. Bangkok: The Duang Prateep Foundation.

Chin, Siew Sim. 1987. 'Coping in the City: A Study of Low-Income Households in Three Squatter Settlements in Bangkok, Thailand'. Unpublished M.Sc. Thesis, Asian Institute of Technology, Bangkok.

Green, Patricia Jennifer. 1990. 'Psychological Impacts of Slum Eviction: Women in Bangkok'. Unpublished M.Sc. Thesis, University of Waikato.

Korff, Rudiger. 1986. *Bangkok: Urban System and Everyday Life*. Saarbrucken: Breitenb-ach Publishers.

Morell, Susan and **David Morell**. 1972. *Six Slums in Bangkok: Problems of Life and Options for Action*. Bangkok: UNICEF.

National Housing Authority. 1991. *Slum Development*. Bangkok: NHA.

National Statistical Office. No date. Preliminary Report 1990 Population and Housing Census. Bangkok: National Statistical Office, Office of the Prime Minister.

PADCO/National Housing Authority. 1987. *The Land and Housing Markets of Bangkok: Strategies for Public-Sector Participation*, Volume 1, Final Report and Volume 11, Technical Reports. Bangkok: PADCO.

PADCO/Land Institute Foundation. 1990. *Bangkok Land and Housing Market Assessment*. Bangkok: PADCO.

Panroj Islam, Prachumporn. 1987. 'Land Sharing for Tenure Security in Bangkok Slum Housing Settlements'. Unpublished M.Sc. Thesis, Asian Institute of Technology, Bangkok.

Panroj Islam, Prachumporn and **Kioe Sheng Yap**. 1989. 'Land Sharing as a Low Income Housing Policy: An Analysis of its Potential', *Habitat International* 13 (1), pp. 117–26.

Pornchokchai, Sopon. 1984. 'A Study of House Renters in Four Bangkok Slum-Housing Settlements', Unpublished M.Sc. Thesis, Asian Institute of Technology, Bangkok.

———. 1985. *1020 Bangkok Slums: Evidence, Analysis, Critics*. Bangkok: School of Urban Community Research and Actions.

Shahand, A., M. Tekie and **K.E. Weber**. 1986. *The Role of Women in Slum Improvement: A Comparative Study of the Squatter Settlements at Klong Toey and Wat Yai Sri Suphan in Bangkok*. Bangkok: Division of Human Settlements Development, Asian Institute of Technology.

Tanphiphat, Sidhijai. 1983. 'Immediate Measures for Increasing the Supply of Land for Low-Income Housing in Bangkok', in Shlomo Angel, Raymon W. Archer, Sidhijai Tanphiphat and Emiel A. Wegelin (eds.), *Land for Housing the Poor*. Singapore: Select Books, pp. 375–92.

Thailand Development Research Institute. No date. *National Urban Development Policy Framework, Final Report Area 2: Urban Population, Employment Distribution and Settlement Patterns*. Bangkok: Thailand Development Research Institute.

Thorbek, Susanne. 1987. *Voices from the City: Women in Bangkok*. London: Zed Books.

United Nations Centre for Human Settlements (Habitat). 1986. *Rehabilitation of Inner City Areas: Feasible Strategies*. Nairobi: United Nations Centre for Human Settlements (Habitat).

Vorratnchaiphan, Chamniern Paul. 1988. 'Local Authorities, the Urban Poor and their Settlements in the Regional Growth Centers of Thailand'. Paper submitted to the International Workshop on Housing in Bangkok. Post Graduate Centre Human Settlements, Katholieke Universiteit Leuven.

Wonghanchao, Warin. 1987. 'Thailand', in Seong-Kyu Ha (ed.), *Housing Policy and Practice in Asia*. London: Croom Helm, pp. 175–94.

Yamklinfung, Prasert. 1973. *The Needs and Problems of Children and Youth in Four Slums in Bangkok*. Bangkok: UNICEF and CUSSRI.

Yap, Kioe Sheng. 1989 'Some Low-Income Housing Delivery Subsystems in Bangkok, Thailand', *Environment and Urbanization 1(2)*, pp. 27–37.
———. 1992. *Low-Income Housing in Bangkok: A Review of Some Housing Sub-Markets*. Bangkok: Division of Human Settlements Development, Asian Institute of Technology.

12

The Logic of Urban Development and Slum Settlements: The People's Republic of China

On-Kwok Lai

Human settlement problems in the socialist world are exceptional in many ways when compared with the trajectories of urban development in the Third World. This is particularly true because of the global ideological struggles between capitalism and socialism since the end of World War II. Many international organizations, e.g., the United Nations Development Program and the World Bank, could rarely influence the synergy of slum settlements in socialist polity. As a result, the case of the People's Republic of China (PRC) is quite idiosyncratic compared to human settlement problems and processes in other Third World countries.

In contrast to the capitalist case, the problem of slum settlements has undergone another set of developments in the socialist polity of the People's Republic of China. As we shall demonstrate in this descriptive study, the urban development patterns and slum formations are, to a large extent, shaped by socialist state policy (and control) in cities and villages, in the course of demographic changes and dynamics. As socialist ideals and their state mechanisms were the major variables in determining the way in which socioeconomic progress took place on the one hand, and the possible development of underdevelopment in socialist cities—the slum settlements—on the other, we will adopt a statist approach (Skocpol 1979, 1985). The description will show that the formation of slum settlements is unintentionally shaped by state policy and the alternative state strategies to ameliorate the related problems, to examine the case of China.[1]

By emphasizing the role of the socialist state in shaping slum settlements, we are in no way to pretend or predict that no societal forces, say, via individual self-help home building, helped to solve the housing problems (Hegedus 1987; Musil 1987). Also, to illustrate the way in which slum settlements and state policy developed in China, we tend to adopt the living conditions approach—the degree of adequate basic infrastructure, i.e., the permanence of housing and fresh water supplies—in defining the slum settlements (United Nations 1971).[2]

China was and still is a developing country. Relatively poor housing conditions are in fact part of the people's lives. On the one hand these were historically determined and, on the other hand, the pursuit of a 'self-reliance' socialist policy in national development with a planned economy have both helped to shape the permanence of the relative poor living conditions. In general, the living conditions in the urban sector, despite higher incomes of city people and their access to public services, were more problematic than their rural counterparts. For example, Tables 12.1 and 12.2 show that not less than half of the urban population lived in a standard space of 4 sq m or less per person before 1978 (Kwok and Chu 1987).[3]

Table 12.1: Living Conditions of Urban and Rural Residents, 1950–88

Years	Floor space of newly-built residential buildings for staff and workers in urban areas (1,000,000 sq m)		Floor space of newly-built houses in rural areas (1,000,000,000 sq m)	Living space per capita (sq m)	
	Through capital construction by state-owned units	Through updating and transformation and other investment by state-owned units and investment by urban collective units.		Urban	Rural
1950–88	1324	N.A.	N.A.	N.A.	
1978	38		0.1	4.2	8.1
1979–88	792	268	6.8	N.A.	N.A.
1979	63	2	0.4	4.4	8.1
1980	82	10	0.5	5.0	9.4
1981	79	19	0.6	5.3	10.2
1982	90	28	0.6	5.6	10.7
1983	81	34	0.7	5.9	11.6
1984	77	30	0.6	6.3	13.6
1985	96	29	0.7	7.5	14.7
1986	89	32	1.0	8.0	15.3
1987	69	41	0.9	8.5	16.0
1988	66	43	0.8	8.8	16.6

Source: State Statistical Bureau of the PRC, 1989. *China: Statistical Yearbook 1989*. Beijing: State Statistical Bureau of PRC, p. 689.

To understand the socialist state's policy initiatives and responses to poor living conditions, historically, we have to examine the macro strategy of national development in general and the differential policies in rural and urban sectors in particular. For elaboration, we have used a period schema in highlighting how and when the Chinese government tackled this problem.

Table 12.2: Summary of General Housing Survey, 1985–86

Urban Living Space

	Small cities (with less than 200,000 people)	Medium-sized cities (with 200,000-500,000 people)	Large cities (with 500,000-1 million people)	Extra-large cities (with over 1 million people)	
Number of cities surveyed	177	94	30	22	323 (Total)
Per capita living space (M^2/ person)	6.65	6.08	6.19	5.86	6.10 (Average)

Average Per capita Living Space in the Provinces with the Highest Figures and the Lowest Figures

	Whole province	Small cities	Medium-sized cities	Large cities	Extra large cities
Six provinces	7.19	7.25	6.84	7.41	7.35
Zhejiang	7.64	7.38	7.17	7.87	8.07
Fujiang	7.49	7.69	5.52	8.10	
Hunan	7.11	6.88	6.85	7.81	
Sichuan	7.11	7.39	6.82		7.14
Heibei	7.10	7.07	6.81	7.33	
Jiangsu	7.07	6.18	6.98	6.94	7.38
Three Provinces	4.85	4.88	4.87	4.79	4.86
Heilongjiang	4.98	4.99	4.93	5.04	4.92
Jilin	4.93	4.81	4.92	4.87	5.03
Liaoning	4.71	4.82	4.78	4.31	4.80

Source: State Statistical Bureau, *Beijing Review*, 30 (19), 11 May 1987, quoted in Fong (1987, p. 4).

PERIODS OF URBAN DEVELOPMENT

The degree of urbanization is generally measured in terms of urban population and its growth rate. When these characteristics are known it is possible to devise a strategy—urban policy initiatives—to administer urbanization. It follows that the monitoring of the urbanization process is not just revealing the synergistic effects of and with other sectoral or distributive policies (Renaud 1981; Lim 1988), but also determines the way to tackle the housing question.

For the period between 1949 and 1992, China's urban policy has undergone zigzag changes and could be broadly periodized into three major distinctive phases: phase I, from the founding of the PRC in 1949 to the end of the First Five Year Plan period; phase II, from the Great Leap Forward to the termination of the Cultural Revolution; phase III, from 1978 to 1992.[4]

Phase I (1949–57), a pragmatic phase of development (Galtung 1987), was characterized by an urban-based Stalinist development strategy for rapid urbanization, and hence vigorous growth of the urban population. The level of urbanization increased by one-half, from 10.6 percent in 1949 to 15.4 percent in 1957. The urban population nearly doubled from 57.6 million to 99.5 million. The urban population grew at an average rate of 7.6 percent a year, while the annual population growth rate was just about 2.2 percent.[5]

Phase II (1958–77), a dogmatic phase, was featured by a Maoist rural-based development strategy and controlled urbanization policy: stabilization of urban population. Antiurban measures were taken. In these years, China's urban population increased at a modest average growth rate of 3.1 percent (while the annual population grew at 1.9 percent), from 107.2 million to 163 million. The level of urbanization was stabilized for the entire period with a marginal increase of 1.1 percent, from 16.3 percent in 1958 to 17.4 percent in 1976 (Chan and Xu 1985; Xu 1984).

Phase III (1978–92) was more than a return of phase I's pragmatic and urban-based development. A 'modernization' and 'open door' policy were pursued. Unlike phase I's strategy, a more balanced development of agriculture and industry was advocated. The ideological influences of Maoism and Marxism were diminishing but not insignificant as manifested in the anti-bourgeois campaign of 1986, Tienanmen Square in 1989 and its aftermath. Hence, urbanization regained its momentum. Within six years from 1977 to 1982, urban population increased a quarter from 166.7 million to 211.5 million, and the level of urbanization rose from 17.6 percent to 20.8 percent. The average annual growth rate of urban population (4.4 percent) exceeded the annual population growth rate (1.3 percent) by 3.1 percent. It was a period characterized by contradictory policies with socialist objectives of equality, on one hand, and economic objectives of rapid development, on the other.

EXTENT AND PATTERN OF
SLUM SETTLEMENTS IN CHINA

Having outlined this urban scenario, we attempt to delineate the extent and pattern of slum settlements in China. But before we do that, the problem in defining and identifying what is a slum settlement in the Chinese context must be acknowledged. In actuality, the determination of the level of poor conditions of urban housing in China is difficult because of lack of information, conflicting figures, different methodologies and data sources, which in turn, lead to confusion. To solve this definitional problem, we shall follow the change in the spatial-administrative unit or city (*shi*), as Ma and Cui (1987) propose that the appropriate estimation of China's urbanization level should *only* include the nonagricultural population of the designated *cities* and *towns*. And we shall check with studies on poor conditions of living. This parameter is used to estimate the extent of slum settlements.

The Legacy of Treaty-Port Slum Settlements

Most of the major infrastructure—housing—in Chinese cities was developed via, directly or indirectly, the treaty port authorities in the pre-1949 period, despite the fact that in Maoist analysis, capitalism and cities in China were perceived as potentially reactionary and alien (Mao 1954, p. 22). The urbanization process happened early in the treaty ports. Slum settlements had developed within a network of premodern and modern socioeconomic enterprises (Fei 1953): the breaking up of the traditional sector in rural township, the related (uncontrolled) migration from villages to cities, and the deteriorating living conditions. Ironically, it occurred in the modernized cities (Kuhn 1970; Mann 1984, pp. 92–93; Murphey 1980a/b; Buck 1978). This pattern of development resembled in many aspects, the development of slum settlements in the developing countries elsewhere (Butterworth and Chance 1981).

Slum Clearance and Development with Nation Building, 1949–57

The new socialist government put much effort in the early period (1949–52) of this phase in clearing up slum settlements for city development and providing the minimal basic infrastructure in cities (Fong 1987). But this strategy was aimed to settle or control the urban population rather than to improve their living conditions. In actuality, the rate of clearance of slum areas was very much determined by the necessity for other infrastructure development; the slum settlements usually were tolerated with some simple in-site improvement works. In other words, the relocation of people for national development purposes, due to infrastructure projects' development, took priority over the improvement of living conditions in slums. Three structural constraints were felt in this period: (*1*) the acute shortage of housing, (*2*) people's tolerance of poor conditions with aspirations for a better society, and (*3*) the urge to build up the new socialist economic base in China.

It is fair to say that existing (previously uncontrolled) slum settlements in this period were kept under control via in-site service improvement. But the new regional policy in developing *growth poles*[6] in the First Five Year Plan (FYP, 1952–57) had contributed to the worsening of housing conditions, and unintentionally shaped the development of slum settlements in these key point cities, ironically, with a revolutionary label that denoted some sense of a new socialist ideal type of city. Since the new [quasi-slum] settlements in these growth poles had been underinvested in quality terms, they contributed much to the process of ghettoization when not much funding nor spiritual supports were available for the maintenance of housing as years went by.

Revolutionary Undertone of Slums (1958–77)

This period was characterized by a dogmatic national development strategy that was in line with the Maoist ideals of the Cultural Revolution. In comparative terms, Maoist rural-based development strategy and controlled urbanization policy had lessened the extent of rural-to-urban migration and in turn reduced the burden on urban housing. However, the existing poor conditions of living in the urban sector, housing in particular, were not improved because first, the available funding for collective enterprises was limited, and second, the revolutionary spirit and ideals, to a large extent, discouraged an individual's efforts in improving his/her material life, if not encouraging the very essence of proletariat life—poor!

More serious was the fact of the deterioration of housing conditions in the existing urban settlements in general and slums in particular, and the ghettoization of the supposedly new districts built after 1949 because less investments were put into the maintenance of existing housing stocks.[7] The neglect of both qualitative and quantitative aspects of housing conditions is clearly shown in the yearly investment (from 1958–78) in this sector which accounted for less than 7 percent of the total investment on capital construction.[8]

This underinvestment in the housing sector was due to Chinese Marxist's interpretation that housing only serves the purpose of collective consumption rather than nation building on the one hand, and on the other hand, the cultural critiques on petty bourgeoisie—property ownership—enabled some form of 'capital accumulation of the Chinese Communist Party [CCP] members' since the early 1960s when the economy was once booming for improvement in living conditions.

In short, this period was characterized by a politically constituted undertone of slum settlements and this form of living environment cultivated the necessary conditions for the Cultural Revolution on the way to a new socialist utopia.

Dualistic Settlement in a Planned Economy, 1978–91

With a liberation strategy which emphasizes both 'open door' and Four 'Modernizations' to pursue national economic development within a socialist polity, the introduction of market elements in a planned economy was experimented with in various arenas. The major characteristics of the problematic slum settlements were structurally linked to: (*1*) the enhanced mobility of people in search of better living conditions, (*2*) housing and living conditions considered as a separate entity which were no longer subsumed under production and its enterprises, and (*3*) development and subsequent consolidation of the commodification of private housing sector.

From 1978 to 1983, the major dynamics of economic reform took place in the rural sector and to a large extent, an improvement in the living conditions was made in the villages and towns which contributed to the stable urban population. On the other hand, the increase in the autonomy of production enterprises enabled the better performed ones to make investments in maintaining their housing stocks.[9] With more autonomy given to production enterprises and the development of individual enterprises in the cities since 1983, the mobility of people from rural areas to cities was obviously increased. These conditions contributed to the increasing volume of mobile population into major cities and Special Economic Zones (SEZs)[10] where economic prosperity developed. For example, the daily mobile population of Guangzhou is 1 million out of its population of 6 million! The daily mobile population (the blind flow) and their accumulation in the most prosperous cities and towns have created various problems for the urban managers. The new type of slum settlements were developing in numerous SEZs.[11] Due to the booming economy of the SEZs, temporary or guest labors were attracted to the SEZs but they were mostly housed in a temporary shelter, e.g., the construction sites.

At the end of the 1980s, the Chinese authorities also approved the opening up of the property market in the SEZs where local and foreign people were allowed to invest in housing stocks. This measure implied a more commercially and externally oriented city development strategy. Slum settlements in the potentially profitable areas were thus cleared for property and city development, and the displacement of people to other slums was observed as the rental charges, in most cases, followed the property values. The classic question on development, as in other countries, is raised: who benefits from urban renewal?

The duality of slum settlements in the late 1980s refers to two regulatory, albeit not equally, dynamic forces underlying the urban question between state or collective enterprises' housing and private property market, formal housing and informal slum settlements, mobile and static settlement patterns, interconnected by a contradictory network which follows the profit making principle within the framework of a planned economy. In short, the portrait of the city development process in other developing countries is being reproduced recently in China's newly formed SEZs.

EXPLAINING SLUM
FORMATION—RECENT INTERPRETATIONS

As analyzed, the formation of urban slum settlements is very much related to two arenas of development in: (1) demographic variables, and (2) state policies in urban, rural, and other functional sectors, within a given historically determined set of housing conditions. In this section, some propositions to explain the phenomenon will be discussed.

The Deurbanization Process and Slum Settlements

By 1952 the rural–urban migration had increased at an alarming rate. The urban population grew by 14 million in four years from 1949. The rate of annual urban growth reached 7.6 percent while the average population growth was just 2.2 percent. Nearly half of the urban growth was contributed by migration (Chen 1973, p. 68).[12] This shaped the crisis in the cities. Policy measures had to be taken to ease the burden on the urban sector.

From 1949 to 1957, slums were kept and, to a lesser extent, developed out of decentralization-cum-consolidation strategy, as more than half of all investment was allocated to inland regions (Roll and Yeh 1975). By 1958, the inland cities increased their industrial production from 1/4 in 1949 to 1/3 of the national total (Richman 1969). But the increase of production in inner cities by increase of labor concentration was at the cost of crowded living conditions and underdeveloped infrastructure.

During this period, the population of the key point cities grew to a considerable extent (Wang 1957). The average annual urban growth was 7.6 percent—well above the nationwide annual growth average of 2.3 percent in the same period. In the First Five Year Plan the migration was caused by the attractiveness of industrial employment and the considerable rural–urban gap of living standards rather than the depression or collectivization in rural areas (Farina 1980, p. 488). The pull factor of better economic life chances for workers in urban sectors thus shaped the formation, if not the permanence, of slum settlements in Chinese cities. Furthermore, since poor living conditions were being argued as the proletarian way of living, the state enterprises were less willing to reinvest in housing enterprises.

The pro-rural development strategy adopted during the period 1960–77 was deurbanized in nature[13] and this had effectively checked the rural–urban migration. But the synergistic effects of the Cultural Revolution had led to the deterioration of housing conditions. This further led to the formation of urban slum settlements. The causes of slum settlements in the 1980s had changed as the dualistic urbanization processes took place in the cities that were subjected to market operation within a planned economy.[14] This duality will most likely shape the course of human settlements in Chinese cities.

Production Biased Over Slum Permanence

Housing was being considered by the Chinese socialists as serving a consumption, not a production function. Economic growth, in this sense, depends a lot on the actual production rather than good housing for the reproduction of labor supplies. This production bias thesis is quite common among socialist countries that leads to the intentional underdevelopment of consumer goods, and the deterioration of living conditions. Slum settlements, in a comparative sense, are not uncommon. Since most of the housing development decisions and housing stocks were in the hands of state or collective production enterprises which had a bias against the possible improvement of housing conditions vis-a-vis production per se, it is not surprising that housing stocks, once developed but without much maintenance, tended to become quasi-slum settlements in the long run.

Furthermore, the organization of production units in a hierarchical form (i.e., vertical-functional linkage instead of horizontal-locality based networking) had limited the capability of the city government to change the existing land use for the improvement of slum settlements. It has been shown in some functionally concentrated localities, e.g., the iron and steel industry in Shanghai, that the locality-based government had not much authority to improve the slum district if the building and housing of the district's population remained the responsibility of the Ministry of Metallurgy. One implication that could be deduced from this logic, is that the higher the functional differentiation of production a city has, the more difficult it is for the local government to solve the housing problem because it is bounded by various structural constraints formed by the production based enterprises.

The case of China is unique. The production bias of the Chinese Marxists, in tackling the problem of slum settlements, was further complicated by Maoist's ideal type of societal development, namely his (and his followers') interpretation of material life and poverty.

Maoist Interpretations of Material Life and Poverty

The Maoist ideal of/for 'poor and nothingness' (no property) has posed a hindrance for the improvement of living conditions for its own sake. In

Maoist terms, to be revolutionary, people should be kept as close to a minimal subsistence level as possible so that the communal spirit could be enhanced in fighting for their collective survival. The Maoist search for the spiritual (vis-a-vis material), if not revolutionary ideal, to a certain extent, resembles the ideal formulation of human beings found in the traditional Confucian thoughts: spiritual over material life. For the Maoist, the major revolutionary power is derived not from good living conditions, but rather the reverse setting (to a certain extent, slum settlements) in which a cultural critique and subsequent (endless) proletariat revolution can emerge (Mao 1954, 1956).

In the name of the socialist ideal, the living conditions of people were disregarded. The establishment of a commune system was a key feature in the Great Leap Forward (1958–60) and rural industrialization, and was regarded as a Chinese version of the Paris Commune (Meisner 1982, p. 193; Salaff 1967). The people's communes were multifunctional entities, and more or less self-sufficient units to achieve the goal of 'self-reliance'. Despite the various contributions of the commune system, they were mostly at the level of marginal subsistence and people lived in quasi-slum settlements. These reform policy initiatives provide a plausible explanation for the tendency of China's development of underdevelopment.

Socialist State's Strategy for Tackling Slum Settlements

To recapitulate, various measures used by the PRC in controlling or eradicating slum settlements had, instead of confronting the slums issue, other aims and intentions.

The growth of large cities was prevented by strict migration control through work permits, control over housing and forced out-migration (Renaud 1987, p. 69). To a certain extent the slum settlements were being kept within a manageable extent, but the feasibility for improvement was much determined by the hierarchically organized production units. The basic question for these production (rather than housing) managers is: *to what extent can these state or collective enterprises generate enough revenue for housing improvement or maintenance*?

In other words, the rustication (send down) movement coupled with the Hukou (resident-register) system was part of the overall strategy of socialist nation development. The unintended consequence was the shifting of slum settlements. Hence, the transfer of officials, intelligentsia, and discontented youth was considered a means to both economic and political ends.[15]

Mass mobilization and decentralization of power in both cities and countryside—a utopian socialist project—had been attempted. The effects were the shift of the poorest or powerless (and their slum settlements) to the countryside. But the problem of poor living conditions had not been directly tackled. Similarly, mass deportation of peasants was tried but was not effective due to the lack of coordination of the measures.

As early as 1954, the government launched a series of urban policy measures to curtail the continuing increase of urban population. Both passive and active deurbanization measures were used (Kirkby 1985, pp. 24–28). First, regarding the 'sending down' policy—a key 'active' measure. Despite their various forms, the common purpose was to maintain 'a stable and manageable urban polity in a situation of severely constrained central investments in the nonproductive urban fabric and insufficiencies in grain supply' (ibid., p. 32). Usually, these actions were supplemented by the imposition of tough measures to restrain urban population growth (ibid., p. 21, p. 121).[16] The obvious case is the one child policy in cities started in the 1970s. But these measures were not effective.

Apart from problems of overcongestion, diseconomies of scale of large cities also forced the government to adopt a new policy initiative to limit the size of cities (Tian 1958, pp. 26–27). Hence, the development of satellite towns (population 50,000 to 200,000) near to the major urban centers (e.g., Minhang, south of Shanghai) within a manageable scale was also promoted.[17] But they were less effective in improving the housing conditions. In this particular context the policies were pro-rural and antimetropole. Deurbanization, and despecialization of urban and rural sector provided short-term solutions (if not a cover-up) of the problems of overpopulation, rapid urbanization, urban unemployment, and the regional disparities the CCP faced.

The effectiveness of the mentioned strategies is self-explanatory, if we consider the development of slum settlements discussed previously and critically examine the socioeconomic development of the PRC in the last four decades. In other words, the discussed strategies have limited effect on solving the problem of slum settlements within the context of China's low economic base, closure of its socioeconomic system and the related political movements embedded in it. New sets of urban agendas and the related policies being issued only reflect the changing sociopolitical conditions!

EPILOGUE: BACK TO THE FUTURE?

The 1978–92 period is one of contradictions: between the socialist ideals of elimination of socioeconomic disparities (between town and the countryside, and between and within regions) and the economic goals for rapid development. Contradictory goals resulted in contradictory policies (Renaud 1981; Lim 1988). Foreign investment in the coastal regions has rejuvenated urban liberalism, if not enhanced its 'counterrevolutionary' sentiments, and opposition to the CCP's hegemony.

National and ideologically oriented state strategy for development, in the PRC, has missed its significant impact on locality, at least in improving citizen's living standard or controlling the slum settlements. The recent development of a dualistic urban structure in the supposedly prosperous cities of China must not be taken lightly because the living conditions of people improved at a differentiated rate, if not in a polarized pattern.[18] This dualistic urban structure will most likely shape settlement patterns in Chinese cities in the future.

Perhaps it is right to argue that the paradigmatic change in the post-1976 period has been subjected to a drastic transformation owing to a fundamental breakdown of the socialist system but without the acknowledgement of it by the traditional communists. The so-called Chinese version of socialism is so abstract for the Marxists. Does it—the contradiction of economic freedom and party control—mean that the Chinese political ideology is in flux or withering away? (Meisner 1982, p. 225; Brugger 1985).

More importantly, Chinese socialism is too far away from limited autonomy, after 43 years of hegemonic communism, of the SEZs' citizens who return. Nor does it follow the logic of profit making which the global investors used to have. Social phenomena in China today are contradictory. These contradictory variables will most likely reinforce slum settlements or the shifting of them between regions. A century-old question comes back again: in what way(s) should China be developed for the betterment of people in the course of the search for better living conditions?

At this historical juncture, China is on its way to becoming a part of the international world via increasing trade and a rapidly developing economy. It is highly probable that many opportunities for involvement of international organizations such as the World Bank or the United Nations Development Program in slum settlements in China will open up. The question of how to deal with the legacy of the urban question in socialist countries is a global challenge for all of us.

NOTES

1. The term 'slum settlements' is used instead of 'squatters' because the latter term implies a legal sense of breaching (individual, capitalist) property rights that is not compatible with socialist paradigmatic interpretation of collective or state ownership.
2. It should be pointed out that, not until recently, China has rarely made known the extent and distribution of urban slum settlements. Instead, for various reasons, they described slum settlements in terms of housing shortage or worsening of living conditions in very general, if not abstract, statements.

3. See Tables 12.1 and 12.2 for illustration.
4. There have been different periodizations on China's urban policy. Cell (1980) observes two major periods; Lau (1987) notes three periods; Buck (1981) divides it into seven periods; Kwok (1981) identifies four distinct periods. For a full discussion, see Lai and Lai (1991).
5. Demographic statistics on China have always been problematic. The information is either unreliable, or inadequate, or impossible to make interperiod comparisons due to changes in the definition of urban population. Chan and Xu (1985), Ma and Cui (1987). For our paper here, if not otherwise stated, demographic data are derived from State Statistical Bureau, PRC (1986, 1992).
6. The key point cities, e.g., Lanzhou, Baotou, formed part of the 'concentrated-decentralization' strategy and functioned as 'regional *growth poles*'. As argued, the development impulses of these *growth poles* could be filtered down the settlement hierarchy by forward and backward linkages. Thus the small cities and the countryside could be benefited. Nevertheless, the 'urban bias' of the Soviet development model was implicit, in which large cities were favored and had profound effects on the nation as a whole.
7. In actuality, the maintenance of housing stocks has rarely come up on the development agenda of state, collective, and individual enterprises in the turbulence of the Cultural Revolution.
8. This figure is according to my own calculation derived from State Statistical Bureau (1986) and Longman (1987).
9. Most of the housing stocks in China, before 1980, were managed and owned by collective or state enterprises.
10. Special Economic Zones (SEZs) in Guangdong province (Shenzhen, Zhuhai, Shantou) and Fujian province (Xiamen) were established in 1981.
11. According to [*Renmin Ribao*] (People's Daily, 15 October 1986), the fourteen cities are: Dalian, Qinghuangdao, Tianjin, Yantai, Qingdao, Liangyungan, Nantung, Shanghai, Ningbo, Wenzhou, Fuzhou, Guangzhou, Zhanjiang, and Beihai.
12. The problem was addressed by a number of directives issued by the central government, see reports in *Renmin Ribao* (People's Daily, 18 April 1953; 15 March 1954).
13. Substantial evidences seemingly confirm that the post-1949 China was and is still not totally antiurban. Furthermore, our view is that a distinction between 'deurbanism' and 'antiurbanism' should be drawn. We would choose the former term to describe the history of post-1949 China's urban policy (Kirkby 1985; Kwok 1987 a/b).
14. To illustrate this dualistic process, the rent difference between private and state sector in Guangzhou is about 1000 percent.
15. Farina (1980) suggests other aims of the 'sending down' namely, for the promotion of technical and cultural level in the countryside, reduction of tension in urban areas, and rational distribution of population and intellectuals.
16. For a detailed account on national development policy, see Mao (1961, pp. 364-65) compared with Liu (1949).
17. The socioeconomic consequences of the Soviet model were questioned by the CCP in 1958, in particular, the widening of the political, economic, and cultural gulf between the modernizing cities and the backward countryside (Meisner 1982, pp. 67); apart from the fact that the Soviet model demanded considerable social overheads.
18. See recent studies on Chinese social development, SSSDPG (1991), Luo (1991), Chan (1991).

REFERENCES

Brugger, B. (ed.). 1985. *Chinese Marxism in Flux 1978-1984*. London: Croom Helm.

Buck, D.D. 1978. *Urban Change in China—Politics and Development in Tsinan, Shan-tuna. 1890-1949*. Madison: The University of Wisconsin Press, pp. 221-43.

———. 1981. 'Policies Favoring the Growth of Smaller Urban Places in the People's Republic of China, 1949-1979', in L.J.C. Ma and E.W. Hanten (eds.), *Urban Development in Modern China*. Boulder: Westview Press.

Butterworth, D. and **J.K. Chance.** 1981. *Latin American Urbanization*. Cambridge: Cambridge University Press.

Cell, C.P. 1980, 'The Urban–Rural Contradiction in the Maoist Era: The Pattern of De-urbanization in China', *Comparative Urban Research 73*, pp. 48–69.

Chan, C.L.W. 1991. 'The Community-Based Urban Welfare Delivery System of the PRC in the Midst of Economic Reforms: The Guanazhou Experience'. Unpublished Ph.D. thesis, University of Hong Kong, Hong Kong.

Chan, K.W. and **X.Q. Xu.** 1985. 'Urban Population Growth and Urbanization in China Since 1949: Reconstructing a Baseline', *China Quarterly 104*, pp. 583–613.

Chen, C.S. 1973. 'Population Growth and Urbanization in China, 1953–70', *Geographical Review 63 (1)*, pp. 55–72.

Farina, M.B. 1980. 'Urbanization, De-urbanization and Class Struggle in China, 1949–79'. *International Journal of Urban & Regional Research 4 (4)*, pp. 484–501.

Fei, X.T. 1953. *China's Gentry: Essays in Urban–Rural Relations*. Chicago: University of Chicago Press.

Fong, P.K.W. 1987. 'The Commercialization of Housing in a Socialist State: An Attempt to Solve China's Urban Housing Problem'. Discussion Paper, Center of Urban Studies & Urban Planning, University of Hong Kong, Hong Kong.

Galtung, J. 1987. 'The Chinese Path to Development', in B. Glaeser (ed.), *Learning From China—Development and Environment in Third World Countries*. London: Allen & Unwin, pp. 32–55.

Hegedus, J. 1987. 'Reconsidering the Role of State and Market in Socialist Housing System', *International Journal of Urban and Regional Research 11 (1)*, pp. 27–36.

Kirkby, R.J.R. 1985. *Urbanization in China—Town and Country in a Developing Economy, 1949-2000 A.D.* London: Croom Helm.

Kuhn, P.A. 1970. *Rebellion and its Enemies in Late Imperial China*. Cambridge, MA: Harvard University Press.

Kwok, R.Y.W. 1981. 'Trends of Urban Planning and Development in China', in L.J.C. Ma and E.W. Hanten (eds.) *Urban Development in Modern China*. Boulder: Westview Press, pp. 339–52.

———. 1987a, 'Metropolitan Development in China: Struggle Between Two Contradictions', Working Paper: November, 1987, Center of Urban Studies & Urban Planning, University of Hong Kong.

———. 1987b. 'Recent Urban Policy and Development in China', *Town Planning Review 58 (4)*, pp. 383–99.

Kwok, R.Y.W. and **D.Y.W. Chu.** 1987. 'Urban Housing Provision In China after 1978'. Discussion Paper, Center of Urban Studies & Urban Planning, University of Hong Kong.

Lai, O K. and **T-K. Lai, ,** 1991. 'Socialist State Planning Reconsidered: Regional Policy in China, 1949-1989', *Environment and Planning C: Government and Policy 9*, pp. 207-24.

Lau, C.C. 1987. 'Urban China in Transition: The Impact of Economic Reforms', in J.C.H. Chai and C..K. Leung (eds.), *China's Economic Reforms*, Occasional Paper No. 73. Hong Kong: University of Hong Kong, pp. 43-56.

Lim, G-C. 1988. 'Theory and Taxonomy of Sectoral, Distributional, and Spatial Policies', *Environment and Planning C: Government and Policy 6*, pp. 225–36.

Longman Publishers, 1987. *China Urban Statistics 1986*. Hong Kong: Longman Publishers.

Luo, B. 1991. 'A Sociological Reflection on the Anti- Poverty', *She Hui Xuev An Jiu* (Sociological Studies) *4*, pp. 65–69.

Ma, L.J.C. and G. Cui. 1987. 'Administrative Changes and Urban Population in China', *Annals of the Association of American Geographers 77 (3)*, pp. 373–95.

Mann, S. 1984. 'Urbanization and Historical Change in China', *Modern China 10 (1)*, pp. 70–113.

Mao T-T, [1939] (1954). *The Chinese Revolution and the Chinese Communist Party*. Peking: Foreign Languages Press.

———. 1961. 'Report to the Second Plenary Session of the Seventh Central Committee of the Communist Party of China, 5 March 1949', *Mao Tse-tung, Selected Works*, Vol. 4. Peking: Foreign Languages Press, pp. 305–74.

Meisner, M. 1982. *Marxism, Maoism and Utopianism*. Madison: The University of Wisconsin Press.

Murphey, R. 1980a. *The Fading of Mao's Vision: City and Country in China's Development*. New York: Methuen.

———. 1980b. 'The Urban Road to Development', in C.K. Leung and N. Ginsburg (eds.), *China—Urbanization and National Development*. Chicago: Department of Geography, University of Chicago.

Musil, J. 1987. 'Housing Policy and Socio-Spatial Structure of Cities in a Socialist Country— Example of Prague', *International Journal of Urban and Regional Research 11 (1)*, pp. 79-99.

Renaud, B. 1981. *National Urbanization Policy in Developing Countries*. Oxford: Oxford University Press.

———. 1987. 'Urban Development Policies in Developing Countries', in G.S. Tolley and V. Thomas (eds.), *The Economics of Urbanization and Urban Policies in Developing Countries—A World Bank Symposium*. Washington D.C.: World Bank, pp. 301–35.

Richman, B.M. 1969. *Industrial Society in Communist China*. New York: Random House.

Roll, C.R. and Yeh, K.C. 1975. 'Balance in Inland and Coastal Industrial Development', in *China: A Reassessment of the Economy, Joint Economic Committee, U.S. Congress*. Washington D.C.: U.S. Government Printing Office, 10 July 1975.

Salaff, J. 1967. 'The Urban Communes and Anti-City Experiment in Communist China', *China Quarterly 29*, pp. 82–110.

Skocpol, T. 1979. *States and Social Revolutions. A Comparative Analysis of France, Russia and China*. Cambridge: Cambridge University Press.

———. 1985. 'Bringing the State Back', in P. B. Evan, D. Reuschemeyer an T. Skocpol (eds.), *Strategies of Analysis in Current Research*. Cambridge: Cambridge University Press.

State Statistical Bureau, PRC. 1986. *Statistical Yearbook of China 1986*. Beijing: State Statistical Bureau.

———. 1992. *Statistical Yearbook of China 1986*. Beijing: State Statistical Bureau.

The Synthetical Study of Social Development Project Group (SSSDPG). 1991. 'A Synthetical Analysis of China's Social Development in the Structural Transition Period', *She Hui Xuey an Jiu* (Sociological Studies), *4*, pp. 74–93.

Tian, S. 1958. 'Guanyu Chengshi Fazhan Guimunde Yanjiu (Research on the Sizes of Cities)', *Jihua Jingji*, pp. 26–27.

United Nations, 1971. *Improvement of Slum & Uncontrolled Settlements.* New York: United Nations.

Wang, G.W. 1957. 'How to Organize Agricultural Labor Power', *Jihua Jingji (Planned Economy), 8 (13),* pp. 6–13.

Xu, X.Q. 1984. 'Characteristics of Urbanization of China—Changes and Causes of Urban Population Growth and Distribution', *Asian Geographers 3 (1),* pp. 15–28.

PART IV

HOUSING UNDER LOW LEVELS OF HUMAN DEVELOPMENT

A comparison of the range on the Index for countries in the medium and high groups shows a remarkable drop. Countries in the first group are ranked in the 80s. Countries in the medium group are ranked in the 70s. The countries in the low group are ranked in the 30s on the Index. They all have improved over the expected rank based upon GNP, with the exception of Egypt. It has a substantial negative (–10) which indicates a very poor distribution of resources with regard to social development problems. Therefore, despite the low-level of economic development, these are countries which have dedicated resources to social development. The result has been an improvement in life expectancy, literacy, and income.

Not many of these countries have comparative improvement scores. Egypt (.140) is in the 40th percentile group from the top. Pakistan (.130) is in the 50th percentile group. India is in the 60th percentile group from the top and Ghana is in the 90th percentile group from the top. So there is a wide-range of improvements for societies of low human development for which information is available.

The recounting of strategies with regard to housing problems in each of the country case studies reflects the international solution in vogue at the time. Chapter 13 on Egypt by Ahmed Soliman is no exception. A self-help housing strategy, following Turner's influential writing, was also utilized in Egypt; followed by sites-and-services, upgrading, core housing, and wet cores. These various attempts failed, Soliman reports, due to lengthy negotiations, lack of political will, inadequate cost recovery, unsuitability of site location or incorrect implementation. After going through the process of discovering that heavy government involvement in self-help did not produce the desired result, there was a proposal to move in the direction of the new World Bank policy as described in Chapter 2, namely the new partnership of the government, the professional builders, and the squatters. Soliman describes these changes in strategy within the context of the particular forms of development of squatter and illegal subdivision in Egypt.

The next three chapters, describing the housing situation in the three African nations, are studies in contrast. The case of Zambia reflects high-levels of urbanization associated with colonial exploitation of natural mineral resources and the early commodification of housing and land tenure. The case of Tanzania illustrates the attempts to solve the problems of land and housing in a socialist mode. Ghana, in contrast with the other two cases, describes housing and land tenure where traditional tribal and communal elements have remained strong. The adaptation of rural housing traditions to urban settings and the particular problems which result are in contrast to the other two African countries.

Chapter 14 on Zambia by Ann Schlyter exemplifies the cyclical process of government attitudes towards the provision of housing for its citizens. Zambia, with a continuing deterioration in its economic situation due to changes in its demands for exports, and continued inability of the government administration to come up with an effective strategy for providing housing to the general public, has gone from squatter clearance policies right after independence in 1964 to squatter clearance policies with the election of the new government in 1990. In between there were periods of upgrading (some with World Bank and Western government help), legalization, and some legitimate expansion through provision of plots for self-built housing.

However, economic and political realities continue to affect housing. The lack of economic development means that the housing which is built and improved is never maintained. The result is a larger and larger share of housing sliding into the category of 'slum' housing. The cyclical process continues when there is no change in the political or economic situation.

In Tanzania, Chapter 15, where 60 to 82 percent of all urban housing is of the spontaneous settlement variety, the government has tried slum clearance and redevelopment, provision of mass housing by the national housing corporation, squatter upgrading, sites-and-services programmes, housing finance for low-income households, housing cooperatives, and employer funded housing. A.C. Mosha reports that due to problems of new squatter housing outpacing the upgrading two-to-one, too much of bureaucracy for self-help to function, cooperatives never developing beyond the formation stage, too much money and work required up-front by programs, the slow pace of the programs, the long bureaucratic process of planning, surveying, and servicing, along with the red tape and black market involved, slow to nonexistent compensation for relocation, the difficulty of obtaining housing loans, the shift of plots to middle-income households and no cost recovery resulted in the biggest project (supported by the World Bank) not being completed.

Despite these difficulties, the author of the chapter recommends that attempts be made to solve some of these problems but that upgrading, sites-and-services and self-help with better physical planning of squatter areas continue as the rate of spontaneous settlements has not abated. He recommends that the process remains in place because that is the only way houses are getting built, and that the government should try to improve that process somewhat.

In definite contrast to Zambia and Tanzania, Chapter 16 describes how housing in Ghana has largely remained under the control of traditional family and tribal relationships. The result is a high incidence of illegal housing, i.e., land and housing not registered with the local government or noncompliance with development regulations. However, it has nevertheless remained in the hands of families and used as the basis for the provision of urban housing for a wide-range of individuals through either a family connection or by renting. One consequence is that spontaneous or squatter housing is almost non-existent as the family/tribal groups are vigilant in protection of their right to use their land. The other major consequence is a large integrated family in the typical housing compound in Ghana. Tipple and Korboe have provided an excellent contrast with other African and nonAfrican societies in the difference that land tenure can make in the control and provision of housing.

While the system of land tenure in Ghana controls squatting, the problem of housing quality remains. The authors endorse the continuation of the present system of housing provision, but with an emphasis upon effective means of making more housing available and of providing upgrading and services, without seriously altering what they report to be a system not in need of fixing.

The two Asian countries of Pakistan and India contain a quarter of the world's current population. Increasingly urban, the attempts to deal with problems of housing poverty contain important lessons for national and international activities. Drawing upon the operational research relationship established between the Amsterdam Free University and Karachi University, Emiel Wegelin in Chapter 17, is able to both describe problems in the provision of housing in Pakistan and prescribe solutions. The main problem, he concludes, is 'scarcity of good governance'. Backed by studies of housing in Pakistan by the World Bank, the Asian Development Bank, and a large internal study by the Pakistan government, he is able to list the problems that continue to plague the upgrading and legalization process in *kachi abadies* and in the deteriorated central parts of the major cities.

The key problem for illegal and squatter housing is one of making land available to the right people, in the right places and at the right time. A solution to that problem lies in auctioning the land to private developers— taking the government out of the process as much as possible. The upgrading and improvement of central city slums, he concludes, is not possible without a change in the tax laws to market rather than rental value and a major program of property valuation. The latter, he notes, does not currently have political support.

Sridharan's description and analysis of housing poverty in India, Chapter 18, is from the broad policy and program perspective. He emphasizes the key role of the informal economy in the whole process of urbanization and the build-up of squatter settlements and slums. India, he shows, followed the standard cycle of initial response of clearance and relocation (generally to distant sites lacking adequate services), to site-and-service activities, and then gradually to the growing recognition that the government bureaucracies had to be minimized in the process and participation from the neighborhoods to be increased if housing goals were to be met. With the help of the World Bank and UNICEF, several programs of upgrading were initiated. As with programs elsewhere, bureaucratic red tape, corruption, and lack of a clear understanding of the problem prevented their implementation.

Sridharan takes a broad rather than an operational view when he emphasizes the need for controls on population growth, a renewed economic effort by the private sector, recognition of information housing as a national asset, and training for people in poverty. At the operational level he suggests greater community organization efforts, a pay-for-services approach, and the rationalization of the land tenure process.

13

A Tale of
Informal Housing in Egypt

Ahmed M. Soliman

In the past few decades, Egypt has seen rapid population growth, imbalance in the distribution of resources and income, and spread of poverty. In the meantime, the magnitude and complexity of the urbanization process associated with a lack of government funds has expanded enormously, creating a real housing problem for the urban poor. To a large extent, for the past few years conventional public housing has been the only official approach adopted in Egypt, but this has been insufficient to meet the increasing demands of the urban poor. The result has been brought about by several problems within the urban centers.

Lately, conventional wisdom (Ward 1982) was applied in Egypt in which self-help was, and continues to be, strongly influenced by the government. This approach was insufficient in servicing the bottom strata of the poorest people such as was hoped. The main objective of this paper is to provide more insights into the current situation of the squatters, and the associated mechanisms which led to the creation of these areas in Egyptian cities. More broadly, the paper seeks to highlight the interrelation between urban development constraints and the factors influencing the formulation of informal settlements and their relative impact upon the urban poor. The conclusions emphasize the three magnets of the problem and how to organize them to make best use of the available resources in Egypt in order to ameliorate the conditions within squatters' settlements on the one hand, and to accelerate housing production on the other.

URBAN DEVELOPMENT CONSTRAINTS

In the recent past, four factors peculiar to the Egyptian environment and to the Egyptian techniques of overcoming the problems of development processes, were emergent. First, Egypt's population is currently more than 58 million and is growing by nearly 2.8 percent each year—nearly one and a half million annually (CAPMAS 1991). Egypt's population will nearly double to 103 million by 2020 (*Time* 1989). More than four and a half out of ten Egyptians now live in an urban place. In addition, Egypt's high overall density and a cultural pattern that favors concentrated rural settlements in preference to scattered farmsteads combine to create a statistical fiction of overurbanization.

Second, overconcentration of the population in a primate city, the national capital housing the machinery of government, is a problem in Egypt. The primacy of Cairo as well as a kind of dual primacy is striking about the distribution of cities in Egypt (Abu-Lughod 1964) where Cairo and Alexandria are far bigger than the rest of the distribution. Both cities comprise 40 percent of the total urban population, and the remaining population is distributed in around 157 secondary and small cities (Soliman 1990). Unfortunately, this record of spatial concentration has not occurred without side effects; beyond a certain 'optimal' city size, urban scale diseconomies, notably congestion, begin to (i) impair the efficient functioning of the urban core, (ii) create visible social problems, and (iii) an inefficient use of the urban periphery in the form of residential sprawl.

Third, the picture of overurbanization, either formal (by the state) or informal (by the private developers and the state), in Egypt is distorted by problems of definitions of the urban: many urban places are simply swollen villages, crowding being induced by the peculiar agricultural circumstances of the Nile delta. In a country where more than 58 million persons are crowded on only four percent of the one million sq km large national territory—mainly along the narrow alluvial valley bordering the Nile and into the wider but still circumscribed far off the delta, a rural or squatting settlement can easily attain a minimum population of 30,000 persons without basically altering in appearance or assuming any of the functions generally associated with urbanism. Many squatter settlements perforce absorb an increased rural population, thus becoming unusually large but are as yet still rural communities mistermed urban centers or urban villages. The Nile delta contains nearly 36.8 million people, upper Egypt nearly 20.5 million, and the frontier region contains 0.7 million (CAPMAS 1990). Thus, in view of the problem of accommodating over 21 million in Egypt in the coming ten years, a significant proportion of the expected increase would live in rural areas which might destroy the delta region, the richest agricultural area in Egypt.

Finally, the salient physical changes in the urban areas are the output of the changing economic situation, and the growth of development in Egypt. The consequences of this were the spread of the built-up areas in the major urban centers and the development of continuous built-up areas between intermediate and small sized cities. The new built-up areas around the traditional, compact city cores or on the cities' periphery are characterized by a new pattern of spontaneous housing development or informal physical growth. This informal growth could act as a hybrid type between squatter and formal housing types, and is called *semiinformal* housing (Soliman 1989). This type of housing is similar in appearance to that of the squatter and formal sectors but contravenes fewer legal standards; as a result the units become more socially and politically acceptable. Also, it is considered ostensibly conventional in nature but has some degree of illegality. Most of the resources allocated informal housing areas have resulted from informal economic activities which are ways of doing things outside the official channels. These are characterized by: (*i*) reliance on indigenous illegal resources; (*ii*) small scale of informal operation; (*iii*) labor-intensive and adapted technology; (*iv*) skills acquired outside the formal system; and (*v*) unregulated and competitive markets (Lee-Smith and Stren 1991).

FACTORS INFLUENCING THE FORMULATION OF INFORMAL SETTLEMENTS

The uncontrolled settlements have occurred in the absence of affordable housing for low-income groups, lack of a national urban policy and the weakness of planning controls.

The scarcity of affordable housing for low-income groups might be attributed to the following reasons. First, the current total Egyptian population is more than 58 million inhabitants, making around 11.6 million families. On the other hand, in 1986 it is estimated that the total housing units in Egypt was around 11.31 million, in which 5.86 million are allocated in urban areas, and 5.45 million in rural areas. The average annual housing production between 1986 and 1992, shown in Table 13.1, is around 180,000 housing units. However, the total housing production in the last seven years is 1.26

Table 13.1: Annual Housing Production in Egypt between 1952 and 1988

No. of Housing	No. of Years	Annual Housing	
Years	Units Completion (1000)	For Housing Construction	Construction (1000)
1/7/1952–30/6/1960	31.8	8.0	3.975
1/7/1960–31/12/1976	434.587	16.8	26.338
1/1/1977–30/6/1982	652.323	5.5	118.604
1/7/1982–30/6/1987	879.188	5.0	175.837
1/7/1987–30/6/1988	184.803	1.0	184.803

Source: Housing in Egypt (1989), the Ministry of Development, New Communities, Housing, and Utilization, Cairo.

million housing units (Housing in Egypt 1989, p. 67). Therefore, the total housing stock in Egypt is around 12.57 million housing units. These figures give a surplus of nearly one million housing units. Most of these units fall within the category of luxury classification and are located mainly in the primate cities (Cairo and Alexandria) and major urban areas. These units are kept vacant for future use or for the purpose of speculation. Hence, these units are considered outside the housing market in Egypt, and do not meet the requirements of the urban poor or lie beyond the affordability of the urban poor.

Second, taking the average annual housing production in the last five years and the current Egyptian population (58 million people), it seems that the average housing production per 1,000 people is around 3.2 housing units which is very low and does not match the annual population growth.

Third, several studies (for example Soliman 1987, 1988, 1989), indicated that at least 11.2 million people or 20 percent of the total Egyptian population are in settlements as shown in Table 13.2. On the other hand, 75–80 percent of the total housing production is built by informal private developers (Mourad 1985; Davidson 1984; Soliman 1988). This type of housing is spread all over Egypt on the periphery of the urban areas, and is characterized by lack of basic services, scramble physical conditions, and social illness.

Table 13.2: Recognised Squatter Settlements in Selected Egyptian Cities

City	Total Population (in million)	No. of Recognised Squatter Areas	Total Population of Squatter Areas (in million)	Percentage
Cairo	16.0	16.0	7.00	43
Alexandria	4.0	15.0	0.60	15
Helwan	0.3	7.0	0.10	33
Ismailia	0.7	6.0	0.15	22
Aswan	0.8	4.0	0.15	20
Suez	0.55	4.0	0.10	18
Port Said	0.60	n.a.	0.12	20
Tanta	0.50	n.a.	0.10	20

* A recent calculation by the author depended on the previous figures recorded in Soliman (1988) and Capmas (1990).
Source: Al-Ahram, Egyptian Newspaper (1992a, 1991b).

To sum up, the previous facts indicate that there is a housing crisis in Egypt, in both quantity and quality. Bearing in mind the limited public budget allocated to housing investment, and the fact that the share of state housing would not exceed 10 percent of the total annual housing production, Table 13.3 shows that this would increase the dependence on private developers in providing the much needed housing production in the coming two decades. On the other hand, the increase in construction costs, the price of building materials associated with the influence of rent control, scarcity, and rising of land prices, create concrete obstacles for the private developers in contributing probably to formal housing production. Therefore, housing crises in Egypt can not only be tackled by the state, but the private developers are also the main producers of the ample proportion of housing supply. However, housing crises are concentrated in the urban agglomeration of places such as Cairo and Alexandria. Low-income groups, civil servants, and the urban poor are the strata most hit by the housing crises in Egypt.

Table 13.3: Housing Production in Egypt between 1960 and 1991

Type of Housing Year	Public Units (1000)	Percent	Private Units (1000)	Percent	Total	Population Increase (million)
1960–65	109.725	58	79.586	42	189.311	3.740
1966–70	56.110	32	119.670	68	175.780	3.000
1974–75	33.898	31	76.438	69	110.336	3.900
1976–80	89.738	19	369.095	81	458.833	5.700
1981–86	166.841	18	769.793	82	936.634	6.000
1987–91	n.a.		n.a.		900.000	8.200
Total	**456.312**		**1,414.582**		**2,770.894**	**30.54**

Source: The Ministry of Development, New Communities, Housing and Utilization, Cairo, 1991.

Second, the lack of a national urban planning policy has contributed to the spontaneous growth of cities by rural immigrants. The spread of the urban centers to the surrounding areas is considered to be a natural process: stretching, spreading out, overflow, arbitrary growth, etc., originating in an ecological phenomenon. Thus, for example, expressions like invasion into agricultural areas or state lands, conquering of areas, occupying key positions, squatting on public land, etc., have been widely used in most Egyptian cities, and are related to perceptions of the struggle of immigrants to settle in the urban areas, and at the same time, to tackle the shortage of housing for low-income groups. Finally, the arbitrary physical development acquired the installation of basic services to alleviate the health hazards, but at the same time, required a lump sum of money which was to be paid by the government. Therefore, while on the one hand the arbitrary physical growth put further financial burden on the government, it destroyed the homogeneity of the natural growth of the cities, and weakened the planning control over the urban areas, on the other. Cairo city seems to be a spontaneous city with leaks in some planned districts, or a city surrounded by a ring of uncontrolled residential areas.

The inappropriate planning control has accelerated the formulation of informal housing areas especially in the periphery of the urban centers. Despite the fact that the government introduced the urban planning law in

1982, there are many defects which are encouraging or helping the establishment of uncontrolled housing areas. This law did not clearly identify the urban areas, and even the regulation for establishing a new housing area outside the city boundary is left vague. On the other hand, the urban planning law No. 3, decree No. 13 stated that the built-up area should not exceed 60 percent of the total size of the land plot. This has encouraged the private developers to escape from inner city areas, and accumulate agricultural areas for the purpose of speculation, to avoid the continuous increase in land prices within the city, and escape from following the regulation of planning law in order to make the best use of their land plots. Also, decree No. 50 stated that the subdivider should install the various services at his own cost to his parcel as a condition to obtain a formal license for the subdivision. To sustain the low price of the land plots, the private developers together with the subdividers, preferred to invade the periphery areas of the urban centers to avoid paying extra and to make them affordable for the low-income groups.

This spontaneous growth has been associated with social and economic segregation in the urban areas, and has separated the old quarters within the Egyptian cities from the new areas. The spatial growth in Egypt has been divided into specific functional sections devoted to transportation, commerce, administration, education, manufacturing and into three major counter-magnets: the primate cities, the new established regions, and secondary cities as shown in Figure 13.1. This sprawl growth is therefore characterized by the following: (*i*) rapid encroachment of arable land by uncontrolled physical growth, mainly housing development; (*ii*) lack of technical infrastructure such as transport network, water supply and sewerage in informal urbanized areas of the cities; (*iii*) low degree of coordination between public development projects and the ongoing informal urbanization; and (*iv*) weak performance of the urban economy of most medium sized towns due to lack of economic resources apart from agriculture, a small degree of backward and forward linkages between economic sectors, and finally lack of cultural activities and the weak performance of political activities due to which towns could not probably contribute at the national level. Consequently, small and medium sized towns do not provide the basic services for their own population in a sufficient way thereby forcing themselves to orient towards the economically more advanced locations of the primate cities.

Figure 13.1 Spontaneous Growth in Egypt

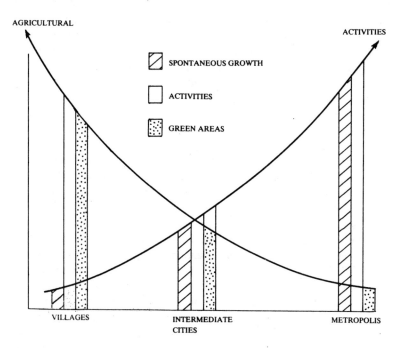

CHARACTERISTICS OF SQUATTER SETTLEMENTS

The physical characteristics of squatter settlements in Egypt are related to common features and differences between them, government intervention, and the residents' role in adapting to their environment.

In relation to the first issue, squatter settlements had some similarities in their physical features, which are, a limited location, a main road as a strong edge limiting future expansion, privileges of various services such as water and electricity supplies in the old parts of squatting areas, and finally, lack of social and public facilities such as schools and clinics. There are differences in housing heights and the width of streets, and in the sanitary services installed within squatter settlements.

These similarities and variations add up to the fact that some areas are in a good physical condition as compared to others. This is related to three variables, first, the different economic situation of one settlement from the other, and second, the different circumstances under which squatter settlements were created. The latter could be expressed in two different ways. Some squatter settlements such as El Dekhila and Ezbet Abou Soliman areas, Alexandria, have been invaded by illegal subdivision of the land without government intervention, while in El Sideen and Ezbet Metras areas, Alexandria, the invasion of the site was organized by the government, or at least the initial development was begun by official bodies such as Hagar El Nawateyah area, Alexandria (Soliman 1993), and Manshiet Naser in Cairo. Such invasions are usually introduced by official bodies as temporary residential areas, or for a specific use for a certain function for a certain time, where most of such development did not follow the basis of establishing a residential area. Second, in some areas such as El Dekhila (Alexandria), Manshiet Naser (Cairo), and Naseriyh areas (Aswan) (Al Ahram 1992a), the settlers originally had a good background knowledge of construction and consequently, they organized and subdivided the land illegally on the basis of their requirements and this has continued to the present day.

The third variable is the phenomenon of land invasion by the squatters. Land was often obtained through the medium of land invasion, a process frequently encouraged by the government opposition parties alike (El Kadi 1988). Land invasion within squatter settlements in Egypt took place as soon as land tenure was in doubt, during the transaction of land property between various governorates, the transformation of the economy or regulation, and during national or local election time within the country. The latter phenomenon is attributed to be the most effective in the formulation of squatter settlements in Egypt, where the largest settlements being established take advantage of political pressure. The process of land invasion within informal residential areas involves three types of invasions as shown in Figure 13.2 namely, organized invasion, a collective invasion, and scattered invasion (Soliman 1992b). This process of land invasion has offered accessible land at a reasonable price and equally increased the availability of the rented flats (the percentage varied from 20 to 30 percent of the total housing production in squatting areas) at affordable rates for the urban poor.

Three aspects of the residents' role in their environment were noticed (Soliman 1991). First, the presence of a hierarchy of use, meeting spaces and scattered layout were related significantly to the residents' social, economic, and climatic considerations and were violated by governmental public housing—closely spaced and in straight rows—which was also rejected by the residents. Second, the pattern and the space form was created by the residents themselves without government or professional intervention. The settlers were their own architects and they formed their settlements according to their needs and requirements. Furthermore, the settlers within the state's housing

Figure 13.2 Land Invasion in Egypt

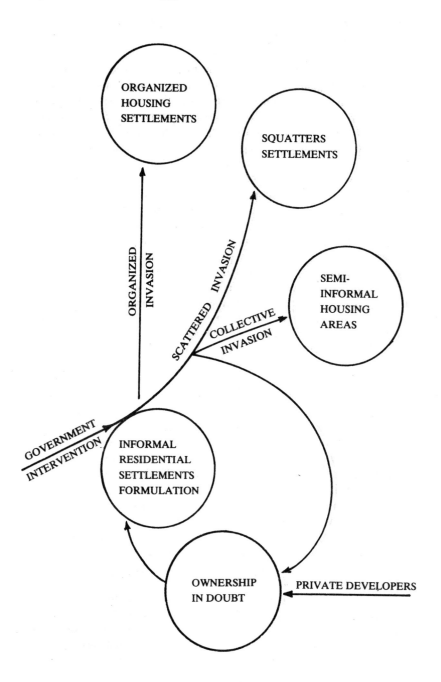

units squatted on vacant public areas in front of their housing blocks, added new spaces, and converted their units to suit their requirements (Steinberg 1984; Tipple, Wilkinson and Nour 1985). In other words, they constituted self-reliant communities, where people decide together on how to shape their common destinies. All decisions about what to build and how to build it, were in the hands of the users, which is representing the principle of community participation. Also, the women's role in sustaining and managing their duties within their units and environment improved the relationship among the residents of the community on the one hand, and increased the level of household's income on the other. Third, the hierarchy of circulation systems within the areas is similar to their area of origin, where their cultural and traditional ties lie. They constructed their physical environment basically in a manner similar to what they have in their villages. The result was a traditional rural pattern with a variation of spatial proportion relating to street widths, building facades, and a hierarchy of space with limited access. In short, the squatters are capable of achieving and providing greater flexibility in their physical environment as compared to what is found in organized areas.

The socioeconomic characteristics of the residents within squatting areas have five key issues. First, the population and household data have identified a low level of special status related to a lack of social facilities within the squatting areas. This lack of social facilities has resulted in a reduction in education (55 percent of the total population is illiterate), there are increased health hazards, a high birth rate, and overcrowding in the areas. Second, the significant of accessibility to job opportunities has played a major role in the success of the development of squatting areas, for example, Manshiet Nasser (Cairo) (Hadjitheodorou 1981), El Nasserieyh (Aswan), and the seven spontaneous settlements in Helwan (*Al Ahram* 1992b). Due to the growth of industry close to the squatting areas, there were increased potentialities for both skilled and unskilled workers in finding suitable job opportunities capable of absorbing a variety of work forces. Third, the decision to enter squatter areas is made on the basis of economic factors, cultural attitudes, and the quality of the physical environment. A high percentage of the residents in squatting areas immigrated directly to the areas without a stop-over in other sectors of the city. Fourth, not all residents of squatter areas are considered poor, but one-third of the total population are living below the poverty line (Soliman 1985). Finally, formal legal and administrative procedures do not exist within the squatter areas, the result being a free rent market, an increase in the housing production, and the institution of key money.

A variation of housing types has been produced in squatting areas in Egypt, shown in Figure 13.3, to suit the varied needs and resources of the residents. Of particular significance is the fact that the residents have adopted

Figure 13.3 House Plot and Built Area on Typical Sites

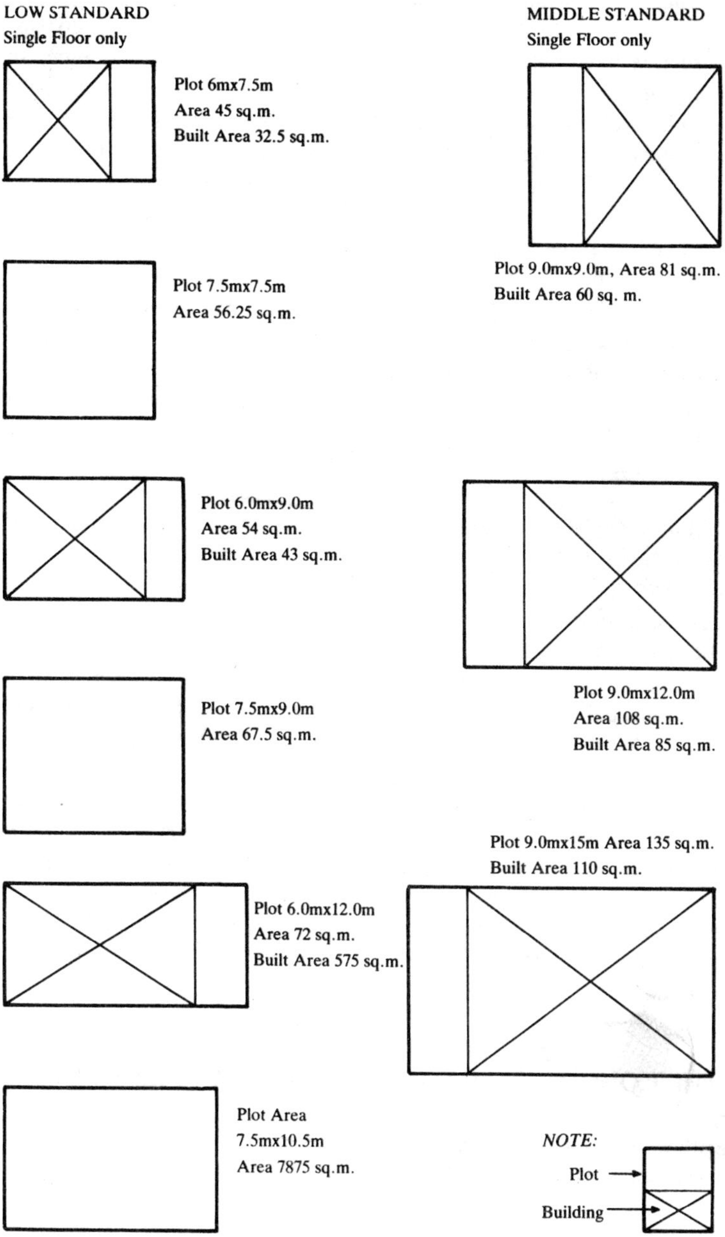

LOW STANDARD
Single Floor only

MIDDLE STANDARD
Single Floor only

Plot 6mx7.5m
Area 45 sq.m.
Built Area 32.5 sq.m.

Plot 9.0mx9.0m, Area 81 sq.m.
Built Area 60 sq. m.

Plot 7.5mx7.5m
Area 56.25 sq.m.

Plot 6.0mx9.0m
Area 54 sq.m.
Built Area 43 sq.m.

Plot 7.5mx9.0m
Area 67.5 sq.m.

Plot 9.0mx12.0m
Area 108 sq.m.
Built Area 85 sq.m.

Plot 9.0mx15m Area 135 sq.m.
Built Area 110 sq.m.

Plot 6.0mx12.0m
Area 72 sq.m.
Built Area 575 sq.m.

Plot Area
7.5mx10.5m
Area 7875 sq.m.

NOTE:

Plot →

Building →

their own methods and their own procedures to provide suitable shelter for themselves. There were three lessons obtained from squatting areas in managing their housing development. First, the variation of housing types, their quality, and the level of investment and improvements on housing construction have not been tailored solely on the basis of the degree of security of tenure. Factors such as the condition of the site's soil, the economic level of the residents, the quality of the environment, and the level of consolidation among the residents are more important. Second, the design and standard of the houses within squatter areas have been tailored according to the residents' requirements (Dix et al. 1992), and the resources are simply not available to provide either high standards or large plots for all. Third, the flexibility of the implementation process in the form of local planning conventions' (Soliman 1987) piecemeal growth and short time span, have all led to increased housing production through freedom from restrictive planning control within squatting areas, and control by the residents' decisions. The squatter has his own control over the nature of local housing, instead of an alien, and he will continue to respond to his emergent socioeconomic circumstances at a faster speed than the formal and organized areas. Finally, despite the fact that land prices have increased in the last decade, and few opportunities exist for purchasing cheap plots, the process of obtaining land plots at cheap rates is possible only through informal arrangements. The informal arrangement depends on the households' needs, aspirations, capital resources, and most important of all, the friendly terms of payments between the buyers and the purchasers.

Fourth, many people who are identified as too poor to participate in conventional public housing market in the absence of massive subsidies, and are unable to afford the cheapest housing units in the public sectors, are at the same time, able to direct their limited resources of all types and invest them into much more efficient and cost-effective way than the public body had ever been able to accomplish. The relatively small or limited sum of money which was invested in housing production seemed to be utilized much more effectively. However, the level of consolidation, land plot size, quality of housing unit, level of social amenities, cost, type, and methods of implementation, as Figure 13.4 shows, are all directly related to the flow and level of income among the squatters.

STRATEGIES TO AMELIORATE
THE CONDITIONS WITHIN SQUATTER SETTLEMENTS

The transformation of socioeconomic development at the national level had an overt and covert impact upon the urban centers in Egypt, as well as on

Figure 13.4 Scattered, Collective, and Consolidated Developments

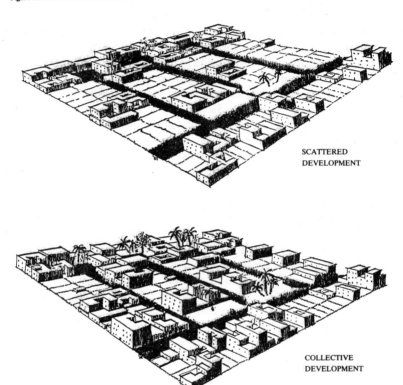

SCATTERED
DEVELOPMENT

COLLECTIVE
DEVELOPMENT

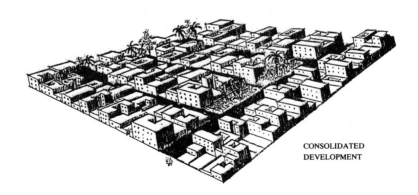

CONSOLIDATED
DEVELOPMENT

housing production. This impact has led to several pressing urban problems such as inadequate services (water, electricity supply, and sewerage system), inappropriate communication and transportation facilities, increasing land values, environmental pollution, and the deterioration and shortages of housing. Limited government intervention (or its overt and covert role) within the squatter settlements could be illustrated by the following aspects. First, the government has provided off-site services (either water taps or electricity supply) in squatter settlements, while the residents installed basic facilities on plots themselves. Second, a lack of social and public facilities within squatter areas indicated that the government had no influence over these areas, while on the other hand, the government encouraged the establishment of self-sufficient religious centers within squatter areas. Third, a lack of site planning for the uncontrolled areas in the government planning offices showed that the state, to a certain extent, had excluded those areas from planning control which led to physical autonomy within such areas. Finally, despite the fact that land-ownership indicated that the government had no complete official control over the areas the government, on the other hand, allowed the residents to remain on their plots after paying a symbolic charge. The state became involved in modifying the housing system, and encouraged, or at least associated itself with residential growth in the periphery of the urban centers (Soliman 1992). The official authorities played a crucial role in squatter settlements' formulation through various phases of residential development. Most of the uncontrolled or preinformal residential areas witnessed three steps of expansion as represented in Figure 13.4: scattered, collective, and consolidated where the government had its effect in each stage. There are various reasons as to why a government should become involved in housing. Perhaps the most common are humanitarian, functionalist, social control, and finally human rights (Leckie 1989) considerations. It became one of government's main tasks to ensure that human rights (and other rights) are met. Meeting housing needs is the justification that most Third World governments use for their housing policies. The debate within the government centers on who is in need of housing, what constitutes an adequate housing, how best to ensure that those in need obtain adequate housing, and how should the government resources be spent to fulfill housing needs. However, Egyptian housing policy had witnessed various actions through three periods: the 1956 to 1970 period of extensive intervention, the 1970–80 period of active but ad hoc intervention, and the beginning of the 1980 when the state played an arbitrary role where housing markets fluctuated.

In the mid-1970s, the recognition of the role played by the informal sector become an indispensable part of housing production in Egypt, in which at least 75 percent of housing construction was built by the uncontrolled sector. This was primarily encouraged by the foreign aid agencies with the government acknowledging the huge potentialities of the squatters and informal sector to help solve the scarcity of housing for low income-groups, if it were wisely managed (Toppin and Couch 1982; Davidson and Payne 1983; Gilbert and Ward 1985; Goethert 1985).

In 1979, the government set up a national housing plan to overcome the problem of housing, and projected 3.6 million housing units to be built by the year 2000. Adequate shelter for all was the declared objective to be achieved through private and public sectors. One of the main issues to be tackled is taking account of the invisible resources of the urban poor and guide their efforts to participate probably in housing construction. The idea was a shift of focus from providing completely subsidized housing to providing other means of housing either in goods or services or both. It aimed to develop a policy instrument capable of meeting the needs of the urban poor at the lowest income, and to encourage the residents themselves to produce a cheap and reasonable housing unit and the basic infrastructure which accompanies it. As a consequence, sites-and-services and upgrading programs, core housing and wet core units have been developed to house the urban poor (Davidson 1981, 1983, 1984). Many projects have been introduced in different Egyptian cities, for example, Alexandria, Ismailia, Helwan, Aswan, Cairo, Alexandria, and two new towns: El Sadat and Tenth of Rammadan.

However, many of the schemes did not develop further than designs; others changed their objectives after one stage or the other and ended up as typical government constructed housing. It is argued that contemporary international policies were unsuccessful in meeting the needs of the urban poor. The reasons were: the lengthy negotiation procedures, lack of political will, inadequate cost recovery, unsuitability of site location in terms of job opportunities and social services, and finally the incorrect implementation process (Soliman 1988). This resulted in a situation of confrontation rather than collaboration. Also, the predetermined standards which assume the existence of a predetermined structure of socioeconomic groups results in mismatches and conflicts which have a direct and negative effect on environment quality.

In 1989, the prime ministry interpreted these new informal established areas as cancer settlements, belonging neither to the city nor to the village, and the inherited social illness and scramble conditions. In the recent past, many conferences have been held in Egypt, for example, Shelter and Urbanization, 1990, Policies and Housing System, 1992, indicated that it is time to guide public and private resources either in kind or in cash, taking into account the valuable efforts of the urban poor as a major resource in housing construction. Therefore, the evaluation for sites-and-services and upgrading programs was undertaken, and policy makers came to the conclusion that a more supportive attitude from the government towards the housing of the urban poor was needed.

However, the policy shifted back to old conventional durable housing. There was an agreement between the central and local authorities on the structural conditions of the dwelling as a main factor which strongly affects the quality of the dwelling. Therefore, the state introduced incomplete housing units which left the inner spaces unfinished. The residents themselves were to complete them according to their needs, requirements, and affordabilities. This policy did not achieve its goals, and the dwellings produced became too expensive for the urban low-income groups.

Lately, the government has realized that the majority of the population are living in illegal residential settlements, and that many Third World countries have followed the international policy of tackling their housing problems with programs which are dependent upon the economic ability of the residents.

Hence, the government's policy makers have emerged with new trends which depend upon the essence of sustainable development as a means to satisfy the present needs of people without compromising on the ability of future generations to meet their requirements. The enhancement of the economic situation in Egypt continues to play an important role in addressing 'the needs satisfaction' component of sustainable development. And it depends upon the ability of national economies to accelerate economic growth, and subsequently, enhance the standard of living of the Egyptian population.

CONCLUSIONS

In the last few decades, the potential of residents within squatter areas has been investigated by many scholars such as Abrams (1964), Turner (1976), and Gilbert and Ward (1985). Most of the researchers indicated that the invisible efforts of the urban poor should be raised and guided in a manner that the philosophy of self-built and other related policies are enhanced. Lately, many governments in Third World countries have come to the realization that even these new policies do not serve the bottom strata of the urban poor as it was hoped.

In Egypt, as in the rest of many Third World countries, there is no clear housing policy for accommodating the urban poor. The Egyptian housing policy took the form of arbitration, and has had no clear plan or strategy to overcome the housing problem for the urban poor. It is quite clear that the change of presidency, and even more, changing of the official cabinet, either the prime ministry or the popular assembly, has a major effect on formulating the housing policy within the country. Therefore, political will is one of the key issues by which one could encourage or discourage the housing production, either formally or informally, within the country.

Most scholars agreed on the three magnets of the problem: the state, the professional and the urban poor. Therefore, a suitable means can be evolved through a new balance of intervention by all the parties involved. It could be developed through a joint venture project, with cooperation between the government, the professionals, and the poor.

It should be realistic in terms of its possible implementation and accomplishment and in meeting local and national needs. The balance should be related, as spelt out in Figure 13.5, in large part to the financial and physical autonomy of squatting areas with limited intervention of both government and professionals, and greater involvement of the residents.

Figure 13.5 The Role of the Participants and Fields of Operation

	PARTICIPANTS		
	Government	**Professionals**	**Squatters**
Affordability	A minimum monetary share to start the project.	The collective commodity must be broken down into parts that can be made available separately to the residents	Through the residents' savings or efforts or both
Land	Providing land at a reasonable price	Determine an appropriate legal title, and introduce different location within the city	The residents should conserve resources obtained
Political Commitment	National organization for low-income housing	A channel between the community and the official bodies	–Council leaders –Sector leaders –Tenants' association
Access to Resources	Providing basic off-plots services	Organization of the collective commodity which the residents can use in their own way	Providing in-plot services
Flexible Community	Housing authority act on national and local levels	To make rules that liberate by setting practice limits to what people may do	Trained development officers to administer construction process
Quality	Training centers for building industry	Specialists of any kind must act to increase the decision making power of those they serve	Incremental process

Because funds are limited in Egypt, the government should provide the essentials required by the urban poor rather than things they can provide for themselves. In other words, the government can play a constructive role in the housing process by enabling the urban poor to have access to the major components of housing or a reasonable access to resources, which is essentially an economic and political problem rather than a technical one. The role of the professionals or those in a position to influence investments made by the government, would be to provide technical assistance by acting as a communication channel between the government bodies and the community, in order to increase the decision making powers of the urban poor they serve, and not their own powers. The role of the people would be the investment of money and effort by individuals or by groups in erecting their own settlements.

The concept underlying the above programs is sustainable development. It is integrated with economic, social, and ecological dimensions to which the enabling approach is added. By coordinating and improving the efficiency of the combined efforts of all actors in the shelter sector, one may directly address the economic dimension. Enablement also has a strong social aspect; there is a growing recognition that participation and development are inseparable, since popular priorities and demands greatly influence the development of effective and flexible enablement.

The program described in the foregoing section would give the government and the professionals the opportunity to guide the poor to squat in areas where they would like them to squat without causing a collapse in the urban fabric. It would also give the opportunity to the residents to act outside the procedures of normal planning controls and achieve their own standards which would result in creating a suitable environment by their own efforts. Last, but not least, the government has been convinced that such an approach is a good one, and has given the green light for starting five residential settlements organized around the concept of enablement in the greater Cairo region (Soliman 1993).

REFERENCES

Abrams, C. 1964. *Man's Struggle for Shelter in an Urbanizing World.* Cambridge, Mass: MIT Press.
Abu-Lughod, J. 1964. 'Urbanization in Egypt: Present State and Future Prospects', *Economic Development and Cultural Change, 13 (3)*, pp. 313–43.
Al Ahram. 1992a. 4 March.
———. 1992b. 6 June.
CAPMAS. 1990. Central Agency for Public Mobilization and Statistics, Population Census, Cairo.

CAPMAS. 1991. Central Agency for Public Mobilization and Statistics, Population Census, Cairo.

Davidson, F. 1981. 'Ismailia: From Master Plan to Implementation', *Third World Planning Review 3*, pp. 161–78.

———. 1983. 'Ismailia: Combined Upgrading and Sites and Services Projects in Egypt', in G. Payne (ed.), *Low-income Housing in the Developing World*. Chichester: Wiley.

———. 1984. 'Ismailia: Combined Upgrading and Sites and Services Projects in Egypt', in G. Payne (ed.), *Low Income Housing in the Developing World*. Bath: John Wiley & Sons, pp. 125–48.

Davidson, F. and G. Payne. 1983. *Urban Projects Manual: A Guide to Preparing Upgrading and New Development Projects Accessible to Low-Income Groups*. Liverpool: Liverpool University Press.

Dix, G., G. Parry, McNeilly, with the cooperation of A. Soliman, E. Amer and M. Hasgag. 1992. *Housing in Alexandria*. Liverpool: Liverpool University Press.

El Kadi, G. 1988. 'Market Mechanisms and Spontaneous Urbanization in Egypt', *International Journal of Urban and Regional Research 12 (1)*, pp. 25–37.

Gilbert, A. and P. Ward. 1985. *Housing, the State, and the Poor*. Cambridge University Press.

Goethert, R. 1985. 'Sites and Services.' *Architecture Review 8*, pp. 28–31.

Hadjiheodorou, N.M. 1981. 'An Institutional Framework for the Upgrading Process of Manshiet Nasser in Cairo, Egypt', *Ekistics 48 (286)*, pp. 71–78.

Housing in Egypt. 1989. The Ministry of Development, New Communities, Housing and Utilization, Cairo.

Lee-Smith, D. and R. Stren. 1991. 'New Perspectives on African Urban Management', *Environment and Urbanization Journal 3 (1)*, pp. 23–36.

Leckie, S. 1989. 'Housing as a Human Right', *Environment and Urbanization 1 (2)*, pp. 90–108.

Mourad, M. 1985. Egypt, *Architecture Review 8*, pp. 21–22.

Soliman, A. 1985. 'The Poor in Search of Shelter: An Examination of Squatter Settlements in Alexandria, Egypt'. Unpublished Ph. D Thesis, Liverpool University.

———. 1987. 'Informal Land Acquisition and the Urban Poor in Alexandria', *Third World Planning Review 9*, pp. 21–39.

———. 1988. 'Housing the Urban Poor in Egypt: A Critique of Present Policies', *International Journal of Urban and Regional Research 12 (1)*, pp. 65–86.

———. 1989. 'Housing Mechanisms in Egypt: A Critique', *The Netherlands Journal of Housing and Environmental Research 4 (1)*, pp. 31–50.

———. 1990. 'Intermediate Cities in Egypt: Their Roles in Urban Development'. Paper presented at the Conference on Urban Development in Egypt, Cairo, 15–18 December.

———. 1991. 'Approaches to Urban Low-Income Housing in the Developing Countries', in D. Ingemann (ed.), *Metropolis In Ascendancy: Housing and Population. Housing and Construction Vitoria*. Melbourne, Vitoria, pp. 123–32.

———. 1992. 'The State, The Private Developers, and the Urban Poor.' Paper presented in Policies and Housing Systems for Low-Income Communities Conference held in General Organization for Housing, Building and Planning Research, 23–27 February, Cairo.

———. 1992b. 'Housing Consolidation and the Urban Poor: Hagar El Nawateyah, Alexandria', *Environment and Urbanization 4 (2)*, pp. 184–95.

———. 1993. 'A Complimentary Prize of a Competition of "Sheltering the Homeless"'. Ministry of Development, New Communities, Housing, Public Utilities, Cairo.

Steinberg, F. 1984. 'Ain El Sira in Cairo: The Architecture of Poverty', *Open House International 9 (2)*, pp. 35–41.

Time. 1989. No. 1, 2 January.

Tipple, R., N. Wilkinson and M. Nour. 1985. 'The Transformation of Workers City: Helwan', *Open House International 10 (3)*, pp. 25–34.

Toppin, D. and S. Couch. 1982. 'Back to Brick, El Heker, Ismailia', *Architects Journal 176 (27)*, pp. 50–53.

Turner, J. 1976. *Housing by People*. London: Marion Boyars Publishers Ltd.

Turner, J. and R. Fichter. 1972. *Freedom to Build*. New York: The Macmillan Company.

Ward, P. 1982. 'Informal Housing: Conventional Wisdoms Reappraised', *Built Environment 8*, pp. 84–94.

14

Squatter and Slum Settlements in Zambia

Ann Schlyter

What in Zambia is adequate to define as squatter and slum settlements? Central in most definitions of squatter settlements is a degree of illegality. Slums are sometimes defined by a process of deterioration, while at times the term is used for any housing area of low standard.

According to the Third National Development Plan (Republic of Zambia 1979) 98 percent of the population can only afford housing of low or very low standard. Indeed, the standard of housing for the majority of the population is low in urban as well as rural areas. This paper will analyze urban housing only. Many housing areas of various types are of low standard and, especially during the last decade, in a process of deterioration, thus fit within the definition of slums.

But what is the point of calling the homes of most urban inhabitants squatter and slum settlements? In fact, many Zambians react to the use of these terms as a derogation. All those inhabitants and local leaders, who are fighting for legalization or improvements of their housing areas are anxious to get rid of these kinds of labels. They want to stress the positive possibilities of their neighborhoods.

On the other hand, the poor reality is undeniable. Idealizations do not make the plight of the inhabitants more easy to carry, but they make it easier for politicians and other decision makers to close their eyes and continue to do nothing substantial to ameliorate the situation. With all respect for the struggle of the creative inhabitants of the neighborhoods of the Zambian towns, an attempt has been made to describe the housing conditions of the majority of the urban dwellers of Zambia under the heading of squatter and slum settlements.

EARLY URBAN DEVELOPMENT

Zambia was colonized and administrated by the British South Africa Company. For commercial mining of copper and other minerals, an African labor force was needed. A hut tax was introduced with the end of forcing men to be laborers and to contribute to the company's revenues. With the introduction of attractive goods, such as better tools, Africans came to *white* settlements in order to earn and buy. The first documented informal settlement was Malota in Livingstone in 1911 (Mashamba 1990).

The large mines and many other employers provided housing. Very often, only land was provided and the workers had to erect their own shelters. In the 1920s, laws were passed to control the influx of Africans to towns, to tie housing to employment, and to place responsibility for the supply of housing on the local authorities. The workers were regarded as guest workers who were supposed to maintain their rural home.

In 1935, the capital was moved to a virgin site along the rail lines between the old capital of Livingstone and the copperbelt. Though not in the original plans for the city Lusaka, some municipal housing areas were built for Africans, but there were also private locations. Influx control proved difficult to enforce, especially with private landlords, so some of these locations became uncontrolled settlements early (Mashamba 1990).

In the 1950s, family housing was built in some large municipal housing areas. Occupancy rights continued to be tied to employment which left a number of job seekers, and what are called presently informal sector workers, among them many women, to provide for themselves under insecure conditions. The construction and farm workers' compounds in the outskirts of the towns became cores around which squatter areas grew.

POST-INDEPENDENT URBAN DEVELOPMENT

Already at the time of independence in 1964, Zambia was the most urbanized country in Sub-Saharan Africa with the exception of South Africa. More than a fifth of the population was living in urban areas. With the removal of restrictions on movement, which had been applied by the colonial government, an explosion of urban growth followed. The annual growth rate of the urban population was almost 9 percent, and the growth was even more rapid in Lusaka and in some of the copperbelt towns.

Most migrants had to build their own houses in informal settlements as never more than some thousands of low cost houses were produced with governmental authorization each year (Robertson 1978). The population of squatter compounds in Lusaka increased from 20,000 in 1963 to 64,800 three years later. In the early seventies, almost half of the population in Lusaka lived in squatter settlements. In the industrial towns on the copperbelt the rate was even higher. In Kitwe, for example, three-fourths of the population lived in squatter areas (Kasongo 1987).

Nevertheless, urban planning proceeded as if this was not the case (Rakodi 1987). The consultants working with the Lusaka Development Plan assumed good houses and one or two cars for every household (Doxiadis 1975). Based on such assumptions it is not surprising that little of the plan has been implemented. Rakodi (1988) points out the considerable differences between the towns in Zambia, and warns against the danger of drawing conclusions only on Lusaka's experiences. Lack of economic and administrative capacity within local authorities causes failures of implementation, also of plans based on much more realistic assumptions.

During the 1970s and early 1980s, more than a third of Lusaka's squatter population was affected by a series of huge upgrading projects, financed by the World Bank and by bilateral organizations such as the German organization GTZ. There was no second generation of huge, externally funded urban projects. The upgrading included legalization, improvements and also new developments in the so-called overspill areas. Upgrading based on national and local resources, and capacities were planned in other towns. However, outside Lusaka the policy was not implemented in more than a few marginal projects.

Deterioration during the Eighties

Ndulo (1989) points at the low annual growth of the official urban housing stock of about 2 percent in the early 1980s, while the urban population growth was still almost 7 percent. All the new households, formed to a large degree, by young people born in town, had the alternative of either squeezing themselves into existing settlements and houses or building new squatter areas. The conditions in all types of housing areas for poor people have drastically deteriorated during the last decade. Lack of basic service and maintenance finally, in 1990, led to cholera and dysentery outbreaks. The urban population increased by more than a million during the 1980s, a period during which very few low or very low cost houses were legally built. It is therefore surprizing to find a low figure in the Fourth National Development Plan (Republic of Zambia 1989) on population in informal settlements: one and a quarter of a million or a third of the urban population.

More than half of the Zambian population is urban, 52 percent of a total 7,800,000 inhabitants, according to the 1990 census (Central Statistical Office 1990). The migration to towns has slowed down with the economic recession, and the census indicates a slight decrease in annual growth rate of urban areas. Towns continue to grow mainly because of a high internal birth rate.

MAIN CHARACTERISTICS OF SQUATTERS AND SLUMS

In this presentation a distinction has been made between the smaller village-like squatter areas and larger urban ones. There is no definite difference, it is partly a question of development over time. The upgraded areas have been squatter areas but are now legal like other high density areas. However, there are differences that motivate a distinction. Finally a few notes are made on employer's housing. All these types of housing are not necessarily slums, it depends on the quality. Each of these five types of housing areas will be characterized by their social and physical development.

Village-like Squatter Settlements

One of the earliest forms of informal urban housing provision was the transformation of villages adjacent to urban areas. Existing rural villages were urbanized in their composition. The inhabitants turned to urban employment, and newcomers working in the town moved in. The settlement was extended in the same physical form as a rural village.

Villages like this grew without being squatter areas in the sense of illegality. The chiefs and the headmen who had control over all Reserve and Trust land, planned and applied some degree of building control (Knapp et al. 1982). Houses were built in sun-dried mud bricks, not the traditional 'pole-and-dagga' technique, and early after independence the thatched roofs were commonly replaced by the corrugated iron sheets, at least in the towns along the line of rail.

There were also new settlements built like villages with houses grouped around a common open space and no fences dividing the public and private space. Also, the organization of the settlements was similar with a headman controlling the land. In case the settlements were built on state or private land the political leader took on the role of an urban headman.

Thus a type of customary organization was maintained even though the population might have belonged to many different ethnic groups. Knapp (1982) who studied two squatter villages outside the small town of Kasama emphasized the lack of ethnic conflicts. The inhabitants consisted to a large part of elderly workers who had retired from work, the younger ones were more mobile and looking for jobs.

The smaller settlements were not as dense as the larger ones, and usually there was a land available for cultivation in a small-scale to supplement wage work incomes. Lack of water, sanitation, and garbage disposal might be a more critical health hazard in large settlements. But at the same time, the inhabitants of the smaller settlements are often worse off regarding access to infrastructure and social service. Ngenda (1992) claims that the squatters adjacent to mine townships are the worst slums in Zambia. The mines have traditionally been very strict in evicting squatters as soon as they appear, and the bad conditions might have to do with the very insecure conditions.

Larger Urban Squatter Settlements

The huge squatter areas in Lusaka and in some Copperbelt towns might have begun as village-like settlements. In Lusaka, many squatter settlements grew to the size of about 50,000 inhabitants, while in other towns, for example Kitwe, the settlement pattern was characterized by many small settlements (Mashamba 1990). Settlements vary due to their history and context.

My studies of a large settlement in Lusaka, George, show that the original density was developed with a consensus between the settlers and the local leaders. Even before the land began to be limited, the same density of about 50 houses per hectare was applied. With increasing population, infilling of new houses was done, and the existing houses were extended until the open space was minimal (Schlyter 1991, p. 74). The population has to eke out its living on urban income generating activities as land is not available for cultivation. Health hazards increase with size and density, and people complain about the density.

Still in 1989, 87 percent of household heads in a Lusaka neighborhood sample were born in a village (Ogura 1991). The conventional view of squatter areas as built by migrants arriving from the countryside is, obviously, true to a certain degree. In George, during the time of rapid expansion, the house builders had usually lived for a period in the town as lodgers. The move to build a house of their own was regarded as positive progress.

All inhabitants in the squatter areas are not poor in the Zambian context. Poverty is widespread, that is not to be denied, but there are a wide range of income groups inhabiting the areas. A most striking social characteristic of the Lusaka squatter settlements is the fact that they are ethnically mixed. Family bonds are maintained in town, but most of my informants in George found it preferable to have the relatives at some distance. Ngulube (1989) claims to have found ethnic clustering, and he is right in that there are squatter areas in which a certain ethnic group is overrepresented in number. It seems, however, as if ethnic affiliation is only one of several interrelated factors such as employment, income, religion, and politics.

Depending on location of the housing area in the city the number of industrial workers, marketeers or domestic workers vary considerably. Before the one-party state, most housing areas became dominated by one of the parties. There are very few indications of clustering according to language.

There are areas where people originating from Zaire or Zimbabwe are overrepresented, but these communities are built on grounds of common entrepreneurship or religion rather than ethnicity (Jules-Rosette 1988).

In rural areas in Zambia it is common that a growing family has many one-room houses separating teenagers of different sex, and special members of the family. In urban squatter areas, most families began to build a one-room house. Additional residential space was added to that room. The residential culture changed from one family in one, or in a number of, one-room houses to many families in a multiroomed house.

No studies of the new squatter settlements built in the 1980s are available. As in earlier periods, it can be anticipated that the newcomers and builders are either elderly people who have moved from their homes tied to employment while retired, or young people born in towns and desperate for a home. It is also likely that the rate of women-headed households is high. It is not likely that the rural character reappears in these settlements of urban population. It is also not likely that they invest much in the houses as an anti-squatter policy has been prevailing since the mid-eighties. Today you will not find the positive feeling of building a house and a nation which was so strong in George in the 1960s. Today it is rather a question of hiding to survive.

Upgraded Areas

The upgrading of squatters in Lusaka was not followed by an exchange of inhabitants. For several reasons, such as the scale of the projects covering a majority of the squatters, the relatively low standard of improvements, the general deterioration of household economy, etc., no so-called gentrification took place. The population changes gradually over the years with the increase of tenants and lodgers, and with the grown-up children remaining in the house of their parents due to no alternatives.

The physical components of the upgrading in Lusaka included water, roads, and some service buildings such as schools, and community centers. Blocks of 25 houses were defined among the existing houses, and the level of standard was defined so that every group of 25 houses would have a standpipe and access to a road. Pit latrines were maintained as the only type of sanitation. The main roads got security lighting, but a proposed system of dustbin collection was never put in use (Rakodi and Schlyter 1981).

The houses were to be built by the owners themselves. There are examples of mud brick houses which have been standing for more than thirty years. Nevertheless, mud brick houses are regarded as temporary structures, and houseowners aim at rebuilding in concrete blocks. Bit by bit, houseowners

A bedroom interior in a mud brick house in a squatter area. The house is now 25 years old.

Five families of altogether 25 persons live in this seven-roomed house in an upgraded area. The owner's family of six occupies two rooms.

In 12 years this house has been only half-finished in an overspill area.

Semi-detached house in the municipal housing area Matero.

improve their houses. Some manage to do it in a shorter period, while others have to live in half-finished structures for years.

A kitchen interior in a upgraded area. The house is partly rebuilt in concrete blocks.

After legalization, infilling of new separate structures was not allowed. The rebuilding of houses from small one-family houses to larger multifamily houses nevertheless made the residential density increase from about 250 to 350 persons per hectare. These figures are not high in international comparison, but are considered too high by the inhabitants according to their frame of reference.

Increased population pressure and lack of maintenance have also rapidly torn down the physical improvements. The roads after ten years of upgrading are in a bad shape, many of the standpipes do not work and the open space has shrunk considerably (Schlyter 1991). Legalization meant an integration of the areas into the responsibility of the local government but only after a cholera outbreak in 1990 was something done. A number of communal latrines were built. However, without maintenance they did not work for long and could be seen only as tragic monuments of the incapability of handling the problems.

An outdoor kitchen in a house rebuilt in concrete blocks but of poor quality.

High Density Areas

The concept of high density refers to formal rental as well as homeownership housing areas. Most homeownership areas can hardly be included in a description of slums, as they are middle-income areas. Exceptions are the so-called overspill areas. These areas were developed during the upgrading outside the squatter settlements in order to receive the families that had to be moved due to the construction of water pipelines and roads. The overspill areas were planned in blocks in an orderly pattern of streets in straight lines.

The standard was otherwise the same as in the old upgraded settlement: no sewerage but pit latrines and 25 houses to one standpipe. The families got no compensation for their old houses but were provided support in the form of a loan delivered in building materials. Most families were happy to get the chance to improve their condition by moving into what more looked like a 'proper high density area'.

The general low-level of income makes the progress of house building in the overspill areas rather slow. Ten years after the resettlement, there are houseowners who have managed to build two rooms only, but improvements are made steadily.

A majority of the houses are owner-occupied, but the number of lodgers might outnumber the members of the owner's family. An increasing number of houses are let to tenants. This can be viewed as an ongoing commercialization of housing. However, in a way it is sign of the opposite situation. Very few houses are sold. An absentee houseowner does not want to sell so he lets the house instead. The landlord usually only owns one house, a house where he has lived.

Most rental housing areas were built in the 1950s in the familiar matchbox type of planning. There are a variety of standards. Many areas have individual water and flush toilets, if not originally provided so added in an upgrading, as communal toilets were very unpopular. The houses have been let at a subsidized rent and maintenance has been severely mismanaged. Lacking the residents' continuous care of the structures the appearance of some of these areas is more like slums than squatter areas.

A tenant in a municipal rental house has to be permanently employed at least when the house is allocated. Though the rate of the unemployed and informal sector workers is higher in squatter areas than in the municipal ones, there is no sharp class boundary between the two types of areas. Ngulube's (1989) observation that there is a high-level of interaction between the occupants of high density and squatter areas is confirmed by my own studies. In the 1970s, a skilled and established worker could prefer a large house of his own in a squatter area to a small and deteriorating rental house in the municipal housing area.

Employers' Housing

Since colonial time there is a strong tradition of employers to supply or subsidize housing for the employees. Many of the inhabitants in the municipal rental housing have their tenure tied to employment. The government has built separate high density housing areas for the police, railway workers, etc. Many of them are severely run down, and the railway's compound in Lusaka is on the list of being turned down (*Daily Mail* 1992). Also middle- and high-income government officials get heavily subsidized houses in low density areas, a fact contributing to the difficulties of dismantling the system of housing subsidies.

The largest type of housing run by the employers are the mine townships. In 1988, in Kitwe, for example, the mine housing stock counted about 12,000 houses, almost half of the total formal housing stock. Many of the mines on the Copperbelt are about to close down as they are empties, and there will be severe problems related to the survival of the urban areas as such. In the shadow of these problems the appalling conditions in many of the townships have not been put on any agenda for action.

The bad housing conditions of domestic workers are often forgotten, as they are not gathered in slum townships. Domestic workers probably make up for the largest single profession in Zambia, with about 100,000 employees (Hansen 1990). Some are not provided with accommodation, others live in the same house as the employer's family, while many male domestic workers live with their families on the premises of the employer. There are 23,630 domestic quarters registered in the Fourth National Development Plan (Republic of Zambia 1989). The houses are situated in the low density areas on the back side of the gardens. The standard of houses is often low, especially when compared with the main house on the same plot: one room and no electricity.

REVIEW OF RESEARCH

Zambia has a rich tradition of urban research, or rather there are a number of different traditions. One originated in the 1950s when the Rhodes-Livingstone Institute was among the leading centers of anthropological and ethnographic studies of social change. The concept of social networks was elaborated and studied in urban areas (Mitchell 1969).

In the 1970s, much research was carried out in urban areas in a completely different tradition. This time it was done by architects and planners with the perspective of environmental improvement. Many of these studies were directly tied to the upgrading projects; the World Bank had a special evaluation team. A series of working papers were presented by the Lusaka Housing Project Evaluation Team. Some of them are listed among the references (Banda 1978; Mulenga 1978; Rakodi 1978; Singini 1978).

Other studies during this period were, like my studies in George (Lundgren, Schlyter and Schlyter 1969; Schlyter and Schlyter 1980) independent but still with a planning and policy perspective. Not less than 120 studies are listed with the key words of squatters or squatter upgrading in a bibliography on human settlements in Zambia (Schlyter and Chanda 1982). Since then the research field has not attracted much interest.

Longitudinal community studies have been carried out in four of Lusaka's poor townships. In the 1960s a broad study was carried out of urban adaptation in the squatter area of Chawama. Ten years later Muller (1979) made a follow-up study. Hansen (1981) has focused on married women in Mtendere and Jules-Rosette (1981, 1988) on a religious sect in Marrapodi. Both have a broad anthropological approach and they make holistic analyses of the townships. My own studies in George focus more in detail on changes in physical structures, use of space, and the households' relations to their houses (Schlyter 1991).

There was no school of architecture and planning in Zambia until the School of Environmental Studies started in the 1980s. The School has been short of research resources. Students have carried out studies as part of their education but few have been available to a broader public.

Occasionally, studies on housing have been presented within other disciplines of the University of Zambia, such as Law (Mulimbwa 1980) or Economics (Ndulo 1986). However, there are rather few among the over 1,000 titles in the bibliography of Zambiana Theses and Dissertations (Mwanza 1990) that indicate an interest in urban residential environment. Similarly, neither housing nor any related key word is listed within the subject index of the bibliography on *Women in Zambia* (Chitambo 1991). Recently a research program focusing on the gender aspect of housing has been initiated (Munalula 1992; Mcwan'gi and Chitambo 1992; Ngenda 1992).

STRATEGIES TO AMELIORATE THE CONDITIONS

All households are involved in the struggle for decent living conditions. Some persons can present elaborated strategies to ameliorate these conditions. Most people in the shanty town are not outspoken in such a way. Many people live on the margin of existence and their efforts are not more far-reaching than food for the next day. It is in an analysis of the actual actions taken by many inhabitants in George and in townships in other countries, that have been identified in various patterns of actions that can be called strategies.

Governments may declare their intention to improve conditions for the inhabitants and voters. Sometimes the policymakers elaborate upon strategies on how to go ahead with the task but what is implemented, what is really happening on the ground, might be far from the declarations. When writing about governmental housing strategies it is, therefore, important to see beyond the declared strategies and analyze the implemented policy.

Inhabitants' Strategies

People apply strategies with the aim of improving their housing conditions, but at the same time, the house or accommodation is itself a means in the various strategies they elaborate for survival.

An increasing number of households have to live as tenants or lodgers. Many young couples and young women with children who do not, because of housing shortage, manage to form a household of their own but have to stay as dependents in their father's house. The extended families under one roof are not traditional in Zambia. On the contrary, many situations which conflict with custom are created. A lodging room or a rented house in a squatter area has been the means available for several generations of poor Zambians in their strategies for household formation.

The renting strategy, the strategy to become a tenant in a formal housing area, is applied by many as the rent is heavily subsidized and they get a relatively high quality of dwelling for a low price. To rent a squatter area is not economically beneficial as the costs are relatively high for a low quality of dwelling. The renting strategy is applied in squatter areas as a temporary solution or because it is the only one available.

The builders of houses in squatter areas, who put their savings and their work into a house, apply a homeownership strategy. For periods, squatters had felt a safety of tenure, though this is not the case now. Building one's own house is an aim as it provides a home. It is also a means for the survival strategies. A house in squatter area is more or less free of charge as soon as the investment is made. A family with insecure monthly income applies a low-monthly-charges strategy.

A house is central in many income generating strategies. Rooms can be let and business can be developed. The study of women householders reveals that a house of their own was of special importance when they developed home-based business. Production in small lodging rooms often disturbed the landlord, and when moving around in different lodging rooms their customers could not find them. Furthermore, it was only with permanent living that the women could develop the supportive network of neighboring women which was so important for them.

Poor people in insecure employment are reluctant to be in debt. They cannot risk to lose everything in case of lacking income for a period. They are, therefore, less interested in the possibility of taking a loan than what is often anticipated. They apply the building 'bit by bit' strategy and improve in the path they can manage (Schlyter 1988).

Unfortunately, poor people in Zambia have almost no chance to apply for the homeownership strategy outside the upgraded or overspill areas. Security of tenure is central as a house of one's own is an investment for the future for old age and coming generations. Even if many households plan to retire in the rural areas (Ogura 1991), a house of their own gives them a freedom of choice. Ageing couples and widows can get a better position as dependents of their children, if they can offer a house for all of them to live in. The house is central in arrange-for-old-age strategy.

As a collective measure, the inhabitants in squatter areas and slums have used the political organization to put pressure on decisionmakers regarding improvement of the neighborhoods. There are also many examples of how they have engaged themselves in direct action such as digging water pipes. During the last decade they were not very successful in convincing decisionmakers about the fairness of their demands.

Government's Strategies

The first reaction by post-independent politicians on the growing squatter areas was to deny the phenomenon; the second standpoint was to explain it as temporary. Official policy was a bulldozing-and-resettlement strategy; illegal settlements should be removed and the inhabitants moved into site-and-service. The consultants working in the 1960s with the development plan of Lusaka based their work on such presumptions (Doxiadis 1968, 1969). Some squatter areas were also demolished but, as a whole, the bulldozing was quite marginal. In reality a blind-eye strategy was applied.

There was a gap between policy declarations and reality. The capacity of the state to implement the policy was nonexisting. Even in the cases where the houses were actually bulldozed, the resettlement failed and people were left homeless (Jules-Rosette 1988). The contractions can only be understood in the light of the general political situation. Zambia was in the post-independent period a multiparty state, and the sympathy of the squatter inhabitants was crucial for success in elections.

With the one-party state introduced in 1972, the political base of the ruling party, United National Independence Party (UNIP), in the squatter areas restricted the bulldozing policy to some areas dominated by dissidents. Instead, lobbying for legalization and improvements of the areas was strong and supported by some civil servants and nongovernmental organizations. In 1974, the government signed an agreement with the World Bank on upgrading of the major squatter areas in Lusaka. Further bilateral aid projects continued the upgrading strategy in the next few years.

The improvement was dramatic and positive to the inhabitants, but criticism was also heard: the appearance of the areas was still the same old muddy compounds. The inhabitants were asked to pay a monthly fee; it was not large but became a political issue when local party leaders campaigned against it. The failure to get cost recovery was enough to stop further World Bank projects. Declarations on the strategy of upgrading on indigenous funds were never implemented. Lack of funds together with the incapacity of managing local projects were important contributing factors to the sudden stop of the policy.

No concrete alternative strategy was ever formulated. A homeownership strategy was declared resulting in a total stop for building of rental housing but fewer legal plots or houses than were ever supplied. The Fourth National Development Plan concludes that formal homeownership in urban areas remained the privilege of a small percentage of the households, while informal homeownership had increased significantly despite the existence of legal tools making it possible to grant licenses to squatters (Republic of Zambia 1989, p. 286).

Under the structural adjustment policy there was no room for governmental investments in housing. To what extent the withdrawn food subsidies, the introduction of school fees, etc., influenced the living conditions of urban neighborhoods is not yet established (Mudenda 1991). New shelters had to be built for the increasing number of households. On the local level party leaders were allowed to make plans and distribute plots for self-help, an activity without which the rate of homelessness would have been even worse. The people in the UNIP controlled areas felt secure of their tenure. Many of them were not even aware of their illegal status. They had been appointed a site by a party leader who was regarded an urban headman with the right to control land development, parallel to the rights of the village headman. Through an official anti-squatter policy the main strategy applied was again a blind-eye or a laissez-faire strategy.

CONCLUSIONS:
STATUS AND FUTURE OF THE SETTLEMENTS

In 1991, the Movement for Multiparty Democracy (MMD) won the election and a new government came into power in Zambia. One of the very first actions carried out by this MMD government was to demolish a housing area and a market. Directives were issued to district councils to form effective squatter control units to curb the mushrooming illegal settlements. *Times of Zambia* (1991) reported that 5,000 families were made homeless in Kanyama in Lusaka. The houseowners had got the plots from UNIP leaders and the former governor had promised to regularize the allocation of the plots but that had never been done.

· The new government declared during these first weeks in power that no houses were to be built without proper surveying and pegging. There have been no reports on any discussions on the possibility of using the Housing (Statutory and Improvement Areas) Act of 1974 which makes it possible to legalize and upgrade squatter settlements. The government seems to have adopted the old bulldozing strategy towards squatters. A resettlement strategy was promised but never decently implemented.

The Minister of Local Government and Housing maintained in an interview in *Daily Mail* (1992) that illegal squatters will not be compensated, but that a more human method of handling the problems will be developed. Further, he presented a prefabrication strategy for the production of new units. Six thousand houses were planned to be built in Lusaka, 2,000 in Kitwe, and as many in Ndola.

The housing stock in high density areas was to a great extent in disrepair. Old areas from early colonial times were since long planned to be demolished; this action is also high on the agenda of the new government. Houses in three such areas in Lusaka were going to be demolished according to the *Daily Mail* interview. The old houses, some to them round, would be replaced by 590 conventionally built houses. The sitting residents were offered the choice of renting a new house or getting some compensation. The government claimed to have offered K1 million to help develop plots elsewhere for those unable to pay the rent in the new housing scheme, such as old people. In March 1993, the author visited one of the rebuilt areas, Chileiyee. According to the residents in the new houses, there were no previous residents living in the new houses. No one had heard about any resettlement plots.

The fact that conventionally built houses although subsidized only can be afforded by a small percentage of the total population has not been dealt with by the new government. The heavily subsidized rental housing has been criticized by the World Bank and other observers for spoiling the market and raising unrealistic expectations on housing. The Minister of Local Government and Housing agreed in the *Daily Mail* interview that it is madness that a house that costs K200 today would cost K5,000 tomorrow. In his opinion, the local government which has announced such an increase only tried to cover up for its own inefficiency. It might be so, but it still remains to be seen if and how subsidies will be withdrawn.

In order to generate funds to build new houses it has been proposed that the local governments should sell out the old rental houses (Ngenda 1992). Some of the high density areas are in an attractive central location so a gentrification is to be expected even if the sitting tenants will be given the first chance to buy.

In spite of widespread poverty in the upgraded areas, there is an amazing building activity going on with extensions and improvements of existing houses. The same can be said about the overspill areas. The people in these areas are the great suppliers of housing for the growing population, but at the cost of their own environment. Only a massive supply of plots for simple houses to be built or a more relaxed view on new squatters can ease the pressure put on the legal areas.

In many areas, during the one-party period, the local party was functioning well as a neighborhood organization, often in conflict with the central party. There was a degree of democracy in the sense that leaders who did not fulfill what the inhabitants asked from them could not be sure of being re-elected. With the multiparty state, the single-party structure in the townships has to be disperse. One can speculate on what will come instead. Probably, churches and nongovernmental organizations will come to play a more important role in grass-roots mobilization.

Whether the poor men and women in the Zambian squatter and slum areas will manage to influence decisions better in a multiparty system remains to be seen. In the one-party system, women organized in the name of the party, worked as unpaid social workers in their own neighborhoods, but had little influence on the policy-making. It has been shown that women put higher priority on improvements of homes and neighborhoods than men do. There were few women in policy-making position before (Central Statistical Office 1991), and no obvious change in this respect has been noted during the time of the new government.

The new government inherited the country in a state of 'rapidly deteriorating fiscal position, accelerating inflation, chronic shortage of exchange and essential imported inputs, and a proliferation of black market activities' (Republic of Zambia 1991). With a deteriorated housing stock and tremendous housing shortage there are no easy strategies to apply. The measures taken so far have not addressed the mass need of cheap shelter.

REFERENCES

Banda, Matthias C. 1978. *Community Participation in the Upgrading Process.* Lusaka: Lusaka Housing Project Evaluation Team.

Central Statistical Office. 1990. *Census of Population, Housing and Agriculture: Preliminary Report.* Lusaka.

———. 1991. *Women and Men in Zambia. Facts and Figures.* Lusaka.

Chitambo, A.M. (ed.). 1991. *Women in Zambia: A Bibliographical Guide and Directory.* Lusaka: UNZA Press.

Daily Mail. 1992. 'Free Houses Coming—Sata', 24 July.

Doxiadis Associates. 1968. *Rehousing of Squatters.* Kafue Estate Ltd.

———. 1969. *A Special Programme of Action for Resettlement of Squatters. I. Lusaka.* Prepared for the Ministry of Local Government.

Doxiadis Associates. 1975. *The City of Lusaka Development Plan: Written Analysis.* Prepared for the Ministry of Local Government and Housing.

Hansen, Karen Tranberg. 1981. *Continuity and Change of New Urban Economic Activities, Mtendere Township 1971 and 1981.* Lusaka: Institute for African Studies, University of Zambia.

————. 1990. 'Part of the Household Inventory: Men Servants in Zambia', in Roger Sanjek and Shellee Colen (eds.), *At Work in Homes: Household Workers in World Perspective.* American Ethnological Society Monograph Series No. 3, pp. 119–45.

Jules-Rosette, Bennetta. 1981. *Symbols of Change: Urban Transition in a Zambian Community.* Norwood: Ablex Publishing Corporation.

————. 1988. 'A Zambian Squatter Complex: Cultural Variables in Urban Relocation', in R.A. Obudho and Constance C. Mhlanga (eds.), *Slum and Squatter Settlements in Sub-Saharan Africa.* New York: Praeger Publishers, pp. 191–204.

Kasongo, B.A. 1987. 'Development Strategies for the Homeless Shanty Town Dwellers: The Case of City Kitwe, Zambia', *African Urban Quarterly 2(3)*, (Nairobi), Special issue on Shelter and Homelessness in Africa, pp. 298–310.

Knapp, Eberhard, Lore Koppenhofer, Joseph Oenarto, and **Dietmar Ziller.** 1982. *Wohnproblem in der Dritten Welt* (Housing Problems in the Third World). Arbeitsbericht 39. Stuttgart: Stadtebauliches Institut im Fachbereich 1 Architektur und Stadtplanung der Universitat Stuttgart.

Lundgren, Thomas, Ann Schlyter, and **Thomas Schlyter.** 1969. *Kapwepwe Compound—A Study of An Unauthorized Settlement in Lusaka, Zambia.* Lund: University of Lund.

Mashamba, Mudzibairi Sylvester. 1990. 'The Informal Housing Sector and its Development in Zambia'. Unpublished manuscript, School of Architecture, University of Newcastle upon Tyne, United Kingdom.

Mcwan'gi, Mubiana and **Angela Chitambo.** 1992. 'The Social and Physical Conditions of Nannies in a High Cost Residential Area in Lusaka'. Unpublished manuscript, research proposal to the program Gender Research on Urbanization, Planning, Housing and Everyday Life, Lusaka.

Mitchell, J. Clyde (ed.). 1969. *Social Networks in Urban Situations: Analyses of Personal Relationships in Central African Towns.* Manchester: The University Press.

Mudenda, Sylvia J. 1991. 'Social Dimensions of Structural Adjustment in Zambia: Urban Women's Work and Structural Adjustment'. Unpublished document, Institute for African Studies, Review Workshop, 14–16 November.

Mulenga, Alfred. 1978. *A Descriptive Analogy of the Physical Resettlement Process.* Lusaka: Lusaka Housing Project Evaluation Team.

Mulimbwa, Anthony Cyril. 1980. *Urban Law and Housing Policy in Zambia.* Lusaka: Faculty of Law, University of Zambia.

Muller, Maria S. 1979. *Chawama—To Make a Good Place Better: The Socio-Economic History of a Squatter Settlement in Lusaka, Zambia,* DPU Working Paper No. 8. London: Development Planning Unit, Bartlett School of Architecture and Planning, University College.

Munalula, Margaret Mulela. 1992. 'Urbanization and its Effect on Women's Rights to Property and the Choice of Law'. Unpublished manuscript, research proposal to the program Gender Research on Urbanization, Planning, Housing and Everyday Life, Lusaka.

Mwanza, Ilse (ed.). 1990. *Bibliography of Zambiana and Theses and Dissertations from 1930 to 1989.* Lusaka: The University of Zambia, Institute for African Studies.

Ndulo, Manenga. 1986. 'Patterns of Housing Demand in a Low Income Economy: The Case of Urban Zambia', *Eastern African Economic Review 2 (1),* pp. 68–76.

————. 1989. 'Housing and Youth Unemployment: Experiences of Low Income Urban

Households in Zambia', in Kwaku Osei-Hwedie and Muna Ndulo (eds.), *Studies in Youth and Development*. Lusaka: Multimedia Publications, pp. 160–71.

Ngenda, Gertrude. 1992. 'Towards a Comprehensive Housing Policy'. Unpublished manuscript, Lusaka.

———. 1992. 'Squatters and Squatter Upgrading'. Unpublished manuscript, research proposal to the program Gender Research on Urbanization, Planning, Housing and Everyday life. Lusaka.

Ngulube, M.J. 1989. *Some Aspects of Growing Up in Zambia*. Lusaka: Nalinga Consultancy/Sol-Consult A/S Ltd.

Ogura, Mitsuo. 1991. 'Rural–Urban Migration in Zambia and Migrant Ties to Home Villages', *The Developing Economies 29 (2)*, pp. 145–65.

Rakodi, Carole. 1978. *George 1976: Initial Results of the Preliminary Sample Survey. Operational and Policy Implications*. Working Paper No. 4. Lusaka: Lusaka Housing Project Evaluation Team.

———. 1987. 'Urban Plan Preparation in Lusaka', *Habitat International 11 (4)*, pp. 95–111.

———. 1988. 'The Local State and Urban Local Government in Zambia', *Public Administration and Development 8*, pp. 27–46.

Rakodi, Carole and Ann Schlyter. 1981. *Upgrading in Lusaka—Participation and Physical Changes*. Stockholm: Swedish Council for Building Research.

Republic of Zambia. 1979. *Third National Development Plan 1979–83*. Lusaka: Office of the President.

———. 1989. *New Economic Recovery Program: Fourth National Development Plan 1989–1993*. Vol 1. Lusaka: Office of the President.

———. 1991. *New Economic Recovery Program: Economic and Financial Policy Framework 1991–1993*. Ministry of Finance and NCDP.

Robertson, J.T. 1978. *The Housing Sector—Perspective and Prospects*. Lusaka: Ministry of Local Government and Housing, pp. 21–47.

Schlyter, Ann. 1987. 'Commercialization in an Upgraded Squatter Settlement in Lusaka, Zambia', *Trialog 13 (14)*, (Darmstadt), pp. 24–29 and *African Urban Quarterly* (Nairobi), Special Issue on Shelter and Homelessness, pp. 287–97.

———. 1988. *Women Householders and Housing Strategies: The Case of George, Zambia*. SB: 14, Gavle: The National Swedish Institute for Building Research.

———. 1991. *Twenty Years of Development in George, Zambia*. D8: 1991. Stockholm: Swedish Council for Building Research.

Schlyter, Ann and Thomas Schlyter. 1980. *George—The Development of a Squatter Settlement in Lusaka, Zambia*. D3: 1980, Gavle: The National Swedish Institute for Building Research.

Schlyter, Ann and Jairus Chanda. 1982. *Bibliography on Human Settlements with Emphasis on Households and Residential Environment—Zambia*. D14: 1982. Stockholm: Swedish Council for Building Research.

Singini, R.E. 1978. *George 1978: Primary Surveys I and II: Comparison and their Operational and Policy Implications*. Working Paper No. 21. Lusaka: Lusaka Housing Project Evaluation Team.

Times of Zambia. 1991. 'Lusaka Demolishes Illegal Homes: 5,000 Families Left in the Cold'.

15

Squatter and Slum Settlements in Tanzania

A.C. Mosha

The history of urbanization is relatively new, dating back to the late 1800s when a few settlements were established in the country as a result of coastal trade with Arabia and India, trade with the Portuguese and of course the now infamous slave trade. With colonization, first by the Germans and later by the British, several other settlements were created (mainly for administrative purposes) under various ordinances.

From 1900, the level of urbanization still remained relatively low only to gather momentum in the 1970s and 1980s. Up to 1948, only 2.5 percent of the national population was urban. Towns were very small in size and population due to introduction of laws by the colonial government which restricted Africans from moving permanently into towns. There was a removal of this law in 1945, after it became clear that the number of Africans coming into the urban areas were contributing to the economic development of the nation. To illustrate this, it can be seen that between 1900–48, the capital, Dar-es-Salaam's urban population grew from 20,000 to 70,000 people recording an annual growth rate of 3 percent. During the same period the rate of growth of the other towns was insignificant. In 1948, the total mainland population was 7,400,000 people of which 183,000 were living in urban areas.

The rate of urbanization then rose to 6 percent in 1967; 13 percent in 1978 and over 18 percent in 1990. This is modest when compared to the rest of the East African nations whose ratio was 23 percent; and 36 percent for Africa in general. Various predictions indicate that if present trends continue, Tanzania's urban centers could easily fall between 30–47 percent of the total national population with populations ranging from eight to 15 million.

Since independence in 1961, Tanzania has been experiencing a higher rate of urbanization than before due to a rapid national growth, massive rural–urban migration, and improvement of transportation and communication networks. The feeling of freedom after independence, coupled with a growth pole strategy introduced in the Second Five Year Plan (1964–69), an industrial decentralization program, and a decentralization of government in 1972, speeded up the urbanization process. Table 15.1 shows that in terms of absolute numbers, the urban population was recorded as 364,076 in 1957, 686, 550 in 1967 and 2,060,000 in 1978 (Ntagazwa 1988).

Table 15.1: Urban Population Growth in Tanzania

Year	Urban Population			Annual Growth Rate from Previous Period Year	
	Total Population	Number	% of Total	National	Urban
1948	7,480,429	183,862	2.5	–	–
1957	8,788,466	364,072	4.1	1.8	7.9
1967	11,958,654	685,547	5.7	3.1	6.5
1978	17,048,329	2,173,816	12.7	3.3	11.1
2001	35,900,000	8,300,000	23.1	3.3 (low)	6.0[*]
		15,800,000	44.0	(High)	9.0[*]

[*] Estimates
Sources: Egero & Henin (1973); Government of Tanzania (1979).

Thus, the urban areas have been growing in population at almost three times the rate of rural areas. However, given the small size of Tanzania's original urban base, this rapid growth has put tremendous pressure on an already hard-pressed government to provide employment, and of course housing (Mosha 1990a).

With fast urbanization, more than 10 percent of housing provision, especially from the public sector has now proved to be a trickle, so that most people now live in unplanned settlements and slums. The government's resources have dwindled dramatically since the 1970s due to harsh economic conditions with falling real incomes and high inflation (Table 15.2).

Table 15.2: Economic Indicators, Tanzania, 1976–87

	Years						
	1976	1982	1983	1984	1985	1986	1987
GDP, current prices Tshs. million	21.652	52.546	62.608	78.143	108.083	143.034	198.101
GDP. 1976 prices Tshs. million	21.652	23.439	22.882	23.656	24.278	25.178	26.142
Per capita income, current prices	1328	2737	3162	3812	5027	6531	8765
Per capita income, prices, Tshs.	1328	1221	1155	1154	1129	1149	1157
Price Index for urban dwellers 1977 = 100	85.1	253.9	322.6	432.7	585.4	775.2	1007.4

Source: Economic Survey, 1987.

It is estimated by various writers that 60–82 percent of all urban housing across the nation is in spontaneous settlements (Mosha 1990).

The problem of housing has been tackled by both the colonial and post-independence governments with the introduction of several strategies, policies, and programs, but to date success seems to have eluded them.

As seen above, the colonial government tried to slow the pace of Africans coming into towns by legislation and physical repatriation (East African Royal Commission 1953–1955; Stren 1975; Kalabamu 1980) but with little success. After independence, the government tried the following strategies: slum clearance and redevelopment in the 1960s; mass housing through the National Housing Corporation; squatter upgrading; sites-and-services programs; housing finance for low incomes, first through the First Permanent Building Society, later through the Tanzania Housing Bank; and the establishment of housing cooperatives and employers' funded schemes (Materu 1986; Kalabamu 1984; Grohns 1972; Stren 1975; Kulaba 1981 and Mghweno 1984). Today, the government is relying very much on parastatal housing, government housing allowances, and mostly private initiatives.

In spite of all of these housing schemes and programs, the problem of housing has persisted with slums mushrooming everywhere like a cancer devouring both land in the city and the periphery of towns. To make matters worse, even some of the earlier planned areas are slowly turning into slums due in part to the lack of maintenance and repair; poor and overused infrastructure and great laxity in development control which have allowed lots of changes of use or new developments to take place without planning permission from the local authorities.

Vast residential, commercial, and industrial areas are slowly turning into ghettoes, full of squalor and filth, reeling under mounds of uncollected rubbish and overflowing sewers. The threat of an environmental disaster is now looming over vast areas of the main towns across the country.

CHARACTERISTICS OF
THE SLUMS AND SQUATTER SETTLEMENTS

The Extent and Pattern of the Problem

With urbanization has come a big demand for shelter nationwide and the established institutions have not been able to cope. In the First Five Year Plan (1964–69), the cumulative shortfall for new urban conventional housing was 37,000 units. The figure increased during the Second and Third Five Year Plans (i.e., 1969–81) when it was found to be 250,000. In 1990, the figure had risen to 450,000 units. If the same trend of housing deficit continues by the year 2000, the deficit will be 2.2 million units.

Nationally, between 40 and 70 percent of all urban population live in squatter areas (Mghweno 1984; Kalabamu 1980). The present annual growth rate of squatter settlements in the major urban centers is estimated at 22–25 percent per year (Kulaba 1989). Between 1974–81 during the implementation of a squatter upgrading program, squatter population had increased by about 900,000. Past studies have shown that squatter developers construct a total of minimum 16,000 houses per annum in urban areas, which is an average of 65 percent of all urban housing (Ministry of Lands, Housing and Urban Development 1980).

In Dar-es-Salaam itself, squatter houses increased at an annual rate of 16 percent between 1965–69, rising to 24 percent in 1969–74 (Mghweno 1979; Stren 1975). By 1972, the figure had risen to 44 percent and by 1978 to 62 percent. Current estimates put it close to 70 percent.

Even in the new capital, Dodoma squatting has been on the increase. In 1976, it was estimated that there were 21,565 persons living in 2,770 informal houses. By 1988, in spite of a strong policy barring uncontrolled settlements, there were 35,690 persons living in 2,880 informal houses. Squatter areas now provide accommodation for approximately 30 percent of Dodoma's population (Mosha 1990). In all towns, these settlements represent invaluable resources both in terms of housing and labor.

Factors that have Led to Squatting and Lack of Plots in Formal Areas

The long process involved in obtaining a surveyed plot has been the main reason that has forced a lot of low-income people to look for land in squatter areas. Before independence, a relatively modest demand for high density, low cost plots in the towns was adequately met through issuance of a short-term renewable right of occupancy by the government or through the leasing of land by private owners for a yearly rent. After independence, with the termination of freehold rights to land, the burden of satisfying a much greater demand for such plots fell entirely on the government. In most towns, the issuing of the right of occupancy has been inadequate to meet the demand for plots.

For example, Table 15.3 shows that in Dar-es-Salaam between 1973 and 1984, there were 11,938 plot applications, but only 2,443 plots were surveyed and allocated. This shows a shortfall of about 80 percent. Up to today the situation has not improved; if anything, it has gotten worse. Confronted with such backlogs, individuals who need housing cannot just sit and wait for ever. They quickly obtain plots in an informal way.

Table 15.3: Demand and Supply of Surveyed Plots in Dar-es-Salaam: 1977–86

Year	Accumulated Number of Applications	Surveyed Plots		Plots Allocated	Outstanding Demand (Applications)
		Target	Actual		
1977	17,200	8,300	2,394	2,113	15,087
1978	18,400	4,250	1,911	1,865	16,535
1979	18,900	8,300	3,214	3,604	15,296
1980	19,350	8,500	1,209	1,198	18,152
1981	20,000	5,280	1,502	1,490	18,510
1982	22,296	12,106	4,010	3,388	18,908
1983	23,896	5,765	2,621	1,660	22,236
1984	24,000	12,065	3,050	1,528	22,472
1985	25,000	9,288	3,740	2,000	23,000
1986	28,000	9,095	3,974	1,718	26,282
Total	N/A	82,859	27,625	20,564	N/A

Source: Kironde (1988).

Although squatters who obtain land informally have no legal documents to support their claims, they appear to feel that they have some clearly defined rights.

Legal/Administrative Factors

Within townships or in areas where township boundaries have expanded to embrace land held under traditional tenure, all land must be registered according to the Freehold Titles (Conversion) and Government Leases Act of 1963. Since all land is now vested in the state, every user of land must have a right of occupancy issued by the commissioner of lands. A second legal requirement arises from the Town and Country Planning Ordinance of 1956 according to which all buildings in declared 'Planning Areas' must receive planning consent from the local authority. Only those with legal titles to their land can apply for planning consent. If land is developed without planning consent, the local authority has the power under section 72 (Town and Country Planning Ordinance) to order demolition. If the demolition order is not compiled with, the local authority can enter the land, demolish any unauthorized structures, and recover expenses. However, the procedure prescribed under the law for people unlawfully occupying land (squatters) is too slow and cumbersome to be effective and this encourages more people to squat. For example, an attempt to control squatting administratively in Dar-es-Salaam was initiated in March 1969, with the establishment of a cadre of 'land rangers' under the legal section of the lands division. A similar group was established in Dodoma in 1976. Unfortunately in both cases, the attempt met with limited success as it was afflicted by four problems: First, the squatters often resorted to evasive practices—such as building at night or threats of violence when harassed by rangers. Second, the rangers felt that they only had a moral authority to evict squatters. Third, some party leaders at the local level appeared to be involved in the selling of plots to prospective squatters. Fourth, the land rangers or their authorities could not offer squatters alternative surveyed plots (Mosha 1990).

Economic Factors

Most people build in squatter areas for rental purposes to make a living. Since land cannot be found in formal areas, and the banks' interest rates have been low and most of the low-income earners have not been using the banks for their savings, squatter housing has undoubtedly been an important channel for investment in an economic system where there are limited alternative opportunities. Further, in squatter areas, no land costs are involved, like rates and service charges to the local authority. So, it is economically cheap to build in squatter areas.

Poor System of Compensation

The current system of compensation can also be cited as another factor that has led to squatting. Whenever the government wants to move squatters from a piece of land, compensation in the form of cash payments is made for the development. In most cases, since the government is cash strapped, it can take several months if not years before the affected are ever paid and the relocation process is started. Second, the cash settlement has also created a small class of 'speculative squatters' who deliberately build in areas where compensation is about to be paid.

REVIEW OF AVAILABLE RESEARCH IN TANZANIA

Quite a lot of research findings on slums and squatter settlements have come out in the last two decades or so, but, by and large, little has been published. Even the published material is sometimes not even accessible to practicing professionals or decision makers for feedback purposes and further research. The following review gives a short account of the major works on this subject.

The causes and effects of urbanization in Tanzania in so far as they lead to the creation of slums and squatter settlements have been well-documented by various authors (Claeson and Egero 1971; E.A.R.C. 1955; Stren 1982, 1975; Kulaba 1981; Mosha 1988, 1989; Mtiro 1988; Sutton 1970). All writers agree on the fact that urbanization is growing at an alarming rate leading to squatting on large-scale.

Several reasons have been advanced as to why squatting has proliferated so much in the urban areas. These include a failure on the part of government and local authorities to provide adequate housing; red tape in getting plots; lack of money to pay compensation for those who need to be relocated; poor system of allocating land; and failure of cost recovery measures in sites-and-services programs (Kironde 1991; Mosha 1990; Segal 1988; Simba 1988 and Tenga 1988).

Further, lack of a clear policy of housing for the low-income group has also been cited by writers like Kalabamu 1980, 1984; Government of Tanzania 1982; Kulaba 1981; Kikenya 1975; and Kironde 1979.

Finally, the lack of housing finance either from government or the private sector has been one of the major contributing factors (Mtiro 1988; Kulaba 1982). They later trace the history of institutions providing housing finance in Tanzania from the colonial era till the 1970s. They conclude that apart from housing built directly by the government and industry for its employers, and the several financial employers, services which sprang up and faded away from time to time fell into one of the following: government efforts to directly channel finance into housing for low-income groups; government efforts to create a market for mortgage loans in the border areas between the commercial and subcommercial housing sectors, and private institutions to serve what little effective demand for mortgage loans there was.

Practical and extensive recommendations on how to ameliorate the problem of squatters in the urban areas have been made by several writers and organizations. These include, inter alia, Mghweno 1979, 1984; Materu 1988; Gurh 1983; Kalabamu 1980; Mosha 1988 and Tenga 1988. Unfortunately a lot of the ideas given have not been acted upon. Instead of addressing the causes of the slum problems, the authorities seem to be busy dealing with the symptoms.

The result is that slums and squatter settlements are growing daily, now nearing 60–70 percent of total urban housing (Mghweno 1979; Stren 1975; Dwyer 1975; Kalabamu 1992; Materu 1988).

To deal with squatters the government introduced all sorts of programs ranging from forceful repatriation, slum clearance, squatter upgrading, provision of serviced land with core housing and parastatal housing. Several writers have written on slum clearance and its problems (Kulaba 1976; Mghweno 1979; Grohns 1972). In his study of the slum clearance of Dar-es-Salaam, Grohns concludes that it did not achieve much in terms of the earlier objectives. Kulaba also came up with the same conclusion and did suggest upgrading as an alternative with less serious impacts.

Upgrading and sites-and-services programs later became the obvious choice and although introduced in a number of towns, the impact was not much because it only scratched the surface of the problem of low-income housing (Siebolds and Steinberg 1982; Kalabamu 1991; Magembe and Rodell 1983; Kulaba 1982; Mghweno 1979; Mosha 1988; Kamulali 1985; World Bank 1978; MLHUD 1978). Although hailed as the solution to squatting, the program was slow in implementation due to a variety of reasons including poor planning, execution, and mismanagement (Peterson 1988; Kulaba 1981; World Bank 1978; MLHUD 1977; Crooke 1985; Kironde 1988). Even then, it has come to light that to date low-income earners have not benefitted much from this program. Instead middle-income earners have encroached on their territory (MLHUD 1978; Mgullu 1978; Seleki 1979; Stren 1982; Nkya 1980; Blunt 1977; Mosha 1988). A majority of squatters allocated plots in the sites-and-services programs have sold their plots and have gone back to squat on virgin land on the periphery of the urban areas hence perpetuating the problem. Materu 1988 notes that vigorous screening criteria notwithstanding, 60 percent of the site-and-service plots in Morogoro town are owned by middle-income people. Kamulali 1985 suggests that for Nyakato in Mwanza municipality, only 20 percent of the beneficiaries were low-income households. Kulaba 1985 suggests that only 30 percent of the people in Sinza site-and-service area, Dar-es-Salaam were low income. Reasons advanced for this state of affairs include bureaucracy, high initial fees (Blunt 1977; Mgullu 1978; Jensen and Wandel 1984; Stren 1975) or too high housing standards set for these areas (Kulaba 1985; Muzo 1984 and Kironde 1991).

Yet another shot at the problem of low-income housing has been the introduction of cooperative housing introduced in the 1970s to go hand in hand with sites-and-services. As with the other programs, success to date has been very limited (Economic Commission of Africa 1972; Kulaba, Uisso and Mwaiselage 1987). So the problem has been going on with no viable solution in hand. Today, even the once planned areas are turning into slums as maintenance has almost but ceased due to lack of funds, poor management, and a host of other problems. Thus the picture of urban housing is very bleak indeed.

STRATEGIES TO AMELIORATE SLUMS AND SQUATTING IN TANZANIA

The previous section just touched in passing the various attempts made by the government to solve the problem of squatting. In the following section each of the solutions will be examined in detail highlighting both successes and failures of these programs.

Slum Clearance and Redevelopment

A 'slum' is a relative term and denotes areas in which housing is crowded, neglected, deteriorated, and often obsolete (Clinard 1966). This definition when used for a country like Tanzania where peoples' incomes are low but the people live happily may not necessarily be true. All the same, from independence in 1961 to 1972, the Tanzanian government, like so many other Third World countries, jumped on the bandwagon that asserted that squatter settlements played no role in national development and would thus be done away with. These centers were viewed as centers of crime, hooliganism, unemployment, vandalism, etc. This view was supported in the 1967 Dar-es-Salaam master plan and reinforced by a Serman study team in 1967–68 which produced a report on clearance of a slum in Dar-es-Salaam.

The government quickly introduced a slum clearance program with three aims: political, sanitary, and social. The political aim was stated in 1963 when the President of Tanzania, Julius K. Nyerere declared that the government would immediately do something spectacular to improve the housing conditions in the capital, Dar-es-Salaam. The pulling down of some of the worst houses in the town center and the quick building of new houses had without doubt a strong demonstrative influence (Grohns 1972).

The more important and perhaps central aim of slum clearance was the improvement of public health, because this is to a large extent dependent on housing conditions. This meant that squatter settlements were to be pulled down to be replaced with high standard, modern, high cost and contractor-built dwelling units to be rented by the low-income people who were displaced in the redevelopment exercise.

The third, the social aim, is far more difficult to describe. The less the privacy that exists for families for individuals within or without families, the greater the danger of social tensions within the population which lives in overcrowded quarters, between these groups and the more privileged social groups.

The renewal exercise was to begin in Dar-es-Salaam, where a master plan had just recommended massive redevelopment, and later spread nationwide. A newly established National Housing Corporation (NHC) was entrusted with the building, as scheduled, 1,000 houses a year. Up to May 1969, 4,500 houses were completed all in Dar-es-Salaam, so it was estimated that NHC should have been able to fulfil the target of 5,000 houses defined in the First Five Year Plan (1964–69).

This efficient implementation of the Five Year Plan was made possible by a rigorous policy of steady reduction of building costs and financial aid of 10 million Deutschemarks from West Germany which also sent helpers from the German Volunteer Service.

In spite of these efforts, it was obvious that 1,000 houses which were replacing old houses, were not sufficient to solve the problem of slum clearance in Dar-es-Salaam. At least 6,000 houses should have been built for the low-income groups. The Master Plan proposed for the first stage of the plan, 1969–74, involved a relocation of 2,469 units in 12 squatter areas.

Similar redevelopment programs were proposed for the other major towns in the country, for example, Ngamiani in Tanga, Nagarenaro in Arusha, Majengo in Moshi, Mbeya and Mwanza but somehow for a long time things never got off the ground in these areas as the exercise that had started in Dar-es-Salaam proved that the program was costly both in terms of new construction and finding money for compensation, as also inappropriate socially (Mosha 1979). The program had reduced the urban housing stock, and destroyed the squatters' investment in shelter, the self-help and co-operative potential existing in squatter areas, and the social ties among the squatter population.

Several evaluation exercises of this program were carried out and in most cases the negative impacts of renewal were overwhelming. In Dar-es-Salaam, for example, rents for the NHC housing units were 20 percent of the salary of low-income earners. So, most just left to set up their camps elsewhere in the city suburbs. However, those who moved in the new houses felt better—cleanliness, better airflow, better light, electricity, water supply, and less incidence of disease (Grohns 1972).

It has also been argued by some writers (Kulaba 1976) that the redevelopment schemes encouraged speculation in land and property development which then led to more squatting. The argument is that at the time of the slum and squatter clearance program, prices of building materials and the cost of labor were very low compared to current prices. With attractive compensation given to owners of demolished properties, cheap, abundant, and easily available building materials, encouraged more and more people to squat especially on planned land ripe for development in anticipation of receiving compensation which they could use to build larger and better houses. Many areas were invaded and residential structures were quickly erected overnight or in a few days.

Thus due to its inherent problems, the government in 1972, abandoned this mass redevelopment scheme preferring to do it on a selective basis. To replace this scheme the government introduced slum upgrading in which squatter settlements were not to be demolished but to be improved and provided with services and infrastructure. This policy continues till the present day.

SQUATTER UPGRADING
AND SITES-AND-SERVICES PROGRAMS

Upgrading is a housing process in which the main emphasis is on upgrading the housing stock through a combination of house construction or improvement loans, technical assistance, secure tenure, the reduction of densities, and so on.

In Tanzania, upgrading was seen as one way of legalizing the then informal houses which had sprouted almost everywhere in the urban environment. It was supposed to create a better health program for the slum-dwellers by bringing in better sanitation, better infrastructure, and social facilities like clinics, schools and community halls.

With the help of a World Bank loan, a squatter upgrading and sites-and-services program was launched in the early 1970s in Dar-es-Salaam and later spread to four other towns and eventually to most other big urban centers in the country. The upgrading program was two-pronged—improvement of slums on the one hand, and on the other, making land and core housing (sites-and-services) available to the urban poor and those displaced from the earlier program of slum clearance or upgrading.

The government appointed the Ministry of Lands, Housing and Urban Development as the executing agency. A sites-and-services project division was immediately established to handle the work of planning and implementing the upgrading program and the production of plots for the sites-and-services program. The project was to be implemented in three phases: phase one, 1973–76; phase two, 1976–80; and phase three, 1980–85.

In phase one, the International Development Agency of the World Bank provided a loan of US$ 16.7 million. This was to provide about 9,000 new sites-and-serviced plots and improvements encompassing full infrastructural services, a slab and core foundation benefitting approximately 160,000 low-income residents in Dar-es-Salaam, Mwanza, and Mbeya.

Under the phase two project, Table 15.4 shows costing over US$ 29.3 million, more than 315,000 low-income urban dwellers were to benefit by providing improvements to over 50 percent of the 1976 then existing squatter houses and satisfying 75 percent of the need for new plots in five major towns viz., Dar-es-Salaam, Tanga, Tabora, Morogoro, and Iringa. In order to reach more people, standards were lowered and this time core concentration was more on infrastructure provision and public services. Five towns were selected for this phase, Dar-es-Salaam, Morogoro, Tabora, Tanga, and Iringa.

Phase three which was prepared based on lessons drawn from the previous two phases, was intended to cover Morogoro, Arusha, Dodoma and of course Dar-es-salaam.

Table 15.4: Tanzania: Squatter Improvement Projects

Towns	Phase One		Phase Two	
	Serviced Plots	Houses in Squatter Areas	Serviced Plots	Houses in Squatter Areas
Dar-es-salaam	6,182	7,600	14,150	9,138
Mwanza	1,900	None	None	None
Mbeya	850	1,200	None	None
Iringa	None	None	1,770	1,088
Morogoro	None	None	810	2,069
Tabora	None	None	925	2,784
Tanga	None	None	1,300	732
Total	8,932	8,800	18,955	15,811

Source: Government of Tanzania Second National Sites and Services Project, Dar-es-Salaam, Government Printer, June 1977, Annex 1, Table 3.

Through these programs a good percentage of the urban poor did get social, economic, and physical infrastructure they were either short of or did not have at all. Squatters could get title for their land and loans for house construction were given either in monetary terms or in kind.

AN EVALUATION OF THE PROGRAM

The phase one program did succeed in upgrading 11,000 houses in squatter settlements, servicing 10,600 plots nationwide with Dar-es-Salaam taking the lion's share of 7,450, Mwanza with 2,300 and Mbeya with 850. Further, the government legalized squatter landholdings by providing them with rights of occupancy while at the same time removing the stigma of temporary classification from squatter houses.

The number of people who were reached by the project in phase two was not less than 90,000 in Dar-es-Salaam; 8,500 in Tanga; 28,000 in Tabora; 19,200 in Iringa and 16,000 in Monogoro (Mosha 1988). It can be said that this is a notable success, in view of the magnitude of the problem facing the government.

Phase three had a shaky start as the World Bank had decided to withhold funds due to poor management of the schemes. The government decided to continue with the program, this time concentrating all its efforts in Dar-es-Salaam alone. Altogether 3,000 plots were surveyed in Tegeta and Tabata between 1987–89. Most work was centered on planning, surveying, and allocation of plots. The only infrastructure provided was trunk water mains and main roads and in some cases even these were not provided. In upgrading areas, evaluations of properties affected by upgrading schemes were done, but due to lack of funds for compensation, very few people have actually moved to a new site. Even those who have been given new plots in the sites-and-services areas, cannot develop them due to lack of water and electricity.

During this period the Directorate of sites-and-services shifted its emphasis and included the middle- and even the high-income earners in the allocation of plots sounding a death-knell for the low-income earners who were to benefit from the whole program. Due to a series of management problems, the unit was dissolved in 1989, its top management allocated other duties, and its duties put under the Town Planning Directorate who are now just trying to untangle the mess left behind.

FAILURES

While some notable successes in upgrading and provision of plots for the urban poor have been recorded, there have also been failures in reaching the target. Studies point to the unforeseen upsurge in squatter population as the main reason for its failure. Over the span of the program, 1974 to 1981, squatter population had increased by about 900,000, whereas the sites-and-services program was estimated to cater to some 467,000 people only. Thus, development of new squatters in various urban areas has far outpaced efforts taken so far to improve existing settlements and contain their further development.

Second, the sites-and-services and upgrading program failed in its objective of encouraging self-help. The integrated systems of controls tended to involve families in bureaucratic tangles leading to little achievement by individuals. Some families even went as far as preferring to build their houses following their own plans rather than those of the agency. Even maintenance of the facilities and infrastructure in many upgraded sites is done by contractors. Most of the 15 housing cooperatives that started in different project areas did not go beyond their formative stages. Lack of management and proper organization accompanied by undefined regulations have been cited as the main reasons for failures of the housing cooperatives (Kulaba, Uisso and Mwaiselage 1987).

Third, the creation of the sites-and-services program can be blamed partially on poor planning of the projects right from the start. For example, it has been observed that plot leases required families to build expensive core houses within six months of allocation or give up their plot. A family could use a plan supplied by the housing bank or pay an architect to prepare an alternative that satisfied the same material standards as the bank's plans. The building requirements adopted called for material costing between one and one-and-half times the annual cash incomes of eligible families. Thus the program was typical in that its design carefully circumscribed self-help and gradual construction while agencies relaxed building codes to permit incomplete houses and simplified housing plans to facilitate the use of unskilled labor. The plans required that a large part of the final infrastructure and the house had to be built before occupation.

Fourth, the slow pace of the program can also be cited as a reason that has led to more squatting. For example, of the total sites-and-services plots surveyed, serviced, and allocated by 1979, only 54 percent were fully developed by 1983 (Kironde 1988). About 43 percent of the plots were partially developed while only 3 percent were fully developed. In Dar-es-Salaam's Kijitonyama and Sinza site-and-service areas, after 15 years since the introduction of the program only 60 percent of the plots were occupied.

The main culprit for the slow rate of development is the long bureaucratic procedure of planning, surveying, and servicing of plots. Second, the red tape in allocation. In Dar-es-Salaam alone, 27,625 plots were made available for allocation between 1977 and 1986, but only around 9,000 were allocated in that period despite over 26,000 applications at the end of 1986 (Kironde 1988). This left a thriving black market for land by some of the unscrupulous officers. Third, the process of plot development is very slow taking up to six years instead of one to two years to complete a house.

Fifth, the process and method of compensation is inappropriate and slow. The compensation paid to displacees is usually not based on the market value of the properties demolished. As a result, it has been found that most displacees cannot build a house of high standards as required by the program. As a result those who fail to develop their plots have to relinquish them and look for either rental property or start squatting afresh. Further, lack of money to pay compensation has been quite common, leaving prospective displacees with anxiety as they cannot continue to improve the properties expected to be demolished. So they continue living in even poorer environments.

Sixth, loans for house construction have not been all that easy to get because of low incomes. Several reasons have been advanced for this: most people are still ignorant of the procedures and other conditions required before getting loans, and even if they have the knowledge, the procedure for getting loans is long and complex, and also there are several expenses and conditions involved that are well beyond the capacity of the low-income person to meet.

Seventh, with time and some elements of greed, the project's target seems to have been missed, with a fairly big number of the plots going to middle-income persons. Several studies done in Dar-es-Salaam, Mwanza, Morogoro, Mbeya and Arusha have all shown that plots either change hands from low-income earners or are directly allocated by the unit to middle- or even high-income earners.

In planning the new site-and-service areas, the World Bank brought in a precondition which called for higher densities and cost effectiveness in implementing the project. This resulted in the reduction of plot sizes from 300–400 sq m to 288 sq m (12m x 24m) much to the disgruntlement of the target population. In addition, apart from plot sizes the sizes of open spaces, road widths, rights of the way of other infrastructure, etc., were also reduced. Under these new standards, the plots were just enough for a modest two-roomed house plus the accompanying septic tank and soak away pits. A factor that was disregarded by these standards was that low-income persons who occupied such areas needed a little bit of extra space within the compound for market gardening or for just growing vegetables for survival. Hence, these plots have become rather unpopular and have in fact led to some residents invading open spaces in their neighborhoods for market-gardening purposes growing maize, vegetables, sweet potatoes, spinach, and similar crops. Efforts by the local authorities to stop these people from invading these areas have failed. This amply demonstrates the insensitiveness of imported standards on the culture and norms of local people.

Finally, cost recovery has been almost nil due to a poor system of collection and management of the funds. Thus the project is difficult to replicate as each time new financial resources have to be found, and with the state of economy being what it is today, such funds are not easily forthcoming.

THE FUTURE OF SLUMS AND SQUATTER SETTLEMENTS

With the economy of the country still in doldrums and urbanization on the increase, what can be expected is that slums will persist and even more planned areas will continue to deteriorate into slums. Further, as the government lacks the capability for providing serviced land for housing, squatting will always appear desirable enough to attract additional settlements. Squatter settlements which reflect local housing markets and local cultural patterns are here to stay and are not marginal any more. The nation has to come up with a housing policy that accepts the existence and importance of these settlements to national development. If well-continued and integrated into national development policies and programs, these settlements have a huge potential to contribute to the general development of the nation.

In general, it then seems that the only option is to continue with more squatter upgrading and the sites-and-services programs; putting some constraints in the spatial distribution of additional squatters; and better form of physical planning of residential areas in order to incorporate those features of unplanned areas that form the physical basis for viable urban life styles in

Tanzania. Further, there is more need for self-help through individual family efforts; easier channels of finance for housing by the low-income people; and by making it easier to develop the land.

What is needed to achieve better results than what has hitherto been attempted is to involve the communities as much as possible in planning and improving their slums, and better management so that plots can be designed, surveyed, and allocated fast enough. Red tape in plot allocation and plot development should also be removed. Further, standards of construction should be lowered so that people can build with whatever material they have, with improvements to come later. There are already a lot of cheap building materials developed by the Building Research Bureau and used in model houses in the entire country, but these are hardly used by the low-income groups mainly due to lack of information and prejudice. Dissemination of information on appropriate building materials should be encouraged.

Further, the country should encourage more self-help in housing as this is the least costly and probably the only viable alternative left. The least that can be done is to assist, teach and show local communities how best they can help themselves. This requires training of an adequate number of extension workers (professionals, sub-professionals, and craftsmen) of the right kind and level who will work with and assist local communities in solving their problems. It also requires training trainers who will keep on training the extension workers needed in the office and in the field.

Physical planners too have a role to play. The high incidence of planned areas turning into slums, e.g., by agricultural practices or the emergence of other informal activities suggests that planned areas will increase in attractiveness if they are conceptualized in terms of the living patterns exhibited by residents of unplanned areas (Segal 1988). This means that a significant portion of the residents will seek part of their livelihood outside the formal cash economy by raising their own food, or supplement their incomes by raising small quantities of cash crops or have a stall in front of their yards to sell this or that. This has to be supplemented with proper development control to ensure that such environments follow proper standards of health and safety.

Local authorities should improve ways to raising funds and managing them in order to check urban growth and improve urban environments. Failure of this will encourage more decay of the urban fabric leading to slums.

Finally, the government should put more effort in channelling the meager financial resources they have into housing for low-income persons by revamping the services of the Tanzania Housing Bank. The Bank should be better managed to reach more people. In a similar manner, private financial institutions like the commercial banks and insurance companies could get involved in providing loans for housing for the middle- to high-income people so that government can be left to deal with the urban poor. This way all sectors will be satisfied.

REFERENCES

Blunt, A. 1977. 'Some Problems that Arose in Phase 1 of the Sites-and-Services Project'. Final report of consultant in charge of monitoring and evaluation, Dar-es-Salaam (mimeo.).

Claeson, C.F. and B. Egero. 1971. Movement to Towns in Tanzania: Tables and Comments. BRALUP Research Notes no. 11, University of Dar-es-Salaam.

Clinard, Marshall. 1966. *Slums and Community Development.* New York: Free Press.

Crooke, P. (ed.). 1985. 'Management of Sites-and-Services and Squatter Upgrading Housing Areas'. Occasional Paper. Center for Housing Studies, Ardhi Salaam (mimeo.).

Dwyer, D.J. 1975. *People and Housing in Third World Cities.* London: Longman.

East African Royal Commission 1953-1955 Report. London: HMSO.

Economic Commission of Africa. 1972. 'Cooperative Housing Pilot Project: Dar-es-Salaam, Tanzania'. Addis Ababa: United Nations Economic Commission of Africa.

Egero, B. and R.A. Henin (eds.). 1973. *The Population of Tanzania.* Dar-es-Salaam: BRALUP and Bureau of Statistics.

Fimbo, G.M. 1988. 'Planned Urban Development versus Customary Law in Tanzania'. Paper presented at the CAP Africa Regional Conference held at Ardhi Institute DSM, 16–21 May 1988.

Government of Tanzania. 1979. *Preliminary Results of the 1978 Population Census.* Dar-es-Salaam: General Statistical Office.

———. 1982. *The New National Housing Policy.* Dar-es-Salaam: Government Printer.

Grohns, G. 1972. 'Slum Clearance in Dar-es-Salaam', in J. Hutton (ed.), *Urban Challenge in East Africa.* Nairobi: East African Publishing House.

Gurh, I. 1983. 'Co-operatives in State Housing Programs Alternative for Low-income Groups', in R.J. Skinner and M.J. Rodell (eds.), *People, Poverty and Shelter.* London: Methuen.

James, R.W. 1979. *Land Tenure and Policy in Tanzania.* Nairobi: East African Literature Bureau.

Jensen, E. and S. Wandel. 1984. 'Squatter Upgrading and Sites-and-Services Programs in Tanzania'. Ardhi Institute (mimeo.).

Kalabamu, F.T. 1980. 'Evolution of Urban Housing Policy in Tanzania'. Unpublished thesis, University of Edinburgh.

———. 1984. 'A Review of Tanzania's New Housing Policy'. *Habitat International 8 (2),* pp. 95–102.

———. 1991. 'Towards a Simplified Sites and Services Approach: Lessons from Tanzania'. Conference paper, International Housing Research, Oslo, 24–27 June.

———. 1992. 'Tanzania: Developing Urban Residential Land', *Journal of Urban Affairs 14 (1),* pp. 61–78.

Kamulali, T.W.P. 1985. 'Site-and-Services in Tanzania: A Case Study in Nyakato, Mwanza Municipality', in P. Crooke (ed.), *Management of Site-and-Services and Squatter Upgrading Housing Areas,* pp. 43–47.

Kikenya, J.D. 1975. 'National Housing Corporation: Progress in Housing the Masses', *Tanzania Notes and Records 76,* 1985–1990.

Kironde, J.M.L. 1979. 'Urban Housing Policy in Tanzania. A Critical Appraisal'. MSc Thesis, University of Salford.

Kironde, J. 1988. 'Providing Land for Development'. Paper presented at the CAP Africa Regional Conference held at Ardhi Institute, Dar-es-Salaam, 16–21 May.

———. 1991. 'Sites and Services in Tanzania', *Habitat International 15 (1/2)*, pp. 27–38.

Kulaba, S.M. 1976. 'Urban Redevelopment Policies in Dar- es-Salaam'. Unpublished M.A. Dissertation, University of Nottingham, UK.

———. 1981. *Housing, Socialism and National Development in Tanzania*. Dar-es-Salaam: CHS (Tanzania) Occasional Paper No. 7.

———. 1982. 'Urban Growth and Management of Urban Reform in Tanzania'. Paper presented at a conference on Urban Reform, IDRC Nairobi, Kenya. April.

———. 1985. 'Managing Rapid Urban Growth Through Sites and Services and Squatter Upgrading Housing in Tanzania', in P. Crooke (ed.), *Management of Sites-and-Services and Squatter Upgrading Areas*, pp. 31–37.

———. 1989. 'Local Government and the Management of Urban Services in Tanzania', in R.E. Stren and R.R. White (eds.), *African Cities in Crisis*. Boulder, CO: Westview Press.

Kulaba, S.M., L. Uisso, and A. Mwaiselage. 1987. 'The Provision of Shelter and Infrastructure through Cooperative Action in Tanzania: A Case Study of Sigara and Mwenge Co-operatives in Dar-es-Salaam'. Ardhi Institute, CHS (mimeo.).

Laquian, A.A. 1983. 'Sites and Services and Shelter: An Evaluation', *Habitat International 7*, pp. 211–25.

Magembe, E.J.A. and M.J. Rodell. 1983. 'Housing Production in Selected Areas of Dar-es-Salaam, Tanzania. A Comparative Study of Sites-and-Services, Squatter and Upgrading Areas', Dar-es- Salaam, Ardhi Institute (mimeo.).

Majani, B.B.K. 1985. 'The Concept of the National Sites-and-Services and Squatter Upgrading Project in Tanzania', in P. Crooke (ed.) *Management of Sites-and-Services and Squatter Upgrading Housing Areas*, pp. 19–30.

Materu, J.S. 1986. 'Tanzania Sites and Services Projects: A Case Study of Implementation', *Third World Planning Review 8 (2)*, pp. 121–38.

———. 1988. 'The Myth of the Progressive Development Model in Housing Provision: The Case of Tanzania'. Paper presented at the CAP Africa Regional Conference, Ardhi Institute, DSM, 16–21 May.

Mghweno, J.M. 1979. 'Human Settlement Upgrading Process, Problems and Solutions—Brief on Squatter Upgrading in Tanzania'. Paper presented at a Symposium of Planning Human Settlement and Development, Dar-es-Salaam.

———. 1984. 'Tanzania's Surveyed Plots Program', in G. Payne (ed.), *Low-income Housing in the Developing World: The Role of Sites and Services and Settlement Upgrading*. Chichester: John Wiley.

Mgullu, F.P. 1978. 'Housing. A Study of Tanzania's National Sites-and-Services Scheme'. M.A. Thesis, University of Dar-es-Salaam.

MLHUD (Ministry for Lands, Housing and Urban Development). 1975. *Dar-es-Salaam Master Plan*. Govt. Printer.

———. 1977. *The National Sites and Services Program, Phase 1 Project Review + Phase II Project Proposals*, DSM.

———. 1978. 'Reducing Housing Costs'. Housing Development Division and Building Research Unit, Dar-es-Salaam (mimeo.).

Mlindwa. C.V.Y. 1981. 'Achievements, Problems and Possibilities for Implementing Tabora Master Plan'. Paper presented at a Conference on Plan Implementation and Human Settlements Administration in Tanzania, Dar-es-Salaam, 21-26 September.

Mosha, A.C. 1979. 'The Process of Urbanization in Tanzania'. Workshop paper DSE, West Berlin.

————. 1980. 'Towards a National Housing Policy, Ardhi Institute (mimeo.).

————. 1988. 'Slum and Squatter Settlements in Mainland Tanzania', in Obudho and Mhlanga (eds.), *Slum and Squatter settlements in Sub-Saharan Africa*. New York: Praeger.

————. 1989. 'Urban Planning in Tanzania at the Cross Roads'. *RUPSEA Journal 1 (1)*, pp. 3–10.

————. 1990. 'Population and Uncontrolled Urban Settlements in Tanzania'. Ardhi Institute Occasional Paper No. 12.

————. 1990. 'Urbanization and the Environment'. Ardhi Institute Occasional Paper.

Mtiro, I.J. 1988. 'Urban Development and Planning in Tanzania'. Paper presented at the CAP Africa Regional Conference, Dar-es-Salaam, 16–21 May.

Mtui, S.L. 1983. 'Neighborhood Plans Implementation in Dar-es-Salaam'. Unpublished thesis, Ardhi Institute, Dar-es-Salaam.

Muzo, R.K. 1984. 'The Administration and Financing of Urban Councils in Tanzania', *Journal of Building and Land Development 2*, pp. 29–37.

Ntagazwa, A.D. 1988. 'Statement of the Honorable Minister of Lands, Natural Resources and Tourism', CAP Conference, Ardhi Institute, 16–21 may.

Obudho, R.A. and Mhlanga 1988. *Slum and Squatter Settlements in Sub-Saharan Africa*. New York: Praeger.

Petersen, E. 1988. 'Master Planning and Development Assumption'. Paper presented at the CAP conference, Ardhi Institute, 16–21 May.

Segal, E.S. 1988. 'Spontaneous and Planned Housing in Dar-es-Salaam', in Obudho and Mhlanga' (eds.), *Slums and Squatter Settlements in Sub-Saharan Africa.*

Seleki, B.A. 1979. 'Sites and Services Project for Low Income People in Tanzania'. Diploma Dissertation, DPU, University College, London.

Siebolds, P. and F. Steinberg. 1982. 'Tanzania: Sites and Services', *Habitat International 6*, pp. 116–25.

Simba, I.C. 1988. 'Availability of Land for Urban Development: Case of Dar-es-Salaam'. Paper presented at the CAP Africa Regional Conference held at Ardhi Institute, 16–21 May.

Stren, R.E. 1975. *Urban Inequality and Housing Policy in Tanzania: The Problem of Squatting.* Berkeley: University of California Institute of International Studies.

————. 1982. 'Underdevelopment, Urban Squatting and the State Bureaucracy. A Case of Tanzania', *Canadian Journal of African Studies 16*, pp. 69–92.

Tenga, R.W. 1988. 'Land Policy and Law in Tanzania'. Paper presented at the CAP Africa Regional Conference, Dar-es-Salaam, 16–21 May.

Turner, J.F.C. 1972. 'Uncontrolled Urban Settlements: Problems and Policies', in G. Breese (ed.), *The City in Newly Developing Countries: Readings on Urbanism and Urbanization.* Englewood Cliffs, NJ: Prentice-Hall.

World Bank. 1978. 'Sites and Services and Upgrading: A Review of World Bank Assisted Projects'. Urban Projects Dept.

16

Housing Poverty in Ghana

A. Graham Tipple and David Korboe

In the two decades preceding 1984, the Ghanaian economy experienced a consistent downward slide (Rado 1986; World Bank 1990). Though a bold economic recovery program has succeeded in reversing the trend, incomes are still very low. In Accra, HUDA (1990) found a mean household expenditure of about C60,000 (about $170) per month. Even with most urban households devoting over 60 percent of their gross expenditures to food alone, the general state of nutrition is poor (Ghana 1990; UNDP 1991a) and there is little left over for housing and other expenditure. Similar to other West African countries, Ghana has a long tradition of urban settlement both in the coastal towns and inland, most notably, perhaps, in the historic city of Kumasi which had a population of 12,000 to 15,000 when visited by Bowdich (1819) in 1817. According to the 1984 census of population (Ghana 1987), there were 12.3 million people in Ghana of whom 3.9 million lived in towns with 5,000 or more inhabitants. Accra, the capital, had an estimated population of 1.2 million (Ghana 1987)[1] in 1984, while Kumasi accommodates in excess of 700,000 people (Malpezzi et al. 1990a). Most Ghanaian towns and cities have a moderately dense core of mixed residential and commercial uses encircling a central open-air market. In this core will usually be found most of the town's public buildings, the more established commercial concerns, and the oldest and most crowded housing. As housing is generally not marketed in West Africa, most of these houses are jointly owned by successors of the original owner and, though extremely precious to the owning family, they may be quite decrepit (Amole et al. 1993; Korboe 1993). Outside this core may be a few sections specifically set aside for government residences or publicly-built estates developed along Western lines. There are also areas of private elite housing, and similarly, some neighborhoods of low-income compounds. Contrary to claims in UNCHS (1982, p. 50), low-income squatting is rare in Ghana.

Apart from the government-built and high cost areas, there are large sections which are unquestionably diverse and impossible to classify in a polarized (e.g., slum or high quality; legal or squatter) manner. Even in such parts, however, it is common for those houses built in higher construction standards to be located closer to the main roads where public utilities are more accessible (Stanley 1975). The more poorly built houses (i.e., the majority situated farther away from mains servicing) tend to be very badly serviced.

EXTENT AND PATTERN OF
HOUSING POVERTY IN GHANA

The characteristics which would commonly be applied to 'slums', and may be expected in squatter housing, would include poor and deteriorating structural conditions. In urban Ghana, these characteristics are found in combination in large areas and singly (but in extreme forms) in most areas. The HUDA (1990) study of Greater Accra categorized housing stress in terms of occupancy, access to kitchen, toilet, water, etc., and the number of people with whom these were shared. The study ranked two of its seven sectors as high stress but together these formed two-thirds of the accommodation in Accra. The majority of households occupy only one room—47 percent in Accra (HUDA 1990); 73 percent in Kumasi (Malpezzi et al. 1990a—only owner households appear to routinely occupy two or more rooms (Tipple and Willis 1991). According to the Ghana Living Standards Survey (GLSS) (Ghana 1990), mean living area per person in urban areas outside Accra is only 6.8 sq m. However, it is doubtful whether most people would regard their housing areas as 'slums'; these are simply the normal conditions which prevail in most parts of Ghanaian cities.

As O'Connor (1983) notes, the urban setting in Africa often incorporates some quite distinctly rural characteristics. Lifestyles, culture, and sometimes even visual qualities are not easily distinguishable. Indeed, in the cities of Ghana, most of the land continues to be owned by tribal communities and large lineages rather than the state. By tradition, such community and ancestral lands are inalienable (Rattray 1929; Meek 1952); only the minority of individually acquired freeholds may be sold without encumbrance. The former (corporate lands) are administered by locally resident custodian chiefs and family heads respectively on behalf of the whole community, including those yet to be born (Ollennu 1962).

As the guardians of the land and their people are vigilant over their heritage, squatters are unlikely to get very far in their house building efforts before they are identified and summarily removed. The authors have no record of any instances where low-income squatting has occurred on a significant scale except on government-owned land in the Tema New Town area (Sebuava 1980). Insofar as permission for leasehold occupancy has been sought from, and the customary tribute paid to, the relevant custodian chief or family head, access is authorized and plots are quite rightfully occupied

(Peil 1976; Tipple 1984; Konadu-Agyemang 1991). If these titles are lacking anything in legality, it is likely to be with respect to formal registration or to complying with the development laid down in local development plans—either being in areas zoned for nonresidential uses or not complying with the approved layout (Peil 1976).

For this reason, low-income invasions are rare. What little squatting there is tends, unlike in most other parts of the world, to be restricted to the extreme top of the market involving some of the most expensive properties in Accra. There is a large area in the north of Accra where land was acquired by the SMC[2] government in the 1970s for a major sports complex. Since the fall of that government in 1979, land has been reallocated by the former owning families as if it were never acquired by the government.[3] Squatting was possible here because the land is officially state-owned and the squatters themselves are among the most influential citizens of Accra. Efforts are currently being made to regularize the landholdings in the area and to provide routes for access roads in a way which is familiar in low-income areas of other countries.

In terms of design, most nongovernment-built low-income housing takes the form of the single-storey compound (Merrill 1989). A multistorey variation which is similar to the single-storey version also exists but it has a staircase in the courtyard and a balcony access to upper floors. The compound has its origins in the rural hinterland where lineage groups occupy large (sometimes half-hectare) homesteads built around a bare patch of ground. With urbanization, the traditional form has been exported to the towns and cities and adapted to respond to the demands of the urban economy. Often built of earth and constructed around the immediate periphery of the plot rather than centrally, the typical compound is illegal under urban building regulations. However, the compound utilizes land quite efficiently, providing flexible accommodation (in terms of single- or multiple-roomed units) along with densities of between 100 and 400 persons per hectare in single storey development.

In the urban arena, where compounds are not occupied exclusively by kin, tenant households are partially fulfilling the role of kinsmen in a context of domestic landlordism (Clark 1984; Korboe 1992; Schildkrout 1978). On an average, one-half of the ten to 15 inward-facing rooms on each storey will be occupied by the owner and his kinsmen. The rest are rented out room by room to tenants who share whatever limited services there are with the owning family. In Kumasi, 84 percent of households occupy housing in this manner compared to 16 percent who have self-contained apartments or villas (Tipple and Willis 1991).

Single-storey compounds tend to be built incrementally, with the odd room or two being added when funding permits (Sutherland 1981). With the scarcity of credit avenues, it very often takes ten years or more to complete a compound. In an as yet unpublished work, Korboe has found that such extension activity accounted for 53 percent of the rooms in his survey of two periurban areas of Kumasi. In addition, Malpezzi et al. (1990a) show that the growth in accommodation in Kumasi over the 1980–86 period owed more to additional rooms on existing houses than to new starts.

Relatively few households are of owner occupiers: 15 percent in the capital, Accra (Ghana 1990)[4] and 10 percent in Kumasi (Tipple and Willis 1991). However, many households enjoy rent free accommodation because they are related to the living owner or have inherited a share in their house from a deceased relative; in both Accra and Kumasi, about 25 percent of households live in such 'family house' accommodation (HUDA 1990; Tipple and Willis 1991). Amole et al. (forthcoming) describe how important this family housing is to the poorer members of Ghanaian urban society in the sense that it provides the type of low or no cost accommodation found in the squatter areas of other countries.

The lack of squatter housing or areas which are easily demarcated as 'slums' does not mean that there is no poor quality housing in urban Ghana. Large areas of the city, though legally owned, are developed in an unauthorized manner and other areas are unserviced or have services only of a meager level. As Hellen et al. (1991) show, unauthorized development of houses cannot automatically be blamed for poor housing conditions. Many of the areas which scored badly in six health-related variables were peripheral villages situated beyond the end of the urban mains service lines. However, the newer houses in these areas are strongly built and relatively well provided with bathrooms and toilets; some are among the most palatial in the city, built ahead of, and awaiting, the provision of services.

Urban rents, except in some parts of Accra, are low by international standards. Using expenditure as a proxy for income, rents were a median of about 2 percent of income in both Kumasi and Accra (Malpezzi et al. 1990a; HUDA 1990) at a time when historically very effective rent control has been (unofficially) relaxed (Tipple 1988a). Within the houses let room by room, relationships between residents tend to be strong, resulting in a supportive community. Housing areas tend not to be distinguished by single-income group occupation; this heterogeneity of income being particularly pronounced in Muslim dominated areas (Schildkrout 1978).

About two-thirds of the housing in Accra is included in the two sectors shown in Table 16.1. The data from areas in both cities show the predominance of crowding with over three persons per room being the rule rather than the exception in mainly single-roomed accommodation. As Tipple and Willis

(1991) show, virtually the only way that a household can obtain more than one room in a compound house is to be the owner.

Table 16.1: Measures of Crowding

	Accra: Central High Density Areas	Accra: Peripheral Low-Income Housing Areas	Kumasi: Whole City
Mean rooms occupied per household	1.6	1.6	1.6
Mean persons per room	3.6	3.1	3.3
Percentage households occupying a single room	49.7	50.0	73.2
Mean persons per house	29.5	34.2	31.2
Mean households per house	5.2	6.8	6.9

Sources: Accra, HUDA (1990); Kumasi, Malpezzi et al. (1990a).

As most people share housing facilities with everyone in the house, the number of people and households in the house indicates the level of the use of toilets, taps, bathrooms, and kitchens which are available. Additional data on the number of people sharing these services in some peripheral housing areas can be found in Table 16.2. In many houses, even one tap or toilet may not be provided and then occupants use public taps or toilets shared by hundreds or thousands of users.

Table 16.2: Access to Selected Domestic Services Surveyed
(Peripheral Low-Income Housing)

Location and Measure	Bath	Kitchen	Toilet	Tap
Accra: High density, low cost housing areas				
Persons per unit	16.7	38.3	27.2	n.i.
No. of units per house	1.55	0.87	1.23	n.i.
Kumasi: Mossi Zongo and Atonsu low cost housing areas				
Persons per unit	28.4	50.1[a]	101.9	155.6
Households per unit	5.5	9.7	19.7	30.1

[a] The statistic for persons sharing a kitchen suggests a higher degree of stress than is the case in reality. Few males participate in food preparation, and compound kitchens are used mainly for the storage of bulky cookware.

Source: Accra, HUDA (1990); Korboe (1992).

Interestingly, illegality (in the form of nonregistration) is not unique to low-income housing. Owing mainly to the cumbersome nature of registration procedures, only an insignificant fraction of all land transactions are ever formalized (Asiama 1979; UNDP 1991b). Bentsi-Enchill (1964) describes this form of tenure as 'proprietary occupancy' indicating that the security of an unregistered interest is subject solely to the sincerity of the grantor. While there are undoubtedly many chiefs whose integrity is unquestionable, there are also vast opportunities to exploit the role of the custodian. Cases of double or multiple allocation are common, as indeed are instances of misappropriation of land proceeds. There are few urban areas where the vast wealth derived from land leasing has benefited the owning communities in a substantial way.

As in the case in Nigeria, however, traditional allocation of customarily held plots is likely to be more equitable than other, more modern systems (see Okpala 1977). Thus, a policy of wholesale nationalization may not be in the best interests of the poorer and socially less esteemed classes.

REVIEW OF AVAILABLE RESEARCH ON GHANA

Useful insights on housing for the Ghanaian poor can be gained from urban literature on West Africa as a whole. Gugler and Flanagan (1978) and Peil and Sada (1984) are useful. In addition, Peil (1976) is an important contextual work as it gives the reasons for those settlements which an outsider might expect to be squatter settlements are, in fact, legal in land tenure.

A bibliography of housing in Ghana (Tipple 1988b) lists 1,005 titles with some relevance to housing. The Department of Planning at the University of Science and Technology (UST), Kumasi, has a considerable stock of BA Special Studies dealing with housing, most of which concentrate on one neighborhood, or one component of the housing process generalized over more than a single locality. In addition, both the Department of Housing and Planning Research at UST and the Building and Road Research Institute in Kumasi have produced occasional reports on housing in 'slum areas' (notably Abloh 1976; Houlberg and Nimako 1973). In addition, anthropological studies of particular groups have important sections dealing with housing conditions. Notable among these are Hinderink and Sterkenburg (1975) on Cape Coast; Schildkrout's (1978) work on the Mossi people living in Kumasi; Stanley (1975 and 1980) on northern migrants also in Kumasi; Kilson (1974) on the Ga people in Accra; and Sanjek (1982) on Adabraka in Accra. An international comparison of low-income housing areas carried out at the University of Darmstadt and UNCHS included areas in Kumasi (Schmitter 1979; UNCHS 1982).

The largest body of research into Ghanaian housing conditions in recent years has been conducted by Tipple and a group of associates at the University of Newcastle upon Tyne (Tipple 1987). The World Bank International Review of Rent Control adopted Kumasi as a case study and generated a considerable body of work (including Tipple 1988a; Tipple and Willis 1989; Malpezzi et al. 1990a and b; Willis et al. 1990a). Additional assistance from the Leverhulme Trust enabled further analysis of the data (Tipple and Willis 1991 and 1992; Willis and Tipple 1991a and b; Willis 1991; Hellen et al. 1991).

The Ghana Living Standards Survey (Ghana 1990) gives some preliminary information on housing in urban areas. Housing conditions in Accra are documented in HUDA (1990), although obtaining copies is so difficult that the latter cannot be regarded as being in the public domain. Studies of particular areas include Afrane (1990), Intsiful (1989) and Korboe (1992). Konadu-Agyemang's (1991) recent work on why low-income households do not occupy land illegally is particularly pertinent in the context of this book. Recent papers by Amole et al. (1993) and Korboe (1993) discuss the place of 'family housing', a growing component in slum areas in Ghana.

STRATEGIES TO AMELIORATE THE CONDITIONS IN THESE SETTLEMENTS AND THEIR CRITIQUES

Most local practitioners and housing institutions (e.g., Ghana 1987 and HUDA 1990) propose self-contained housing for all. Most also argue a case for wholesale owner-occupancy as an immediate target. However, neither of these is prudent or even practical under current economic conditions. Not only is the combined cost of a lease on land and the price of constructing a self-contained villa on the periphery of the large urban centers way beyond the pocket of most households but also the majority of Ghanaians would regard the small house which they can afford to be too small for their requirements. In addition, self-contained villa development requires very extensive tracts of land, producing relatively low density development. Furthermore, it encourages large households as those with claims on the owner will join his/her household within the interior of a villa (which is designed for one household) in contrast to the ability to form a different household in a part of the compound house. Joining a household in a villa increases the number of dependents who are to some extent supported by the main occupant which, in turn, reduces per capita incomes and, therefore, increases the likelihood of hardship. On the other hand, households in a compound are likely to be more independent.

Densely settled central-city areas tend to be the heart of the traditional city. Most of the oldest and most crowded houses in these cores are jointly owned by large lineages and occupied by the poorest members of the urban society (Amole et al. 1993; Korboe 1993). Thus proposals for upgrading central-city areas should take account of the special circumstances imposed by 'family houses'. Efforts to provide roads and other services should deprive no one of their family plot if possible. Unlike in other countries, more plots slightly affected are preferable to a few completely affected. In addition, families who lose part of their land can be more fruitfully compensated by additional services (water supply into the house, for example) rather than by cash which is easily dissipated by the family head without helping poorer family members.

Even in peripheral self-help settlements in Ghana—for which Turner (1968) hypothesizes significantly high proportions of owners—renting is the majority tenure. In Mossi Zongo and Atonsu, for example, tenant households outnumber owner households by a factor of 6:1 (Korboe 1992). This high tenancy rate has negative implications for upgrading as the proportion of households who can realistically be expected to freely invest their labor and financial resources is low (Tipple 1988c).

Another important consideration in the upgrading equation is the harshness of Ghanaian rent controls. Throughout the 1980s, Ghana operated one of the most stringent rent control regimes worldwide (*The Urban Edge* 1991). For a room in a compound or any other shared house, the monthly rent prescribed by legislation (Ghana 1986) is 300 Cedis, equivalent in 1992 to $0.70 or the cost of two bottles of Coca-Cola. Yet, because owners typically support larger households, many are actually worse-off than their tenants on a per capita basis (Tipple and Willis 1991; Korboe 1992).

On such rents as those described, landlords cannot be expected to carry out required maintenance or service upgrading. Indirectly too, the authority of landlords to deal effectively with irresponsible tenants has been severely curtailed by rent control practice. Thus landlords cannot oblige their tenants to share in upgrading costs. As a result, the burden of financing an upgrading project could easily fall fully on the small proportion of not-so-affluent owners. In Ghana's well-known pilot upgrading scheme (the Maamobi East Pocket Infrastructure Development Project), infrastructure standards have not been based on the households' willingness or ability to pay. While some relatively cheap community toilets and refuse skips have been provided, the standard of roads and other technical services are unduly high.

Some ameliorative policies have been suggested as a result of the work on rent control and rental housing, based mainly on the need to encourage new housing starts and renovation of existing stock. Malpezzi et al. (1990a) proposed that rent controls should be removed in a 'floating-up-and-out' exercise where rental levels would be increased by more than inflation for a fixed number of years until market rents are reached. Rents on new properties should be immediately decontrolled. This would have the effect of raising rents for most households probably by at least a factor of three but rent-to-income ratios would still be within the 10 to 20 percent range for most households. There would be a need for some assistance for those at the lower end of the income scale but many at the bottom end of the housing market would find their rents actually falling because their accommodation is so poor as not to merit the current rent levels.[5] Simultaneously, there would be a need for removal of the bottle-necks in the supply system so that new housing could be built quickly to prevent the rationing of driving rents which are higher than the housing conditions would merit. The new housing, on which economic rents would be accrued, may be sufficiently attractive to prospective landlords to reestablish urban housing as a popular investment (Tipple and Willis 1992).

Tipple and Willis (1991) also show that the owners of compounds are sufficiently similar to their tenants to suggest that it would be much simpler to encourage current nonowners to become owners of houses shared with tenants than to induce them to invest in the self-contained houses which are currently the target of housing policy.

On finance, existing credit schemes are limited to the elites and formal sector workers; people who are registered with the Social Security and National Insurance Trust (SSNIT) as pensionable workers who have formally registered plots, and can afford an architect or competent designer to draw plans for approval by the planning authority. Almost every owner in the compound housing neighborhoods (i.e., those about whom we refer in this chapter) would be outside formal credit schemes. In addition, formal credit tends to neglect consolidation (upgrading and extension) which tends to happen in the compound neighborhoods as a credible source of supply in spite of the major contribution which it makes to the low-income housing stock.

As is common in low-income settlements, collateral can be a great problem for would-be borrowers in Ghana. However, the very marked and culturally-based reluctance to sell real property should be enough to allow an existing house to stand as collateral against a loan for extension, even where there are only proprietary occupancy rights to the land. So great is the fear of disgrace if default forced a sale, that most of such loans would be safe.

The water supply corporation (GWSC) is currently confined by a state-controlled pricing policy which does not cover the cost of water supply, and its connection costs do not encourage the corporation to extend the mains network. In the current centrally regulated system, the corporation cannot recover costs of plant rehabilitation or mains extension. A change in pricing policy to cover the economic cost of water supplied (plus an operating profit), and a flat connection charge would reduce the distance between water mains and houses and increase the viability of providing water to all houses (see Tipple 1988c).

Current land rents and the property rates do not take adequate account of the cost of urban development. Thus, the District Councils and Metropolitan Authorities are insufficiently funded to keep pace with the demands for infrastructure and services (particularly waste disposal). The current exercise in improving land registration procedures should be extended to arrange for a larger share of money to be paid to landholders which should go into the cost of urban infrastructure development.

CONCLUSIONS:
STATUS AND FUTURE OF THESE SETTLEMENTS

It is important that the areas dealt with in this chapter should not be thought of as a problem because they contain almost the only housing affordable by the majority of Ghanaians. The needs are too great for the government or any currently extant formal sector developer to provide more than an insignificant fraction. Thus, the compound house neighborhoods built through informal and often unauthorized mechanisms are likely to be major sources of current and new housing for decades to come.

Although their servicing and physical condition require improvement, the areas under consideration here present a major resource for the future housing of urban dwellers in the majority, low-income group. Housing resources could achieve considerable improvement in these areas if they were targeted towards encouraging the construction of housing for the owner, some tenants, and/or a few family members. Where houses already exist, policy should aim at improving and extending it within a budget which does not exclude the very people who need to benefit. The most important change in housing circumstances for occupants of such housing is that there be much more housing; more rooms and more services available; and a greater variety of housing choices so that the majority have choices with respect to location and occupying more than one room.

NOTES

1. Note as no more up-to-date information is available, we will use the Ghana census figure for 1984. However, this is done with some caution as our work in Kumasi led us to have serious doubts about the census estimate of 490,000 there.
2. The Supreme Military Council Government which was removed by the 4 June 1979 coup.
3. It must be noted that government is notoriously slow in paying compensation for land which is compulsorily acquired and that family property is subject to multiple claims as to who is entitled to receive such compensation. Thus, those parties who originally owned the land can claim that it has never been properly acquired by the government and their claim is very difficult to refute.
4. Though HUDA (1990) found 24 percent in their sample in Greater Accra Metropolitan Area which includes some rural settlements.
5. Malpezzi et al. (1990) contains a detailed discussion of the costs and benefits of rent controls for owners and renters, and some predictive material on who may lose and by how much if rents were to reflect free market conditions. They show that not all rents would rise, *ceteris paribus*, especially if supply bottle-necks were effectively removed.

REFERENCES

Abloh, F.A. 1976. *Housing Areas in a Ghanaian Urban Centre, Kumasi*. Kumasi: Department of Housing and Planning Research, University of Science and Technology.

Afrane, S.K. 1990. 'Job Creation in Residential Areas: A Comparative Study of Public and Private Residential Communities in Kumasi, Ghana', in M. Raj and P. Nientied (eds.), *Housing and Income in Third World Development*. London: Aspect Publishing, pp. 41–54.

Amole, B., D. Korboe and A.G. Tipple. 1993. 'The Family House in West Africa: A Forgotten Resource for Policy Makers?' *Third World Planning Review 15 (4)*, pp. 317–29.

Asiama, S.O. 1979. 'Social Analysis, Urbanisation and Land Reform in Ghana'. Unpublished Ph.D. Dissertation, University of Birmingham.

Bentsi-Enchill, K. 1964. *Ghana Land Law*. London: Sweet and Maxwell.

Bowdich, T.E. 1819. *Mission from Cape Coast to Ashantee*. London: J. Murray (reprinted by Frank Cass and Co., 1966).

Clark, G. 1984. 'The Position of Asante Women Traders in Kumasi Central Market'. Unpublished Ph.D. Dissertation, University of Cambridge.

Ghana, Government of. 1986. *Rent Control Law*. PNDC Law 138 (as amended by LI 1318).

———. 1987. *National Housing Policy and Action Plan, 1987–90*. Accra: Ministry of Works and Housing.

———. 1990. 'Ghana Living Standards Survey'. Accra: Statistical Service.

Gugler, J. and W.G. Flanagan. 1978. *Urbanization and Social Change in West Africa*. Cambridge: Cambridge University Press.

Hellen, J.A., A.G. Tipple and M.A. Prince. 1991. 'Environmental Risk Assessment in a Tropical City: An Application of Housing and Household Data from Kumasi, Ghana', in E. Hinz, *Geomedizinische und biogeographische Aspekte der Kranlheitsverbeitun: und Gesundheitsversorgung in Industrie-und Entwicklungslandern*. Frankfurt am Main: Peter Lang.

Hinderink, J. and J. Sterkenburg. 1975. *Anatomy of an African town: A Socio-economic Study of Cape Coast*. Ghana, Utrecht: Geographical Institute, University of Utrecht.

Houlberg, P. and **J. Nimako**. 1973. 'Unauthorised Housing in Kumasi'. Draft Report, Department of Housing and Planning Research, University of Science and Technology, Kumasi.

HUDA (Housing and Urban Development Associates). 1990. 'Housing Needs Assessment Study, Final Report'. Accra: Ministry of Local Government, Government of Ghana.

Intsiful, G.W.K. 1989. 'Towards Adequate Housing in Ghana: The Case of Ayija Township and the Asawasi Housing Estate in the City of Kumasi'. Unpublished Ph.D. Dissertation, University of Michigan.

Kilson, M. 1974. *African Urban Kinsmen: The Ga of Central Accra*. London: C. Hurst and Co.

Konadu-Agyemang, K.O. 1991. 'Reflections on the Absence of Squatter Settlements in West African Cities: The Case of Kumasi, Ghana', *Urban Studies 28 (1)*, pp. 139–51.

Korboe, D. 1992. 'Multihabitation: An Analysis of Residence in a West African City', *Open House International 17 (1)*, pp. 45–53.

———. 1993. 'Family Houses in Ghanaian Cities: To Be or Not to Be?' *Urban Studies 29 (7)*, pp. 1159–72.

Malpezzi, S.J., A.G. Tipple and **K.G. Willis**. 1990a. 'Costs and Benefits of Rent Control: A Case Study in Kumasi, Ghana'. Washington, DC, World Bank Discussion Paper No. 74.

———. 1990b. 'An Econometric and Cultural Analysis of Rent Control in Kumasi, Ghana', *Urban Studies 27 (2)*, pp. 241–58.

Meek, C. 1952. 'Some Social Aspects of Land Tenure in Africa', *Supplement to the Journal of African Administration* (October), pp. 15–21.

Merrill, S. 1989. *The Evolution of Donor Policies for the Shelter Sector: Lessons Learned and a Case Study of Ghana*. Cambridge, MA: Abt Associates.

O'Connor, A.M. 1983. *The African City*. London: Hutchinson University Press.

Ollennu, N.A. 1962. *Principles of Customary Land Law in Ghana*. London: Sweet and Maxwell.

Okpala, D.C.I. 1977. 'The Potentials and Perils of Public Land Ownership and Management: A Case Study of the Lagos Executive Development Board (Nigeria), 1928–72'. Unpublished Ph.D. Dissertation, Massachusetts Institute of Technology.

Peil, M. 1976. 'African Squatter Settlements—A Comparative Study'. *Urban Studies 13 (1)*, pp. 155–66.

Peil, M. and **P.O. Sada**. 1984. *African Urban Society*. London: Wiley.

Rado, E. 1986. 'Notes Towards a Political Economy of Ghana Today', *African Affairs 85 (341)*, pp. 563–72.

Rattray, R.S. 1929. *Ashanti Law and Constitution*. London and Kumasi: London University Press and Basel Mission Book Depot.

Sanjek, R. 1982. 'The Organisation of Households in Adabraka: Towards a Wider Comparative Perspective', *Comparative Studies in Society and History*, January, pp. 57–103.

Sebuava. 1980. 'A Causal Model of the Squatter Settlement: A Study of Tema Manhean'. Unpublished BSc Dissertation, Department of Planning, University of Science and Technology, Kumasi.

Schildkrout, E. 1978. *People of the Zono: The Transformation of Ethnic Identities in Ghana*. Cambridge: Cambridge University Press.

Schmitter, J.P. 1979. 'Economic Effects of Housing in Developing Countries: Field Study in Ghana, Part A, Analysis of Two Settlements in Kumasi'. Darmstadt, Institute of Tropical Building and Planning, Technical University.

Stanley, J.M. 1975. 'The Legality of Ayija, A Case Study of Development Procedures in a Suburb of Kumasi'. Research Report No. 2, Department of Planning, University of Science and Technology, Kumasi.

———. 1980. 'Migrant Settlement in West Africa: The Case of Ayija, Kumasi'. Unpublished Ph.D. Dissertation, University of Glasgow.

Sutherland, R. 1981. 'The Outdoor Room: A Study of the Use of Outdoor Space in Ghanaian

Architecture'. Unpublished MSc Dissertation, University of Science and Technology, Kumasi.

Tipple, A.G. 1984. 'Towards a Culturally Acceptable Housing Strategy: The Case of Kumasi, Ghana'. Unpublished Ph.D. Dissertation, University of Newcastle upon Tyne.

———. 1985. 'Housing Problems and Fields for Intervention in Ghana', *African Urban Studies 21* (Spring), pp. 5–13.

———. 1987. *The Development of Housing Policy in Kumasi, Ghana, 1901 to 1981: With an Analysis of The Current Housing Stock*. Newcastle upon Tyne: Centre for Architectural Research and Development Overseas, University of Newcastle upon Tyne.

———. 1988a. *The History and Practice of Rent Control in Kumasi., Ghana*. Washington DC., Infrastructure, Water and Urban Development Department Working Paper, No. 88-1, World Bank.

———. 1988b. *A Bibliography of Housing in Ghana*. Newcastle upon Tyne: Centre for Architectural Research and Development Overseas.

———. 1988c. 'Upgrading and Culture in Kumasi: Problems and Possibilities', in R.A. Obudho and C.C. Mhlanga (eds.), *Slum and Squatter Settlement in Sub-Saharan Africa: Towards a Planning Strategy*. New York, Praeger, pp. 71–88.

Tipple, A.G. and **J.A. Hellen.** 1989. 'Priorities for Public Utilities and Housing Improvements in Kumasi, Ghana: An Empirical Assessment based on Six Variables', in G. Salem and E. Jeanee Paris (eds.), ORSTOM, pp. 199–226.

Tipple, A.G. and **K.G. Willis.** 1989. 'The Effects on Households and Housing of Strict Public Intervention in a Private Housing Market', *Geoforum 20 (1)*, pp. 15–26.

———. 1991. 'Tenure Choice in Kumasi, Ghana', *Third World Planning Review 13 (1)*, pp. 27–45.

———. 1992. 'Why should Ghanaians build Houses in Urban Areas?' *Cities*, pp. 60–74.

Turner, J.F.C. 1968. 'Housing Priorities, Settlement Patterns and Urban Development in Modernising Countries', *Journal of the American Institute of Planners*, pp. 354–63.

The Urban Edge. 1991. 'Rent Control: Pros and Cons', *15 (6)*.

UNCHS (Habitat). 1982. *Survey of Slums and Squatter Settlements*. Dublin: Tycooly International Publishing.

UNDP. 1991a. *Human Development Report*. New York: Oxford University Press.

———. 1991b. *Urban Management Program*. Nairobi: UNCHS.

Willis, K.G. and **A.G. Tipple** 1991a. 'Discriminant Analysis: Tenure Choice and Demand for Housing Services in Kumasi, Ghana', in A.G. Tipple and K.G. Willis (eds.), *Housing the Poor in The Developing World: Methods of Analysis. Case Studies and Policies*. London: Routledge, pp. 126–42.

———. 1991b. 'Economics of Multihabitation: Housing Conditions, Household Occupancy, and Household Structure Under Rent Control, Inflation and Non-marketability of Property Rights', *World Development 19 (12)*, pp. 1705–20.

World Bank. 1990. 'Ghana Housing Sector Review: Sustaining the Structural Adjustment Program, A Shelter Strategy for Ghana'. Washington DC., Infrastructure Operations Division, World Bank.

17

Squatter and Slum Settlements in Pakistan: Issues and Policy Challenges*

Emiel A. Wegelin

The backdrop to the prevalence of squatter and slum settlements is formed by the unabating pressure of urban population growth. Although recent overall population census data are not available (the 1991 census was aborted in Sindh province, while in other provinces numerous instances of manipulation of the field counts were reported; the results for these provinces have not been tabulated and published to date), all available data suggest that urban population growth in Pakistan is among the highest in Asia.

Table 17.1 illustrates the rapid growth of urban areas in Pakistan in the 1980s. Urban areas were projected to grow at a rate of around 77 percent during 1981–93, while the overall population was expected to grow at a rate of 43 percent over the same period, implying annual growth rates of 4.9 percent and 3.1 percent respectively. This indicates both a high level of natural population growth and a high level of rural–urban transformation (rural–urban migration as well as urban area expansion and transformation of villages into small towns).

Table 17.1: Trends in Urban Population in Pakistan by Region
(million)

	Actual 1981	*Estimate 1989*	*Projected 1993*
Punjab	13.1	19.4	23.5
Sind	8.2	12.0	14.4
NWFP	1.7	2.4	2.8
Baluchistan	0.7	1.0	1.1
FATA	–	–	–
Islamabad	0.2	0.3	0.4
Total urban population	23.8	35.1	42.2
Total population	84.3	107.0	120.9
Urban share (%)	28.2	32.8	34.9

Source: *Economic Survey 1989/90*.

*Comments by Jan van der Linden (Amsterdam Free University) on an earlier draft of this chapter are gratefully acknowledged.

According to the World Development Report 1992, annual population growth rates of urban areas in Pakistan were 4.3 percent during 1965–80 and 4.6 percent from 1980–90 (IBRD 1992). Punjab is the province where the majority of the urban dwellers reside, but Sindh (largely due to the influence of Karachi) is the most urbanized province, with 43 percent of the provincial population living in urban areas.[1]

In the absence of reliable data one may quibble over the exact magnitudes; yet, it is clear that the absolute numbers involved are very substantial: the above urban population growth projections for 1989–93 imply an average addition of about 250,000 urban households per annum during this period.

Urban Land and Municipal Services Delivery

Recent comprehensive data are not available, but data for individual cities suggest that urban services provision and provision of serviced plots in urban areas have not been adequate to keep up with population growth (see e.g., IBRD, 1985 and 1988). There is thus no reason to suppose that the pattern displayed in Table 17.2 below for the 1970–80 period has changed fundamentally in the subsequent decade.

Table 17.2: Access to Water and Sanitation

Percentage of Urban Households with House Connections (Water)		Percentage of Urban Households Served by Public Stand Post (Water)		Percentage of Urban Households Served by Water Supply		Percentage of Urban Households Served by Sewage or Other Systems
1970	1980	1970	1980	1970	1980	1980
34	30	41	42	76	72	42

Source: UNCHS, Global Report (1987).

Although the extent of service delivery tends to gradually improve over time in already settled areas, the government is clearly unable to provide for adequate amounts of urban land serviced with municipal services and other civic amenities (let alone housing) to meet the shelter requirements of the large number of new households, even if there were no provision for backlogs. This means that the urban population must essentially fend for itself to meet its shelter and urban services needs, i.e., market solutions are relied upon. Those who can afford to, turn to solutions within the formal housing sector with standards adhering to planning and building codes. This, however, is not possible for a sizeable and increasing segment of the urban population, who therefore depend on 'informal' solutions at lower quality levels, resulting in the emergence of slums and squatter settlements as well as densification of existing low-income housing areas, particularly in the inner cities. This is largely caused by the failure of public land development agencies to deliver. In fact, the operations of such agencies in the major urban areas have tended to stultify the operation of the urban land market and obstruct affordable supply of urban land to the poor and middle-income groups, rather than enhance it.

MAIN CHARACTERISTICS: EXTENT AND PATTERNS OF SQUATTER AND SLUM SETTLEMENTS IN PAKISTAN

Katchi Abadies

The settlements most commonly referred to as the equivalent of slum settlements are called 'katchi abadies', literally translated as nonpermanent/substandard settlements. In actual fact, housing standards in katchi abadies vary greatly; their common denominator is that they emerged as a result of an uncontrolled shelter development process and that neighborhood layout and building quality did not necessarily adhere to prescribed standards. This is partly caused by the fact that, at least initially, residents did not have a legal title to the land.

The Government of Pakistan estimated in 1988 that there were at that time a total number of 2,322 katchi abadies on 43,145 acres of land (37,510 acres of government land and 5,635 of private land) with an estimated population of about six million people or about 18 percent of the 1988 urban population (Planning Commission, Government of Pakistan, Seventh Five Year Plan 1988–93, p. 238). About 60 percent of these katchi abadies with about 63 percent of katchi abadi population were located in the Sindh province. This is partly due to the influence of Karachi, the largest urban center and the commercial capital of the country, with an estimated population of about eight million in 1989, or 23 percent of the country's urban population (which, as noted above, contributes very substantially to making Sindh the most urbanized province). It also relates to the pattern of land-ownership at the fringes of the growing urban areas: in the desert areas of southern Sindh particularly, there are generally few agricultural land title claims, and hence substantial tracts of state land by default. In contrast, in the fertile Punjab, changes from rural to urban land uses generally take place on privately titled land.

The varying nature of housing quality in katchi abadies depends largely on the financial capability of the individual household concerned, their perceived security of land tenure and their length of stay in the settlement. Housing development is mostly incremental in nature as formal housing finance is not generally available to the residents in the absence of the possibility to use a formal land title as collateral. As a result of this, gradual upgrading and expansion of houses take place as constrained by the households' cash savings and/or ability to borrow informally. Apart from such land and financing problems, major problems in katchi abadies consist of the absence or inadequacy of municipal infrastructure such as water supply, urban roads and street lighting, garbage collection and disposal, drainage and flood protection, as well as social services such as primary health care and primary education.

It is important to note that while this was fairly prevalent in the 1950s and 1960s, in more recent times not many of the katchi abadies have come about as a result of spontaneous settlement or large-scale organized invasions. Increasingly, the most prevalent formation pattern has become the illegal subdivision of (government) land by middlemen/brokers with connections/protection in the government land controlling agencies (Nientied and Van der Linden 1985; Nientied 1987, p. 165). Such illegal subdivision is often characterized by relatively spacious and regular land layouts, anticipating, so to speak, the public provision of infrastructure and ultimate legalization of tenure.

Homeownership is the most common type of residential arrangement in katchi abadies, with only about 20–25 percent of households renting their house, even though financial commitments are less of a long-term burden in the latter case. As settlements consolidate, become legalized and integrate more in the overall urban fabric, this percentage tends to increase over time. There are two predominant motives for the relatively limited extent of renting, consisting of the general appreciation of the asset value of housing in times of acute need (insurance motive), and a more cultural dimension relating to the need for privacy, particularly for women. Additionally, renting arrangements have often not been trouble-free. With rent control and eviction protection clauses formally on the statute books, rental arrangements have generally been agreed upon an informal basis, providing substantial uncertainty to both parties, unless there are other ties between landlord and tenant (Van der Linden 1989).

Inner-City Slums

Slum formation of quite a different nature occurs in the inner-city areas of the major urban areas, particularly Lahore and Karachi, where much of the existing housing stock is subject to increasing densification (Kalim 1988). The original housing stock is often rental housing, neglected by its owners for a variety of motives, ranging from lack of interest due to low returns on investment in rehabilitation or reconstruction to speculative motives to hasten the process of decay in the hope to cash in on subsequent redevelopment.

The process of decay is further stimulated by the fact that these areas are generally still subject to rent control legislation, which acts as a further disincentive to the owners to provide adequate maintenance, let alone to engage in any serious upgrading. As nominal rents are very low, there is substantial informal market premium on the occupancy of such units: tenancy rights are sold for a large sum of 'key' money, which in case of moving is then passed on by the outgoing tenant to the next one (this is called the 'puggri' or tea money system).

There is an additional fiscal disincentive which makes this situation even more difficult to reform, as property tax assessment and collection are carried out on the Net Annual Rental Value (NARV) basis. As owners cannot evict tenants and collect very low controlled rents, the present property tax system reinforces the status quo in that it reduces the incentive for owners to redevelop, which in turn contributes further to the process of decay.

Poverty, Ethnicity, and Length of Stay

While it is fair to say that katchi abadies and inner-city slums form the dominant housing environment of the urban poor (some of the urban poor live in the few government-provided housing schemes or in employer-provided quarters), the reverse is not necessarily true: levels of income and quality of housing in these areas are often quite varied, and it would be wrong to portray katchi abadies as ghettos of the urban poor. Indeed, there is substantial evidence that, due to inadequate legal urban land supply, middle-class families' occupancy in katchi abadies is on the increase (Van der Linden 1990).

There is also considerable variation in terms of ethnicity and length of stay among slum residents. Obviously a big wave of immigrants settled in the late 1940s as a result of the 1947 partition of colonial India. This had an impact on settlement patterns in the inner-city areas and provided an early impetus to the emergence of katchi abadies, particularly in Karachi and Lahore. Apart from that, separate sections within katchi abadies can generally be distinguished along areas of geographical origin within present day Pakistan.

REVIEW OF AVAILABLE RESEARCH

Substantial research on slum characteristics in Karachi has been carried out in the 1960s and 1970s in a cooperation agreement between the Amsterdam Free University and Karachi University, ultimately resulting in recommendations to local agencies on slum upgrading by the mid-1970s. An upgrading policy was adopted and dovetailed with further research and technical assistance. These efforts were drastically curtailed around 1980, when it appeared at the time, that the political events prevented reasonable progress in policy implementation; even under the best of circumstances this would have been difficult in view of the linkages to overall urban and municipal government issues (Wegelin 1979). Concerns of sustainability of slum upgrading efforts led to calls for cost recovery and concern with municipal capability to manage the upgrading program. Cost recovery options related primarily to direct or indirect cost recovery related to land titling. This raised questions on the effectiveness of the land leasing process carried out by the local government as part of the upgrading program (Wegelin 1983) and the effectiveness of the property tax system (particularly in view of the outdated property valuations and numerous exemptions). Cost recovery options for chargeable services such as water supply and sewerage led to reviews of the sustainability of the city-wide water supply and sewerage service network.

Hence, one of the major lessons learnt were that slum upgrading should not be looked at and implemented in isolation from broader urban issues, such as municipal infrastructure and services delivery, municipal management and finance, and urban land management (see Schoorl, Van der Linden and Yap 1983 for an account of the research done, the areas covered, and difficulties encountered). Furthermore, it is questionable if it could be carried out successfully in isolation from issues in other sectors such as the financial sector (considering the identified constraints in housing and municipal finance). Research work on slums and slum upgrading carried out at more modest levels in other cities of Pakistan came to similar conclusions (for Lahore, see e.g., Qadeer 1983 and Kardar 1990), as did similar operational research carried out elsewhere (see UNCHS 1987, Chapter 13 for a generalized summary of findings).

Perhaps in response to this call for a broader scope of policy research and action, substantial amount of broader urban policy research has been carried out during the 1980s, the most ambitious of which undoubtedly was the National Human Settlements Policy Study, carried out for the Government of Pakistan by a local consulting firm during 1983–86 (see PEPAC 1986). This monumental study attempted to estimate the national human settlements development requirements over a 20 year time horizon, the estimated costs of various alternative development scenarios, the investment pool of resources available for urban development during this time period and attempted to determine the magnitude of any possible resource gap. The study also identified urban centers with strong potential for cost effective growth.

While the study struggled with very serious data limitations and had to make several rather heroic assumptions, its output has been used in several other, more operational studies, particularly the urban development studies carried out by the Asian Development Bank (ADB 1985 and 1986). The World Bank had carried out an earlier (1983) urban sector review study for Sindh province. Based on these sector studies both development banks supported several urban development projects in Pakistan (covering activities in Karachi, Lahore, Peshawar, and several secondary cities in the Punjab and N.W.F.P.), all of which had slum upgrading components in them, embedded in broader framework to overcome/ameliorate urban problems in the cities concerned. These projects also included further studies, addressing mostly institutional and financial weaknesses of local implementing agencies, i.e., provincial government departments, water agencies, local corporations, and development authorities. Additionally, several thematic studies were commissioned, of which a major example is the urban land management study for Karachi (1990).

Also for Karachi, a major review of its master plan had been carried out under UNCHS auspices during 1988–91 (PADCO/PEPAC 1991).

What has become clear from all these studies is the central importance of an effective urban land supply in determining settlement patterns. The serious deficiencies in urban land supply through public land development agencies in the major urban centers have contributed to rapid land price increases, and, hence, have acted as a driving force in pushing increasing segments of the urban population to informal settlement patterns (see Van der Linden [1990] for a vivid description of these processes in Lahore and Karachi).

STRATEGIES TO AMELIORATE ENVIRONMENTAL CONDITIONS IN KATCHI ABADIES

Upgrading and Regularisation

Much of the research work during the 1960s and 1970s on katchi abadies was on influencing government policy away from a legalistic approach focusing on the illegality of the settlements to an awareness that there were no realistically implementable options other than in situ area upgrading. As a matter of policy this was broadly accepted by the second half of the 1970s, but, as noted above, the practical implementation left much to be desired. Local policy perceptions at that time matched the increasing advocacy of slum upgrading by international agencies, particularly the World Bank. The Bank planned to finance one of its earlier slum upgrading projects in Lyari, Karachi from 1977 onwards, supported with advisory technical assistance provided by the Netherlands government. The project, unfortunately, was not implemented, as the Bank withdrew its support, following a disagreement with the government in early 1977 (when the project had already fully been prepared with UNDP assistance) over the project's cost recovery strategy from enhanced land lease charges. Nevertheless, it is encouraging that in spite of the political changes in Pakistan since then, the basic policy orientation has not essentially changed. A dual strategy is being implemented comprising (i) the provision of long-term leasehold tenure rights (generally for 99 years) to katchi abadi residents and, (ii) the provision of civic amenities and municipal infrastructure. In the present Seventh Five Year Plan 1988–93, attention is paid to augmenting the delivery system for such components by giving a larger role to community groups and NGOs. From the mid-1980s the implementation of this approach has been supported by the two major international development banks, i.e., the World Bank and the Asian Development Bank through projects in Karachi, Lahore (including the upgrading of Lahore's walled city), Peshawar, and secondary cities in Punjab and Northwest Frontier Province, as noted in the foregoing section.

Of the major implementation difficulties (discussed subsequently), a major problem consisted of the apparent incongruence between the need for cost recovery and the need to keep solutions affordable for the urban poor. Fuelled by populist political sentiments, this has resulted in land lease rates which do not reflect the cost of developed urban land and low tariffs for billable services such as water supply, sewerage, and solid waste removal. These were equally insufficient to cover costs of provision. This obviously adversely affects the sustainability of serviced urban land supply and the supply of the public services.

Simultaneously, the poor often pay substantially higher prices in the informal market for urban land and services (particularly water supply), indicating an ability and willingness to pay market prices (admittedly at lower consumption levels).

In an obvious situation of scarcity, the below-market administrative pricing practice is, of course, open to abuse and corruption, and leads to the emergence of middlemen, brokers, and vendors. This tends to run contrary to the ostensibly intended result, as it reduces the likelihood of the urban poor to gain adequate access to land and services. Mitra and Nientied (1989) suggest that large-scale, transparent legal provision at a cost plus price is also likely to be a cheaper solution for the katchi abadi dwellers than the present pattern of provision.

In some cities, notably Karachi, where public land-ownership is predominant (about 94 percent of urban land is in public ownership), implementation of the strategy was further hampered by the fact that the occupants who often acquired their land through the illegal land subdivision process, rightly perceived that their leaders and/or middlemen would successfully be able to use their influence to protect them from eviction (out of enlightened self-interest). Hence the occupants' perceived security of land tenure was high, even without a formal land lease title. The leasing procedure is cumbersome, requiring some nine administrative steps and the collection and preparation of a substantial number of documents in support of the lease application. These factors combined removed much of the incentive on the part of the occupants to be quick in taking out a land lease from the Karachi Metropolitan Corporation. Sultan and Van der Linden (1991) demonstrate that this affects not so much the willingness to take a lease, but rather the urgency to do so and hence the speed with which the leasing process is initiated and completed. This further weakens the cost recovery (and hence replicability) potential of the approach.

Similar problems were encountered in Lahore, but these were compounded by further delays resulting from katchi abadi land acquisition procedures, as most regularizable areas in Lahore are on private land (Kardar 1990, Chapter 15).

Nevertheless, in spite of these problems, longitudinal studies in two major katchi abadies in Karachi (see Sultan and Van der Linden 1991 for a summary review) suggest substantial positive features:

a) In both settlements, infrastructure provision improved dramatically over time, leading to improved sanitary conditions, improved health conditions, and reduced infant mortality.

b) Individual households have made substantial complementary investments in improving and extending their houses (this appears to be a common positive feature of upgrading programs as reported on in Skinner et al. 1987); partly as a result of this property values in the settlements have increased substantially, at more than double the rate of inflation, providing a significant social safety net for the owner-occupants.

c) Rental values have increased significantly too, but this has not led to an (expected) exodus of renters (who generally have a weaker socioeconomic profile than owner-occupants); more generally, turnover of population was low and not significantly different from that in other areas (this again is in keeping with results found elsewhere—see Skinner et al. 1987).

d) Ultimately residents will take leases in spite of the above cited difficulties: given the existing levels of de facto security of tenure and supply barriers, it may not have the same priority as home improvements, but a steady gradual increase in the percentage of households with leases is in evidence.

The overall picture that emerges is that of a moderate acceleration of the normal, organic process of settlement formation and consolidation. While this gradual development misses some of the cost recovery and efficiency opportunities that a more rapid and concerted approach would have offered, it has at least avoided some of the undesirable by-products, such as displacement of the poorer residents.

However, a major problem arises from the fact that a substantial segment of the country's katchi abadies is considered to be unregularizable, either for physical reasons (e.g., if located in river beds, on steep hills) or for administrative reasons (settlements established after a certain date, initially May 1978, now March 1985, are considered encroachments and therefore not regularizable). Additionally, in the upgrading process there is often a need for relocating some households which are affected by road realignments or have to make way for other infrastructural facilities in the area. While first priority would obviously be to try and relocate such households within the settlement itself, this is not always feasible.

Sites-and-Services

On both the above counts, there is need for a complementary strategy of development of new serviced sites for shelter. This approach has been tried in most of the major cities of Pakistan, but its implementation went sour on account of several reasons (see Kinhill Engineers 1990, Chapter 4; Kardar 1990, Chapters 7–10; Van der Linden 1990):

a) Lack of coordination of trunk infrastructure design with planning of individual schemes as a result of which schemes could not be provided with water and access; the resulting delays in allocation and occupation have adversely affected the cash flow of the implementing agencies which theoretically work on a 'no profit-no loss' basis.

b) Unduly high planning and infrastructure standards, leading to high cost levels per unit.

c) Administrative plot allocation policies, which resulted in (subsidized) plots ending up in the hands of land speculators rather than the displaced katchi abadi occupants.

The end result has generally been that not enough plots have been developed, that they were often in the wrong places, developed at high costs, partly occupied and pre-empted by groups for which the implicit subsidies were not intended; in the process the development agencies which relied on land development for their financial sustainability bankrupted themselves (the most notable case is that of the Karachi Development Authority, which as a result of this—largely political—mismanagement is barely able to pay its staff salaries).

For these reasons the sites-and-services approach has not, as elsewhere, been supported by international donor agencies. Particularly the World Bank and the Asian Development Bank have ongoing discussions with the government on ways to remedy the above deficiencies in the sites-and-services approach. However, as no operational agreement could be reached until recently, this has not as yet led to financial support from the international donor community.

Yet a few examples of good practice have emerged recently (e.g., Khuda ki Basti in Hyderabad—see Siddiqui and Khan 1990; Van der Linden 1992; Kalim 1983 in Karachi), which suggest that the sites-and-services approach retains its validity, but that the rules of the games should be as simple and transparent as possible to avoid the above management problems. Reforms on interagency coordination, standards, plot pricing and, allocation procedures agreed upon by the Government of Sindh and the World Bank in early 1993 in the context of the proposed Sindh Special Development Program suggest that international donor support for the sites-and-services strategy may become more likely in the near future.

Inner-City Redevelopment

To date no concerted efforts have been embarked upon to address the inner-cities' issues, except that property tax assessment has recognized the existence of the 'puggri' system in that 'puggri' payments can be incorporated in determining a property's NARV (Kalim 1988, p. 66). While a building code is in force to protect the residents, it is normally not enforced in the sense of forcing the owners to maintain and upgrade their property: rather, it is used to certify the process of decay by declaring buildings as unfit for human habitation long after such buildings have become dangerous to live in. Indeed, fatal accidents in building collapses are not uncommon in most of the cities.

CONCLUSION: THE FUTURE OF SLUM AREAS

The population dynamics in Pakistan will, for the next decades to come, ensure a continuing rapid urban population build-up. While Pakistan is fortunate in that it suffers less than other developing countries from the primacy syndrome, and therefore its population growth will be rather spatially balanced, it will still mean an urban population growth of about 4–5 percent per annum and a concomitant need to develop new shelter opportunities. Considering the strengths and weaknesses of the approaches employed by the government to meet this challenge uptill now, katchi abadi growth will continue unabated. The inner-cities' decay and reduction of residential opportunities will also continue at their current pace, as there are no realistic intervening mechanisms in place to arrest it.

The crux of the problem is the scarcity of good governance; if one may assume that this will remain a scarce commodity in years to come (and there is no reason to believe otherwise), even though some fairly radical programs to address this have been embarked on recently, like the World Bank supported Sindh Special Development Program referred to earlier, it is imperative to utilize this limited capacity in as effective a manner as possible. This will mean a reinforced emphasis on the role of the (local) government as an enabler, rather than a provider, and even this enabling role will have to be exercised with considerable restraint. The best that may be expected is that local government interventions may improve slightly and accelerate organic settlement patterns as they have unfolded during the past decades since independence.

In the area of slum upgrading this will mean a more effective and streamlined support of the informal market systems governing the establishment and consolidation of katchi abadies. This will include improved coordination with the provision of trunk infrastructure; enhancing the role of community based NGOs in infrastructure provision and increasing the role of the commercial banking system in the land leasing process and in cost recovery for billable services; and dovetailing this with improved housing (upgrading) finance options.

In new sites-and-services development the concerned government agencies and their potential clients would be better-off if the agencies would auction off conditional land development rights to the private sector. This may not be limited to conventional large tracts of virgin lands, but may also apply to 'infill' locations, and, more generally, to smaller bundles of plots than is now commonly done. Essential conditionalities would comprise adherence to a prescribed set of layout planning and engineering standards, ensuring access to trunk infrastructure, development timing, and public auctioning of serviced plots.

Both slum upgrading and sites-and-services development could be implemented much more effectively, if the urban land supply system could be made to work more transparently and quickly. As Van der Linden (1990) illustrates dramatically for Lahore and Karachi, this is an area where improved governance is needed most of all.

A reform of the property tax system (i.e., to recover costs of upgrading through capturing part of the benefits of increased land values following upgrading and to remove artificial constraints on the redevelopment of the inner-city housing stock) is long overdue: early actions required are to shift the assessment system to a capital value instead of a rental value basis, eliminate or substantially reduce the numerous exemptions, and most important of all, to embark on a massive property valuation exercise (which in view of its large-scale will have to be largely notional initially, based on selective benchmark sampling). Many of the required valuation, assessment, and collection activities can be carried out efficiently and profitably by the private sector under contract with the local government, as has been done with the collection of octroi (local import tax) in Karachi.

Particularly for the inner-cities' areas, there is no sense in retaining the (provincial) Rent Control Ordinances which are currently in force, as they do not serve any useful purpose, but merely act as a disincentive on private investment. Abolition of rent control would also create opportunities for more creative tenure arrangements in inner-cities' areas, such as tenants' cooperatives and condominium-type arrangements (Kalim 1988, pp. 68–70). This, however, will also require legislative backup which is currently absent.

NOTES

1. However, the definition of urban population as used by the Government of Pakistan is unusually wide; any community with a population of more than 5,000 inhabitants is defined as urban. Even smaller communities may be declared urban under certain conditions.

REFERENCES

Asian Development Bank. 1985. *Strategies for Economic Growth and Development—The Bank's Role in Pakistan*. Manila.
———. 1986. *Pakistan Urban Sector Profile Study*. Manila.
Government of Pakistan, Ministry of Finance. *Economic Survey 1989/90*.
International Bank for Reconstruction and Development (IBRD). 1983. *Pakistan: Sind Urban Sector Memorandum*, Report No. 4503—PAK.
———. 1985. Staff Appraisal Report, *Karachi Special Development Project*, Report No. 5772—PAK, November.
———. 1988. Staff Appraisal Report, *Punjab Urban Development Project*, Report No. 7018—PAK, March.
———. 1992. *1992 World Development Report*. Washington, D.C.
Kalim, S. Iqbal. 1983. 'Incorporating Slumdwellers into Redevelopment Schemes', in S. Angel, R.W. Archer, S. Tanpiphat and E.A. Wegelin (eds.), *Land for Housing the Poor*. Singapore: Select Books.
———. 1988. *The Inner City Tenant: The Missing Category in Housing Policy*. Working Paper No. 19, Alumni Paper Series, East–West Center Association, August.

Kardar, Shahid. 1990. 'Institutional and Legal Arrangements for Administration of Urban Land: The Case of Lahore'. Report prepared for UNCHS (Habitat).

Kinhill Engineers/NESPAK. 1990. *Karachi Urban Land Management Study*, Final Report. Karachi, December.

Linden, Jan van der. 1989. 'Rental Housing of the Urban Poor in Pakistan: Characteristics and Some Trends'. Paper prepared for the Expert Group Meeting on Rental Housing in Developing Countries, Rotterdam, October.

————. 1990. 'The Limited Impact of Some "Major Determinants" of the Land Market: Supply of Land for Housing in Lahore and Karachi, Pakistan'. Paper presented at the European Conference on Asian Studies, Amsterdam, June.

————. 1992. 'Back to the Roots: Successful Implementation of Sites-and-Services', in Kosta Mathey (ed.). *Beyond Self-help Housing*. London: Mansell, pp. 341–52.

Mitra, B.C. and **Peter Nientied**. 1989. *Land Supply and Housing Expenses for Low-income Families: A Rationale for Government Intervention*, Urban Research Working Paper No. 19. Amsterdam: Free University.

Nientied, Peter. 1987. 'Practice and Theory of Urban Policy in the Third World: Low-Income Housing in Karachi'. Ph.D. dissertation, Amsterdam: Free University.

Nientied, Peter and **Jan Van der Linden**. 1985. 'Legal and Illegal Plot Development: A Rationale for Illegal Sub-division of Land in Karachi', *Nagarlok XVIII (1)*, Jan–March, pp. 132–45.

PADCO/PEPAC. 1991. *Karachi Master Plan 2000*, Final Report.

PEPAC. 1986. 'National Human Settlements Policy Study', draft final report, Lahore.

Planning Commission. 1987. *Seventh Five Year Plan 1988–93 and Perspective Plan 1988–2003*. Islamabad: Government of Pakistan.

Quadeer, Mohammad A. 1983. *Lahore, Urban Development in the Third World*. Lahore: Vanguard Books.

Schoorl, J.W., J.Van der Linden and **K.S. Yap** (eds.) 1983. *Between Basti Dwellers and Bureaucrats—Lessons in Squatter Settlement Upgrading in Karachi*. Oxford: Pergamon Press.

Siddiqui, T.A. and **M.A. Khan**. 1990. 'Land Supply to the Urban Poor: Hyderabad's Incremental Development Scheme', in P. Baross and J. Van der Linden (eds.), *The Transformation of Land Supply Systems in Third World Cities*. Aldershot: Avebury, pp. 309–25.

Skinner, Reinhard J., John L. Taylor and **Emiel A. Wegelin** (eds.). 1987. *Shelter Upgrading for the Urban Poor—Evaluation of Third World Experience*. Manila: Island Publishing House.

Sultan, Jawaid and **Jan van der Linden**. 1991. *Squatment Upgrading in Karachi—A Review of Longitudinal Research on Policy, Implementation and Impacts*, Urban Research Working Paper No. 27, Amsterdam: Free University.

United Nations Center for Human Settlements (Habitat). 1987. *Global Report on Human Settlement 1986*. New York: Oxford University Press.

Wegelin, Emiel A. 1979. 'Slum Improvements in Karachi: Look Back in Despair', *Pakistan Economist 19 (26)*, 30 June, pp. 5–6.

————. 1983. 'The Economics of Land Tenure Regularization in Katchi Abadi Improvement', in J.W. Schoorl, J. van der Linden and K.S. Yap (eds.), *Between Basti Dwellers and Bureaucrats—Lessons In Squatter Settlement Upgrading in Karachi*. Oxford: Pergamon Press.

18

Indian Slums:
Problems, Policies and Issues

N. Sridharan

Slums and squatters have become an important component of urban planning in the Third World. Particularly in a country like India (the second
largest populated country in the world), the stagnating agricultural and
industrial sectors are pulling down the growth trends of the economy thus
pushing the rural underemployed and unemployed laborers to the urban areas
in anticipation of a better income and life-style. The urban centers, particularly the metropolitan centers of India have become enclaves of economic
power, thanks to the dualistic process of development, which attracts and
depends upon the migrated rural labor for its own day-to-day economic
survival. Thus the urban slums, in economic terms, contribute a significant
quantity of labor force to the urban labor market and generate adequate
income not only to sustain the urban economy but also to attract more and
more migrants towards these urban economic enclaves. It is not only the
rural–urban income differentials, as perceived by physical and demographic
planners, that activate the 'push' and 'pull' factors, but other factors such as
access to basic facilities and amenities, access to institutional and political
power, etc., also trigger off the rural–urban as well as the urban–urban
migration.

The present study is divided into four parts. Part I analyzes the lopsided
urbanization in India with increasing metropolitanization and the resultant
slum/squatter growth. Much research has been done on Indian slums recently, which is reviewed in Part II. Part III evaluates the government policies
and programs towards slums and squatters over the plan period. The final
part raises the policy issues which are relevant for future planning.

INDIAN URBANIZATION

The growth rate of the urban population during the decade 1981–91 has
slowed down to 36.19 percent as compared to 46.14 percent during the census
decade 1971–81. However, in terms of percentage of population living in the
urban centers there was a marginal increase in 1991 (25.72 percent) from that
of 1981 (23.34 percent). All this does not deter the extent of concentration

of urban population within the urban centers. In fact, the number of metropolitan centers (having 1,000,000 population) increased from 12 in 1981 to 23 in 1991. The extent of concentration of urban population can be seen from Table 18.1.

Table 18.1: Urban Population Concentration in India, 1901–91

Census Year	All Classes	Class I*	II*	III*	IV*	V*	VI*	Total Urban Population (in million)	% Urban to Total Population
1901	100.00 (1811)	26.00 (24)	11.29 (43)	15.64 (130)	20.83 (391)	20.14 (744)	6.10 (479)	25.85	10.84
1911	100.00 (1754)	27.48 (23)	10.51 (40)	16.40 (135)	19.73 (364)	19.31 (707)	6.57 (485)	25.94	10.29
1921	100.00 (1894)	29.70 (29)	10.39 (45)	15.92 (145)	18.29 (370)	18.67 (734)	7.03 (571)	28.08	11.18
1931	100.00 (2017)	31.20 (35)	11.65 (56)	16.80 (183)	18.00 (434)	17.14 (800)	5.21 (509)	33.45	11.99
1941	100.00 (2190)	38.23 (49)	11.42 (74)	16.35 (242)	15.78 (498)	15.08 (920)	3.14 (407)	44.15	13.86
1951	100.00 (2795)	44.63 (76)	9.96 (91)	15.72 (327)	13.63 (608)	12.97 (1124)	3.09 (569)	62.44	17.29
1961	100.00 (2270)	51.42 (102)	11.23 (129)	16.94 (437)	12.77 (719)	6.87 (711)	0.77 (172)	78.93	17.97
1971	100.00 (2476)	57.24 (148)	10.92 (173)	16.01 (558)	10.94 (827)	4.45 (623)	0.44 (147)	109.11	19.91
1981	100.00 (3245)	60.42 (216)	11.63 (270)	14.33 (738)	9.54 (1053)	3.58 (739)	0.50 (229)	159.46	23.34
1991	100.00 (3609)	65.20 (296)	10.95 (341)	13.19 (927)	7.77 (1135)	2.60 (725)	0.29 (185)	217.17	25.72

Notes: a) Figures in brackets are number of settlements in each size class.
b) Figures without bracket are percentage to total urban population.
*c) Census of India classifies a town according to population size, which are as follows:
Class I—1,00,000 & above, Class II—50,000–99,999, Class III—20,000–49,999, Class IV—10,000–19,999, Class V—5,000–9,999 and Class VI—Less than 5,000 pop.
Source: Census of India—1991. Statement 14 and 17, pp. 30 and 32.
Paper–2 of 1991, Provisional Population totals: Rural–urban distribution.

Table 18.1 shows that the number of class I towns/cities with the exception of 1911 has been steady till 1951 and thereafter increased rapidly. As many as 80 cities have been added during 1981–91 raising the number to 296 in 1991. A similar trend has been noticed in the case of cities relating to class II, III and IV. In sharp contrast, the number of class V towns which increased to 1,124 in 1951 from 744 in 1901, declined drastically to 725 in 1991. Similarly class VI towns declined to 185 in 1991.

The table also reveals that from a mere 26 percent in 1901, the percentage share of class I cities' population to total urban population has increased to 65 percent in 1991. This itself shows the predominance of class I towns among the towns. This factor is accompanied with decreasing number of class V and VI towns which in fact can act as a transit point for a rural–urban migrant. Many schemes such as Integrated Development of Small and Medium Towns (IDSMT) were envisaged during the census decade 1981–91, but the results were not fruitful.

Within the class I cities also, all of them do not have an equal amount of population living in them. The race for a predominant position continues among class I cities with the metros emerging as leaders. This is depicted in Table 18.2.

Table 18.2: Metropolitan Emergence and Concentration of
Population Within Class I Cities, 1991

Population Size	No. of Urban Agglomeration Cities	Total Population in 1991	% of Population of Class I Cities
Class I (Total)	300	1,39,730,050	100.00
M1 (Less than 200,000)	167	22,939,086	16.42
M2 (200,000–299,999)	40	9,606,814	6.88
M3 (300,000–499,999)	40	15,586,157	11.15
M4 (500,000–999,999)	30	20,936,734	14.98
M5 (1,000,000 & above)	23	70,661,259	52.57
(i) 1,000,000–1,999,999)	14	17,175,849	12.29
(ii) 2,000,000–4,999,999)	5	16,260,762	11.64
(iii) 5,000,000 & above	4*	37,224,648	28.64

* Of which two (Bombay & Calcutta) have more than 10,000,000 plus population.
Source: Cencus of India—1991, Paper 2 of 1991, Provisional Tables, p. 35.

Table 18.2 reveals that of the class I cities, metro centers, i.e., M 5 in the table, account for 52.57 percent of class I centers population. Except M1, the population concentration declines from M5 to M1. Perusal of the table also reflects the fact that out of the 23 metros in 1991, just four metros (5,000,000 and above in the table) accounted for 28.64 percent of class I cities' population. This clearly shows that even though the growth rate of urban population declined during the decade 1981–91, the heavy concentration of population in the metros continued unabated resulting in many problems such as slum formation, urban poverty and unemployment.

As the population census of India does not cover the persons living in slums, it is difficult to present the extent of population concentration in the metropolitan slums at the same point of time. No effort has been made by any local authority to systematically gather information on the growth of squatters/slum settlements and the number of people living in the slums. Only in exceptional cases as in the case of Delhi, the capital of India, efforts are made to collect such statistics due to political compulsions. The available statistics for Delhi show that (see Table 18.3) the total population increased almost six times from 1951 to 1991.

Table 18.3: Growth of Delhi's Population, 1901–91

Year	Area in Sq Km	Urban Population	% Growth
1901	43	208,575	–
1911	43	232,837	12
1921	168	304,420	31
1931	170	447,442	47
1941	170	695,686	56
1951	196	1,437,134	107
1961	326	2,359,408	64
1971	446	3,647,023	55
1981	592	5,770,000	58
1991	592	8,427,083	46

Source: Census of India, 1981 & 1991 (Prov.).

Simultaneously the number of slums increased by a little over twenty times during the same period (see Table 18.4).

Table 18.4: Growth of Slums in Delhi

Year	No. of Slums[†]	Percentage Growth
1951	12,749	–
1956	22,415	76
1961	42,815	91
1966	42,668	–0
1971	62,594	47
1973	98,438	57
1977	20,000[*]	–392
1981	98,709	394
1983	129,000	31
1985	150,000	16
1987	171,000	14
1988	210,000	23
1991	259,344	23

[†] Can be counted as number of slum households.
[*] The decrease is due to large-scale slum clearance.
Source: Delhi Development Authority, 1992, 'Growth of Slums in Delhi', New Delhi (mimeo.).

Similarly in Dar-es-Salaam, the slum population accounted for 34 percent even before the 1970s. The situation in Latin American countries was no better with the proportion of slum population ranging from 10 percent to 50 percent or more. Moreover, Delhi's case clearly shows that socioeconomic aspects outweigh other aspects in slum location/formation. To illustrate, in Delhi, of the five major planning zones, a heavy concentration of slums is found in the South and North zones where the major employment centers are located (see Table 18.5). This clearly shows that along with the heavy concentration of slums in the metros, within the metro too, employment centers attract and act as a catalyst for slum concentration. This science is not at all different in other metro centers.

Table 18.5: Zonewise Position of Slums

Zone	No. of Slum Clusters	Average Slums/Clusters	No. of Slums in the Cluster
East zone	123	341	41,958
Central zone	93	235	21,877
North zone	227	290	65,901
West zone	204	209	42,573
South zone	282	309	87,305
Total	929	1,384	2,59,614

Source: DDA, Slum Wing, May 1992.

A recent study of Asia's biggest slum 'Dharavi' in Bombay shows that Dharavi is vibrant with all its daily sociocultural and economic activities and this one slum alone accommodates for almost 60 percent of Bombay's population.[1] In Calcutta, another million plus city, a study conducted by the Calcutta Metropolitan Development Authority shows that almost 50 percent of the pavement dwellers are located in the Central Business District (CBD).[2] All this reaffirms the fact that the metropolitan economy offers a better prospect for the rural migrants in terms of employment, income, and other important aspects of life.

REVIEW OF EARLIER STUDIES

Unfortunately, even the tests for identifying a slum in India were those prescribed by the Association of Public Housing Authorities of America.[3] The Supreme Court,[4] the highest judiciary body of India, fixing the responsibility of providing the housing on the government, reiterated that 'if the government cannot provide *pucca* houses to the people, they have the liberty to live wherever they can and in whatever way they can'. In fact, the political sensitivity of the slums guides the policy approaches that are required for slum improvement, relocation, etc. A recent (August 1992) decision of the Delhi administration, the decision making authority on Delhi's fate, is a pertinent example of this political sensitivity. The slums of Delhi hitherto looked after by the slum wing of Delhi Development Authority (DDA), an autonomous body with full powers to plan and implement programs on slums, was shifted from DDA to Delhi Administration under the control of the Lieutenant Governor of Delhi. This decision was made considering the approaching election for the Delhi metropolitan council in which the slums form the vote banks for different parties. Naturally, unplanned and ad hoc provision of some basic services in the slums will bring back some more votes to the parties concerned. Another study,[5] criticizing the relocation policy of the government observes that 'the policy ignored the Indian climate and way of living'. It further states that the voice of reason has not found favor and crores of rupees are still being dumped in fruitless projects.

A series of research studies (1990) sponsored by Human Settlement Management Institute were conducted by Neelima Risbud,[6] Meera and Dinesh Mehta,[7] Vijay Jagannathan and Animesa Halder,[8] Solomon Benjamin,[9] and Mulkh Raj and Banashree Mitra[10] looked into the income, employment, and housing linkages. However, these studies restricted their proposals to physical planning approach and fell short of an integrated approach to the slum problem. Andrea Menefee Singh and Alfred De Souza's study (1980) of the urban poor in major cities of India was in fact the first exercise on slums at such a macro level, putting together almost all aspects of the slum problem.

However, the findings of any of these studies did not get reflected in the official documents in the form of policy statements. The government policy on clearance remained the same. Many of these studies fall short as they analyzed only the economic or social or physical aspect of the slum life and none of them came out with an integrated solution.

GOVERNMENT'S APPROACH

The Government of India, rather than evolving a policy of its own towards the slum, was heavily dependent upon the experiences of other countries in dealing with the slum problem. Unfortunately, the land of millions, never had a housing policy till recently. The first ever Draft National Housing Policy[11] announced in 1988, has already seen through three revisions clearly indicating the ad hocism in policy planning towards housing in general and slums in particular. This is party due to the low priority given to housing and urban development in the Five Year Plans of India. Except in the Fifth Five Year Plan (4.3 percent) none of the Five Year Plans allocated more than four percent of the total planned outlay to urban development which includes housing (see Table 17.6). As regards housing, hardly one percent or little more than one percent is allocated, which got reflected in the growing housing shortage and increasing slums in the urban areas of India. Added to this, provision of housing was thought of to be the duty of the government only and not enough encouragement was given to private initiatives in this area. Only of late (1988), tax concessions were given for investment on housing. In the existing administrative set-up, housing comes under the state list, i.e., to be looked after by the state governments and not by the center. This division of responsibility enshrined in the Constitution protects the center in not allocating much to housing and the resource crunch faced by the state governments all the more neglects housing in this set-up. As regards policy towards slums and squatters, the Government of India started off with a negative approach of slum clearance way back in the First Five Year Plan (1951–56) which continues in one form or the other even now. In fact the percentage outlay allocated for slum clearance gradually increased to as high as 19 percent in the Fourth Five Year Plan and thereafter heavy emphasis was given to organized sector housing, i.e., housing for regular salary earners according to their income group, rental housing schemes, police housing, industrial workers' housing, etc. thereby relegating the slum problem to the background.

Under the Slum Clearance Scheme (May 1956), state governments were required to acquire slum areas for demolition and clearance. To begin with, the slum clearance effort was mainly concentrated in six cities, viz., Bombay, Calcutta, Delhi, Madras, Kanpur, and Ahmedabad. However, from the Third Five Year Plan, it was proposed that slum clearance and improvement work could be taken up wherever the state government considered a slum problem existed in an acute form. The entire scheme was carried on till the Supreme Court stalled the Bombay Municipal Corporation's move to clear the slums of Bombay in the late 1980s. However, none of the states could succeed in implementing this scheme because of (*i*) the delay in acquiring slum areas; (*ii*) nonavailability of alternative sites near the places of work; and (*iii*) the increasing cost of dislocation for the poor. In fact the poor slum-dwellers suffered in two ways. On the one hand, their travel time and cost increased because of dislocation, and on the other hand, their earnings got reduced due to decreased working hours. This was seldom understood by the physical planners.

While the First and the Second Plan considered slums as a housing problem of low-income groups and thus designed social housing schemes and also adopted legislative measures for slum clearance and prevention, the Third Plan indicated a change of strategy. As per the global thinking on 'low cost housing' to meet the housing demand of the low-income group, the Indian government also thought that by reducing the design/space standards, the cost would automatically decrease, to be affordable by the slum-dwellers.

Unfortunately, thereafter the physical planning strategies designed for Delhi, the capital of India, were blindly followed by other urban centers of India irrespective of their applicability. The Third Plan stressed that the housing standards be reviewed to bring them within the reach of low-income groups.

The Fourth Plan (1969–74) continued with the earlier approach towards slums in the first two years of the plan period. However, for the first time it was accepted by the planners that the slum clearance approach would not be effective and it would be necessary to try and ameliorate the living conditions of slum-dwellers as an immediate measure. For this the Calcutta Bustee Improvement programs were taken as a model to be followed in other urban centers of India. The Calcutta Bustee (Slum) Improvement program was directed towards economic regeneration of the city within the limited resources and to optimize the use of such resources. This program closely followed the approaches experimented with in Columbia, like 'Barrio Popular' which entirely changed the earlier thinking on slums. In consonance with this, a new scheme at the national level called Environmental Improvement of Slums (1972) was initiated. This was accompanied by the World Bank sponsored scheme of Integrated Urban Development Program (1974) which considered slums as a part of the total development of the metro centers. Though the employment generation aspect of slum development has been incorporated in the successive development plans prepared by the World Bank initiated Urban Development Programs, for cities like Madras Metropolitan Area, Kanpur, etc., not much progress has been made in this regard.

The Fifth Plan, in order to evolve a healthier pattern of human settlements advocated an Integrated Urban Development Program. The scheme suggested the state governments to establish development authorities in order to undertake self-generating and self-financing urban development. Central government through the state governments provided the seed capital for developing a revolving fund which could be utilized for land acquisition, etc. This direct intervention in the land market by the development authorities for monopoly gains resulted in further segregation and neglect of the poor. In fact this kind of large-scale acquiring, developing, and disposition of land is somewhat unique at least in the Asian context.

Yet another scheme, viz., Integrated Development of Small and Medium Towns (IDSMT) was introduced in the Sixth Five Year Plan in order to tackle the macro issues of rural to urban and urban to urban migrations and to reduce the dependency on metros. Under the scheme, the central government extended a loan to the state governments on a matching basis for development on infrastructure and to provide economic momentum in the small and medium towns. Selection of the towns was left to the state authorities. The entire scheme was to be implemented by the local authorities. The initial outlay for the scheme was Rs. 96 crores which was reduced to Rs. 88 crores under the Seventh and Eighth Plans. A quick look at the data available shows that Rs. 56.83 crores released during the Sixth Plan was for the development of 235 towns in 24 states and union territories. A sum of Rs. 75.30 crores released by the center in the first four years of the Seventh Plan could cover only 145 towns. The number of towns to be covered during 1992–93 and the remaining part of the Eighth Plan would still be fewer in view of the costs going up and the allocations not being enhanced. The maximum benefit from the scheme appears to have been derived by Tamil Nadu, Madhya Pradesh, and Maharashtra which were highly urbanized. With an inflation rate of around 12 to 15 percent per annum and reducing budgetary allocation, the per capita availability of funds for a town and its effective utilization is nullified. Neither the scheme could check the rate of migration nor could it provide employment opportunities to the poor in the small and medium sized towns.

In the Seventh Five Year Plan period, it was felt that more assistance had to be given to the urban poor in order to upgrade their quality of life, especially the women and children. A new program called The Urban Basic Services (UBS) was launched in 1986 as a centrally sponsored scheme with UNICEF assistance. The most crucial element in the UBS program is financial and technical assistance of the UNICEF in its design and execution. The UNICEF assistance was available only to those towns, where:

1. the target slum population is at least 10,000;
2. urbanization rate is disturbing and basic services are not available to a large segment of the slum population; and,
3. state and municipal authorities are in agreement to provide counterpart resources and sufficient supervisory and infrastructural facilities including the assignment of a senior municipal officer to manage the implementation of the project

What singles out UBS strategy from others is its stress on community participation and people's involvement in their own development. A recent study (Town and Country Planning Organisation 1989) highlighted the following issues:

1. In several states program implementation was delayed unnecessarily due to reasons ranging from nonrelease of funds by the state governments to nonapproval of supervisory posts.
2. Delays also occurred as a result of the state governments not being prepared psychologically and attitudinally to undertake such a participatory

program. In fact, none of the earlier plans or programs had considered the concept of people's participation particularly the urban poor's participation. The new philosophy of working with the poor rather than working for them envisaged in the UBS received limited acceptance by the planners and the administrators.

3. Lack of municipal support was an evident constraint in several districts. The municipalities lacked staff, capacity, and finance to get the program going.

4. District administration also concentrated on the program implementation to district headquarters rather than taking the program to other urban centers.

5. Institutional reviews seem to be biased towards examining fund utilization and visible output activities such as water supply and sanitation, at the expense of more long term gains that can be obtained if Neighborhood Committees are properly organized, energized and supported. Neighborhood Committees are the pivot of the UBS strategy. If this pivot is not energized the strategy of working with the urban poor will fall apart.

This quick evaluation shows that even the programs directly meant for the urban slum-dwellers could not be implemented smoothly due to the poor recognition of the authorities about the ability and innovativeness of the slum-dwellers in organizing themselves. The slum-dwellers are often looked down upon as consumers of services rather than as producers. Even in the first interministerial meeting on urbanization in Asia and the Pacific region held in Bangkok on 1 November, 1993, the Indian housing and urban development minister reiterated that 'too much involvement by NGOs in direct decision making might delay decisions'. This itself reveals the official thinking towards popular participation.

Apart from this scheme which was meant to tackle the problems of the urban poor, the government of India, for the first time since the beginning of the planning process, introduced the National Housing Policy in 1988 which aimed at providing housing for all by the year 2000. Considering the acuteness of the housing problem and the resource constraints, the housing policy recognized for the first time the slums as a form of informal housing and outlined policies to organize and equip them with all necessary infrastructural facilities. However, the access of the urban poor to institutional finance for home upgradation for constructing informal houses was not incorporated even in the successive changes that were brought into the policy. A National Housing Bank (NHB) was set up on the lines of the housing banks in Latin American countries, thanks to the housing policy recommendations.

NHB too addressed itself to formal organized sector housing finance requirements, leaving the slum-dwellers where they were. The informal financial circuits for housing were never given due weightage by the policy makers. Neither was the land policy amended to recognize informal housing. This further widened the gap in the society between the rich and the poor. The rich consisting of middle- and high-income groups were given tax concessions, access to institutional finance, etc., for constructing or acquiring their own house. On the other hand the poor neither had the access to housing finance nor were their existing housing considered legal. Even in the changed set-up, the urban slum-dwellers remained where they were and their quality of life seemed to be deteriorating.

The National Commission on Urbanization set up during the Seventh Five Year Plan also looked into the problem of housing the slum-dwellers. The Commission's report (pp. 17–18) submitted in 1988 had the following recommendations for housing the urban poor:

1. Housing policy must aim at increasing the supply of serviced land and low cost shelter, improving and upgrading slums and conserving the existing stock.

2. The State must facilitate housing and ensure access to basic inputs. It should not become a real estate developer.

. 3. The sites and services program should be extended to cover an entire cross-section of society. Besides providing housing, the program should be used to generate employment.

4. Public agencies in the housing sector should be restructured for fulfillment of their new role as facilitators rather than providers of housing.

Incidentally, the Commission's recommendations have yet to be accepted and acted upon. Still, it is sad that even the National Commission on Urbanization desisted from spelling out clear-cut policies towards housing the urban poor. In the new role recommended for public agencies, the urban poor can hardly get any benefit in terms of housing or access to urban employment market. With these kinds of policies and programs towards the slum-dwellers, one wonders, how the objective of 'Housing for all by 2000' is to be fulfilled. The slum-dwellers' plight continues to remain as it was before depending upon the local political exigencies. With the global fever of privatization already imported in the Indian economic scene, the slum-dwellers can hardly have any access to the profit oriented high cost housing market.

POLICY ISSUES

The planning issues involved in slum development are many, as the problems themselves are many and complicated. The solution required is an 'integrated one' which can encompass social, physical, and economic aspects of improving the quality of life of the slum-dwellers. The issues identified are grouped into preventive aspects and curative aspects. The preventive aspects cover the population policy vis-a-vis industrial policy and the overall policy towards housing and poverty alleviation. The curative measures include, among other things, environmental education, developing informal and formal financial systems to finance the economic activities and housing, community participation and provision of infrastructural facilities.

Preventive Aspects

It is worth reiterating that by the turn of this century India's population is expected to cross the 1 billion mark and the target of bringing down the population growth rate to 1.2 percent by then will certainly elude the planners. For years, the government has been putting the cart before the horse, as it were, hoping that population control can be achieved separately and even without literacy and development. It has stubbornly refused to learn not only from the demographic patterns in other countries but also from the examples of some of our own states like Kerala and Tamil Nadu—that population cannot be controlled in a vacuum, that it necessarily follows industrialization and development, urbanization, literacy, and increasing female employment. Though many studies have proved that the population growth rate among the poor is high no systematic effort has been made to bring the poor under the population planning program. Unfortunately, as stated earlier, the family planning programs were implemented in isolation without integrating them with the literacy mission or employment programs. Without an integrated approach, i.e., integrating at least literacy programs with family planning programs, the population of India cannot be controlled. Similarly there is need to have a proper settlement policy. Till 1988, there was no policy on urbanization or the urban settlement pattern. Again, to control rural-urban migration and slum formation in urban centers, proper settlement policy and its integration with industrial policy is a must.

Since the Second Five Year Plan, the industrial policy oriented itself towards large-scale, public sector-based industrialization. The successive industrial policies brought in more and more controls. This restricted the scope of formal sector employment, particularly the industrial sector employment, resulting in the growth of informal sector, with its vicious cycle of low productivity, low income, low savings and low-level of employment genera-tion. The recent policy spelt out in July 1991 and its subsequent changes ushered in the process of industrialization in India into a new era based on hi-tech orientation and liberalization attracting more foreign investments directly to the urban centers. Thus the major metros in India are already in the process of becoming global economic centers attracting more and more labor from the hinterland. Unless the policy orients itself towards industrial decentralization, the metro centers with their increasing slum population will become unlivable. Simultaneously, a proper fillip has to also be given to the employment generation programs in the rural areas as well as in the lower order urban settlements.

The National Housing Policy which is being revised should also consider the informal houses as a national asset instead of treating them as waste generated from urban development. The earlier Draft Policy just paid a lip service to the problem of slum housing. The policy adopted towards the slum has seldom been changed in the successive policies and all the major housing development agencies and the urban development authorities follow the same old approach of relocation, demolition, etc. Unfortunately, even the recently prepared (1990) Perspective Plan—2001, for Delhi also outlined the same old strategy of slum relocation and resettlement as one of its measures towards slum development.

Even the low cost housing solutions prepared by the government spon-sored research centers like Central Building Research Institute (CBRI) or by the nongovernmental organizations could not be implemented to solve the housing problem of the poor in general and slum-dwellers in particular, because of the big industrial lobby which influences the widespread use of concrete structures based on cement, rather than clay or other materials of building construction. Unless the government comes forward to build low cost houses by improving the very same material which the slum-dwellers use at present, the housing problem of the slum-dwellers cannot be solved and even if it is solved it will be at a cost that cannot be acquired by the slum-dwellers.

So far, except through official statistics, the extent of urban poverty is not known. The government figures give only the quantity of population living below the poverty line and safely omit the qualitative aspects of poverty. The so-called urban and rural poverty alleviation programs are implemented only through government departments or through banking sectors which are famous for their bureaucratic delays and corruptions. Moreover, the an-tipoverty programs give the beneficiary a certain amount of money which the beneficiary is supposed to utilize for productive purposes and to generate adequate income to come out of the clutches of poverty. Many studies on antipoverty programs had shown that the beneficiaries did slide back to the below poverty level condition. To set it right, the urban as well as the rural poverty programs are to be linked with manpower policy and adequate training should be given to carry out the economic activities and to generate a continuous income. Moreover, it is necessary to organize the beneficiaries by directly assisting them, thereby avoiding the middlemen. This will improve the living conditions of the poor in the rural areas and detract them from migrating to the urban areas. In the urban areas, though the government has come out with many schemes such as the Self-Employment Program for the Urban Poor (SEPUP) and the Self-Employment scheme for Urban Youth (SEUY), its spatial spread is restricted and often the slum-dwellers are sidelined due to security for loan and other procedural problems. There is an urgent need to revamp the credit delivery system for supporting the informal sector in the urban areas. Starting of small banks, on the lines of world women's banks, and its effective linkage with decentralized centers could go a long way in assisting the informal sector, thereby improving the economic and social condition of the slum-dweller.

CURATIVE ASPECTS

The first and foremost aspect is that of community organization. This along with people's participation dictates the social and economic survival of the slum. The smooth social fabric is often disturbed by the state sponsored slum development and slum relocation. Before initiating any kind of slum development, the slum to be affected should be thoroughly studied and the leaders within the slums should be consulted for the type of development they require. Experiences in Hyderabad (India) and other slum clusters in Delhi (particularly in a slum in south Delhi called Ekta Vihar) show that upgradation through community organization and people's participation yields very good results. Nongovernmental organizations play a vital role in community organization and environmental education. The government should facilitate these organizations by increasing their activities and give funds to them for carrying out any improvement in the slums.

As the income increases the slum-dwellers can afford to pay for the services at least marginally. Mostly the slum-dwellers prefer the community level facilities and services rather than going for private ones. Considering this, the government should initiate different levels to provide services and facilities after undertaking thorough survey of the existing slums and slum dwellers' affordability. Some kind of a levy or a tax or user charge can be thought of at the community level for the community level services provided to them. The local government should utilize the sum thus collected only for slum improvement and should not divert it to other uses.

Land tenure is the major issue in slum development. Close attention must be paid to the legal and administrative aspects along with the political situation before initiating policies directed towards the slums.

Definitely these issues are not exhaustive as there can be many types of slums and many kinds of solutions to their problems. However, the approach to the problem of slum development will remain the same in the Third World in general.

NOTES

1. For a detailed description on Dharavi slum see 'A Slum like No Other' by Christopher Thomas (1992).
2. See for detailed information (Jagannathan and Halder 1990).
3. Till the time Indian government enacted the Slum Clearance Act in the early 1970s, it followed the American standard for identifying the slum.
4. See S.R.O. 1252, Slum Clearance Act schedule, 24 February 1959, 6 July 1960 and 2 March 1963, Table 1. In fact by using the definition stated in this report, the Government Gazetteer of India notified the entire walled city of Delhi and its surroundings as slums. After the master plan exercise this was the first area to be declared as a slum in India.
5. See the paper 'Delhi forever Slums' prepared and presented by N. Chakravarthy and Om Mathur in a national seminar on Housing & Slums way back in 1971 (mimeo copy available with the Delhi Development Authority) for details. However, neither this seminar nor the subsequent court verdicts controlled the demolishing act of the Development Authority. In fact, at one point of time, Delhi Development Authority was nicknamed as Delhi Demolishing Authority due to its policy towards slums and squatters.
6. For details see Risbud (1990).
7. For details see Mehta and Mehta (1990).
8. More analytical work has been done by Jagannathan and Halder (1990).
9. A good case study of Delhi's resettlement colony has been done by Solomon Benjamin. It was published in *Housing and Income Linkages in Third World Urban Development.*
10. Again the authors provide us with a thoroughly analytical case study from Delhi, though it discusses many issues related to income generation and home based economic activity. The policy implications of this study were too sketchy. This study was also published in *Housing and Income Linkages in Third World Urban Development.*
11. In fact even this policy was formulated only because of international compulsions and assistance for housing programs. The policy towards slums and squatters was not openly stated in the Draft Housing Policy and only in the subsequent changes some kind of approach has been outlined.

REFERENCES

Basu, Ashok Ranjan. 1988. *Urban Squatter Housing in the Third World.* Delhi: Mittal Publications.

Chakravarty, N. and Om Mathur. 1971. 'Delhi for Ever Slum'. Paper presented at the National Seminar on Housing and Slums, 24–25 July, Delhi Development Authority, Delhi.

Christopher, Thomas. 1992. 'Dharavi—A Slum Like No Other', *India Magazine 12 (10)*, pp. 28–29, September, Bombay.

Government of India. 1988. 'Draft National Housing Policy', Ministry of Urban Development and Housing, New Delhi, May.

Government of India, Ministry of Urban Development. 1988. 'Report of the National Commission on Urbanization'.

Government of India, Town and Country Planning Organisation. 1989. 'Final Report and Recommendations on Urban Basic Services Program'. New Delhi: Town and Country Planning Organization.

Government of India. *Census of India 1991*. Provisional Population Tables', Paper 1&2 of 1992, Registrar General of India, New Delhi.

Jagannathan, N.V. and **Animesh Halder**. 1990. 'Income and Housing Linkages—A Case Study of Pavement Dwellers in Calcutta', in Mulkh Raj and Peter Nientied (eds.), *Housing and Income in Third World Urban Development*. New Delhi: Oxford and IBH.

Kar, G.C. 1988. 'Economics of Housing: A Case Study', *Indian Institute of Town Planners Journal 29 (2)*, June, pp. 50–52.

Kundu, Amitab. 1991. 'Mixed Environment in Urban Planning—Access of the Poor to Water Supply and Sanitation', *Economic and Political Weekly 26 (37)*, pp. 2167–71.

Lal, Vinay D. 1987. 'National Housing Policy—Building Blocks for Housing', *Economic Times*, 31 March, New Delhi.

Mathur, D.D. 1992. 'Encroachment on Public Lands', *Institute of Town Planners Journal 10 (4)*, June, p. 150.

Mehta, Meera and **Dinesh Mehta**. 'Home Up-gradation and Income Generation from Housing', in Mulkh Raj and Peter Nientied (eds.), *Housing and Income Generation in Third World Urban Development*. New Delhi: Oxford & IBH, pp. 82–115.

Mulkh Raj and **Banashree Mitra**. 1990. 'Households, Housing and Homebased Economic Activities in Low Income Settlements', in Mulkh Raj and Peter Nientied (eds.), *Housing and Income Generation in Third World Urban Development*. New Delhi: Oxford & IBH, pp. 116–34.

Ribero, Edger F.N. 1989. Delhi—2001—Emerging Issues for Housing Development', (mimeo.), Delhi Development Authority.

Risbud, Neelima. 1990. 'Housing and Income Generating Policies for the Urban Poor—Linkages and Limitations (A Case Study of Madhya Pradesh)', in Mulkh Raj and Peter Nientied (eds.), *Housing and Income Generation in Third World Urban Development*. New Delhi: Oxford & IBH, pp. 135–66.

Sandhu, Ranvinder S. 1989. *The City and Its Slums—A Sociological Study*. Amritsar: Guru Nanak Dev University.

Singh, Andrea Menefee and **Alfred De Souza**. 1980. *The Urban Poor—Slum and Pavement Dwellers in Major Cities of India*. Delhi: Manohar Publications.

Solomon, J. Benjamin.. 1990. 'Income and Housing—Understanding Household Productivity within the framework of Urban Structuring', in Mulkh Raj and Peter Nientied (eds.), *Housing and Income Generation in Third World Urban Development*. Oxford & IBH, pp. 167–90.

Sridharan, N. and **R.A. Dongre**. 1992. 'Tale of Four Cities—QOL in Metro Slums'. Unpublished.

Town and Country Planning Organisation. 1989. 'Final Report and Recommendations on Urban Basic Services Program'. New Delhi: Government of India.

Urban Development, Ministry of. 1988. 'Report of the National Commission on Urbanisation'. Government of India.

World Bank. 1989. 'Coping with Involuntary Resettlement'. *The Urban Edge 13(2)*, March.

PART V

CONCLUSION: DIRECTIONS FOR THE FUTURE

Charles L. Choguill, in Chapter 19, summarizes the various attempts at solving the problem of housing poverty in the Third World in the last 40 years. He clearly shows the global trends from one set of assumptions and practices to the next— from clearance and relocation to sites-and-services to upgrading. The World Bank has been a major player in this process and has carried a world of consultants and experts with it. Choguill concludes, however, as has the World Bank as described in Chapter 2, that planners and technicians have to have the skills of a community organizer if rehousing projects are to succeed. The reason for this conclusion is that international agencies and national governments have learned that top-down imposed bureaucratic and technically proficient solutions have not saved the day. On the contrary, such approaches have proved to be substantially ineffective. The shift in emphasis is now to the recognition of the key role of the local participants in the process: local governments as enablers, local neighborhood residents as facilitators, and local entrepreneurs as providers of cost-effective solutions.

PART V

CONCLUSION:
DIRECTIONS FOR THE FUTURE

19

The Future of Planned Urban Development in the Third World: New Directions

Charles L. Choguill

Over the last 40 years, there has been an enormous increase in the level of urbanization in the Third World. Whereas in 1950, less than 300 million people in developing countries lived in urban areas, by 1985 this figure had reached 1.1 billion. Estimates for the year 2000 suggest that nearly 1.9 billion people in developing countries will live in towns and cities, representing two-thirds of the world's urban population (United Nations Center for Human Settlements 1987, p. 23).

The results of this massive growth have, and will continue to be, profound. It is expected that by the year 2000, eight of the 10 largest urban agglomerations will be in the developing world. By that time there is no reason to doubt that the largest of the agglomerations would have assumed gargantuan proportions, with Mexico City approaching 26 million, Sao Paulo at 24 million and Bombay and Calcutta both having populations of over 16 million. Although actual urban growth rates are declining, given the growing size of the base upon which such percentages are calculated, the actual numbers involved in urban growth are still extremely large.

This urban growth results in a number of serious problems. These include high-levels of urban unemployment and underemployment, extreme pressures upon urban services and infrastructure, congestion, pollution as well as other forms of environmental deterioration, and significant shortfalls in the provision of housing for new urban residents.

Over the last 30 years, shelter has frequently been viewed as the primary weapon in the Third World's fight to improve living conditions among this rapidly growing number of urban poor. As a result, a bewildering array of policies have been initiated in various countries as a means of improving the size of the housing stock, almost all with disappointing results. Consequently, recent urban development programs appear to be moving in new directions, with increasing emphasis being placed on the provision of low cost infrastructural schemes, and as a result, environmental improvements.

The purpose of this chapter is to examine the processes that have been followed to meet the challenge of rapid urban growth and to explore the success of such processes. This in turn may well have implications for the skills required of planners who will be working in the developing world in future.

HOUSING POLICY FOR DEVELOPMENT

Prior to the 1960s, development economists gave a fairly low priority to housing issues in the national development planning process. The reason for this was straightforward: the sector was considered to be unproductive. Instead, such economists favored investment priorities which were directed at industry, energy generation, and transport, sectors which were viewed as growth generating and hence able to pay for themselves over time.

In the 1960s, however, the low priority according to housing began to change, although this did not necessarily mean that more housing would result. Although we can see the contributions of people like Charles Abrams (1964) beginning to emerge into the urbanization and housing debate, the loudest voice heard was far more likely to be that of Oscar Lewis (1951, 1961, 1966), the American anthropologist who was interested in determining how individuals at the very bottom of the economic pecking order viewed their position and the future that they saw for themselves and their children. Most of us are familiar with Lewis' concept of the 'culture of poverty', with the attendant characteristics of fatalism, helplessness, dependence, and inferiority. Certainly his suggestions had enormous appeal for those governments which had little intention of doing anything for the poor anyway as it provided an apparent reason for their inaction but this also appealed to the wealthy elites who sought justification for their own position. After all, carried to extreme, the arguments concerned with the culture of poverty suggested that the poor were poor because they were poor and it was their fault. Only an irresponsible government, it was argued, would spend scarce resources on such a group to provide them with housing when the money could be spent on nation building investments such as industry and transportation systems.

By the late 1960s, however, housing policy with respect to the poor was clearly in a transitional stage. Largely as a result of the studies and contributions by John Turner (1967, 1976) and William Mangin (1963, 1967), the ideas concerned with the culture of poverty, although very influential in their effect upon development aid policy of certain donors, were relatively short-lived. The Turner and Mangin arguments are well-known. This dynamic duo argued that the poor were just as rational as the middle- and upper-income classes in terms of their response to a situation, but that the squatter shack which had been viewed by Lewis as an evidence of social malaise, was in fact a rational step on the way to self-improvement. Turner argued strongly that if the poor could be given security of tenure for a plot of land in a favorable location, then through progressive improvement the squatter shack would be transformed into a respectable house and would represent the savings of the particular family involved.

To the governments of developing countries which were faced with almost daily demands by the poor to do something to improve their situation, the arguments of Turner and Mangin had tremendous appeal. Clearly self-improvement implied self-help and to many governments, self-help is a free good. Such policies seemed to offer to hard pressed governments a way of solving housing problems on the cheap. Any government, regardless of whether it is of a developed or developing country, places very high priority on anything that can be done on the cheap.

Theoretical ideas appeal tremendously to academics, but have little relevance for governments and aid agencies. Before self-help could fulfil its role as the facilitator of housing provision, it was necessary to incorporate it into some kind of a concrete housing policy. As Abrams (1964, p. 174) had suggested as early as 1964, and in fact other writers had suggested even earlier, one proposed way of obtaining these advantages was through the design of sites-and-services projects. Schemes of this kind involve the provision of tracts of urban land which are divided into plots and provided with basic supporting services. A title to the plots could be either sold or leased to those who wished to build their own houses on them. The World Bank became deeply involved in supporting sites-and-services schemes throughout the developing world and by 1983, had funded more than 70 such projects (Cohen 1983, p. 91).

In retrospect, it is clearly obvious that the major advantage of the sites-and-services approach may have been that it provided quite an economic way of formally shifting the housing burden from the government, which had not coped with it very well anyway, to the households in need of shelter who had traditionally been the key movers in the field.

Certain inherent disadvantages became associated with the approach of sites-and-services as well. Almost inevitably, the most significant of these had to do with costs.

THE PROBLEM OF COST

Once it is realized that the World Bank was involved in sites-and-services schemes, it should come as no surprise to learn that full cost recovery became a central principle in the design of shelter projects for the urban poor as this is one of the golden tenets of the World Bank for any of its lending projects. It follows as well, that approaches to the reduction of various costs concerned with such programs would become increasingly important as the development of this particular approach to shelter provision progressed.

A central issue in the cost recovery/cost control processes was the problem of building standards. The problem of setting standards is a long-standing issue in most developing countries and in fact one still finds standards currently in use in certain countries, particularly in the British Commonwealth, which date back to colonial times and all too often reflect the present day standards in use by the former colonizer. Although most analysts may agree that standards of some sort are required for fire prevention, public health, structural safety, and possibly aesthetics, apparently very few seem to realize that as standards rise, so do costs. Whereas developed countries may well be able to afford high standards in construction and layout to achieve perfectly understandable aims, it does not necessarily follow that a Third World nation should adopt these Western standards which might be totally inappropriate to its own climatic, cultural, and economic circumstances (Mabogunje, Hardoy and Misra 1978).

The result of the imposition of such standards inevitably means that costs begin to rise. As this occurs, it becomes increasingly difficult for poor families, the target group for such shelter provisions, to meet the repayments required under full cost recovery policies and as a result, their hold on such property is in jeopardy. In one sense, in cases of this sort, the entire issue is related to the degree of involvement of the government. Recall that at the beginning of the sites-and-services discussion, it was pointed out that self-help could be viewed as one way for governments to avoid any involvement in the housing provision. However, once self-help becomes institutionalized, very often the government agencies feel that the people involved in conceiving the houses and providing the self-help to build them cannot possibly do it without some sort of guidance from above. Once a government begins to get its fingers into the pie, these costs begin to rise with dire consequences. From the point of view of the poor, two extreme points along this continuum of possible points of government involvement would seem to be optimal. The first of these, at one extreme of the continuum, is for governments to build the houses and give them to the poor free of charge. The second point on the continuum, at the opposite extreme and no doubt somewhat less desirable to recipients, is for the government to stay out of the shelter provision altogether and to merely let people get on with providing their own houses with guarantees of secure tenure. To governments, on the other hand, although the former may be financially unfeasible, the latter seems to be bureaucratically undesirable. The result is a middle of the continuum compromise which increases costs but puts constraints on the freedom of the people involved.

It is the land standards that seem to cause one of the most serious cost problems associated with projects of this type. In low-income housing projects which are organized by the government, plot sizes are frequently larger than necessary as planners wish to avoid the potential criticism of building slums. There also seems to be a tendency for the land provision to be designed not for the low cost structures being built at the time, but for some imaginary standard twenty years in the future. As a result, too much land is used and land prices are bid. Although the cost of land as a percentage of total housing cost per unit varies widely, it can be substantial. As Grimes (1976, p. 43) has noted, 'cost breakdowns for middle- and low-income housing in selected cities—Ahmedabad, Hong Kong, Madras, Mexico City, Nairobi, and Seoul—of developing countries demonstrate that land makes up 12 to 46 percent of the total cost for a single family public housing unit and from 2 to 15 percent for multifamily units'.

Another problem sometimes occurs if land standards are set too high. In central city areas, pressure on the poor on existing land resources is usually the greatest due to their understandable desire to be near the employment opportunities that exist at those points. Projects in such areas which provide excessive plot sizes often result in the residents subdividing the plots by themselves and renting or selling them to others. This is particularly dangerous when full economic costs are charged for the plot. It leads to overcrowding and possibly even slum creation which the authorities were attempting to avoid (Choguill 1985).

If a genuine land provision is included within the project design, then such projects are frequently relegated to the periphery of the area, the only place such acreages are available, and this results in even worse problems for the project's recipients. Since most jobs in the informal sector are found in the center of the town, a peripheral location does little more than add to the cost of transport of the project participants and reduces the desirability of the projects for them.

CRITERIA FOR PARTICIPATION

The inability to control project costs on sites-and-services schemes as a result of government intervention into the shelter field, frequently results in strict criteria about who is and who should not be admitted to such a program. After reviewing its own shelter projects in El Salvador, the Philippines, Senegal, and Zambia, the World Bank (Kearne and Parriss 1982) concluded that such projects were affordable by families down to the 20th income percentile.

Although strictly interpreted, this means that one-fifth of the income distribution is excluded from participation in such projects, in reality, given the small number of people at such low incomes who might through one means or another gain admission into the projects, such exclusion usually means something closer to the bottom 40 percent of that distribution.

The exclusion provisions are often quite explicit. For example, in the World Bank's E1 Salvador sites-and-services project, partially as a result of a design income range, participation probably extended down to between the 17th and 24th income percentiles, although the majority were from the third, fourth and fifth income decile (Kearne and Parriss 1982, p. 2). The Indian project at Kanpur was specifically designed for households with incomes between the 15th and 42nd income percentiles (Swan, Wegelin and Panchee 1983, p. 19).

In other cases the constraints which led to exclusion can be more subtle. In the first Tanzanian National Sites-and-Service Project, again financed by the World Bank, applicants for construction loans who needed to build their own accommodation were required to have a saving amounting to Tsh. 2,290 in order to qualify for money from the Tanzanian Housing Bank. As the average income of the low-income groups was not more than Tsh. 380 per month, this requirement was an almost insurmountable barrier for the poor (Bamberger 1982, pp. 39–40).

The selectivity that results from such financial constraints can be devastating to shanty town economies. Peattie (1982) argues that such projects tend to cream off the more established members of the working class, leaving behind in the unorganized system those who are less successful. An advantage of the heterogeneous economic mix in such communities is that demand for goods and services tends to trickle down from the more successful to the less successful. If the high-income groups are removed from the community to participate in sites-and-services schemes, the result may be the creation of what Peattie (1982, p. 133) refers to as a 'sharply defined underclass'.

It is apparent that although sites-and-services may offer certain advantages in housing development programs, in terms of incomes of the target population, it is still an expensive approach to the solution of the shelter problem. Partly as a result of this, the World Bank shifted its own emphasis from, to use Blair's (1983, p. 143) terminology, 'retailer' to 'wholesaler' in urban development finance, from lending for specific projects to something more like 'lending directly to strengthen national and government created metropolitan authorities so that they can choose projects themselves'. At present, only two national governments, Tanzania and Sudan, are known to incorporate sites-and-services as part of their national housing policy.

Instead, the search goes on for cheaper alternatives and one such alternative is the upgrading of existing communities.

THE ROLE OF UPGRADING

Upgrading schemes are usually designed for areas of the city which are already built up, such as the edges of central or commercial areas. The objective here is to transform areas which though are frequently developed outside the legal system, continue to provide residences which are convenient for employment opportunities and are popular with their occupiers. Rather than resort to total clearance, emphasis is directed towards the installation of infrastructure, such as water and sewers, possibly to the rearrangement of at least some parts of the layout, the extension of whichever social services may be available, the legislation of tenure, and sometimes to the provision of financial and building assistance which could be used to improve houses and business premises.

Martin (1983, p. 52) identifies four advantages of upgrading. First, it preserves existing economic system and opportunities for the urban poor. Second, it preserves the low cost housing stock already in existence at its present location. Third, it preserves the community structure and the safeguards that already exist for the family and the community group. Finally, the alternative, resettlement, is socially disruptive, usually occurs at a less favorable location, involves high community costs, and reduces access to informal employment.

Although upgrading is sometimes considered to be a relatively recent addition in the arsenal of weapons available to improve urban areas, the approach has, in fact, been used for a number of years. One such example was the Kampung Improvement Program in Indonesia which began during the First Five Year Development Plan in 1969 as an attempt to improve neighborhoods in Jakarta. Because of its initial success, the scope of its content has been widened over time and the methods have been applied to other cities (US Agency for International Development 1986). The program has succeeded in providing minimum infrastructure to a large number of beneficiaries, including footpaths, secondary roads, surface drainage ditches, water supply systems and public standpipes, individual toilets (mainly pit privies and some community toilets), and rubbish collection facilities. Education and health facilities have also been built. These items have been provided at an investment of US$ 59 per person at the 1976 prices, which represents very good value when compared with the alternative approaches.

Although upgrading has in recent years been attempted by a wide range of governments, it has received relatively little attention in the academic literature on housing and planning. This is indeed unfortunate, as without doubt the per unit cost of improvement is much lower than can be achieved in the sites-and-services approach. As Yeh (1981, p. 209) has observed, existing case studies of upgrading are essentially noncomparative, in part because of the diversity of settlements that exist. However, despite the problems caused by diversity, the strengths of such an approach appear to be clear-cut and given the potential economic advantages, it would be expected that upgrading should become increasingly popular as a way of improving existing shanty towns.

THE EMERGING IMPORTANCE OF INFRASTRUCTURE

Even upgrading involves costs which may be beyond the capabilities of a number of national governments. As a result, some authorities have experimented with even cheaper approaches. In Tanzania and Zambia, for example, an experiment in 'sites-without-services' has been carried out. Obviously this particular approach is based very firmly on the assumption that if secure tenure is provided through self-help, beneficiaries in such projects will construct not only their houses, but also infrastructure. The importance of infrastructure was also to be noted in the discussion on upgrading where, for example, in the Kampung Improvement Program of Indonesia, infrastructure was the major improvement that was provided. In fact, the whole issue of infrastructure is receiving increasing attention due to its extreme importance in reducing morbidity, improving health, providing a basis for environmental improvement, and possibly most important of all, in reducing the drudgery and labor that is an inherent part of living in low-income communities (McGerry 1987, p. 15).

One reason for this increasing concern with infrastructure, in particular water supply, sewerage disposal, and drainage, is that many cities of the developing world are woefully undersupplied with such equipment. Perhaps an extreme example of this is Dhaka, Bangladesh, with a population of somewhat over 3,000,000, but which has a piped water supply which reaches only 67,000 houses and a sewerage disposal system with only 8,500 connections (Choguill 1988). The Dhaka situation is by no means atypical of cities in the developing world. The United Nations Center for Human Settlements (1987, p. 79) recently reported that in 1983, no more than 57 percent of the African urban population had access to drinking water supply as compared to 65 percent of the urban population in the Asian and Pacific region and 78 percent of the Latin American and Caribbean urban population. In rural areas, the figures were much lower.

One reason for the low provision of services is the high cost of providing utilities to communities in developing countries. In a recent study, Franceys and Cotton (1989) analyse eight housing projects in four different countries.

In these studies they concluded that the average investment cost in infrastructure was 64 percent of the total site development cost, but this percentage varied from 54 to 70 percent. The authors suggested that one of the reasons for the high cost of this infrastructure was that it was usually designed by engineers according to conventional standards and byelaws appropriate for contractor built middle-income housing. This seems to suggest that in designing for low-income communities, a unique form of infrastructure may be required. Indeed, it is possible to differentiate between 'town systems', that is water and sewage disposal systems built using conventional Western technology, and 'low cost systems', a category which may be based on appropriate technology, such as hand pumps, pour-flush latrines, and similar approaches. The failure to recognize this important distinction has in the past frequently led to wasted investments (Choguill, Cotton and Franceys 1991).

Although infrastructure based on such intermediate technology can be considered by some to be inferior to the more expensive, engineer designed equipment, there is little doubt that the low cost approach meets the basic objectives with respect to the health of such infrastructure. At the same time, successful low cost approaches frequently involve the self-help of the recipients in the planning, design, and implementation phases of such a project (Choguill 1991). It follows that whereas engineer designed systems in developing countries are frequently plagued with maintenance problems of one sort or another, the same does not hold true of the low technology approach. Sophisticated infrastructure which cannot be maintained produces no benefits and when used in low-income neighborhoods, often deteriorates very quickly. Franceys and Cotton (1989, p. 104) suggest that the ideal approach to infrastructure provision is 'to maximize the involvement and responsibility of householders and minimize the role of the urban authority and/or any external agency'.

Although some might argue that the emphasis placed on the role of infrastructure is a classic case of planning imperialism and that such activities should be left to engineering specialists, it is argued here that the physical planner must be involved in such development. The skills required to develop housing areas which incorporate low technology infrastructure still involve land use planning, but also the ability to promote community development from below and an understanding of the economics of housing development. There is no reason to believe that such skills are incompatible with those of physical planning. Although engineers must be involved in these processes, there has been a tendency in the past for them to seek high technology solutions to the problems they face, and again, this may be one area where the planner can be of use in the development debate because of his own training in more human-related fields.

Thus, it is difficult to avoid the conclusion that the current emphasis on low cost infrastructure based on appropriate technology is little more than a natural progression which begins with the 'culture of property', passes through 'progressive improvement', 'self-help' and 'upgrading' and has finally become a variant of approaches to 'community development'. Urban physical planning has been involved in each step of this progression. Although new skills may be required if the planner is to continue his involvement, such has been the case of each step of the progression.

CONCLUSIONS

In this chapter an attempt has been made to trace the major policy influences and instruments which have had an effect on Third World urban improvement programs, particularly housing, over recent years. It has been a period of significant change. As noted, in the 1960s, those charged with housing responsibilities interpreted their task as one of building houses for the poor. The houses produced were very often inappropriate for the needs of the target population and were, unless generously subsidized, very expensive as well. Under the influence of the writings of Turner and Mangin, by the end of the decade there began a gradual withdrawal of government involvement in housing provision and a greater reliance on self-help principles. In terms of government housing policy, these ideas were translated into sites-and-services schemes and slum upgrading programs. Certain problems associated with the approach have been identified and considered within this paper. As a result of these problems, increasing emphasis has been placed on the role of infrastructure on urban development within the developing world.

Three conclusions would seem to follow from the analysis which has been presented:

First, it is apparent that the government has not been particularly successful in meeting the shelter requirements of the urban populations of developing countries. In fact, there appears to be some evidence to suggest that the relationship between involvement of government in shelter provision and the accomplishment of objectives concerned with shelter may be an inverse one. Certainly governments throughout the developing world have grasped at the opportunities to withdraw themselves from direct involvement in shelter provision and it is perhaps unfortunate that residual activities in this field have frequently tended to impede, rather than promote, the achievement of the various objectives with respect to housing and urban development. The most recent developments in this field which have been identified, are in particular, the 'sites without services' approach in which government involvement is almost at minimal levels.

Second, the importance of economic problems and constraints in achieving objectives with respect to housing and urban development are very important indeed. In fact, it has been costs relative to income that have prevented further accomplishments within this area. It must be realized that housing is merely one part of the development process and without a comprehensive approach which will lead to income generation and better jobs for the poor within the community, accomplishments within the housing urban development field are likely to continue to be disappointing. It is only when real incomes are increased that progress within this area can be achieved.

Third, the analysis included in this paper would seem to have certain implications for the skills required of planners who are involved in low-income housing projects. Very often, such planners are equipped with little more than a knowledge of the general principles on land use planning and the knowledge of national laws and regulations which constrain and govern the planning systems in their particular country. If the foregoing interpretation of history in housing and urban development is correct, it would seem that new skills would be required for planners from developing countries. These would involve the skills to promote and coordinate community development, particularly development from below, in contrast to the highly centralized government led efforts that have characterized past endeavors in the field. Anyone who is involved in community development must have the skills of a diplomat. It is evident that economics is a key subject within this area and the skills of economic analysis, particularly with respect to low-income housing and urban development, should be central to their knowledge. Finally, further knowledge of infrastructure, including at least some recognition of the technology of such equipment, would seem to be essential if they are to fulfil their full role as planners in the poorest cities of the developing world.

REFERENCES

Abrams, Charles. 1964. *Housing in the Modern World: Man's Struggle for Shelter in an Urbanizing World.* Cambridge: The MIT Press.

Bamberger, Michael, Bishwapura Sanyal and Nelson Valuerde. 1982. 'Evaluation of Sites and Services Projects: The Experience from Lusaka, Zambia', World Bank Staff Working Paper No. 548.

Blair, Thomas L. 1983. 'World Bank Urban Lending: End of an Era?' *Cities 1 (2)*, pp. 139–45.

Choguill, Charles L. 1985. 'Third World Shelter Policy: Solutions and Problems for Housing the Poor', Department of Town and Regional Planning, University of Sheffield, Occasional Paper No. 55.

Choguill, Charles L. 1988. 'Problems in Providing Low-Income Urban Housing in Bangladesh', *Habitat International 12 (3)*, pp. 29–40.

———. 1991. 'Infrastructure for Low-Income Communities: A Study from Honduras'. Paper presented at the U.K. Overseas Development Administration Sponsored World Habitat Day Seminar, 7 October.

Choguill, Charles L., Andrew Cotton and **Richard Franceys.** 1991. 'The Preparation of a Planning Manual for the Infrastructural Provision of Water Supply, Drainage and Sewage Disposal Based on a Literature Review'. Report to the U.K. Overseas Development Administration by the University of Sheffield Center for Development Planning Studies and the Loughborough University of Technology, Water, Engineering and Development Center.

Cohen, Michael A. 1983. 'The Challenge of Replicability: Towards a New Paradigm for Urban Shelter in Developing Countries', *Regional Development Dialogue 4 (1)*, pp. 90–99.

Franceys, R. and **Andrew Cotton.** 1989. 'Benefits and Sustainability in Infrastructure Provision: India and Sri Lanka'. Paper presented at the Sixth Inter-Schools Conference on Development, University of Sheffield, 18–19 March.

Grimes, Orville F. 1976. *Housing for Low Income Urban Families*. Baltimore: John Hopkins Press for the World Bank.

Kearne, Douglas, H. and **Scott Parriss.** 1982. 'Evolution of Shelter Programs for the Urban Poor: Principal Findings'. World Bank Staff Working Paper No. 547.

Lewis, Oscar. 1951. *Life in a Mexican Village: Tepoztlan Revisited*. Urbana: University of Illinois Press.

———. 1961. *The Children of Sanchez*. New York: Random House.

———. 1966. *Livida: A Puerto Rican Family in the Culture of Poverty*. New York: Random House.

Mabogunje, A.L., J.E. Hardoy and **R.P. Misra.** 1978. *Shelter Provision in Developing Countries: The Influence of Standards and Criteria*. Chichester: John Wiley.

McGerry, M.G. 1987. 'Matching Water Supply Technology to the Needs and Resources of Developing Countries', *Water Resources Journal 154*, pp. 11–19. United Nations Economic and Social Commission for Asia and the Pacific, September.

Mangin, William. 1963. 'Urbanization Case History in Peru', *Architectural Design 33*, August.

———. 1967. 'Latin American Squatter Settlements: A Problem and a Solution', *Latin American Research Review 2*, pp. 65–98.

Martin, R.J. 1983. 'Upgrading', in R.J. Skinner and M.J. Rodell (eds.), *People, Poverty and Shelter: Problems of Self-Help Housing*. London: Methuen.

Peattie, Lisa R. 1982. 'Some Second Thoughts on Sites-and-Services', *Habitat International 6 (1/2)*, pp. 131–40.

Swan, Peter J., Emiel A. Wegelin and **Komol Panchee.** 1983. *Management of Sites and Services Housing Schemes: The Asian Experience*. Chichester: John Wiley.

Turner, John F.C. 1967. 'Barriers and Channels for Housing Development in Modernizing Countries', *Journal of the American Institute of Planners 33 (3)*, pp. 167–80.

———. 1976. *Housing by People*. London: Marion Boyars.

United Nations Center for Human Settlements. 1987. *Global Report on Human Settlements 1986*. Oxford: Oxford University Press.

United States Agency for International Development. 1986. *Integrated Improvement Program for the Urban Poor: An Orientation for Project Design and Implementation 2*. Washington D.C.: USAID.

Yeh, Stephen H.K. 1981. 'On Characteristics of Urban Low-Income Settlements and Improvements Strategies: An Asian Perspective', in United Nations Center for Human Settlements, *The Residential Circumstances of the Urban Poor in Developing Countries*. New York: Praegar Publishers, pp. 191–218.

About the Contributors

Brian C. Aldrich is currently Professor of Sociology at Winona State University in Winona, Minnesota, U.S.A. He is the coeditor of *Housing in Asia: Problems and Perspectives*. He has published work on local habitat defense in the United States and in Southeast Asia. He is currently researching the housing status of the elderly in China.

Ernesto G. Arias is a city planner who received his Ph.D. from the University of Pennsylvania and is an Associate Professor of City and Regional Planning at the New College of Architecture and Planning of the University of Colorado. He cofounded the National Research Program on Sustainable Urban Development (PRODUS) at the University of Costa Rica.

John J. Betancur is an Assistant Professor in the School of Urban Planning and Policy and the Latin American Studies Program at the University of Illinois at Chicago (UIC). He is also associated with the Center for Urban Economic Development (UICUED) at UIC. Professor Betancur has conducted extensive research on spontaneous settlements and economic development in Colombia.

Jaesoon Cho is Associate Professor of the Department of Home Economics Education at Korea National University of Education. Her interests are in the areas of residential mobility, housing for the poor and the elderly, housing education, and housing research methods.

Charles L. Choguill is Professor of Town and Regional Planning at the University of Sheffield and Director of the University's Center for Development Planning Studies. His major research interest is the rapid urbanization in the developing world and the problems this creates, particularly with respect to shelter, urban services, and poverty. He is the Editor of the journal *Habitat International*.

Katharine Coit did her doctorate in urban sociology under the direction of Henri Lefebvre at the University of Nanterre. She was a consultant for UNESCO in collaboration with John Turner in a program concerned with housing the poor. In 1988, UNESCO published her work, *Housing and Development in the Lesser Antilles*. Presently, she is working on a slum upgrading project in Ho-Chi-Minh City.

Jorge A. Gutierrez is a civil engineer who received his Ph.D. from the University of California, Berkeley. He is a Professor of Civil Engineering at the University of Costa Rica and the Director of Research of the National Bamboo Project.

David Korboe qualified as an architect at the University of Science and Technology, Kumasi, Ghana, where he is now a Research Fellow in the Department of Housing and Planning Research. He recently completed his doctoral studies at the Centre for Architectural Research and Development Overseas, University of Newcastle upon Tyne, UK.

On-Kwok Lai is at the Department of Applied Social Studies, The Hong Kong Polytechnic University, Kowloon, Hong Kong. He received his degree from the

University of Bremen and worked in the University of Hong Kong, with academic interests in environmental and urban issues in China, Hong Kong, East Asia, and Europe.

Kosta Mathey is an architect and sociologist. He is Professor of Urban Development at the ISPJAE University in Havana, Cuba. He is editor of *TRIALOG*, the journal on planning and building in the developing world. He is also the editor of a number of books, including *Housing Policies in the Socialist Third World*.

A.C. Mosha is Senior Lecturer at the University of Botswana. He was a town and country planner. He has written extensively on housing for low-income groups, as well as urban management, urban design, and environmental issues.

Jeonghee Park is an Assistant Professor in the Department of Household Management at Mokpo National University. She is interested in housing stratas, changes in urban housing, and housing data analysis.

Keith Pezzoli teaches at the Urban Studies and Planning Program at the University of California, San Diego (UCSD), and also serves as its director for field research. He has worked on issues of human settlements, ecology, and development in Mexico for a decade.

Cedric Pugh has lived and worked in five countries in three continents. His published works cover developing countries, industrialised countries, and the transforming socialist countries of central and eastern Europe. One of Cedric Pugh's recent major books is *Housing and Urbanisation: The Case of India*, published by Sage Publications, New Delhi, in 1990.

Rosendo Pujol is a city planner who received his Ph.D from the University of California, Berkeley. He is a Professor of Civil Engineering at the University of Costa Rica where he co-founded and co-directs the National Research Program on Sustainable Urban Development (PRODUS).

Ranvinder S. Sandhu is a Reader in the Department of Sociology, Guru Nanak Dev University, Amritsar, India. He has written extensively on housing poverty in India. He is the author of *Evaluation and Impact of Slum Improvement Programme in Ludhiana (Punjab)* and *The City and its Slums—A Sociological Study*. He is the co-editor of *Housing in India: Problems, Policy and Perspectives* and *Housing in Asia: Problems and Perspectives*.

Ann Schlyter is an architect and Assistant Professor at the University of Lund. She has conducted longitudinal research on the development of urban settlement and living conditions in George compound, Lusaka, Zambia. At present she is conducting gender research on urbanization, planning, housing, and everyday life with several other researchers in southern Africa.

Alan Smart is a member of the Department of Anthropology at the University of Calgary, Canada. He has conducted field research in Hong Kong and China. He is the author of *Making Room: Squatter Clearance in Hong Kong*, as well as numerous articles on housing-related issues.

Ahmed M. Soliman is Associate Professor of Architecture at the Architecture

Department of the Faculty of Engineering, Alexandria University, Egypt, and Fellow of the University of Liverpool, Civic Design Department, UK. He has worked on informal housing and new towns in Egypt and has published widely on the problems of housing low-income groups in Third World countries.

N. Sridharan is an economist specializing in urban and regional planning. He has written extensively on urban and regional planning, housing, urban finance, and women in development. Currently he is teaching at the School of Planning and Architecture, Delhi. He is the honorary director of the Centre for Research and Training in Poverty Alleviation and Women Welfare (CRATPAW).

Suzana Pasternak Taschner is Professor of Architecture and Planning at the University of Sao Paulo. In addition to her research and teaching activities, she was a consultant to the municipality of Sao Paulo on its master plan. She has also organized the squatter settlements census in Sao Paulo, including the ongoing survey on squatter settlements and slums, together with professors from the Fundacao Instituto de Pesquisas Economicas. She is the author of several books and many articles, including works in Spanish, Portuguese, and English.

A. Graham Tipple is UK trained town planner with experience of working in UK, Zambia, and Ghana. He is the Principal Research Officer in the Centre for Architectural Research and Development Overseas, University of Newcastle upon Tyne. He is the joint editor of *Housing the Poor in the Developing World: Methods of Analysis, Case Studies and Policy*, and a consultant on housing policy for UNCHS (Habitat), ILO, World Bank, and Urbanaid Africa.

Willem van Vliet is a Professor in the New College of Architecture and Planning at the University of Colorado where he is also director of the Center for International Research and Education Projects. His professional interests include urban planning and crossnational analysis of housing policies and practices. He is the author of several books including *The International Handbook of Housing Policies and Practices*.

Emiel A. Wegelin is an urban economist with more than 20 years of experience in shelter and urban development issues in developing countries, mostly in South and Southeast Asia. At the time of writing this contribution, Mr. Wegelin was head of the Human Settlements Economics Department, Netherlands Economic Institute (NEI), Rotterdam, The Netherlands. He is currently coordinator of the global Urban Management Program of the United Nations Centre for Human Settlements (Habitat) in Nairobi, Kenya.

Kioe Sheng Yap teaches in the Human Settlements Development Program at The School of Environment, Resources and Development of the Asian Institute of Technology. He was researched housing in Thailand extensively. He is the author of *Low-Income Housing in Bangkok: A Review of Some Housing Sub-Markets*.